P9-CJN-082

Ethnic Identity

Ethnic Identity
Cultural Continuities and Change

Edited by
GEORGE DE VOS and LOLA ROMANUCCI-ROSS

With a new Introduction

The University of Chicago Press
Chicago and London

This edition published by arrangement with The Wenner-Gren Foundation for Anthropological Research, Inc.

The University of Chicago Press, Chicago 60637
The University of Chicago Press, Ltd., London

 Published 1975
University of Chicago Press edition 1982
Printed in the United States of America

89 88 87 86 85 84 2 3 4 5

Library of Congress Cataloging in Publication Data
Main entry under title:

Ethnic identity.

Papers based on a conference sponsored by the Wenner-Gren Foundation in 1970.
Bibliographical references.
Includes index.
1. Ethnicity—Congresses. 2. Ethnopsychology—Congresses. 3. National characteristics—Congresses. I. De Vos, George A. II. Romanucci-Ross, Lola. III. Wenner-Gren Foundation for Anthropological Research.
GN495.6.E87 1982 305.8 82-15907
ISBN 0-226-14364-3

Contents

Preface

This volume reflects the editors' contention that cultural anthropology must formulate scientific generalizations about the structures and functioning of pluralistic societies as well as about those based on a single cultural tradition. One relatively neglected dimension of pluralistic societies, traditional as well as modern, is ethnicity. The social sciences have identified many forms of classification within societies, from the kinship systems of simple pre-literate, pre-industrial societies, to the stratified economic classes of complex, industrial societies. Ethnic divisions, however, have gone relatively unnoticed. Societies with unitary, homeostatic cultural traditions have been taken as the norm.

A contrary point of view emphasizes the presence in almost every social organization of tensions which result from pressures to unify versus pressures to maintain differences. In fact, most societies give evidence, mythological or otherwise, of some stubborn survival of alien traditions. We would therefore contend that the "normal" condition of many social systems is one of tension and intermittent conflict, of "system perturbation," rather than placid homeostatis. Such a view calls direct attention to the complexities arising out of conflicting, centrifugal tendencies in society. It frustrates the desire to simplify theoretical explanation by emphasizing the integrative, unifying processes of a social system.

The dynamics of disturbance caused by unassimilated ethnic minorities cannot be ignored. Ethnic groups, by maintaining a separate sense of origin, are a persistent irritant producing disequilibrium and change in the total society. Comparative studies of sex role, kinship, class, caste or any other form of social segmentation do not diminish the importance of the generalizations which can be made about ethnic minorities.

This volume grew out of a conference on ethnicity sponsored by the Wenner-Gren Foundation in 1970. The conference brought together distinguished anthropologists who were themselves of diverse ethnic backgrounds. These scientists were invited to discuss ethnicity from perspectives derived from their own research experience in pluralistic societies. Those represented here are particularly partisan to psycho-cultural forms of analysis, since we believe ethnicity is best understood by an approach which takes into account the experiential, subjective forces underlying ethnic identity and its maintenance; macro-cultural forces alone (social structure and cultural history, for example) are inadequate to an understanding of the nature of ethnicity. The first four chapters of this volume define ethnicity and ethnic identity and illustrate the advantages of a psychological as well as a sociological approach. The remaining chapters represent a number of divergent approaches to ethnicity. In their concluding chapter the editors bring together some of the diverse strands of the group discussion which occurred during what proved to be a most intellectually and personally rewarding conference for the participants.

Introduction 1982

Since the Wenner-Gren conference in 1970 that gave rise to the first printing of *Ethnic Identity* in 1975, the comparative approach to ethnicity has burgeoned in both sociology and anthropology. We note with some appreciation that our approach, which emphasizes both the subjective experience and the emblematic aspects of ethnicity, has gained some currency among others considering the subject.

Our emphasis was deliberate. It was not to gainsay the political, economic, and other social features of the history of contrastiveness among people, but to assert that a relative priority must be given to the emotional, even irrational, psychological features underlying one's social identity. In the contemporary world of complex societies, identity is often expressed in ethnic terms. It has been our insistence that ethnicity has both "emic" as well as "etic" approaches. It has a psychological as well as a social level of analysis, and it is irrational and emotional as well as rational and expediential.

In our Chapter 1 we indicated that an ethnic identity is one more-or-less salient aspect of present complexities in social identity. It is more past oriented than present identities related to profession or to citizenship or such future-oriented identities manifest in participation in an ideological or religious movement.

Reviewing some reactions to this volume, we perhaps should have been more explicit as to how the term "ethnic identity" is inherently subjective and conscious whereas other levels of analysis of ethnicity or of ethnic groups are more "structural" and refer to etic concerns with either social or personality structure (see Chart A). Some recent social structural

CHART A Structural and Experiential Approaches to Ethnicity

Levels of Analysis	Mode of Analysis	Major Behavioral Concepts & Governing Concepts (Including Ethnicity)	Positive vs. Negative Functioning	"Dichronic" Historical Dimension
Ecological		Environmental	Ecological Adaptations	Environmental Change
Social structure	Etic	Ethnic or social behavior as representations of social structure *Despres* *Gordon* *Greeley* *Glazer & Moynihan*	Organization/disorganization Cohesion/anomie *Srole*	Social change, changes in technology
Social role interaction	Etic-emic	Patterns of social or ethnic interaction *Barth* *Berreman* *McKay & Lewins* *Burgess*	Patterns of conformity and deviancy in ethnic behavior *De Vos* *Lemert* *Malzberg* *Srole*	Social conflict/accommodation including actions of ethnic interest groups *Berreman* *Cohen* *Bennett* *Glazer & Moynihan* *M. G. Smith* *Burgess*
"Self" in social interaction	Emic	The self—the subjective experience of social or ethnic "identity" *Gans* *De Vos & Ross*	Adaptation/maladaptation *De Vos* Belonging/alienation *Novak* *Erikson*	Changing perceptions of self and society—with changes in the life cycle or changes in social conditions *Brunner* *De Vos* *Patterson* *Schermerhorn*
"Personality," Psychological structure	Etic	Ego mechanisms in identification, fixed patterns in ethnic behavior, expressive emotional styles *De Vos*	Adjustment/maladjustment *Erikson* *Kardiner & Ovesey* *De Vos* "Health"/pathology *Stein* *Inkeles*	Psychosexual development, cognitive development *Bruner* *Inkeles* *Piaget* *Witkin*
Physiological		"Instinctive" patterns	Physiological adjustive functions	Maturation

approaches can analyze whether a given ethnic group is "structurally" or "culturally" assimilated (cf. *16, 17*), whether a particular society is pluralistic or heterogeneous (*28*), and whether ethnic groups are more similar to class or caste divisions or have internal stratification (*8*). One can analyze objectively certain economic/exploitative features in ethnic relations (*6, 28*). Ethnic groups function well as interest groups (*14*). These are all valid approaches but we contend they are not capable of any complete explanation however cogent they are in addressing themselves to salient features of ethnicity within a given group. Conversely, ethnic attitudes and behavior can be analyzed further than we have done in an etic psychological frame of reference as forms of expressive behavior to be understood completely only after an examination of unconscious processes involved in one's ethnicity (*18, 29*). On both a social structural and a psychodynamic level of etic analysis one finds valid issues to be examined and delineated, but again we would contend that neither of these approaches is complete, nor do they address themselves to the experiential level of identity which is our central concern in this volume.

One notes, however, that even among the experiential approaches, there are some whose concern is with the patterning of ethnic interaction rather than with "identity" as a central concept. In the former, interaction is seen in the context of social role expectations on which interaction patterns are based (*3*) or interaction patterns are viewed as forms of boundary maintenance between groups (*1*). These patterns can lead to epidemiological differentiation in respect to deviancy and mental illness (*22*). Patterned anticipations lead to forms of social labeling which in themselves have a determinative effect (*20*). There are patternings of social conflicts and accommodations which can be analyzed in social structural or interactional contexts (*2, 5, 6, 14*). Our approach analyzes the self in social action and is concerned with how the subjective experience of an ethnic identity is related to adaptive behavior that is partially a resultant of underlying structural features of personality. There is need to separate concepts of social maladaptation from those of psychological maladjustment. A principal form of subjective experience in this respect is that of personal alienation (*10, 23*). Changing perceptions of identity occur with changes encountered in a changing society, affecting a person differentially throughout the life cycle (*24, 27*).

In brief, seen in this overall context, ethnicity is defined on four levels of analysis: first, in respect to a social structural level; second, as a pattern of social interaction; third, as a subjective experience of identity; and fourth, as expressed in relatively fixed patterns of behavior and expressive emotional styles. From this global perspective, however, our contributors do in many instances deal with social structure and historical determinants of ethnicity. We suggest that our volume should be supplemented by other readings emphasizing other aspects of patterned behavior related to an understanding of ethnicity. We have chosen the experiential approach because we consider it relatively neglected in many other writings in the social sciences addressing themselves to this topic.

An experiential subjective approach in considering ethnic groups is recent in the anthropological tradition. One notes an interest in acculturation since the 1930s (25), but implicit in most acculturation studies has been the assumption that it is possible to measure by observation, behavior, or material objects how "acculturated" individuals or groups have become. From the late 1930s, those interested in both culture and personality have been concerned with psychological states as well as behavioral traits, but many in this tradition have tended to assume some ultimate assimilation as an adaptive goal. Adjustive psychological or adaptive social difficulties were often considered inherent in remaining "marginal" or not fully identified with the dominant culture and its social system. The concern with eventual assimilation was from early on inherent in the sociological literature on minority groups in America. As represented at the University of Chicago under Robert Redfield, the anthropological tradition regarding a folk-urban continuum or the assimilation of groups into the dominant white society owed a heavy debt to previous sociological studies of the city of Chicago under Park, Burgess, Wirth, and others. These Chicago sociologists concerned themselves with the ecological, economic, and social patterns of growth in a city that was absorbing continuing waves of European immigrants.

Some social scientists became restive about the implicit assumption that American society, so self-consciously diverse in origin, would ultimately achieve total assimilation of its various minorities. An important turnaround point of view was marked by Glazer and Moynihan's *Beyond the Melting Pot* (13). The theoretical crucible had been broken. We had become free to observe that no more in America than elsewhere was assimilation the ultimate solution to social interaction.

A more recent volume edited by Glazer and Moynihan, *Ethnicity: Theory and Experience*, appeared in 1975. It resulted from a 1972 Ford Fokndation conference of distinguished sociologists considering recent trends in ethnicity. Obviously, the topic was in the air, although it is hard to trace origins of ideas since the intercommunication of social scientists is frequent. Glazer and De Vos discussed the subject in Japan in 1969 at another conference (cf. 9) that examined how people of culturally diverse origins but politically dependent or newly independent were adapting to the modern world.

In 1969 Fredrik Barth published *Ethnic Groups and Boundaries*. This work was somewhat revolutionary for anthropologists since he forthrightly pointed out the subjectivity of ethnicity. Using an interactional framework, Barth studied boundary maintaining mechanisms that keepgroups distinct rather than their distinguishing cultural traits. His book is quoted in most subsequent anthropological studies of ethnicity. In stressing the particular virtue of *Ethnic Identity* we differ slightly with Barth, not because we disagree with his basic approach, but because we find that his concept of boundaries as an analogy is somewhat less direct than our approach, which sees ethnic interaction using emblems of contrast. The term "boundary" refers perhaps too much to territory, although it is used in psychology in such terms as "ego boundaries." We find that Barth is not using it in this second manner but is suggesting that ethnic boundaries are kept inside by certain symbolic processes. Since the attributes of ethnicity are more apt to be worn or practiced for others to see, we find the concept of emblematic identity more hueristic.

With respect to the continuing controversy about the saliency of the rational versus the irrational components of ethnicity, we maintain that an ethnic identity is composed of both. On one hand, there are rational expediential usages of a political and economic nature which one finds today in many ethnic groups. On the other hand, there are certain irrational features which can be demonstrated to be counter to the group's immediate or ultimate best interests. It is the fact that there is this tension between the rational and the irrational that creates internal conflict in many individuals—the dilemma of continuity versus change. For example, Patterson (*24*) documents well that in the Caribbean an individual can choose voluntarily to be Puerto Rican or a Jamaican black but moves in and out of an ethnic identification simply by traveling from the homeland to the United States and back again. This is a overgeneralization because the problem resides in why certain Puerto Ricans and certain Jamaicans cannot so readily change but become militant instead. So there are problems with the whole subject of "passing" which cannot be addressed if one does not see ethnic identity as both rational and irrational, and the question of priority of loyalty in individuals and in groups must be addressed.

It is precisely for this reason that in our theoretical statement in Chapter 1 we stress that ethnicity has to be seen as a matter of relative priority in comparison with other forms of identity within any given individual, and indeed, one can characterize groups as demonstrating a relative degree of priority in this respect. Abner Cohen, in some of his writings at least (*6*), is sympathetic to this examined prior ity or degree of allegiance.

James McKay and Frank Lewins (*21*) have sought to distinguish between ethnic awareness and ethnic consciousness. In effect, however, this distinction does not create categories that are relative measures of priority and loyalty in individuals who are conscious of their ethnicity. According to Lewins and McKay, ethnic awareness is simply a statement of knowledge of one's ethnic origins whereas ethnic consciousness appears in situations of conflict and where there is some need for solidarity among individuals of a given ethnic group. In effect their distinction seeks simply to categorize degrees of militancy and ethnic assertion that we contend are actually on a continuum that is informed by a high degree of complexity. Some of our contributors elaborate on this complexity.

It is with gratification that we note the publication of new journals on ethnicity, the *Journal of Ethnic Studies*, *Ethnicity*, and *Ethnic and Racial Studies*. This last journal, first published in 1978, has a number of thoughtful articles seeking to create better theoretical distinctions in conceptualization of ethnicity (*5*, *7*, *12*, *26*, *30*). We found the article by Burgess a particularly well-balanced discussion of the major variables emphasized in one theoretical position or another. She distinguishes well between rational and nonrational approaches to ethnicity. She concludes that there is pervasive evidence of the persistence of ethnic diversity without resorting to "innate primordiality" as is true for some using a sociological approach. The conscious and unconscious determinants underlying individual and group responses or allegiances to ethnic interests must be considered. This is precisely the point made in the conclusion of our volume concerning the necessity to see some form of balance or inbalance between the instrumental and expressive usages of one's ethnic identity.

Burgess also stresses the need for balance between objective and subjective criteria as we have done. She suggests some reasons for the lack of interest in ethnic consciousness until the present time. One reason ethnicity is a relatively contemporary theoretical concern—although ethnic problems certainly have been a salient feature of conflict prior to the 1970s—is that functionalist theory in sociology and anthropology failed to give due weight to conflict and change in stressing stability, consensus and conformity as reasons for social continuity. A second reason was the pervasiveness of the modernization theory that stressed convergence in cultures and an expectancy of diminution of ethnic diversity with modernization. Burgess borrows Milton Gordon's term (*15*, pp. 68–69) in describing a state of mind among social theorists, i.e., the "liberal expectancy" that the features that divide groups will lose their weight in modern and modernizing societies. This expectancy has not been fulfilled. The third reason that Burgess cites for the lack of previous concern with ethnic problems is the saliency of class conflict in theories of conflictful relationships. These theories are in effect versions of a modernization theory which disregards the so-called ethnic reality as an antiquated form of belonging, and states that the ultimate struggle in society is one founded on class. In the late 1970s we observed the manner in which a number of Marxist theoreticians in France seized upon ethnic discontent as a means of marshalling political allegiance to socialist and communist causes, despite some embarrassment to their colleagues.

Since the first printing of *Ethnic Identity*, Lee and De Vos have published *Koreans in Japan: Ethnic Conflict and Accommodation* (*19*) in which the instrumental and expressive frame of analysis discussed in the concluding chapter of the earlier work was applied in detail to the Korean ethnic experience. For those interested in seeing the direct applicability of our theoretical position to a single difficult ethnic situation, we commend this volume, which considers the history of Korean ethnic identity from the early period of contact between Japanese and Koreans that continues as part of the contemporary ethnic identity of those Koreans residing as a minority in Japanese society. One cannot neglect the past in understanding contemporary hostility and conflict. Primary to this understanding is the nature of political interaction and economic exploitation; but as we pointed out in *Ethnic Identity*, this is not the whole story. To understand present conflict one also has to understand the psychological and social cost of a history of minority exploitation, and it is this dimension that is neglected with loss in some of the social structural approaches to ethnicity in the social sciences. While we in general agree with contemporary sociological thought about the present saliency of the "instrumental activities" in ethnic groups in modern states, we also contend that it is incumbent on the social scientist to make a psychocultural analysis, since to understand the behavior of particular groups we need to know their psychological states as well as the simple fact of political and economic exploitation.

Following Geertz, Daniel Bell (*4*) simply summarized the psychological expressive features as "primordial feelings." He agreed that such feelings are operative in ethnic groups and that ethnic groups have become forces in society because they can better than other groups, perhaps, combine "interests" with "affective ties." These interests cross-cut other economic and class perspectives. As he puts it, there is "an emergent expression of primordial feelings chosen by disadvantaged persons as a new mode of seeking political redress" (*4*, p. 169). While Bell recognizes the role of emotional needs, he does not seem to think it within the province of sociological analysis to delve into either the psychological or historical reasons for the how or why of psychological processes involved in human behavior. Suffice for him to examine how ethnic minorities attempt to actualize their instrumental goals and how ethnic movements are powered by strong emotional forces. An adequate theory must stress the insufficiency of such an approach. It's precisely the ingredients of these "primordial feelings" that need to be further analyzed in order to understand both the rational and irrational behavior forthcoming in many ethnic movements. Put in our terminology, we must understand how ethnicity is a complex combination of both the instrumental and expressive that operate within and in turn influence historical-sociological processes within any conflict-ridden changing social structure. A dual framework of analysis must be applied in understanding any given ethnic situation, for example, that of the Koreans in Japan.

In summary, in reviewing recent discussions of ethnicity and ethnic identity, we consider our approach to be a fruitful one, although not a theoretically complete one. But as the title suggests, viewing ethnicity from the standpoint of identity, we believe that the authors we have gathered together in *Ethnic Identity* have points to make that combine to serve as a valid perspective in understanding ethnic conflict and accommodation in contemporary societies.

Some personal and public events have transpired among our contributors since our first printing. Czeslaw Milosz has been awarded a Nobel prize as an outstanding "Polish poet," but as his autobiographically based study of ethnicity in Vilnius, his place of birth, attests, his personal identity is not so simple. The need to come to terms with who one is may result, as in the case of Milosz, in the production of a complex personality who may realize himself through the vehicle of his art.

If one looks carefully at the chapters of our volume and the subjects chosen by our contributors, it becomes evident that we include a group of distinguished individuals who have written objectively about forms of ethnic identity which they themselves have subjectively experienced. It is not necessary that a person be a member of a specific ethnic group to write about ethnic experience, but it certainly deepens the perception; and depending upon the amount of objectification realized, the person may communicate to others more profound understanding.

Margaret Mead is no longer with us—a loss to anthropology and to social science generally. In this volume, she too wrote a document from inside her own culture. She selected for discussion the central challenge of the American identity—a continuing ambivalence over whom to include and exclude as part of heterogeneous American society. The essentially conflictful hyphenated identity of most Americans continues from past to present.

We would like to dedicate this new edition of *Ethnic Identity* to Margaret Mead, who as a social scientist, in investigating beyond her own early boundaries, pioneered in broadening anthropology with a psychocultural approach continued in this volume.

REFERENCES

1. Barth, Fredrik. *Ethnic Groups and Boundaries.* Boston: Little, Brown, 1969.
2. Bennett, John W., ed. *The New Ethnicity: Perspectives from Ethnology.* St. Paul: West Publishing Company, 1975.
3. Berreman, Gerald D. *Caste and Other Inequities: Essays on Inequality.* Merrut: Ved Prakash Vatuk, 1979.
4. Bell, Daniel. "Ethnicity and Social Change." In *Ethnicity: Theory and Experience,* edited by N. Glazer and D. Moynihan, pp. 141–74. Cambridge: Harvard University Press, 1975.
5. Burgess, M. Elaine. "The Resurgence of Ethnicity: Myth or Reality?" In *Ethnic and Racial Studies* 1 (1978): 265–85.
6. Cohen, Abner, ed. *Urban Ethnicity.* London: Tavistock, 1974.
7. Connor, Walker. "A Nation Is a Nation, Is a State, Is an Ethnic Group, Is a . . ." In *Ethnic and Racial Studies* 1 (1978): 377–400.

8. Despres, Leo. "Toward a Theory of Ethnic phenomena." In *Ethnicity and Resource Competition in Plural Societies*, edited by L. Despres, pp. 187–207. The Hague: Mouton, 1978.
9. De Vos, George A., ed. *Responses to Change: Society, Culture and Personality*. New York: D. Van Nostrand, 1976.
10. Erikson, Erik H. *Identity and the Life Cycle*. New York: International Universities Press, 1959.
11. Erikson, Erik H. *Identity: Youth and Crisis*. New York: W. W. Norton, 1968.
12. Gans, Herbert J. "Symbolic Anthropology: The Future of Ethnic Groups and Cultures in America," In *Ethnic and Racial Studies* 2 (1979):1–20.
13. Glazer, Nathan, and Moynihan, Daniel P. *Beyond the Melting Pot*. Cambridge: MIT Press, 1963.
14. Glazer, Nathan, and Moynihan, Daniel P. *Ethnicity: Theory and Experience*. Cambridge: Harvard University Press, 1975.
15. Gordon, Milton. "Toward a General Theory of Racial and Ethnic Relations." In *Ethnicity: Theory and Experience*, edited by N. Glazer and D. P. Moynihan, pp. 84–110. Cambridge: Harvard University Press, 1975.
16. Gordon, Milton. *Human Nature, Class and Ethnicity*. New York: Oxford University Press, 1978.
17. Greeley, Andrew. *Ethnicity in the United States*. New York: Wiley, 1974.
18. Kardiner, Abram, and Ovesey, L. *The Mark of Oppression*. New York: World, 1962.
19. Lee, Changsoo, and De Vos, George A. *Koreans in Japan: Ethnic Conflict and Accommodation*. Berkeley: University of California Press, 1981.
20. Lemert, Edwin M. *Social Pathology*. New York: McGraw-Hill 1951.
21. McKay, James, and Lewins, Frank "Ethnicity and the Ethnic Group: A Conceptual Analysis and Reformulation." In *Ethnic and Racial Studies* 1 (1978):412–27.
22. Malzberg, Benjamin. "Are Immigrants Psychologically Disturbed?" In *Changing Perspectives in Mental Illness*, edited by Stanley C. Plog and Robert B. Edgerton, pp. 395–421. New York: Holt, Rinehart and Winston, 1969.
23. Novak, Michael. *The Rise of the Unmeltable Ethnics*. New York: Macmillan, 1971.
24. Patterson, Orlando. *Ethnic Chauvinism*. New York: Stein and Day, 1977.
25. Redfield, Robert et al. "Memorandum for the Study of Acculturation." *American Anthropologist* 38(1936): 149–52.
26. Richmond, Anthony H. "Migration, Ethnicity and Race Relations," In *Ethnic and Racial Studies* 1(1978):1–18.
27. Schermerhorn, R. A. *Comparative Ethnic Relations*, Phoenix edition. Chicago: University of Chicago Press, 1978.
28. Smith, M. G. *The Plural Society in the British West Indies*. Berkeley: University of California Press, 1965.
29. Stein, Howard F., and Hill, Robert F. *The Ethnic Imperative*. University Park: Pennsylvania State University Press, 1977.
30. White, Naomi Rosh, "Ethnicity, Culture and Cultural Pluralism." In *Ethnic and Racial Studies* 1(1978):139–53.

The Concept of Ethnic Identity

PART ONE

PART ONE

THE CONCEPT OF ETHNIC IDENTITY

The introductory chapter by George De Vos provides a general definition of ethnicity, often defined as the attribute of membership in a group set off by racial, territorial, economic, religious, cultural, aesthetic, or linguistic uniqueness. However, like any other form of social identity, ethnic identity is essentially subjective, a sense of social belonging and ultimate loyalty. The potential for intergroup conflict within pluralistic societies has continued throughout the history of man.

George Devereux takes a complementary approach, separating ethnic identity from ethnic personality. For Devereux, ethnic identity is a form of role attribution, both internal and external. Ethnic personality is what one does more spontaneously as a result of being socialized within an ethnic group from childhood. Devereux supports his thesis with illustrations drawn from the Mohave and Sedang cultures, in which he has done detailed anthropological fieldwork, from the Hungarian culture of his own origin, and from the reconstructed cultural history of Athens and Sparta, on which he has been conducting recent research. His work combines anthropology with classical scholarship, an interest in the philosophy of science, and his considerable experience as a psychoanalyst.

Gerald Berreman attempts to clarify the relationship between the various forms of social identity segmenting complex social structures. He examines

how a subjectively defined sense of ethnic separateness influences other forms of social interaction. He draws for examples on India, perhaps the most complex culturally and socially stratified pluralistic society. Striving to retain its political unity, it remains segmented into myriad subdivisions by race, caste, class, occupation, language and religion. Berreman views identity as a dual question: what is subjectively claimed creates a dynamic tension with what is socially accorded. He concludes from his own field studies that, methodologically, ethnic identity is best studied through an analysis of the subjective meaning of behavior in an interactional social context. Only by intensive participant observation can an anthropologist come closest to understanding what people are expressing verbally and how they act with reference to one another.

Theodore Schwartz relates ethnicity to the basic psychological processes of separation to be found in totemic thought and in ethnic identity, arguing against Lévi-Strauss' reduction of totemism to an illusion. He takes as a case in point the Melanesian inhabitants of the Admiralty Islands, whose culture reveals ample evidence of the force of totemic thought. A totemic form of categorization is also to be found in an emblematic separation of groups into ethnic divisions. Schwartz demonstrates that pluralistic cultures are not solely the result of the modern national state: throughout the stateless Melanesian macro-culture area ethnic groups interpenetrated and lived in juxtaposition with one another long before Western contact. The emphasis on single groups in previous ethnographies has created an illusion of isolate cultures living in separate communities. In fact, there is continual territorial interpenetration and intercommunication despite differences in language, religion, occupational specialization and myths of separate origin. Ethnicity in primitive Melanesia, Schwartz points out, is the endogamous outer ring of relatively safe marriages, just as lineage exogamy defines an inner ring prohibiting incest. Schwartz even finds that ethnic identity was the means by which the boundaries of exophagy ("eating out") were defined, when cannibalism was practiced in the area. His chapter offers elegant evidence that the limits of the concept of ethnic identity has been as problematic for Melanesians, both past and present, as it is for modern man. In either instance, emblems of identity are necessary to secure for the individual his sense of social self.

Ethnic Pluralism: Conflict and Accommodation

GEORGE DE VOS

1

Role of Ethnicity in Social History

A sense of common origin, common beliefs and values, a common sense of survival—in brief, a "common cause"—has been of great importance in uniting men into self-defining in-groups. Growing up together in a social unit, sharing a common verbal and gestural language allows men to develop mutually understood accommodations, which radically diminish situations of possible confrontation and conflict. In mammalian societies generally, ordered systems of individual dominance are a major accommodative device. Given man's capacities for cultural elaboration, he goes further. He can, on the basis of *group definitions of belonging,* develop complex formal systems of individual and group social stratification. These systems are found in many so-called primitive societies as well as in technologically advanced modern states (see *5, 9*).

The cultural bases for social groupings in society are varied. Some of these groupings are defined reciprocally and horizontally; others are stratified vertically, with emphasis on the status of an individual or a group with respect to other persons or groups. Kinship networks, a major form of grouping, very often operate horizontally as forms of reciprocal marital exchange. These networks, however, may also stratify particular intermarrying families as part of a nobility separated from those considered commoners. In more complex social structures both sociologists and anthropologists have become concerned with forms of stratified social groupings, based on occupational status, which may appear as organizing social class structures or as caste systems. Another form of group separation—the subject of this volume—is found most often in composite societies and results from the inclusion of groups of different cultural, or "ethnic," origin.

Lineage, class, or caste forms of social grouping are more socially accommodative than ethnic divisions. Hence, in theories emphasizing concepts of stability and equilibrium, ethnic minorities are relatively neglected. Ethnicity can be a source of considerable conflict, since ethnic groups in many instances do not remain in a fixed position within a stratified system. A separate ethnic identity, when it persists in a group, tends to maintain boundaries, to use the perspective of Fredrik Barth (*1*, p. 15). Like Barth, I think that how and why boundaries are maintained, rather than the cultural content of the separated group, are what one must examine in the study of ethnic relations. I too contend that boundaries are basically psychological in nature, not territorial. These boundaries are maintained by ascription from within as well as from external sources which designate membership according to evaluative characteristics which differ in content depending on the history of contact of the groups involved. The resulting collective sense of separateness may lead to continual accommodation or conflict.

In social stratification systems that emphasize the separate origin of the groups, competition is stronger than in stratified societies emphasizing the common origin of all social strata. Ethnic pluralism implies an internal complexity with more or less unstable boundaries in respect to questions of dominance. These can lead to harsh forms of exploitation and resentment, when the awareness of differences outweighs the sense of belonging between members of separate strata. There may also be less acceptance on the part of ethnic groups of the dominance of another stratum or group, thus leading to periodic overt social conflicts that are no less frequent than those found in the history of politically independent ethnic entities living in neighboring territories. It seems necessary, therefore, in a discussion of ethnicity, to start from a theoretical position that regards some form of conflict as a normal or chronic condition in a pluralistic society. Such social tensions, however, are manifestly different in pluralistic societies than they are in stratified societies composed principally of an ethnically homogeneous populace.

Ethnically plural societies are not new. They have occurred throughout man's history, most often involuntarily as a result of conquest. Today, however, ethnicity has become an important issue in modern states because of the ethnic interpenetration that has resulted from increasing social mobility (related to individual achievement) and from increasing geographic mobility (due to shifting markets for labor).

We are also witnessing a revolution in the recording of social and cultural history. Today's ethnic minorities are not content to remain mute; they too seek to be heard. The defeated and the oppressed are themselves contributing to the writing of history, adding their own interpretations, and, where facts fail, creating or deepening their own sustaining mythologies. Social classes or pariah outcastes relatively invisible in earlier histories are emerging as figures in a larger history of conflict or as subjects in the historical approach that deals with stratification in societies. Whether or not social scientists accept the priority given by some Marxists to economic determinism, there is no doubt that the Marxian philosophy of history has deepened the perception of modern historians, enabling them to recognize the contributions of historically oppressed ethnic and economic groups. Like Freud's approach to personal history, a conflict approach to social history reveals the continuing influence of repressed forces—forces which do not disappear simply because they have been omitted from the official history written by the politically and socially dominant group. The social scientist today, when examining social history, must not only consider the history of the politically successful and hence dominant groups, or to consider stability as the norm of society but must also consider the position of minorities and their influence in the processes of conflict and accommodation continually at work in changing societies.

Ethnic minorities have been present as long as sovereign political states have existed, but ethnic conflict has usually been treated from the standpoint of political struggles for territory rather than from the psycho-cultural viewpoint of what occurs within the individual when he is confronted with the necessity of changing his allegiance to a new master, adopting a new religion, or even acquiring a new language, in order to participate in a dominant political society that is ethnically alien. We have had in the past relatively little concern, for example, with reconstructing the internal crises faced by individual Gauls as they resisted or accepted Roman or Christian influence. Today, however, there is growing interest in those who resisted. It is a sign of the times that the most popular comic book hero in France today is Astérix, a counterculture Gaul whose Druidic potion gives him superhuman powers to help his tiny band of countrymen resist the establishment Romans.

Social science theorists have until recently paid little attention to enduring ethnic or cultural identity as a primary social force comparable to nationalism or class affiliation. Its role in past and present conflicts within complex societies is often neglected by social scientists, who usually concern themselves with the relations between ethnically different but politically autonomous groups. Once a group has been conquered or absorbed politically, the assumption seems to be that its existence in a new political state is of less concern than the state's external relation. From the earliest history of the state, however, there appear many forms of intrasocial tensions arising from ethnic diversity. Such conflict is not limited to empires which acknowledge political hegemony over ethnically heterogeneous groups. It is also continually apparent in states that seek to extend a uniform culture to all its members.

To maintain its focus, this discussion does not deal with conflict between independent cultures, restricting itself instead to a preliminary and partial overview of the nature of ethnic conflict in established pluralistic societies. I shall examine, however briefly, in the course of this introductory chapter, how ethnicity can be used both expressively and instrumentally within a pluralistic society and how it may or may not contribute to social instability.

Even more rarely do social scientists stop to ask why ethnic enclaves persist, sometimes to their own continuing social disadvantage. Yet social theory could certainly benefit from a better understanding of why certain peoples insist on maintaining symbolic forms of cultural differentiation for centuries, despite a lack of political autonomy or even of a particular territory. An adequate answer to this question must involve a psycho-cultural approach. It is perhaps impossible to reconstruct how such processes might have operated in the past, but given the present abundant opportunities to observe such groups first hand, there is no excuse to neglect the question of how ethnic identity functions in a complex stratified social system. Class, caste, and other forms of occupational stratification are most often discussed from a strictly sociological point of view, but the following discussion takes a psycho-cultural approach. One cannot fully understand the force of ethnicity without examining in some detail its influence on the personality of minority group members. It is insufficient to examine ethnic group behavior directly only from the vantage point of social structure or social processes.

The discussion of ethnicity and social stratification which follows relates conflict over allegiance and belonging not only to one's place in the status system, but also to internal conflicts over the priority to be given to past-, present-, or future-oriented forms of self-identity. In his primary sense of belonging, an individual can lean toward one of three orientations: (1) a present-oriented concept of membership as citizens in a particular state or as a member of a specific occupational group; (2) a future-oriented membership in a transcendent, universal religious or political sense; or (3) a past-oriented concept of the self as defined by one's ethnic identity, that is, based on ancestry and origin. It is our contention that the maintenance of this latter form of identity is as powerful a force as class conflict in the shaping of human social history.

ETHNICITY BROADLY DEFINED

There is as yet no acceptable single word in English for the phrase "ethnic group," no word equivalent to "class," "caste," or "family" to describe a group self-consciously united around particular cultural traditions, although French anthropologists have suggested the word *ethne* for technical usage. If one seeks, however, to define those characteristics that comprise an ethnic group, one ultimately discovers that there are no essential characteristics common to all groups usually so designated. This has been equally true for other attempted definitions related to lineage, family, class, or caste. In what follows, the word "usually" must be understood as preceding any generalization. The fact that exceptions to every generalization will come to mind does not render invalid a definition based on those features shared by a group which combine to create a sense of ethnicity for those who include themselves in the group.

An ethnic group is a self-perceived group of people who hold in common a set of traditions not shared by the others with whom they are in contact. Such traditions typically include "folk" religious beliefs and practices, language, a sense of historical continuity, and common ancestry or place of origin. The group's actual history often trails off into legend or mythology, which includes some concept of an unbroken biological-genetic generational continuity, sometimes regarded as giving special characteristics to the group. Endogamy is usual, although various patterns for initiating outsiders into the ethnic group are developed in such a way that they do not disrupt the sense of generational continuity.

Some of the same elements that characterize ethnic membership may seem in some societies to characterize lineage group or caste membership. The subjective definitions differ, however, as do their functions. A lineage group or caste perceives itself as an *interdependent* unit of a society, whereas members of an ethnic group cling to a sense of having been an independent people, in origin at least, whatever the special role they have collectively come to play in a pluralistic society. Thus caste definitions explicitly point to a present system of formal stratification, whereas ethnic definitions refer to a past cultural independence. In contrast, groups formed around universalist religious or political ideologies are oriented to a future society with less explicit or more satisfactory forms of status stratification.

Individuals presently dissatisfied with the social status accorded them as members of a minority group may seek to leave their group. They may choose either to adopt a future-oriented religious or political ideology, thereby gaining admission to a new group, or they may emphasize their ethnic past and exert pressure to change the collective status of the group—as I shall presently discuss in the instances of attempts to escape caste definitions in India and the United States. An alternative to a change in collective status is a change in individual status, which may involve "passing," as I shall also discuss later.

"Racial" Uniqueness

Some sense of genetically inherited differences, real or imagined, is part of the ethnic identity of many groups, as well as being one of the beliefs about an ethnic minority held by those dominant groups who wish to prevent assimilation. The relationships between caste, ethnicity, and racial definitions are complex in many pluralistic societies. Real or supposed genetic differences, when socially recognized as a constituent of stratification, are usually used by dominant groups to maintain a castelike exclusion regardless of the presence or absence of other ethnic distinctions, such as language or religion. A willingness to acculturate completely on the part of a "racially" defined ethnic minority, not only in comportment but also in actual identity, may not be acceptable to the dominant group. The maintenance of a system of stratified exclusion cannot be well rationalized on the basis of ethnic differences alone, but can be better maintained on the basis of genetic heritage. The view that a racial minority genetically is backward and hence less worthy of participation is most often linked to a belief that such backwardness is not to be overcome.

Conversely, if a socially defined racial minority wishes to assimilate but finds that intermarriage or other forms of integration are withheld on the basis of race, the group is forced to select another alternative. It can accept an inferior caste status and a sense of basic inferiority as part of its collective self-definition, or it can define the situation as one of direct political and economic oppression. Or it can define itself symbolically, creating a positive view of its heritage on the basis of cultural as well as racial distinctions, thereby establishing a sense of collective dignity. This in-group ethnic sense can be used in an attempt to escape caste stratification. Thus, an ethnic self-definition on the part of a group in an already ethnically plural society can be used to heighten the relative status of a group vis-a-vis other groups also defined in ethnic terms.

Territoriality

Most ethnic groups have a tradition of territorial or political independence, even though the present members have become part of another, or sometimes several, political entities. In comparing ethnic groups, however, one notes highly different patterns related to the possession of territory as a means of maintaining group cohesion. At one extreme are groups, such as the Japanese, occupying an entire nation; at the other extreme are minorities such as the Jews, who have been without a territory for centuries. In numerically large, politically independent groups, ethnic identity tends to be coextensive with national or regional identity. Social and political problems resulting from continual attempts by groups to extend their territory account for much of the world's political history.

Strictly used, "nationality" is indistinguishable from ethnicity. But in a looser sense, the words "nation" and "nationality" very often encompass diverse groups that have achieved political unification. It can be argued that for many people, national identity and subjective cultural identity cannot be distinguished, especially when ethnic identity and national identity have been one historically. Otherwise, ethnic identity is either a more specific or broader identity than national identity. Identity may take on a local flavor, so that a person defines himself as a Breton rather than a Frenchman, or a Roman rather than an Italian. However, a "German" identity can include Austrians as well as inhabitants of present-day "German" states. Local identifications may or may not entail some feeling of continuity with the past. A Briton of Irish or Welsh descent now residing in London, for example, will continue to have a distinct ethnic identity if in his own eyes his Welsh or Irish origin remains more important than his present affiliation with British citizenship or London residence. The crucial question is the priority given to competing loyalties, for, depending on that priority, a person's social relationships will tend to be quite different.

Some ethnic minorities maintain themselves at least partially by sustaining a hope for political independence or for the recapturing of lost territory. The most striking example of such thinking has been the Jewish vision of re-establishing Israel. There are also other examples of groups, such as the Kurds in Iran, who still hope to reassert their autonomy by recapturing or maintaining a political territorial base. Some such groups inhabit territory that is difficult to penetrate and that therefore enables them to maintain a measure of local autonomy. Tibet has thus recurrently resisted becoming Chinese.

There are a variety of illustrations of partial incorporation of ethnic minorities into larger national units, such as the Scottish and Welsh incorporation into Great Britain. The Soviet Union is an example of a state with continuing tensions resulting from territorial expansion and the incomplete incorporation of widely divergent groups, such as the Latvians and Estonians in Europe and numerous Moslem groups in Asia.

Thus territory may be central to maintain ethnicity, or it may be minimal, or even nonexistent (the wandering gypsies are an extreme example). The degree to which some territorial concept is necessary to the maintenance of ethnic identity, symbolically or actually, must be considered in relation to the use of nonterritorial definitions of ethnic uniqueness and to the use of economic, religious, or other social functions to maintain group cohesion.

Economic Bases

Economic factors contribute in a complex manner to ethnic definitions and identity maintenance. An ethnic minority can be well dispersed within another population and still defend themselves from assimilation by maintaining a certain amount of economic autonomy. Minorities such as the Parsis of India, the Jews of Europe, the overseas Indians and overseas Chinese manage to remain ethnically distinct, at least partially because their community organization has a secure subsistence base anchored in special occupations which they can pursue from one generation to the next. There is, however, a great deal of political ambivalence in some areas about allowing quasi-independent, economically secure ethnic enclaves to persist. The ambiguous role of overseas merchant Indians in Africa and Chinese in Southeast Asia are cases in point.

Ethnic identity is also strongly reinforced when ethnic subgroups are exploited by the socially dominant population, as happens in racially segregated societies such as South Africa, where policies insist on ethnic separation on the basis of some socially defined racial differentiation. Some dominant cultures also find it politically and socially advantageous to maintain minority enclaves. However, these are sometimes defined as special classes, castes, or slave populations rather than simply in terms of their ethnic past.

One recent theory developed by Everett Hagen relates economic, political, and social changes in status on the part of ethnic minorities to general social change (*14*). Hagen finds that a minority group may compensate for a prior downward shift in status by innovative economic activities that lead to a consequent resurgence in the relative status of their members. Such an examination of the relationship between ethnicity and economic power is particularly revealing of the means by which group shifts occur in social position.

Religion

Religion can be a means of abandoning one's ethnic identity by adopting a transcendent worldview, as happens when a member of a non-Christian state converts to Christianity. Or it can support a sense of ethnicity, as in the case of the Welsh Protestants who reject the Church of England. In their studies of revivalist cults among politically subordinate groups, anthropologists have found that religion can be used to mobilize members of a group to deal with a felt threat to their continuing existence or, more directly, to attain a promised change of status through a religiously oriented social revolution. Folk religion very often takes the form of myths about the uniqueness of the group or its genesis. "Nativism" in medical practices—resistance to scientific definitions of disease and a tenacious clinging to traditional curing practices—is another means of maintaining ethnic identity. A written tradition of sacred texts defining the religious faith can also be a strong force in maintaining a sense of identity in each succeeding generation. The use of religion to support ethnic identity is clear in the case of folk beliefs and practices. But universalist faiths such as Buddhism, Christianity, and Islam can also contribute to ethnic group cohesion when sectarian differences become important as a matter of group loyalty and identification.

Religious or ideological conflict in society often has more to do with increasing the power of one's own group than it does with extending the benefits of one's religion to the converts. In fact, throughout history states have exploited religious differences to enhance their power. For this reason religions have often been nationalized, so as to diminish problems of divided loyalty. In this context, it is interesting to note that today's disputes between Marxist-oriented socialist states markedly resemble the past sectarian conflicts within Christianity or Islam. Religious adherence on the part of an ethnic group may also become a symbol of resistance to the dominant group, thereby reducing religious affiliation to simply a means of asserting ethnic identity. Thus many secularized intellectuals in Poland attend church to mark symbolically their allegiance to an independent Poland.

Religious revivalism related to ethnic-cultural maintenance is a widespread feature of contemporary social change. Lanternari generalizes that these are "religions of oppression"—helpless responses to political and economic domination (*17*). Schwartz disagrees with this analysis (*25*). In a cogent psycho-cultural analysis of "cargo cult" phenomena in Melanesia, he sees this form of revivalism as a reaction to disturbances of the Melanesian status system, which was based on economic prestige. The wealth of the Europeans destroyed the traditional economic symbols of Melanesian culture, leading to a collapse of the culture's economic system and a disruption of the Melanesian's self-concept. This disruption of social identity resulted in the phenomenon of the cargo cult, which Schwartz contends was a means of overcoming in symbolic economic terms the disparities of status between Melanesians and Europeans. The millenarian coming of cargo would equalize a status deprivation inflicted by the dominant whites, even when they were not present politically. Schwartz points out that the cargo cult could occur without direct European contact, because mere knowledge of European wealth was sufficient to devalue the Melanesians' previous criteria of economic success. Hence one does not have to call on direct political domination and exploitation to explain Melanesian revivalist cults. A psycho-cultural examination of how a sense of social self-identity relates to a concept of economic-social status is more directly explanatory.

For some groups, religious beliefs about their historical origin and past tribulations provide the vital definition of who they are. When a native religion is destroyed by the imposition of a conquering people's beliefs, the group identity, if it survives at all, receives a severe blow. There can be widespread loss of morale. The status role of adult males, particularly, can be affected by attacks on the indigenous religious system. When sustaining beliefs are undermined by this type of cultural contact, the individual and collective will to survive is weakened, leading to collective anomie. Some groups, such as American Indians, suffer from an inability to believe in themselves, because they have lost faith in their own religious system and its symbols of dignity and status, but at the same time they cannot draw sustenance from the Christianity of their conquerors without giving up their own identity.

For many black Americans the Christian tradition remains a strong integrative force. The preacher or minister, always a social leader, now finds the requirements of his role shifting from accommodation toward confrontation and protest. Some militant blacks, however, have defined Christianity and sometimes Judaism as white racist religions. They have turned instead to Islam, which they see as less racially discriminatory. As an African religion it is not associated with European political oppression, whereas Christianity, in Africa and elsewhere, has been introduced during colonial occupations and used to induce psychological as well as social accommodation to an oppressed status. To forge a new identity, some black Americans have joined new groups such as the Black Muslims, or affiliated directly with an established

Muslim sect. Implicit also in this pro-Arab movement is an anti-Jewish feeling based on the ghetto experience of many blacks, who perceive Jewish merchants as using sharp practices to take advantage of them. Other blacks, while not adopting Islam, find it psychologically easier to identify with their African heritage by simply foregoing Christianity. Their sense of ethnic identity takes precedence over even a universalist definition of Christianity or the secular universalist outlook of Marxism.

Aesthetic Cultural Patterns

Particular cultures afford particular patterns related to aesthetic traditions used symbolically as a basis of self and social identity. Tastes in food, dance traditions, styles of clothing, and definitions of physical beauty are all examples of how cultures identify themselves by aesthetic patterns. In times of ethnic resurgence, greater emphasis is put on aesthetic features related to communication and social communion. The "soul" concept of black Americans is a case in point. Their patterns of communication form a basis for mutual acceptance and identity and include a vocabulary of gestures and formal language differences.

The religious, aesthetic and linguistic features of ethnic identity are related to questions of artistic creativity examined in psycho-cultural terms. Modes of ethnic persistence depend on the capacity to maintain art forms characteristic of a group rather than of an individual. Thus the trend toward world society brings with it a fear of increasing cultural homogeneity. It is not only the cultures of remote parts of New Guinea that are being lost, but the distinctiveness of traditional cultures everywhere. Perhaps the present interest in local folk traditions on the part of modern youth reflects a concern for preserving these rich sources of personal diversity.

Language

Language is often cited as a major component in the maintenance of a separate ethnic identity, and it is undoubtedly true that language constitutes the single most characteristic feature of a separate ethnic identity. But ethnicity is frequently related more to the symbol of a separate language than to its actual use by all members of a group. The Irish use Gaelic as a symbol of their Celtic ethnicity, as do the Scots, but speaking Gaelic is not essential to group membership in either case. Where particular languages have transcended national frontiers, as have English, French, and Spanish, ethnicity is not broadened to include all speakers of the language any more than it encompasses all believers in a common faith or all people with similar life styles.

Group identity can even be maintained by minor differences in linguistic patterns and by styles of gesture. There are a wide variety of ways in which language patterning fluency or lack of fluency in a second language is related to identity maintenance. Changing patterns within groups are related to the sanctioning, positively or negatively, of specific dialects. The reassertion of local versus central political controls is sometimes symbolically indicated by the degree to which local dialect patterns are maintained. This is apparent in European countries such as Italy and has strong influence in such pluralistic states as Indonesia. There is re-emphasis, for example, in England on the maintenance of local speech patterns. Political and economic sanctioning has lessened in Britain, so that one finds it no longer necessary to adopt standard speech or intonation in order to apply for a particular job.

Ethnicity: A Subjective Sense of Continuity in Belonging

In brief, the ethnic identity of a group of people consists of their subjective symbolic or emblematic use of any aspect of culture, in order to differentiate themselves from other groups. These emblems can be imposed from outside or embraced from within. Ethnic features such as language or clothing or food can be considered emblems, for they show others who one is and to what group one belongs. A Christian, for example, wears a cross; a Jew the star of David.

An extreme case, but useful for illustration, is that of the modern American Jew. There is a considerable body of literature written by Jewish intellectuals throughout their history in Europe and in the United States about what it is to be a Jew, and how one reconciles one's sense of ethnicity with citizenship, power, and social status in a prevailingly Christian society. Some recent writers fear that with the attenuation of social discrimination, modern American Jews may soon lose their sense of Jewishness. Already, some individuals who consider themselves Jews have no remaining special linguistic heritage; they no longer adhere to any of the beliefs of Judaism, nor to any customs peculiar to Jewish culture, and they do not believe that Jews comprise any special or distinct racial group. How, then, can they continue to feel that being Jewish is of importance in their sense of social self, or ethnic identity? Apparently it is a difficult task, for today some Jewish youth, although children of non-practicing parents, study Hebrew, visit Israel, join an orthodox synagogue, and reinstitute the rituals of the Sabbath, in order to "find themselves." This example illustrates dramatically the need for a psychological or "emic"* approach to the question of ethnic identity. As a subjective sense of belonging, ethnicity cannot be defined by behavioral criteria alone. Ethnicity is determined by what a person feels about himself, not by how he is observed to behave. Defining oneself in social terms is one basic answer to the human need to belong and to survive.

In a simple independent culture the sense of self is relatively uncomplicated. One's instrumental goals and expressive needs are inseparable. One's sense of belonging and social meaning—past, present, and future—are defined without contradiction in a unified belief system. This unified sense of belonging is disrupted, however, when the state emerges as an institution for governing—when several ethnic groups are coercively unified within a single political framework. Social allegiance is further complicated when future-oriented revolutionary ideologies appear. These are often religious movements that offer a transcendent form of identity more encompassing than currently available definitions.

As indicated earlier, religious movements can appear as revivalist cults that reinterpret symbols of the past in order to reestablish the group, using the old patterns to evoke an image of a better future for its members. Ethnicity, therefore, is in its narrowest sense a feeling of continuity with the past, a feeling that is maintained as an essential part of one's self-definition. Ethnicity is also intimately related to the individual need for collective continuity. The individual senses to some degree a threat to his own survival if his group or lineage is threatened with extinction. Ethnicity, therefore, includes a sense of personal survival in the historical continuity of the group. For this reason, failure to remain in the group leads to feelings of guilt. It is a form of killing inflicted on one's progenitors, including one's parents, who still "live" as long as some symbols of their culture are carried forth into the present and future out of the past. Ethnicity in its deepest psychological level is a sense of survival. If one's group survives, one is assured of survival, even if not in a personal sense.

Transcendental religions or universalist ideologies offer an alternative form of survival by affording a new identity, and a new form of continuity. The reasons for rejection of the old in embracing the new are varied and complex in individual cases. Entering a new religion, or leaving the family, are marked by symbols of death and rebirth in many forms of initiation ceremonies, such as baptism. These symbolic rituals testify to a transition in identity and are a

* An "emic" approach is an attempt on the part of the scientific observer to understand the conceptual system of the observed and to state his observations as best he can within the conceptual framework of the observed. This is opposed to an "etic" approach, which analyzes an observed situation in terms of the external system of the observer.

source of security about survival, whatever the threat of death may be in relinquishing the old identity. Broadly, universalist ideologies and ethnically-oriented social definitions are contrastive and alternative patterns that introduce conflict in complex societies.

BASIC TYPES OF GROUP ALLEGIANCE

Problems of Priority

A sense of social belonging can be achieved by according loyalty to a larger group. In a complex society, the body to which an individual gives his greatest commitment depends on whether he is oriented primarily to the past, the present, or the future (see figure 1). With a present orientation, one's primary loyalty is directed toward his country. Patriotism can be a powerful emotion, making people willing to sacrifice their lives for the "fatherland" or "motherland." Here survival of the nation is more important than personal survival. Although this strength of emotion can bind citizens together, it may,

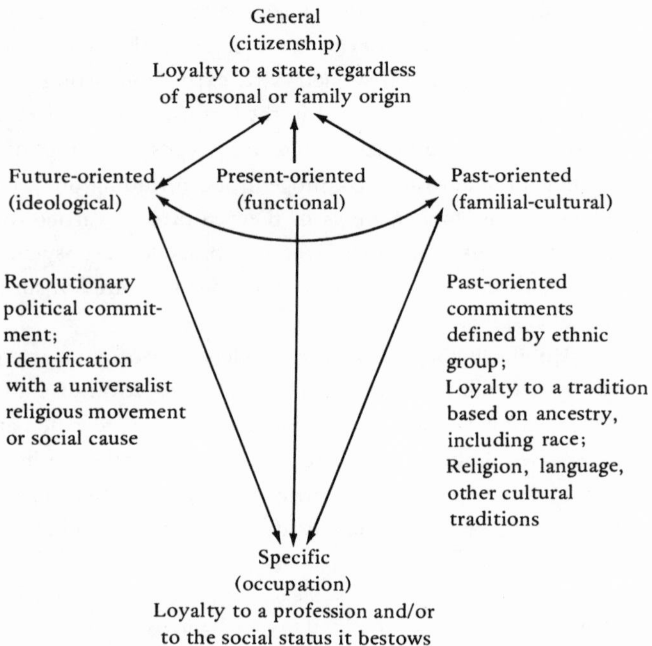

FIGURE 1 **Priority in Belonging: Directions of Conflict and Accommodation Between Types of Group Allegiance**

but does not necessarily, involve any concept of past common origin. The emphasis is on present participation. French citizenship or American citizenship are assimilative legal concepts defining vital and continuing national identity. One does not often hear Italians or Germans speak of citizenship in the same way, perhaps because Italy and Germany lacked a tradition of voluntary in-migration or assimilation of the foreign-born.

A less general and sometimes conflicting form of present-oriented social belonging is identity through participation in an occupation. This identity may conflict with a national identity. When an individual acquires competence in a skill or a profession, his primary commitment shifts to his occupation, or to the social class of his profession. He may identify himself by status as a nobleman or a commoner, or by occupation, as a merchant or a worker, or more specifically as a scientist, a physician, and so on. This identity may be much stronger and more compelling than a national or ethnic allegiance. However, in time of conflict an ethnic or national allegiance may assume priority, such as in the case of some German and Japanese social scientists who distorted professional knowledge in the direction of ethnic-national ideologies in World War II. Present occupation and past ethnic identity can in addition represent caste allegiances.

Individuals who are dissatisfied with the past and the present may adopt a future orientation, attaining a sense of belonging by identification with a cause or a revolutionary movement. These movements may be directly generated by a religious or politico-social ideology. Individuals whose sense of social self is related to a perceived exploitative, unjust or immoral present society may develop a sense of identity that brings them into political conflict with their society. Unrest on the basis of religious or political beliefs may develop in individuals or in groups. Sometimes an ethnic minority will seem to use a future-oriented movement as a vehicle for protest, but in such cases, the actual motivation of participants must be carefully examined. Russians in World War II, for example, are reported to have fought more to defend their ethnic homeland than to defend the ideology of international Communism. The Vietnam war involved ethnic and religious conflicts as much as it involved conflict between international socialism and capitalistic democracy.

In contrast to present- or future-oriented sources of social identity, ethnicity is oriented to special past heritage. It may be congruent with present citizenship in some states, or be quite unrelated to citizenship in others. It may overlap with a future-oriented identity when the two are seen as mutually supportive. But ethnicity, as defined here, is primarily a sense of belonging to a particular ancestry and origin and of sharing a specific religion or language. This primary sense of belonging may or may not be related to political or geographical units, and may or may not bring the individual into conflict with the larger society.

The history of minority peoples and organizations has in general, however, been an unhappy series of conflicts and accommodations arising from the coercive pressures that politically dominant groups exert on their subordinates to gain and to maintain their loyalty. Some members of subordinate groups may seek to change their assigned or ascribed lower status positions to more congenial past or future definitions of self and group. This pressure for change causes instability in stratified societies, which often respond with suppressive measures, seeking sometimes to assimilate the group, causing it to disappear rather than according it more autonomy.

Ethnic Pluralism as a Means of Changing Relative Social Status

The conceptual scheme of forms of social belonging just presented is abstract, but is helpful in understanding why social movements based on group belonging take the particular form they do in given cultural-historical situations. The change of status demanded by black Americans from their reluctant white countrymen affords a good example of how ethnic membership shapes social movements. Gerald Berreman (2) and others have advanced cogent arguments defining how caste concepts govern social relationships not only in India but in the United States, between blacks and whites. In assessing the status of the *burakumin*, the ex-pariahs of Japan, Wagatsuma and I came to a similar conclusion (*9*). Those groups of Indians, Americans and Japanese who have been treated as members of outcaste or pariah groups show numerous similarities in their collective attempts to overcome the effects of caste. However, the differences are striking and reflect overall differences in cultural history and present social structure. They influence the methods taken to change one's status individually and collectively in each instance. The directions taken by their social movements differ depending on the inherent difficulties faced in reconciling class, caste, and ethnic identities.

Both caste and class definitions of self are explicitly related to a system of formal stratification, whereas ethnic definitions imply some less explicit hierarchy, hence are more open to change with shifts of economic or political power. Both ethnic and class self-definitions can constitute a challenge to the state, since loyalty to either one may transcend national boundaries. International Communism, for example, threatens the state by emphasizing the solidarity of the world's working classes, while ethnic groups may threaten it by a struggle for political separation. Some of the present caste groups in India, for example, were originally non-Hindu tribes, but they cannot draw on this past to change their present relative status. Some of these groups, however, have reconstructed their history to create in effect a myth of a past higher status (*23, 24*). Since caste rank is strongly internalized as part of an Indian's identity, freeing oneself from it is very difficult. A socially mobile group in India must therefore constrain others to recognize its right to a higher rank, rather than trying to escape from the caste system altogether. *Harijans* or former untouchables, however, are attempting exactly that by converting from Hinduism to Buddhism, but with questionable success.* Although Indian state policy has taken steps toward establishing non-caste criteria for social ranking, caste is still the most potent influence on social status. Since ethnicity is not an effective means for changing relative status within Indian society, some territorial–ethnic groups such as the Assamese are seeking political autonomy instead.

The United States, on the other hand, is a mixed class-ethnic society with caste–race features. In order to resolve the caste-related conflict as well as social and ideological inconsistencies, the United States is attempting to eliminate caste-race categories in favor of an ideology of ethnic pluralism. There is as a result a reduced commitment to assimilation and a greater emphasis on religious, cultural, and even linguistic pluralism.

Although the point is disputed when put in these terms, the black population in the United States, a former slave caste, is forcing white society to accept Negroes as equals in the competition for social status and economic benefits, a pattern of social adaptation already worked out by the millions of European immigrants into the United States. Black Americans are also redefining themselves in ethnic terms. Among the blacks brought in as slaves, African ethnic traditions persisted as submerged fragments. Now, however, black Americans are reaching back to their African heritage to create an ethnic tradition of their own, separate from that of Europeans and Asians.

There is a seeking out among blacks for means of amplifying all the criteria comprising ethnicity. Definitions of their territorial origins in Africa, and territorial and economic strongholds in present American settings, old folk and religious practices, features of lifestyle, family relationships, and artistic traditions—are researched for their Afro-American flavor. As in all groups concerned with origins as a source of social meaning, where history is insufficient, myths are created. Effort is made to recreate their identity on the basis of cultural continuities rather than on the simplistic caste–racial criteria used in oppressing them. Some blacks, reversing the pejorative

* A universalist faith, Buddhism was born in India as a revolutionary attempt to overcome caste. When caste-oriented Hinduism prevailed, Buddhism retreated out of India. Now again Buddhism is being used for the same revolutionary task which it failed to accomplish in the past. Hindus consider Buddhism ethnically alien, just as some Shintoists in Japan have been anti-Buddhist, resenting its universalist elements.

connotations imposed by Europeans, consider "soul" or "negritude" biologically inherited and the source of special folk features supposedly shared by all of African heritage, but not to be found in Europeans or Asians.

The search for origins goes back to a black history that preceded slavery. The slave past is not denied or hidden but is seen as a transitory stage of exploitation of black Africans as a "people," not as an occupational class. This ethnic definition is presently more powerful as a means of overcoming the disadvantages of caste definitions than any occupational or social class, since these affinities do not as yet cross the caste barrier among white working-class Americans.

By using an ethnic definition of themselves to change their relative status, blacks are pursuing a characteristically American path. Ethnic relationships remain as potential sources of identity and of social participation in America and cut across those patterns generated by the various levels of social class positions and occupations that stratify the society economically and socially.* It is a way to change relative status that works for the blacks, who have now taken the initiative in defining themselves by means of confrontation and militancy. Whites of various ethnic backgrounds, especially on the working-class level, are being forced either to fight back or to find some accommodative redefinition which makes sense to them and which they can accept, while still not admitting blacks totally as in-group social participants. Retreating from overt racist positions, some American urban groups are seeking defensive accommodations or are launching counteroffensives on the level of ethnic groupings. Among the Jews and Italians in New York and the Poles in Pittsburgh, Chicago, and Milwaukee, a sense of ethnic belonging has been rekindled among third-generation working-class members, restoring definitions that had become attenuated by attempts to pass as ordinary Americans.

A great deal of American conformity behavior and concern with loyalty is a reflection of uneasiness over the legitimacy of a claim to be "American" on the part of the second generation of ethnic immigrants. Many ethnics pass by moving to a suburb. Those moving into a good neighborhood in a suburb are very conformity-oriented, since they are new to, and often insecure about,

* This pattern of a dual ethnic-social class identity is found in other so-called hyphenated Americans—Italians, Jews, Irish, Poles, Lithuanians, Armenians, Mexicans, Chinese, Japanese—that are sprinkled throughout various occupational-social class levels in American society and who may or may not maintain overt continuity with their ethnic group as a feature of their social life or as a part of their self-identity. Nathan Glazer and Daniel P. Moynihan in *Beyond the Melting Pot* (Cambridge, Mass.: MIT Press, 1963), point up numerous examples of the persistence of ethnicity despite the American ideology of assimilation.

their claim to middle class status. In particular, white suburbs composed of second generation Americans of European parentage become defensive, fearing collective loss of social status should black families move in. They are realistically afraid that the value of their hard-earned real estate might suffer in a panic exodus of like-minded "neighbors." Among upwardly mobile ethnics there are numerous changes of name to remove the stigma of an unAmerican name. Names with an Anglo-Saxon or Irish sound are preferred. Jews, Poles, and other Eastern Europeans, especially, find ways to truncate or Anglicize their names.

A recent widespread phenomenon is taking place among the third-generation children produced in these suburbs. Now attending American universities, they are searching for ways to recapture a sense of ethnic identity, which their parents failed to transmit to them. Today's youth in general do not respond to WASP social dominance as did F. Scott Fitzgerald when he faced the subtle discrimination of his upper-class classmates at Princeton. The entry of self-conscious racial-minority group militants into American universities has changed the system of ethnic passing practiced there. These young people, seeking out some former ethnic identity as a counterpart to the sense of "soul" espoused by their black classmates, children of parents who carried little ethnic baggage in their search for upward mobility, deeply miss the expressive emotional satisfactions of ethnic belonging.

At this point in American history, past-oriented ethnicity is more appealing to American blacks as a means of reordering their status than is a future-orientation, such as a universalist religion or self-definition as a member of an exploited proletarian class. Black workers are aware that emotional expressive caste attitudes remain a strong part of the spontaneous relationships of the other workers, and that many of these white workers are still ethnics to some degree. He recognizes that Irish get certain jobs, Poles others, and that they too live in special neighborhoods. These American realities are more visible than is the supposed brotherhood among workers that is to remove discrimination. Sometimes the middle-class management of a plant is less discriminatory than the work force. One finds similar caste discrimination in Japan. Despite Marxist militancy, the former Japanese pariahs get little support from majority group Japanese workers. Worker brotherhood, emotionally at least, does not seem to cross the caste barrier (*26*).

The change taking place in socially pluralistic America, therefore, is that social primary group participation is becoming more ethnic oriented, while seeking to eliminate occupational discrimination. The processes occurring in combating the force of caste as a social institution in America are far different from those in India. Out of this use of a new ethnic definition by black Americans is emerging a shared social self-identity which is overcoming internally and externally the negative social definitions which have been internalized accommodatively by large numbers of people in the past.

ETHNICITY AND INDIVIDUAL SOCIAL MOBILITY

Within complex or culturally pluralistic societies as in any stratified society, individuals of inferior status are motivated to change identity by entering some group of superior status. A form of "identity flow" occurs in emulated behavior which characterizes the higher-status groups.

Complex cultures contain differential patterns with respect to how upwardly mobile behavior is learned and how culture is or can be diffused. In Japan, for example, patterns for diffusion of status behavior are related to the apprenticeship experiences of men and women who in their youth work several years for individuals or families of higher status. Women from lower status positions are apprenticed in the houses of upper status persons and learn patterns of acceptable behavior with which they at least partially identify and which they use to evaluate the behavior of members of their own social class. Such judgments may then create internal tensions in lower status persons, inducing them to acquire the more highly valued traits. Status emulation is apparent in the diffusion of warrior or samurai traits to the Japanese population at large, especially when the samurai were abolished as an official class after the restoration of the emperor in 1868.

With the development of mass communication media in Japan, these patterns of diffusion have been radically altered. The source of models for emulation is shifting from immediate personal contacts with people of higher status to an extra-cultural or extra-national frame of reference for all segments of the population. The effects of modern mass media on cultural identity should be thoroughly examined for their influence on evaluative patterns related to ethnic behavior and to other forms of social mobility. As Wagatsuma suggests in his chapter, much of this behavior is a change of reference group rather than of ethnic identity. Modern Japanese youth are "Japanese" even though they wear "mod" clothing or sing country and western music.

In some instances there are reverse romanticizations of submerged ethnic minorities; that is, behavioral traits can be borrowed from more active, less rigidified lower status groups. Such borrowing may symbolically liberate a person in a higher status group from the excessive strictures imposed in assuming an acceptable social role within his own group. Identity diffusion, therefore, does not only take place from upper to lower strata, but from lower to upper or between strata, by borrowing from another ethnic group.

In California, for example, some Japanese-American militant youth, seeking an "ethnic" pattern of confrontation, lacking in their parental tradition, borrow black dialect and its rhetorical inflections directly from members of the black power groups with whom they associate.

With respect to individual upward mobility, maintenance of ethnicity in some societies is obviously characteristic of non-socially mobile lower status individuals who have few other sources for self-acceptance to fall back on. Thus his ethnic background is important in proportion to the number of other sources of status (occupational accomplishment, economic success) that are open to him.

Some ethnic minorities fear that their more successful members will leave them or betray their cause. This fear is justified to some extent, since the capacity to interact with individuals of higher status produces emotional and material rewards that are impossible to gain through association with members of a subordinate group lacking opportunities for obtaining these rewards.

Crises in Alienation

The alienation felt by some successful upwardly mobile individuals may be the result of their having cut so many ties with the past that they have lost a deeper sense of meaning, although the loss may not be apparent until they have time to think about it. The sense of anomie in American society that is commonly attributed to social mobility may often have more to do with the loss of ethnic inheritance than with the simple movement from a lower class to a higher class. It is the movement out of an ethnic group into a new community with new norms that creates the loss of meaning. When occupational success moves a person into an alien group, what is alien to him is often the change in ethnic behavior required, rather than new status behavior as such.

Jews are an ethnic group which has accommodated well to living within another culture while maintaining its integrity. Even the resultant psychological problems do not in the main interfere with social adaptation. Many occupationally successful Jews have adapted well to shifts in social class status without feeling any loss of their ethnic integrity. In fact, Jewish culture looks upon successful individuals as heroic figures. There are many tales of how the Jew who was successful in the alien Christian world was able to maintain his ethnic integrity and bring benefit to his community, rather than using his success for selfish personal reasons. As I shall discuss in respect to patterns of group expulsion as well as passing, other ethnic groups such as Mexican-Americans have no tradition that individual success should benefit the ethnic community, since their culture is so often characterized by deprived social status. Since business success in the United States generally requires capitulation to white standards, blacks and Mexicans often suspect the ethnic ties of those members of their groups who have become successful.

A major source of ethnic identity is found in the cultural traditions related to crises in the life cycle, such as coming of age, marriage, divorce, illness, or death. It is particularly in rites of passage that one finds highly emotional symbolic reinforcement of ethnic patterns. Erik Erikson has delineated well the problem of identity commitment in modern complex societies (*10*). Adulthood is particularly problematic for younger members of minority groups, because of possible difficulties with "identity diffusion."

The situations and the time of life in which members of particular ethnic minorities are subject to alienation probably varies from group to group. Different groups may face overt social problems at different periods of life. These problems, however, may be preceded by less visible intrapsychic conflicts. The Japanese-American may have no apparent difficulty socially in maintaining his ethnic identity and at the same time conforming to the majority society throughout his entire educational experience, although the price of this maintenance is sometimes neurotic psychological patterns. Social crises, however, may not occur until later, when, for example, job requirements demand a type of initiative which the individual has not learned within his tradition.

A Mexican-American child, on the other hand, may experience a social crisis involving potential alienation early in his formal school experience when he is torn between the conflicting demands of the school and the peer group. Either he sides with the peer group, which may lead him into a career of social deviance during adolescence, or he chooses to conform to the role of good student, which may lead to a deep sense of social alienation. In some ethnic groups, the tensions of minority status are visible in the form of socially deviant careers, whereas in other groups, such tensions lead to internalized forms of psychopathology that are not visible to the casual observer (*6*, pp. 328-356).

Patterns of Passing

It is readily observable that in most societies where upward mobility is possible, ethnic minorities continually lose members to the politically, economically, and socially dominant segments. Such mobility not only provides the individual with a means of resolving his social and psychological problems, it also serves to maintain the stability of the society. Individual "evaporation" takes the pressure out of potential social protest movements of dissatisfied groups. When a group is, however, totally blocked in an otherwise mobile society, pressure can build to explosive proportions as it has among racial minority groups in the United States. In most stratified societies social order is maintained by providing sufficient possibilities for individual social mobility, whether this pattern is part of the overtly acknowledged social ideology or not. One cannot judge a society in this respect simply by looking at its formal structure—one must seek out the hidden, sometimes even criminal, means available to individuals bent on changing their status and the status of their families. Some ethnic minorities in the United States, like the Koreans and Chinese in Japan, are overrepresented in organized as well as in individual criminal activity (*7*, pp. 289-325; *8*).

Occupational mobility patterns in modern industrial states are relatively similar, despite differing ideologies about the effects of economic demand on the upward mobility of people with special skills in commerce and industry and the scientific professions. Lipset and Bendix (*19*) demonstrated the similarities between the United States and European countries with respect to occupational-economic mobility, despite highly divergent ideological attitudes. Their criteria for social mobility, however, are not quite adequate. There are observable differences in the patterns of social participation possible to occupationally mobile individuals and their families. In France, for example, the wife of a professionally mobile man does not socialize with those on the same professional level as her husband. This would not be true for wives of occupationally successful Americans. The French children, however, if they attend the proper schools, can often translate their father's success into a higher level of social participation. Social background remains important and hard to disguise in France, although fictions about background are frequent—altering one's name is one of the most frequent devices. But in class and caste societies, occupational mobility does not guarantee change in social participation in any except the most formal circumstances. The "wrong" background is sanctioned against informally, especially by denying access to informal primary social participation. There is therefore in most societies some inducement to disguise one's background, if it would stigmatize one socially. In the managerial class of the contemporary Soviet Union, it is socially disadvantageous to be of bourgeois origin. Every stratified society in one way or another induces passing, that is, disguising the stigma of a disfavored family background.

The term "passing" used in race relations literature is usually applied only to situations in which an individual of partial black African ancestry disappears from his black social classification and reappears as white, if his appearance permits him to do so. By disguising his origins he "passes" unnoticed, in some forms of participation at least, into white society. Wagatsuma and I (*9*) studied this phenomenon in Japan, where members of a former pariah caste cut off contact with family and friends of similar origin, as part of individual attempts at social mobility. In this instance the issue was racial only in that members of this caste are generally but erroneously considered to be biologically, hence racially, different from other Japanese. In studying this phenomenon from a psychological viewpoint in Japan, it became apparent that passing is a general psycho-cultural phenomenon that operates in a similar fashion both socially and psychologically, no matter whether social class, ethnic origin, or racial group is the primary consideration. In each case appearance and behavior are consciously changed into socially acceptable forms, in order to be considered part of a more desirable social group.

But passing is not simply a procedure used for direct social advantage; it also has expressive emotional meaning. A variety of intrapsychic as well as external behavioral maneuvers are involved, which can in turn lead to different types of internal tensions related to alternatives in reference groups and alternatives in degree and pattern of partial incorporation of alien elements into the self. It should be interesting to examine the differences and similarities between passing within one's own society and expatriate forms of alienation. For instance, alienation in Japanese, Chinese, or Indian intellectuals is different each from the other in respect to how they maintain an integrated national identity while incorporating Western values. The crises of "integrity" involving a search for the "real self" have similarities no matter where they occur or under what conditions passing or alienation takes place. In some situations individuals re-identify with their ethnic origins, having found the alienation and malaise involved in maintaining a new identity too much a strain (*9*).

Since passing is usually effected through self-conscious manipulation of behavior, it requires maintaining a facade. To the degree that the facade is not part of oneself there is often an internal duality involving a partially pejorative self-image. The self is thought to have been stigmatized by one's parents, in Goffman's sense of the term (*13*), with some resulting elements of self-hate, or hate of one's progenitors. In psychotherapy, however, the sequence uncovered is often found to be the reverse: first a primary pattern of hate starts within the family, which in turn produces an ambivalence about the self. The individual may then seize upon an available pattern of class differences or ethnic pluralism and use social mobility to attempt a resolution of psychological distress.

In this context it is not possible to discuss the role of conscious and unconscious psychological mechanisms in the original psycho-sexual identification processes which underlie those later processes that form the total social self-identity, of which ethnicity is a central component. I cannot do more here than introduce the topic of individual passing and its personal motivations as a general phenomenon that cannot be ignored in studying social stratification.

Suffice it to say here that people often need to escape what is perceived to be a negative social self-identity. Most individuals who pass are in this sense prejudiced against their group of origin. Passing is used to escape as well from a way of feeling and acting which the individual perceives to be necessary or inescapable for his primary social group. A person sometimes identifies very early with the dress, speech and bodily comportment of a higher social class, viewing the behavior of his own family with distaste. He may even fear that he inescapably possesses traits he dislikes in others of his group. Such an individual seeks new models of comportment and associations outside his own group.

Physical appearance that is in the direction of favorable stereotypes may provide reinforcement for change. A person whose appearance is not conducive to passing may view his own appearance as an irremovable stigma passed on to him by his group. Obvious physical differences make passing difficult but not always impossible, at least from a subjective standpoint. Some black Americans become not Anglo-Saxons but "Hindus." Some Mexican-Americans believe they are socially better off if they pass as Italians.

But in any case, the absolute black-white "racial" distinction is only an extreme among various modes used by class- or race-oriented societies to prevent individuals from passing upward.

The non-U Londoner who has used the word "glasses" instead of "spectacles" has irrevocably revealed his class background to witnesses who by subtle change of demeanor can socially reclassify him thereafter. Such rejection inflicts suffering subjectively proportionate to the felt need for acceptance. There are forms of what is technically called "denial" used by some who seem consciously unaware that they are not passing as far as observers are concerned.

Some of the most poignant incidents related to us about the passing among Japanese outcastes were situations in which the individual deliberately exposed his stigmatized outcaste origin. We presume this was out of a need to escape the intolerable burden of continual disguise. Many individuals sooner or later find it psychologically more tolerable to drop their facade; to "come in from the cold." Some like to avoid identity ambiguity. Instead of exposing themselves to some possible social trauma related to a disguised identity, they use some overt, unmistakable symbol or emblem of identity that signals to others their origins and their continued ethnic or class allegiance. These usages resemble what Erving Goffman would consider the flaunting of a stigma.

Withdrawal and Expulsion

Social mobility does not invariably involve passing as we have described it. Much more often one finds gradual withdrawal from social participation. The economically successful upwardly mobile individual may find that he and/or members of his family no longer feel comfortable with those known in childhood. New experiences develop social perceptions and needs that move him out of his former group. The social alienation is probably in most instances mutual. There may be no shift in identity but a shift in acceptable life style.

In some instances the individual is ostracized by members of his own social group. In Mexican-American or American Indian groups, for example, to be successful economically, or to participate socially with dominant status whites, is by definition to be a "falso" or a deserter. To maintain individual wealth without sharing can be considered a reason for social exclusion. A social group that has experienced "evaporation" can be particularly sensitive to the first signs of a member's behavioral emulation of traits of an outside group. Members from early on may be prevented from taking on other linguistic or social usages by group sanctioning. The individual is made well aware of the threat of expulsion; hence there can be a self-fulfilling prophecy that those who learn "Anglo" behavior, for example, are not to be trusted.

The maintenance of ethnic separation therefore is quite complex, since whether or not a person belongs to an ethnic minority is decided by people outside the group, by the group itself, and by the individual's definition of himself. Self-definition is secondary when the individual has no choice about his group identity, either because the majority group actively prevents his entry into their ranks, or because his own group will not tolerate his leaving their ranks, whether he wants to do so or not. Yet in almost all instances social ambiguities permit some individuals to pass.

The child of a mixed union is almost always put into an ambiguous role, a complex topic which cannot be pursued in depth here. Where racial differences in appearance make some social affirmation of identification important, there can still be room for ambiguity in definition of individuals of mixed ancestry. In Brazil, light-skinned Negroes are in a sense given the choice of passing if they so desire, with the phenomenon of passing treated rather lightly. In the United States, on the other hand, where maintaining the ritual purity of the white group has been important, passing is a serious issue for those whites who fear "tainted blood." It is also a serious concern to the black group, which would like to assert sanctions to keep members loyal. This is a particular point of tension in contemporary American society, not only from the standpoint of subjective self-inclusion as an American black but also because the word "black" has become symbolic of ethnic membership (as contrasted to the word "Negro," which is seen as indicating excessive accommodation to the culture and viewpoint of the dominant white population). Thus the role of light-skinned persons of mixed white-black ancestry has become more difficult, especially since the threat of expulsion has increased with attempts to establish a militant black solidarity.

In the history of ethnic survival, thresholds of leaving or of expulsion vary with social conditions. Groups sometimes feel threatened when assimilation is easy and seek to maintain separation by increased sanctioning from within. At other times discrimination from outside the group makes leaving it difficult. The within-group sanctions to retain members are more or less invisible, but nevertheless remain in force. I shall not attempt here to consider the sanctions by which the majority keeps an ethnic group separate, but will consider very briefly some of the internal sanctions of a group in maintaining itself.

Sanctions of belonging start very early and cannot be separated from the development of the sense of self. The conscious processes involved in the later stages of identity formation are preceded by earlier, automatic processes. The self as it develops in a human being is innately social—it is related to the primary community. Experiences in the family develop a sense of self, but peer group experiences in childhood are also important. In some societies, in fact, peer groups are much more important than the family as a principal mediator of social identity. The peer group is certainly a most exacting socializer, which demands continual symbols of allegiance from those participating. Although childhood gangs in many cases are transitory, they are instrumental in setting standards for language usage, and even for modes of thinking, which may in some instances run counter to parental patterns.

In acculturative situations such as those in New York or Chicago in the early twentieth century, primary social identities reflected, especially in regard to language, more the effect of the peer group than of the home in self-definition. American-born ethnics of that generation identified themselves as "Americans" linguistically, by refusing to speak the language of their parents, and attitudinally, by rejecting many of the expressed values of their parents. They adopted instead the values presented by the mass media and the school, as well as by the predominantly American peer group. Social mobility was part of a positively sanctioned American identity. These children accepted without question the characteristics of those who are today viewed with much more ambivalence—the white Anglo-Saxon Protestants who, as far as many a child in New York knew, all came over on the Mayflower.

One wonders why American education has been so successful in overcoming linguistic pluralism, when other countries encounter so much difficulty in changing the language of minority groups. The explanation may lie in the influence of the peer group at school. Since the school was a meeting ground of peers from different language groups, English became its lingua franca in the early 1900s in the United States. No European ethnic minority children could hold out for a language that separated them from the others at school. In other words, the peer groups were broadly "American" in orientation. The sense of self that developed out of this experience in the sons and daughters of immigrants was of being "American" rather than simply remaining Italian – or Jewish, or Irish – in a new setting. The business of being American was extremely important for the American-born children of immigrant parents at the turn of the twentieth century.

Although the cultural content of their heritage has disappeared, many third-generation youth have developed a longing for a sense of continuity with their past. The recent positive response to the Italian Defense League in New York, despite its rather unsavory founders, is a fair indication of the continuing sense of ethnicity in New York City. The fact is that being an Italian-American has little to do with the Italian language or with most features of Italian culture. Rather, it has to do with a sense of continuity with the past, of group loyalty, and of a similarity of emotional experience within the home which makes the individual look for self-assertion in the form of ethnic group belonging.

Compared with the experiences of the waves of European immigrants, there seems today to be more difficulty in educating children of Mexican-American, Puerto Rican, black or American Indian background. It is evident to me at least that for these children to be amenable to learning majority norms, the influence of their minority peer groups against such norms must be overcome. Threats of expulsion from the ethnic peer group are a strong force against the formal educative processes in the schools. Scattered informal evidence suggests that European schools—for example, in Switzerland—are beginning to encounter similar difficulties in educating ethnic minorities, including the children of migrant workers.

The poor school record of some ethnic minorities may be partly the result of the frequent negative images that majority group teachers hold toward their ethnically or socially different charges. Such difficulties are also caused by the early internalization of negative self-images and by a peer group culture that sanctions against ready compliance with the objectives of the school. Thus for some minority groups, the majority-oriented school can not provide the means of acquiring occupational mobility. The status of the group as a whole tends to remain depressed, offering no variation in class position or social-occupational models with which members of the group can identify and still retain a sense of belonging. By contrast, some groups, such as Jews and Japanese, severely sanction those who do poorly in school. The conforming attitudes of their peers reinforces in these children the need to learn at school (*9* pp. 241-257).

Although this topic has more dimensions than it is possible to consider here, we can say that from a social structural standpoint, at least, early sanctioning to maintain ethnic integrity can cause certain ethnic groups difficulty in changing status through formal education. Within-group self-perpetuation is a partial cause, as is external social discrimination. In some groups, such as Jews and Japanese, there is sufficient support from within to push those who remain identified with their groups toward occupational mobility, while in other groups, such as American Indians, group identity tends to prevent mobility.

ACCOMMODATION TO MINORITY STATUS

The assertion that any low-status ethnic minority or social caste really prefers the position allocated to it is highly questionable. Such assertions nevertheless are often repeated as myths of mutual reassurance by members of dominant groups who suppose their subordinates to be happy with their lot. Any intensive contact with a subordinate group easily dispels such ideas. Nevertheless, a social scientist must account for the social and psychological accommodation found in fairly stable systems, as well as for the eruption of conflict when it occurs. While one cannot accept the notion that externally accommodative behavior on the part of people of subordinate status reflects the true social self-identity of the group's members, neither can one accept the converse Hobbsian notion that a stratified system which often includes ethnic minorities remains stable simply by the threat of force. Some forms of psychological internalization are found among those forced for any period of time into accommodative behavior.

In ethnic minorities, internal psychological accommodations, including internalization of assigned lower social status, differ among individuals and among the groups considered, as the following section illustrates by considering the difference between two forms of accommodation to low status. At one extreme we see debilitating attitudes toward the self manifested by a considerable number of persons in some ethnic minorities; at the other extreme, we see in members of some groups a capacity for deferment of goals of higher status as a culturally available psychological tactic which does not injure one's self-assessment, while providing a means for accommodation to subordinate status.

According to George Herbert Mead, in acquiring a sense of self, one "internalizes a generalized other" (*20*, pp. 152-164). Approaching identity formation from this theory, one would expect a subtle but significant psychological difference between the social internalization of low-status individuals who are members of ethnic groups and those who are not. A lower status member of a stratified society cannot resist some internalization of a negative self-image as a result of the socially prevalent explanations for his group's relative occupational and social inferiority. By remaining oriented to a pattern of evaluation originating in one's ethnic group, however, an individual should be better able to avoid the internalization of attitudes toward himself pressed on him by outsiders. Nevertheless, ethnic identity is of itself no assurance that a negative self-identity can be avoided, if the negative aspects are continually reinforced by discriminatory social attitudes. Ethnic communities must be examined individually to ascertain how they protect or damage the self-evaluation of their members.

To illustrate briefly, the majority population on the West Coast expected second generation Japanese-Americans to fulfill certain stereotypes: they would become ideal houseboys or gardeners, etc., emulating the lower status accommodative occupational roles permitted their parents. In California, where the social discrimination was the strongest, there were even attempts to use legal as well as social means to limit the occupational roles open to Japanese. Such social pressures did not prevent the "Nisei" (the American-born generation) from attaining educational and occupational goals defined by their own families and communities rather than by the outside society (*3*). The period of low status accommodation to social discrimination in the United States has been relatively short. But even more important is that those emigrating to the United States brought with them their own sense of self-respect, as well as cultural attitudes which were useful in overcoming the severe racism of American society.

An estimated 85 percent of Japanese immigrants were from rural areas, but they were not former serfs or peasants in the European sense. In Japan, farmers were a respected class, ranking only after the samurai and ahead of merchants and artisans, regardless of economic fluctuations. The Japanese communities in the United States accorded status to their members which had little or no correspondence to their jobs outside. They did not evaluate themselves on the basis of American attitudes toward them as peasants or immigrant workers or "yellow" Asians. Moreover, they brought with them a future orientation, ready to postpone immediate gratification and to endure adversity. Characteristically, a person would submit to an apprenticeship, with the goal of acquiring status through competence (*4*), just as a traditional Japanese society one was expected to submit to a long apprenticeship, looking forward to status acquired by compliance to a mentor. Japanese also avoided confrontation in working out differences with American discrimination—direct confrontation would only have been used as a last resort. In their recent history, governmental authority both legally and socially has tended to be paternalistic but responsible, making it possible to think of the government as interested in the welfare of the people, rather than hated or feared as exploitative. Compliance was rewarded.

These and other interrelated cultural features help explain the relative lack of confrontation and conflict both in the United States, where West Coast Japanese were put in guarded camps, and in Japan during several years of postwar occupation.

A traditional Japanese does not feel it socially or personally demeaning to be in a subordinate position while he is learning. His sense of integrity is not destroyed by adversity. Japanese immigrants to the United States imparted to their Nisei children a respect for authority, even the authority of an alien society—they were to become loyal citizens. This was not inconsistent with Japanese concepts of loyalty to organizations once one became a member (*21*). Children were taught to conform to regulations imposed in school. Improper behavior would bring injury and shame to parents and to "Japanese." To be Japanese was a matter of deeply felt pride on the part of the immigrant "Issei," whatever attitudes they met on the outside. They therefore imparted an accommodative but future-oriented concept of success. This pattern is less understood by some third generation or "Sansei," youth who are impatient with what they considered the complacency and conformity with which their parents met social discrimination.

The indirect non-confrontational methods of Japanese community leaders in dealing with the racist attitudes of white Americans is well illustrated by an incident in Chicago in 1949. The well-known news commentator Drew Pearson learned that cemeteries in Chicago were refusing to bury Japanese, even if they were Christians. He wished to make a public issue of this act of social discrimination, but members of the Japanese community asked him to refrain, saying that they did not want "dirty publicity"—they would find indirect means of resolving the problem.

Given the terrible problems of dislocation of families in California, our research team failed to find any but a minimal use of public welfare agencies. The Japanese were solving their social problems within their own community. The fact that Japanese did well in American schools attests to group consistency with respect to what was expected. Parents were cohesive reinforcers of tightly sanctioned values in regard to education, while the community itself heavily sanctioned conformist behavior in the schools. The Japanese peer group left no alternative to studying hard in the American schools. Conversely, parental pressures to learn Japanese in Japanese language schools were notably unsuccessful. The peer group pressure was in the other direction, toward an American identity. The written Japanese language was not learned. The response of Japanese children in refusing to learn Japanese was in no way different from that of the children of European immigrants who refused to learn Italian or Polish.

The contrast with the ethnic adaptation of Mexican-Americans is striking. Since Mexico is directly south of the United States, the continuous inmigration encourages the persistence of Mexican ethnicity, including language, a persistence which is not found in those coming from Europe. Nevertheless, the Mexican-American ethnic minority, in contrast to the Japanese, manifests a relative lack of cohesiveness both in the community and in family life. While young Mexican-Americans are seeking a positive ethnic identity, the traditions available are sometimes conflictful and nonsupportive in respect to economic and occupational mobility.

The Mexican traditions are complex, but in general one finds wide status disparities and mutually alienating feelings among Spanish-speaking Americans. American territorial aggrandizement at the expense of Mexico incorporated into the United States Mexican minorities with a variety of internal class and status conflicts that later immigrants have reflected. The internal class, racial and ethnic cleavages are noticeable: those who identify with a Spanish background look down on the Indian culture and people. Others conceive of Mexican ethnicity as membership in "la raza," a special blend of European and Indian. There has been severe exploitation of peons, a depressed peasantry that has known only a society marked by extremes of poverty and wealth. Government authority has a suspicious history. A Mexican feels a need to defend himself from being "taken" or penetrated (*22*). Even within his immediate community he must defend himself against the easily aroused, malevolently perceived envy of neighbors. Social and personal distrust are part of social life. Traditionally, he finds it difficult to conceive of the economic success of one person without seeing it as of necessity taking something away from others. There is in fact a widespread belief in what George Foster terms "the limited good" (*11*).

Within the family one frequently finds distrust between marriage partners. In some lower status Mexican families the child is expected by the mother to take her side against a father who is depicted as drunken, unfaithful and financially irresponsible (*18*). The mother pictures herself as keeping the family together for the sake of her children and as lacking rapport with her husband. This contrasts with the Japanese family, where cohesiveness is based on the mutually supportive status that each parent accords the other. Discord within the Mexican family makes it more difficult to inoculate Mexican children against the discriminatory practices and attitudes of the majority group. Thus Mexican youth in many cases are alienated not only from the majority society but from their own parents, in such a way that their personal development is debilitated. They find themselves performing inadequately both in school or at work. The peer group for growing boys becomes an escape from family tensions. It is oriented against authority and discipline, often taking on a delinquent character. It becomes the principal reference group until marriage, which may in turn lead to the repetition of an unhappy pattern.

To make my point, I have stressed the negative aspects of Mexican-American ethnicity that contrast in my mind with features of Japanese community and family life. I would contend that the vast differences in individual and community response of Mexicans and Japanese both to social discrimination and to occupational opportunity depend very much on ethnic identity, as well as on differential socialization, expected role behavior and the effect of the reference group. These differences are most graphically represented in the respective patterns of school performance and differential rates of delinquency.

Amelioration of the effects of social discrimination in the case of Mexican-Americans depends not only on changing the social attitudes and practices of the majority, but on strengthening the positive integrative function of the family and community. As we have seen, for the Mexican-American an ethnic background has not helped maintain a positive social self identity against majority Anglo attitudes. The Chicano movement is an attempt to develop community pride and cohesiveness, in order to give Mexican identity a more positive meaning. At present, this movement has not been as successful as the ethnic group orientation taking place in the black community.

Among Americans of African ancestry, the relative number of individuals suffering from personal debilitation as a result of American racism is considerable. The "mark of oppression," as Kardiner and Ovesey (*16*) termed it, is widespread, whether one uses indices of addiction to drugs, brittle and unsatisfactory heterosexual relationships, delinquency and crime, or hospitalization for mental illness. The cases cited by Kardiner and Ovesey or the writings of Malcolm X (*15*) are full of psychological problems related to the internalization of a negative self-image. It has been difficult for some black families to provide sufficient psychological and economic security for their young. For all too many, racial oppression penetrated into basic child-parent relationships to the degree that a negative self-image was passed on from parent to child, without the child's even having had any direct contact with the outer white society.

Unfortunately for those who seek to change the effects of discrimination by changing laws or social attitudes, a personal sense of failure among some blacks is not due solely to the force of external discrimination but to the internalization of traits debilitating to intellectual functioning and to the will to achieve. Malcolm X discusses with great integrity and candor the self degradation of his generation, of Negroes who internalized concepts of physical beauty that flatter the white and degrade the black. It is very often the black man's own mother who "puts him down," causing self-hatred and self-rejection. In our book, *Japan's Invisible Race* (*9*), Wagatsuma and I describe similar processes involving unconscious negative self-images that helped debilitate the former *eta* or pariahs of Japan and led to their relative failure in the economically competitive contemporary Japanese society. These internal processes are never separate from the external forms of discrimination which deepen and intensify the inner difficulties experienced by members of disparaged groups.

CONCLUSIONS

In the foregoing presentation I have contended that ethnicity is as important as social class in social theory, that a psycho-cultural approach to social belonging is necessary for understanding social behavior. I have also suggested that a conflict approach to society is more productive in understanding change than one based on formal structure analysis alone. Change is a reality of human history. Stability and order exist in social patterning, but human social groups rarely exist in an unchanging environment with unchanging social forms in total isolation each from the other. I realize I have touched only too briefly on a number of specific topics related to these general contentions.

Seen from one perspective, the history of social life in a culture is a continual rhythm of conflict and accommodation between groups, both external and internal. Stratification allows for some form of accommodation. Those coming to power continually seek a more stabilized allegiance from those subordinate to them. Some theorists who emphasize conflict and coercion in political matters forget, however, to examine the forces that unify individuals into the groups that then struggle with each other for power. Hobbes, in his discussion of the state, leaves us dissatisfied when he sees coercion as the only force keeping individuals united. His psychologically insufficient sociological theory does not examine the forces of collective affirmation and the individually internalized constraints that keep groups—ethnic minorities or nation-states—together and enable them to meet internal or external crises.

Durkheim in his *Elementary Forms of the Religious Life* pointed toward the proper direction for such understanding. He saw man as a social animal who achieves his real and ideal sense of self partially out of his sense of belonging to a group. In a primitive, occupationally undifferentiated society, there is little tension between a sense of social identity with the political community with its primary form of citizenship, and the "church," a sacred representation of primal folk ethnicity. The political and the spiritual communities are one. Within such a community the relatively undifferentiated occupational system affords little basis for divergent concepts of belonging. Hence it is only in more complex social units with their occupational divisions and their amalgamation of groups maintaining a sense of diverse origin that tension develops in the overall sense of belonging. But, depending upon the vagaries of their history, not all societies develop chronic tensions resulting from political incorporation. In some instances of recorded as well as unrecorded history, ethnic groups have indeed disappeared into a unified nation-state, just as nation-states have disappeared by incorporation or dissolution.

In members of more simple communities one usually finds much less evidence of any form of identity crisis as a part of social maturation. The modern widespread existential search for meaning suggests the presence of conflicting alternatives. Modern conceptual systems attempt to relate past cultural traditions to ideological alternatives about the future direction of society and to questions about the degree of allegiance to be paid to the different social units in the system. Those who see individualism as the highest goal sometimes mistakenly assume that individuation or autonomy means a lack of allegiance to any group. They fail to see that modern man is also searching for meaningful and ultimate units of social belonging and a sense of survival through such belonging.

Problems of choice related to occupation or identity occur only in flexible societies with a great deal of internal social mobility. In rigidly stratified societies, the individual's occupation tends to be predetermined, inculcating early a sense of belonging to a primary occupational group. Even this situation may not be completely free of conflict, since the state may apply pressure concerning religious and political adherence, leading to conflicts over loyalty.

Seen from this perspective, human history shows numerous combinations of tension, conflict, and accommodation related to conflicts between loyalty to a past ethnicity, present status or a future idealized concept of society. The sections of this chapter discussed only a few of the topics related to ethnicity and social stratification, and even they need much more detailed examination than it was possible to give here. Other complementary approaches to ethnic identity appear in the following chapters.

REFERENCES

1. Barth, Fredrik. *Ethnic Groups and Boundaries.* Boston: Little, Brown, 1969.
2. Berreman, Gerald. "Structure and Function of Caste Systems" and "Concomitants of Caste Organization." In De Vos and Wagatsuma, *Japan's Invisible Race: Caste and Culture in Personality.* Berkeley: University of California Press, 1967.
3. Caudill, William, and De Vos, George. "Achievement, Culture and Personality, the Case of the Japanese Americans." In *Socialization for Achievement: The Cultural Psychology of The Japanese,* edited by George DeVos. Berkeley: University of California Press, 1972.
4. De Vos, George, ed. *Socialization for Achievement: The Cultural Psychology of The Japanese.* Berkeley: University of California Press, 1973.
5. De Vos, George. "Conflict, Dominance and Exploitation in Human Systems of Social Segregation: Some Theoretical Perspectives from the Study of Personality and Culture." In *Conflicts in Society,* edited by A.V.S. de Reuck and Knight. London: Churchill, 1966.
6. De Vos, George A. "Transcultural Diagnosis of Mental Health by Means of Psychological Tests." In *Ciba Foundation Symposium on Transcultural Psychiatry,* edited by A.V.S. de Reuck and Ruth Porter. London: Churchill, 1965.
7. De Vos, George, and Mizushima, Keiichi. "The Organization and Social Functions of Japanese Gangs." In *Aspects of Social Change in Modern Japan,* edited by R. P. Dore. Princeton: Princeton University Press, 1967.
8. De Vos, George, and Wagatsuma, Hiroshi. "Minority Status and Delinquency in Japan." In *Mental Health Research in Asia and the Pacific,* edited by William Caudill and Tsing Yi-Lin. Honolulu: East-West Center Press, 1969.
9. De Vos, George A., and Wagatsuma, Hiroshi. *Japan's Invisible Race: Caste and Culture in Personality.* Berkeley: University of California Press, 1967.
10. Erikson, Erik H. *Identity, Youth and Crisis.* New York: Norton, 1968.
11. Foster, George. "Peasant Society and the Image of Limited Good." *American Anthropologist.* 1967, pp. 293-315.
12. Glazer, Nathan, and Moynihan, Daniel P. *Beyond the Melting Pot.* Cambridge, Mass: MIT Press, 1963.
13. Goffman, Erving. *Stigma: Notes on the Management of Spoiled Identity.* Englewood Cliffs, N.J.: Prentice Hall, 1963.
14. Hagen, Everett E. *On the Theory of Social Change.* Illinois: Dorsey, 1962.
15. Haley, Alex. *The Autobiography of Malcolm X.* New York: Grove Press, 1966.
16. Kardiner, Abram, and Ovesey, L. *The Mark of Oppression.* New York: World, 1962.

17. Lanternari, V. *The Religions of the Oppressed: A Study of Modern Messianic Cults.* New York: Knopf, 1963.

18. Lewis, Oscar. *Five Families.* New York: Basic Books, 1959.

19. Lipset, Seymour M., and Bendix, Rinehard, edited by William Caudill and Tsing Yi-Lin. *Social Mobility in Industrial Society.* Berkeley: University Press, 1959.

20. Mead, George Herbert. "The I and the Me." In *Mind, Self and Society,* edited by Charles Morris. Chicago: University of Chicago Press, 1934.

21. Nakane, Chie. *Japanese Society.* London: Weidenfeld and Nicolson, 1971.

22. Paz, Octavio. *The Labyrinth of Solitude: Life and Thought in Mexico.* New York: Grove Press, 1961.

23. Rowe, William L. "Social and Economic Mobility in a Low-Caste North Indian Community." Ph.D. dissertation, Cornell University, 1960.

24. Rowe, William L. "Myth as Social Charter: The Assignment of Status in Hindu Caste Origin Stories." Paper presented before the 63rd Annual Meeting of the American Anthropological Association, Detroit, November 20, 1964.

25. Schwartz, Theodore. "Cargo Cult: A Melanesian Type Response to Culture Contact." In *Responses to Change: Adjustment and Adaptation in Personality and Culture,* edited by George De Vos, forthcoming.

26. Totten, George, and Wagatsuma, Hiroshi. "Emancipation: Growth and Transformation of a Political Movement." In *Japan's Invisible Race: Caste and Culture in Personality,* edited by George A. De Vos and Hiroshi Wagatsuma. Berkeley: University of California Press, 1967.

Ethnic Identity: Its Logical Foundations and Its Dysfunctions

GEORGE DEVEREUX

2

THE DOUBLE MEANING OF IDENTITY

In the following chapter I propose to show that ethnic identity (and the operations by which it is determined) can be usefully contrasted with other forms of identity (and the operations by which they are determined). A discussion of this contrast lays the foundations for a rigorous analysis of what I term the dysfunctional-dissociative aspects of ethnic identity. Although I analyze mainly the dissociative (differentiating) and the dysfunctional aspects of ethnic identity, I do not deny the associate (dedifferentiating) and functional aspects of identity. In fact, it is precisely the analysis of the former which permits one to grasp more fully the latter—as the study of neurosis helps one to understand the meaning of normality. These terms will be clarified in the course of the discussion. Throughout this study, the term "class" is used in its mathematical sense only. It is never used in the sense of "social class;" the term "Spartan" denotes only the truly free upper stratum of that city-state—the "equals" (*homoioi*) (*19*).

Identity is the absolute uniqueness of individual A. Non-identity with any other individual is determined by at least one very precise operation which shows A to be the sole member of a class. The result of such an operation can often be expressed by a cardinal or an ordinal number. A cardinal number expresses A's unique weight in x millionths of a milligram. Nothing else has the same weight (except the aggregate of weights used to weigh him on a scale). An ordinal number (masquerading as a cardinal number), such as a social security number, can also uniquely identify A. Practices such as primogeniture and ultimogeniture prove that this type of identification is ancient (*14*). But it is meaningful and unambiguous only if the class contains more than one member. Indeed, if a couple has one child only, that child will in a primogeniture system inherit as "the first born," and in an ultimogeniture system as "the last born." This kind of identity is of little immediate interest to the student of ethnic identity. But A's uniqueness—his total distinguishability in space and time (*24*), implemented by the temporal Ego (*9, 10*)—is of great importance. For in order to have an ethnic identity, one must first be human. Humanness implies a capacity to be unique, for individuation is more characteristic of man than of the amoeba. But the uniqueness of A is a consequence of the exceptional range of his potential behavioral repertoire, which is at the root of his extreme plasticity. This quality is relevant for the student of ethnic identity in two ways: it permits A to assume an ethnic identity and to maintain it operationally under highly variable conditions; and it permits A to change his ethnic identity, when necessary.

Other problems arising out of the relationship between the exceptionally high degree of the individual's uniqueness and between his collective ethnic identity are analyzed below.

An individual's absolute uniqueness is defined by an induplicable accumulation of imprecise determinations. Each of these operations denies A's uniqueness in one respect sufficient to permit him to be assigned, *in that respect*, to a particular class, which has at least one other member. Such an assignment involves a deliberate imprecision which, in principle, is of a specifiable degree.

Case 1: Some women athletes have a female anatomy and are heterosexual, but are genetically "less female" than other women. Their genetic anomaly is disregarded in nearly all sociological operations, yet athletic authorities often question their right to compete with "real" women, for their anomalous genetic make-up appears to give them an unfair advantage in sports.

Case 2: Maria Theresa, quasi-absolute queen of Hungary, Elizabeth II, constitutional queen of England, and Anne of Austria, queen of Louis XIII, can all be assigned to the class "queens," but only by operations of considerable imprecision, i.e., by leaving the concept of "queen" very flexible.

Assigning A to class X by means of a specifiable degree of imprecision—that is, by the affirmation that, in that respect, A is not different from B—*neither affirms nor denies A's total uniqueness* in some *other* respect, such as weight, or the fact that only he discovered the theory of relativity. The identity of A can be unambiguously determined without enumerating all classes to which, within specifiable degrees of imprecision, he may be assigned. The more highly differentiated A is, the fewer of his class-memberships need be enumerated in order to identify him uniquely.

Case 3: One can uniquely identify Freud by saying that he is (a) a member of the class (having two members: Freud and Breuer) whose researches made the discovery of psychoanalysis possible; and (b) one member of (the more numerous) class of persons who actually laid the foundations of the science of psychoanalysis. This class includes Freud, Ferenczi, and Abraham, but excludes Breuer.

Certain conventions tend to rank the classes to which A belongs in terms of their relevance for establishing his identity.

Case 4: Euripides was both a member of the class of all playwrights and of the class of all persons having facial warts, but the former class membership is usually considered more relevant than the latter—because, for example, more persons will be able to name the author of the *Bacchae*, than the person who had x facial warts.

In times of crisis this hierarchy of classes tends to become scrambled.

Case 5: Before Hitler, Einstein's most relevant class membership was "physicist." Under Hitler, at least in Germany, it was "Jew," and Einstein had to take this into account.

In times of crisis it can also happen that only one, or a very few, class memberships of A are considered relevant.

Case 6: Under Hitler, the most relevant class memberships were being a "pure" Aryan and being militarily useful. Initially the Nazi regime did not fully realize the military usefulness of physicists, which led to the flight of many Jewish physicists. By contrast, the military usefulness of generals was recognized: Goering himself declared the half-Jewish general, Milch, an Aryan, while Germany's wartime Japanese allies were honorary Aryans.

These findings give us a first glimpse of the dysfunctional-dissociative aspects of ethnic identity, and of other group identities, but a detailed discussion must be postponed for the moment, in order to contrast "ethnic personality" with "ethnic identity."

ETHNIC PERSONALITY VERSUS ETHNIC IDENTITY

Though in practice ethnic personality and ethnic identity overlap, no satisfactory analysis of ethnic identity is possible unless the two concepts are first sharply defined and carefully contrasted.

Ethnic personality is a conceptual scheme derived inductively from concrete data of two not very distinct types. The first consists of directly observed behavior which, as one's data become more numerous, appear to be typical of and distinctive for a particular group. Such behavior is recognized as not being simply human behavior, since the elements of the total possible human repertoire that it includes are used in a distinctive way. The second type of concrete data is directly observed verbal behavior consisting of generalizations about the ethnic personality by informants acting as self-ethnographers (*13*). Only if such statements are viewed as observable behavior can one lend credence to the Cretan self-ethnographer Epimenides' affirmation that "All Cretans are liars." Bertrand Russell (*39*) has shown that even though Epimenides was a Cretan, and even though by his own account all Cretans are liars, it is possible to accept Epimenides' self-ethnographic generalization as true, for it is a statement about all Cretan statements and therefore does not apply to itself (*19*). In the perspective of ethnic personality, the key word in Epimenides' statement is "liars." The statement cannot be turned around and expressed in the form "All liars are Cretans," even if it could be shown that only Cretans lie, primarily because this latter formulation—even if it were true—would pertain not to the ethnic personality but to a bastard "ethnic identity model." In addition, in Epimenides' statement, the term "Cretan" *could* be defined without reference to ethnic identity—for example, in purely geographical terms. As to the ethnic personality of Cretans, one predicates about it only the trait "liar." This very probably does not suffice to render Cretan ethnic personality distinct from all other ethnic personalities, since it is possible that one could say, also correctly, "All X's are liars," where X denotes an ethnic group not identical with the Cretans.

In principle, an *ethnos* could exist which does not enunciate anything whatever about its ethnic personality. An *ethnos* could also exist which does enunciate generalizations about its ethnic personality, but views them as a formulation of human personality, as distinct from animal behavior only. This could happen in an imaginary tribe so cut off from other tribes for so long, that it had lost any knowledge of the existence of other people.

Only an outside observer would realize that his informant enunciated the group's *ethnic* personality. As I understand it, the Cape York Eskimo formerly somewhat approximated this condition. That some tribes call themselves simply "the people" is also suggestive in this context. But I note the occurrence of an inverse type of "misapprehension." In one instance, the Sedang Moi viewed as a typically Sedang (cleverly legalistic) manipulation of Sedang customs, a universally female act of ingratiation performed by a captive Annamese girl, who certainly had no knowledge whatever of Sedang law and custom.

At times, the generalizations enunciated by informants fit but poorly the findings of the competent observer. Such poor fit is often the result of attempts to represent the ethnic personality as congruent with the ethnic identity, treated in such cases as an ideal model of conduct, which it primarily is not. In many such instances the traits ascribed to the ethnic personality, and believed to be part of the ethnic identity, tend to have the quality of a value judgment.

Case 7: When a missionary told the Arunta about original sin, the Arunta indignantly replied, "All Arunta are good!" And this answer was given even though they occasionally ostracized or punished for badness people whom they recognized to be Aruntas, and who misbehaved in an Arunta manner.

Case 8: There are probably few ethnic personality self-models which do not include the ascription of courage, though manifestly not all *ethnes* are equally warlike.

I will show further on that treating ethnic identity as an ideal self-model, composed of predicative statements is, strictly speaking, an adulterated ethnic identity, already contaminated by the ethnic personality self-model. It is also significant that the logical construct, "ethnic personality," pre-supposes the existence of sets of conjugate and well-articulated ethnic sub-personalities.

Case 9: A Spartan man's ethnic personality differed significantly from that of a Spartan woman, but could not have existed without the latter. The Spartan woman, too, was laconic and dour, but she did not fight in battles; she only encouraged her men to fight, mocked inadequate fighters and bore stoically the death of her men on the battlefield. But one notes that not even one of the 27 cases cited in Plutarch's essay *On the Bravery of Women* (*34*) concerns a Spartan woman.

One can supposedly exhibit the ethnic personality either in a good or a bad way, as in Linton's (*26*) "patterns of misconduct."

Case 10: According to the Israeli sabras, there is a good (*sabra*) and a bad (ghetto Jew) Jewish ethnic personality. The reverse valuation is ascribed to these patterns by the Chassidic Jews of Israel.

Case 11: The militant and the "Uncle Tom" Afro-American ethnic personality models contrast in similar ways.

It is inherent in the notion of ethnic personality that members of the *ethnos* display that ethnic personality both in various ways and to a different degree. This finding leads to the logical problems of "ethnic typicality," admirably analyzed by Bertrand Russell (*38*, cf. *46*): "How shall I define a 'typical Frenchman?' We may define him as one 'possessing all qualities that are possessed by most Frenchmen.' But unless we confine 'all qualities' to such as do not involve a reference to any *totality* [my italics] of qualities, we shall have to observe that most Frenchmen are *not* typical in the above sense, and therefore the definition shows that to be not typical is essential to a typical Frenchman. This is not a logical contradiction, since there is no reason why there should be any typical Frenchman; but it illustrates the need of separating off qualities that involve reference to a totality of qualities from those that do not." Again, with reference to Napoleon, Russell observes, "I must define 'qualities' in such a way that it will not include what I am now saying, i.e., 'having all the "qualities" that make a great general' must not be itself a quality in the sense supposed."

A distinction must also be made between the actualization and the exhibition of ethnic personality in behavior. Much ethnic-personality determined behavior is actualized (manifested) unwittingly and at times without an awareness that the behavior manifests the ethnic personality. Roughly speaking, such behavior is actualized because, owing to conditioning, it follows the line of least resistance and involves the smallest amount of effort, at least for the one who performs it.

Case 12: Though displaying *machismo* is easy for a Cuban, a Hopi may view it as singularly strenuous behavior.

When the ethnic personality is consciously implemented in behavior, it tends to be experienced also as an implementation of the kind of ethnic identity model which is logically already contaminated by the ethnic personality model. In many cases, an unwitting, spontaneous actualization of some aspect of ethnic personality is less easily identifiable as such, than is an act which intentionally exhibits it. An analogy may be helpful here.

Case 13: Consider two sets of photographs. One set shows the faces of persons genuinely experiencing extreme grief, pain or stress; the other set shows the faces of good actors mimicking extreme grief, pain or stress. Psychologists have found that subjects misidentify the expression of a genuinely experienced state more often than a mimicked one. Actual laughter may, for example, be identified as "crying," while the facial expression of a "laughing" actor is generally correctly identified.

One last and extremely important characteristic of ethnic personality must now be noted. Ethnic personality may be defined as a set of usually hierarchized sets of positive (positive = ego ideal) predicative statements, such as "A Spartan is brave, dour, frugal, laconic, etc." All such adjectives are attributes, even when they are negatively worded: "A Spartan is not loquacious." (Super ego.) (5) One often encounters such seemingly negative statements in such formulations of the ethnic personality as: "The Spartan is not loquacious" (like the Athenian, whom he does not wish to resemble); "he is not alcoholic" (like the Helot, whom he despises). I show further on that such negative formulations often reflect historical processes. They highlight the dissociative-differentiating origins of many ethnic personality traits.

Ethnic identity is far more difficult to define in a strictly logical sense than is ethnic personality, because in practice it is so often and so abusively contaminated by the latter. Ethnic identity must first be considered in a rigorously logical manner, even though such a purely logical view of ethnic identity has almost no direct practical applicability. It nonetheless needs to be defined, in order to render understandable both the way in which it becomes contaminated by the ethnic personality and how it functions after being so contaminated.

Ethnic identity is neither logically nor operationally an inductive generalization from data. In the narrowest sense it is not even an ideal model. It is simply a sorting device. It has in principle nothing to do with modes of behavior, be they directly observed by the field worker or enunciated by the informant. But ethnic identity must be enunciable and be enunciated by a self-ethnographer. Let us consider once more Epimenides' statement, "All Cretans are liars." We saw that in the framework of the ethnic personality, the key word is "liars." But in the framework of ethnic identity, the key word is "Cretans," whose existence this statement postulates. In the present frame of reference, "Cretans are those who inhabit Crete" is the equivalent of "All Cretans are liars," for we can consider here only the postulation of the existence of "Cretans"—*independently* of any quality we may attribute to Cretans.

Exactly as in the case of the ethnic personality, we can also imagine an *ethne* whose ethnic identity is identical with its notion of human identity (as distinct from being an animal). But even such a pure ethnic identity can develop only out of a confrontation with and a differentiation from "others," to whom a different ethnic identity is ascribed. In logic, the ascription of an ethnic identity to another need not presuppose any performance or predisposition. Where such an ascription is made, the concept is already impure.

Case 14: A baby born to Spartan parents—an event which, for the newborn, was not a performance but a passive experience—was labelled a Spartan. He had a Spartan ethnic identity. But it was recognized from the start that he would have to acquire a Spartan ethnic personality, through an extremely rigorous training, which all ancient studies of Sparta discuss at great length (*31, 35, 48,* etc.). By contrast, a Mohave baby was held to have a Mohave temperament ("predisposition") already in the womb. In cases of obstetrical difficulties, the shaman could appeal to the unborn child's Mohave personality, to persuade him to be born (*4*). This belief made even birth a performance of the infant and, moreover, a characteristically Mohave performance.

The ethnic identity, being simply a label or sorting device, does not presuppose, at least in theory, the existence of ethnic sub-identities. Spartan men, women, or children were all equally Spartan with respect to their ethnic identity and, moreover, Spartans in the same sense. This implies that, within the framework of pure ethnic identity, one could not be more or less Spartan, nor Spartan in good or bad, male or female ways. One either was a Spartan or one was not. Ethnic identity is an all-or-nothing proposition, to such an extent that the concept of typicality simply does not intervene at any point of the discourse concerning it. (Similarly, any finite integer is either an even or an odd number: 2 is neither more nor less an even number than 6 or 20, nor more typical of the set of all finite even integers than any other even integer.)

In this framework, then, ethnic identity is operationally a sorting device for oneself and for "others," and sociologically, a label which can be attributed or withheld only totally. Hence, it matters not at all, in this frame of reference and at this stage of the analysis, whether A asserts, "I am a Spartan" (with B concurring or dissenting), or whether B asserts, "A is a Spartan" (with A concurring or dissenting). In practice, of course, such things do matter:

Case 15: Brasidas asserted that he was a Spartan, and the Athenians concurred.

Case 16: Roheim asserted that he was a Hungarian, but under Nazi influence most Hungarians dissented and drove him into exile.

Case 17: The Hungarians asserted that, though Hungarian-born, Herzl was a Jew and Herzl concurred.

Case 18: The Nazi-influenced Hungarians asserted: Roheim is a Jew. Roheim dissented so strongly that he arranged to have his coffin covered with a Hungarian flag when he was buried in New York.

The moment anything is predicated about ethnic identity other than "A is, while B is not, an X" (Spartan, Hungarian, Mohave), ethnic identity begins to function as an ideal model, akin at its worst to a kind of superego which is but a residue of traumata that were not mastered when they were endured (5), and at its best to a kind of ego-ideal. Like them, the ideal model can variously be implemented and it may even be quite illegitimately argued that the concept "typical" *can* intervene in discussions of ethnic identity. But underneath it all, the all-or-nothing concept persists. A good example is the difference regularly made between the concepts "spy" and "traitor." A curious example of the latter follows.

Case 19: When Rumania was still a kingdom, its laws recognized the right of a Rumanian to acquire another nationality and even another ethnic identity. Hence, when a foreign-naturalized ex-Rumanian returned to Rumania on a visit, he was not held to be still sufficiently Rumanian to be forcibly inducted into military service. But there was one limitation: he could be penalized, even after his naturalization elsewhere, for service in an army fighting the Rumanian army. Thus we have the case of a Transylvanian Hungarian who becomes through conquest a Rumanian citizen in 1919, but who moved to Hungary and resumed his Hungarian citizenship. If taken prisoner by the Rumanians while serving in the Hungarian armed forces, he could have been penalized for fighting as a Hungarian citizen against his alleged country of birth. But this is admittedly a highly unusual situation.

This all-or-nothing element continues to exist even where there are attempts to postulate partial or hyphenated ethnic identities.

Case 20: The WASP usually claims to have a more genuine American ethnic identity than, let us say, an Italian-American, who also claims an American ethnic identity. But for the sociologist, what matters is that WASP-ness is meaningful only because there also exist non-WASPs. It is an important characteristic of the American ethnic identity model that both WASPs and non-WASPs can and do claim it. This flexibility is inherent in the ideal model of American ethnic identity, and does not modify, for the logician at least, its all-or-nothing character.

The moment one begins to predicate anything about ethnic identity, one is faced with the seeming paradox that one can express one's ethnic identity by turning traitor (as distinct from spy), as far as other members of the *ethnos* are concerned, and that one can even express one's ethnic identity by not expressing it in a certain way.

Case 21: During the eighteenth and nineteenth centuries, a class of Catholic Hungarian aristocrats existed, who claimed Hungarian ethnic identity (conceded by their opponents), but whose entire behavior was not Hungarian. Many of them spoke no Hungarian, lived in Vienna, were close to the Hapsburg court, and believed a total Austrianization of Hungary to be in Hungary's best interests and in their own, as Hungarian aristocrats. It may even be said that they manifested their Hungarian ethnic identity differently from the way Bohemian (Czech) aristocrats, of similar outlook, manifested their Bohemianness, for similar reasons.

It is also necessary to specify that even though a particular conduct may be felt by the observer to be an instance of A's ethnic personality and his ethnic identity (as an ideal model), it expresses ethnic identity from the point of view of the subject only if the performance is intended, or is retrospectively felt, to express it. Training usually made a Spartan "spontaneously" laconic (ethnic *personality*). But if he made a show of his laconism, especially in his contacts with an outsider, in such a way as to exhibit his ethnic identity, his performance was logically inseparable from role playing. I cite in this connection a curious observation.

Case 22: Hundreds of typical Spartan sayings (*36, 37, 38*) have come down to us. Plutarch alone assembled about two hundred of them. All, or nearly all, of them are so typical, or ritualistic, that if one has read twenty or thirty of them, one feels that one has read them all. Allowances must of course be made for Plutarch's selection of these sayings. Nonetheless, I note a curious fact. Though we also possess a number of pithy sayings by such Athenians as Themistocles, Aristides, Pericles, and others, their sayings are not monotonous and are not cited as specimens of typical Athenian wit. They are cited to shed light upon the individual personalities of these great Athenians. In fact, they are typically Athenian precisely by being so very different, for individualism was part of the Athenian ethnic personality and ethnic identity model.

It is also striking that many of the Spartan sayings were addressed to non-Spartans, or concern non-Spartans, or concern Spartans in their relations with foreigners. Since the Spartans themselves were for hundreds of years intellectually unproductive, and since most accounts of Sparta were written by non-Spartans, this finding can be partly explained by assuming that foreigners would hear and report mainly remarks addressed to them by Spartans, or made about them between Spartans. But even when allowances are made for both these factors, it still would seem that Spartans were more laconic in connection with non-Spartans than in daily relations among themselves. I hold, for example, that the extreme and "typical" laconism of these sayings was to a large extent due to role playing, to an "exhibiting" of Spartan ethnic identity (see below, *Case 24*).

I must, for clarity's sake, repeat here something already mentioned in connection with the ethnic personality. Consider an activity which, from the viewpoint of the performer, seems easy and natural because it is an expression of his ethnic personality. If the observer views it as an actualization of that person's ethnic identity, he does more than view it as role playing. He (rightly or wrongly) assumes also that the act intentionally involves more effort than the act which the observer would naturally execute under the "same" circumstances and for the "same" purpose. The observer may even hold that it entails more effort than an ideally economic act seeking to achieve the "same" objective would entail. I place the word "same" in quotes, since owing to cultural evaluations, an activity might not have the same meaning in two cultures. Acquisitive activity in Mohave and in Yurok society is a case in point.

This brings me to the key findings of this paper:

Since the ethnic personality is an inductive generalization from behavioral data and may be held to describe or model accurately some basic aspects of the personality of any X (Mohave, Spartan, etc.), then a particular activity which can be predicted or explained from a knowledge of that ethnic personality must be viewed as a natural manifestation of it. Though the conceptual model of the Spartan ethnic personality was originally constructed out of the observation of certain modes of behavior current in Sparta, those modes of behavior were derivable from it, once that model was constructed. Thus Brasidas was brave because he could not help being brave, given his Spartan ethnic personality. In the framework of ethnic personality he did not act bravely in order to express his Spartan ethnic personality.

Since the ethnic identity is not an inductive generalization from behavioral data, it cannot be held to describe or model accurately any basic aspect of the personality of any X (Mohave, Spartan, etc.). No particular activity can be predicted from a knowledge of the pure ethnic identity (label) or explained in terms of it. No activity can be viewed as a natural actualization of that pure ethnic identity, nor can it be held to express the pure ethnic identity, since, in strict logic, nothing is predicated about ethnic identity except that it exists, or is claimed by or imputed to A. Only when in a logically abusive manner something is predicated about ethnic identity, does it become a model, more or less congruent in its contents with the ethnic personality, but quite distinct from it in terms of its logical status. Once one operates, as one must in practice, with the logically impure ethnic identity model, one can assert that Brasidas was brave in order to instance his Spartan ethnic identity. I note in passing that a number of Spartan sayings, which I cannot cite here, do tend to represent the bravery of some particular Spartan, A, as something which voluntarily expresses his Spartan ethnic *identity,* rather than as something which automatically derives from his Spartan ethnic *personality.*

The explanation which views Brasidas' bravery as an inevitable manifestation of his Spartan personality and the explanation which views it as an intentional expression of his Spartan ethnic identity stand in a relationship of Heisenbergian complementarity to each other. (The nature and socio-psychological importance of complementary explanations cannot be discussed here; they have been analyzed in a series of earlier publication [*9, 13* chaps. 4, 5].) Speaking somewhat loosely, the analysis of Brasidas' bravery in terms of his ethnic personality is primarily a psychological one; its analysis in terms of his ethnic identity is primarily a sociological one.

The preceding paragraphs are the core of this essay's argument; I now pass from the concept of pure ethnic identity, to the logically impure concept of the ethnic identity *model,* about which many predicative statements will be made. But the reader must constantly bear in mind that from this point on "ethnic identity" denotes *not* the pure concept (label), but the impure ethnic identity model, which is more or less congruent, in terms of what is predicated about it, with the inductively formulated ethnic personality.

I conclude this section by citing three types of observations which help one to distinguish fairly easily between behavior voluntarily expressing ethnic identity and behavior which manifests almost automatically the ethnic personality as it really is.

Behavior expressing ethnic identity often disappears as soon as A ceases to be under the eyes of other members of his *ethnos.*

Case 23: An old oracle predicted that "Sparta would perish through greed." Spartans were therefore forbidden to own precious metals, and their houses could be searched for it (*48,* 7.6). Nonetheless, as soon as a Spartan went abroad—for example, as governor (*harmost*) of a subject city—he displayed notorious greed and corruptibility (*37*, p. 220F f.). This suggests that impulses incompatible with the ethnic identity (functioning as a superego) were inhibited, but were nonetheless part of the ethnic personality. (Compare the Mohave belief that the ghost of a very generous man is highly acquisitive and possessive [*11*].)

Behavior expressive of ethnic identity also tends to disappear when a strong upheaval brings about a state of affairs incompatible with the ethnic identity model.

Case 24: As soon as the previously invincible Spartan army was decisively beaten *on land* by a foreign power (the Thebans)—a state of affairs which destroyed forever Sparta's military supremacy in Greece and which was totally unimaginable in terms of Spartan self-definition—the Spartan negotiators for peace displayed such loquacity that the victors mockingly remarked that they had put an end to Spartan laconicity (*36,* p. 193D, etc.).

There is often a tendency to exaggerate, with respect to foreigners, an ethnic identity trait that is less obvious in intra-ethnic relations. Spartan laconism with aliens is an example (*Case 22*). A variant of this process is the exaggeration of the tokens of one's ethnic identity during exile (*Case 18*).

THE FORMATION AND MANIFESTATIONS OF ETHNIC IDENTITY

Logically, ethnic identity involves two symmetrical specifications:

(1) A is an X (Brasidas is a Spartan);

(2) A is not a non-X (Brasidas is not an Athenian).

I have already indicated that an absolutely isolated hypothetical tribe's ethnic identity model is totally congruent with its human identity model. It can cease to overlap with the latter only after the group enters into contact with another group and establishes its difference from the latter.

In the analysis and perhaps in the historical development of the sense of ethnic identity, the statement, "A is not a non-X ('they')," is prior to the statement, "A is an X ('we')." In short, specifications as to what constitutes ethnic identity develop only after an ethnic group recognizes the existence of others who do not belong to the group. At the start, these specifications may conceivably include only certain real (racial, cultural, personality) traits of the group. But it is almost inevitable that these distinguishing traits will eventually acquire also evaluative connotations.

Case 25: The Moi tribes have no generic name for themselves. They differentiate themselves from the non-Moi by referring to themselves both neutrally and accurately as "those who eat from wooden platters." They can also differentiate themselves by attributing to themselves a good trait said not to be characteristic of the non-Moi. One such (formerly correct) trait was "courage in war." Lastly, they differentiate themselves by the admission that they lack some good trait of others: "We don't know how to talk to the buffaloes and therefore cannot yoke them." They even have a myth explaining why they are illiterate.

At times, a tribe may not attribute to themselves a trait which they possess and value, in order to differentiate themselves from others.

Case 26: A Spartan unable to grasp the speech of a Spartan orator would have deemed himself stupid and would have been called stupid by others. Yet, leading Spartans repeatedly and contemptuously professed not to understand the eloquent speeches of non-Spartan envoys (*43,* 1.86; *36,* p. 223D, p. 232E, etc.).

I note in this context an unusual fact.

Case 27: Owing no doubt to linguistic isolation in Europe, the Hungarian word "to explain" actually means "to Hungarianize," to put into Hungarian (*magyarazni*).

I will now give some examples of routine items internal to the race and/or culture, terms which had originally probably no relation to ethnic identity, but which acquired that quality when they began to be used as a means of differentiation, of being X by being non-Y.

Examples of physical traits include the following:

Case 28: The realism of Bushman wall paintings makes easy the identification of the animal species they depict. By contrast, the representation of human beings remained quite schematic until after the country of the Bushmen (who are small and yellowish) was invaded by the Bantu (who are tall and black) (D. F. Bleek). Nonetheless, paintings showing *battles* between the two races do not accentuate the *penis rectus* (*40*) of the Bushmen (castration anxiety?).*

An ordinarily unexploited potential may acquire the quality of a component of ethnic identity and may be arbitrarily held to be ancient.

Case 29: The "Afro" hairstyle seems to me Melanesian rather than African. It does not appear to be traditional in those parts of Africa where Afro-Americans originated. It seems, rather, to reflect a reaction against the former assimilative use of hair straighteners. But there may be more to it than that. The excessive use of inferior hair-straighteners sometimes caused a considerable, if temporary, loss of hair. What little fuzz remained somewhat resembled a scanty "Afro" (*9*). Also, the "Afro" is something most other races cannot duplicate or imitate. It is therefore "Afro" only in the sense that it is not imitable, except artificially, by non-Africans (and non-Melanesians).

Internal cultural traits at times acquire the value of ethnic identity tokens, differentiating the group members from non-members, especially under conditions of stress.

Case 30: The ancient nomadic Hebrews probably had no pigs because pig-breeding was inconvenient for nomads living in a semi-desert. They may therefore be presumed not to have eaten pork simply because they had no pigs. Once settled in Canaan, however, they were among peoples who not only ate pork, but ate it at times ritually, because in their myths (Adonis, etc.) wild boars played a significant role. Thus for the Hebrews, not eating pork became a token of Hebrew ethnic-religious identity. The custom remained the same all along, but acquired a new meaning related to the implementation of dissociative ethnic identity. I note in passing that, even though the Hebrew dietary laws did not enunciate the taboo in that form, they tabooed in effect the flesh of all polymastic animals, perhaps because their neighbors had a polymastic female deity, such as the Artemis of the Ephesians. To my knowledge, this point has not previously been made.

Case 31: In the ninth and tenth centuries, the pagan Hungarians routinely drank fermented mare's milk, for it was their only alcoholic beverage. But they also drank with pleasure the beer and wine they found in sacked Western cities. However, beginning with Hungary's Christianization and Westernization, the Western priests decided to treat kumys-drinking as a pagan practice

* I am not altogether certain of the second half of this statement. One fairly reliable novel and one not altogether reliable informant affirmed that these battle scenes *did* emphasize the *penis rectus.* A specialist, consulted by mail, did not know the answer. My own examination of reproductions in the Rhodes Library, Oxford, yielded negative results, but the books I consulted dated from an age where "obscene" details were obliterated even in some scientific works.

(*9*), just as missionaries in Kenya treated Kikuyu clitoridectomy as a pagan practice, though nothing in the Bible forbids either one. (Note that Strabo [*43*, 16.4.9] asserts, probably erroneously, that Jewish girls were "circumcised.") As a result, certain Hungarians who wished to resist both Christianization and Westernization, defiantly began to drink kumys in a new and different spirit. It became a token of their old-fashioned "pagan Hungarian" ethnic identity. Much the same may be said of obstinate advocacy of clitoridectomy on the part of some educated Kikuyus in response to missionary interference (*22*).

This brings me to what I believe is an overlooked fact.

Case 32: Marie Bonaparte (*1*) divides mankind as a whole into "friends of the clitoris" and "enemies of the clitoris." Now in some areas of Africa, girls are in fact deprived of their clitoris and much of their labia (*1, 2*). But in certain other African tribes girls are encouraged to manipulate and to tug at their external genitals, so as to increase their length and bulk (*2*). To my knowledge, neither of these symmetrical practices has been correlated with the fact that Khoisan women naturally have very long labia, the "Hottentot apron" (*39*). Since the Khoisans formerly lived far to the North of their present habitat, the Hottentot apron of their women may perhaps have inspired both the differentiating (Kikuyu, etc.) practice of female circumcision and the assimilative practice of the artificial lengthening of the labia in other African cultures.

Some of the most striking tokens of the dissociative nature of ethnic identity models are new culture traits that have evolved in the form of an "antagonistic acculturation," a process defined and analyzed by E. M. Loeb and myself (*3*). I can enumerate only a few striking maneuvers of this kind. For example, total imitation in reverse, while not common, does exist.

Case 33: Adult Spartans forced the despised Helots—a subject population "neither slave nor free," as an ancient authority puts it—to get drunk and then exhibited them to Spartan youth as negative models (*31*, 28.4-5), to teach the young Spartans sobriety. I note in passing that this did not suffice to teach King Kleomenes I to be sober, for he had learned to drink undiluted wine from (non-despised) Scythian ambassadors (*20*, 6.84, etc.).

Another example of antagonistic acculturation is partially deviative imitation which consists in evolving practices that deliberately deviate from traits held to be part of the ethnic identity of "others," and become components of one's own ethnic identity.

Case 34: The Bible repeatedly admonishes the Jews in Canaan not to "be like unto" the people surrounding them.

Case 35: G. Vajda (*46*) has shown that after Mohammed lost hope of converting the "people of the Book" (Jews and Christians), he devised a whole series of behavior patterns for Mohammedans, the main purpose of which was to differentiate them from the "unbelievers."

Alloplastic activities involve either the denial or the imposing of distinctive culture traits on others. The dominant group then treats both as tokens of the ethnic identity of the dominated. The yellow Star of David, which the Nazis forced the Jews to wear, is an obvious case. But it is striking that the forbidden trait can be smuggled into the culture of the oppressed *in disguise* and accepted as a token of ethnic identity. Invidiously imposed culture elements can also turn into such tokens.

Case 36: Some Arab states forbade the Jews to ride camels. According to an informant, the Jews compensated for this by rocking themselves like camel riders while praying, but this may be only folklore.

Case 37: The Manchus imposed the pigtail on the Chinese, for whom it soon became a token of ethnic identity.

Case 38: The Chassidim consider certain garments necessary tokens of Jewish ethnic identity, even though they had been invidiously forced upon them by their former Polish overlords.

Case 39: Between 1926 and 1932, I never once saw a French Jewish youth or girl wear the Star of David as a necklace. In 1946, after the Nazi occupation, I saw many French Jewish girls and even boys wear such pendants, but have seen none since my return to France in 1963.

I note in passing that antagonistic acculturation often involves the borrowing of the "other's" means, the better to defeat his ends, and to protect one's own ethnic identity. Sometimes it takes the form of what Kroeber called "stimulus diffusion" (*23*).

Case 40: Sequoya invented the Cherokee alphabet in competition with (and as a result of stimulus diffusion from) the English alphabet.

A particularly interesting example of the implementation of ethnic identity is the acceptance of "ethnic" psychological traits invidiously attributed to certain oppressed groups.

Case 41: Many formerly warlike groups, forced to become despised merchants and then accused of shrewd practices, tend to take pride in being shrewd and deem it a token of their ethnic identity. This is as true of medieval Jews as it is of Armenians in Mohammedan lands, of Levantine Greeks, etc. The Greek hero Odysseus becomes almost caricaturally Levantine in some Greek tragedies (*18, 41, 42*), although of the Homeric poems only one scene of the *Iliad* (*21,* 6.234ff.) depicts a profitable deal "pulled off" in a Levantine manner—the scene in which Glaucus exchanges his golden armor, worth 100 oxen, for Diomedes' bronze armor, worth only nine—a naivete which the poet himself highlights and ridicules.

Case 42: Aside from dire necessity, the development of strong military forces on the part of the Israelis is partly a reaction to their millenary intimidation and partly a conscious return to the ethnic identity model of the pre-Diaspora Jews, whose great military prowess was recognized even by their Hellenistic and Roman conquerors.

I note, *in fine,* that a change in one's ethnic self-definition is at times made possible by an undeviating adherence to one ethnic identity trait.

Case 43: A French Jewish acquaintance, who had fought in the Free French army and had considered military skill an important component of his French ethnic identity, began to feel that he had (also) a Jewish ethnic identity only after the Israelis displayed great valor in battle in 1948, 1956 and 1967. (I suspect, however, that part of this shift in his ethnic identity was due to the 1940 French military disaster and to the antisemitic measures of the Petain regime.)

Several more very important aspects of the implementation of ethnic identity may also be mentioned. Behavior expressing ethnic identity tends to be more ritualistic and monotonous than behavior triggered off by the ethnic personality (see *Case 22*). One cannot but think, in this connection, of a remark Dodds (*15*) made in another context: history repeats itself, but only ritual repeats itself *exactly*. This ethnic identity ritualism may even become exaggerated in times of decline. The Spartans under Roman domination, for example, seem to have played at being Spartans more consistently than they did at the peak of Spartan power, and this despite the likelihood that earlier Spartan sayings probably lost nothing of their typicality in the telling. In the same sense, only a modern-day millionaire can have a 100 percent Louis XIV salon, for the salons of dukes in the time of Louis XIV assuredly also contained Henri IV or Louis XIII heirlooms and portraits of ancestors. In some cases such ethnic role-playing leads to excesses comparable only to the absurdity of eighteenth Century *castrati* singing passionately sensual operatic *roles.*

Ethnic identity is sometimes maximally implemented by those who, by ordinary standards, would not be expected to possess it.

Case 44: The greatest Hungarian Poet, a patriot who died a hero's death as a volunteer in the revolutionary army of 1848–49, was of Serbian extraction, and had Magyarized his name, Petrovitch, to its Hungarian equivalent of Petofi (Peter-son).

Case 45: European public opinion forced the Emperor of Austria to dismiss in disgrace the half-demented Austrian general Haynau, notorious for his brutal repressions in Hungary after the 1848 revolution. Upon his dismissal, Haynau purchased an estate in Hungary, affected the Hungarian national costume and went about proclaiming, "We Hungarians will not allow ourselves to be robbed of our national liberties." It won him no recognition as a possessor of Hungarian ethnic identity. (Compare with the Athenian, Alcibiades, exiled in Sparta, playing at being more Spartan than the native inhabitants of that city.)

The intellectual awareness that a trait, previously felt to be a manifestation of one's ethnic identity, is actually alien, does not necessarily destroy its capacity to be experienced as ethnic.

Case 46: Until Bartok had shown that gypsy music was *not* Hungarian, it was thought to be, and, despite Bartok, continues to be experienced as Hungarian. What little I preserve of a "Hungarian ethnic identity" is more easily aroused by a gypsy *csardas* than by a pentatonic peasant song.

Last, there are very few one-dimensional ethnic identities.

Case 47: I remind the reader once again that in the following discussion the term "Spartan" denotes only the "full" Spartans, the "Equals," who claimed a Hellenic ethnic identity (as contrasted with that of the Barbarians); at times they also claimed a "racial" Doric identity, as did King Anaxandridas, who called his favorite wife's eldest son "Dorieus," meaning "the Dorian." But at other times the Spartans claimed to be successors of the Achaean Atreids, as did the *ephor* Chilon and the son of his kinswoman (by Anaxandridas), King Cleomenes (*19*, 5.72). They validated the latter claim by "discovering" abroad and reburying in Sparta the bones of the Achaean, Orestes, son of Agamemnon and nephew, son-in-law, and heir of Menelaus (*19*, 1.67). Thus Spartan expansionism could be justified either by claiming Dorian (conqueror) identity or else Achaean (legal successor) identity.

The Spartans also claimed a Spartan identity as contrasted with the Athenians, with their Helot serfs, and with Sparta's satellites by maintaining that to be Spartan meant to be a soldier, for only the Spartan was not permitted to be anything but a soldier.

Case 48: At a gathering of the armies of Sparta and its satellites, an ally protested that Sparta had contributed too few soldiers. In response, the Spartan leader asked that all potters, smiths, carpenters, and so on in the assembled armies stand up in turn. Eventually all the allied warriors stood up. Finally, he asked that the professional soldiers stand up, and only the Spartan contingent rose, for they alone were professional soldiers only. This was held to prove that Sparta had contributed more soldiers than anyone else (*37*, p. 214A).

A last aspect of ethnic identity, areal climax, must now be considered. In certain cases the claim to incarnate the areal climax, in Kroeber's sense (*24*) is part of the ethnic identity of more than one *ethnos*. At least two Greek city-states professed to incarnate the essence of Greece.

Case 49: Athens was called "the school of Hellas" by Pericles; a poet hailed it as "the Hellas of Hellas." It deemed itself typical of Greece in the sense in which the finest race horse may be said to typify the species. How different Athens was from other Greek states is shown by the characterizations of Athens by the Corinthian, Spartan, and Athenian orators at a gathering of Sparta and its allies, who had to decide on peace or war with Athens (*44,* 1.68 ff.). In addition, Athens claimed to be the most Greek of all Greek cities because only its people were truly autochthonous, having always lived in Attica (*20,* 1.56; 7.161). This also made them different from other Greek cities, where the pre-Greek (Pelasgian) racial element was minimal. Many of these other cities had, in addition, been overthrown by the invading Dorians at the end of the Achaean period. Yet even Sparta acknowledged at least the eminence, if not pre-eminence, of Athens in Hellas. When Athens lost the Peloponnesian war, one Theban envoy urged that it be dealt with as Athens had dealt with Melos—the city razed, the men slaughtered, the women and children enslaved. At that point, a Phocian envoy, one of Athens' enemies, rose and sang a choral ode from Euripides' *Electra,* and a dour Spartan envoy declared that Sparta was unwilling to destroy the city that had saved Greece during the Persian wars, some 80 years earlier (*31,* 15). At that moment, Athens' ethnic identity, as expressed by its past, became for it a capital reserve.

Sparta—so outlandish by ordinary Greek cultural standards—was also deemed by some to be "ideal Greece," on a very different, and possibly even less valid, grounds. The "real" Spartans were Doric invaders (*19*), while most of Greece was *not* Dorian. No Greek state differed more—in qualitative ways—from the rest of Greek states than did Sparta. Athens, on the other hand, differed from the others mainly *quantitatively*: it had *more* good poets, artists, philosophers, craftsmen, sailors, and so on, than the other Greek states. We may note the curious fact that even though it is generally recognized that the Roman conquerors preserved Sparta as a kind of "reservation for antiquarians," they also preserved Athens as a kind of "reservation for students," as a university town. It is ironic that Sparta became a super-tough reservation when it had ceased to be a military power, and Athens an intellectual reservation when it had ceased to produce first-class minds.

Unlike ethnic personality, ethnic identity nearly always has both a "self" mystique and an "ascribed" mystique. Let us examine a highly peculiar example of such a twofold mystique, a town which was in significant respects a product of outsiders.

Case 50: Several aspects of the mystique of Spartan ethnic identity must be considered.

The self mystique and the ascribed mystique converged in some respects: The Spartans deemed themselves invincible on land, and the Athenians, their enemies, concurred. At the outbreak of the Peloponnesian War, Pericles advised Athens to fight only at sea (*44,* 1.142ff.).

The two mystiques may diverge, at least in their evaluation. The Spartan deemed absolute rectitude a token of his ethnic identity. The Athenians held the Spartan to be totally dishonest, especially when he pretended to be righteous. It suffices to cite here Euripides' characterization of Menelaus, king of Sparta, in his *Andromache* (*17*), a characterization based not upon the image of the Achaean Menelaus of the *Iliad*, but upon the Athenian image of the fifth century B.C. Spartan.

Even where the facts prove both the convergent self mystique and the ascribed mystique to be false, they often continue to be accepted by both in-group and out-group. The myth of Spartan invincibility on land survived their severe defeat by the Athenians at Sphacteria. Plutarch wrote almost 500 years after his own city, Thebes, had forever broken Spartan pre-eminence at Leuctra; yet he too preserved the mystique of the Spartans military superiority to the Theban hoplite; he attributed Sparta's defeat to the genius of a single Theban: Epaminondas (*37,* 214C ff.).

At times an *ethnos* can have a double ethnic-identity self mystique. Thus, Sparta's double (Dorian and Achaean) ethnic identity and mystique led only to alternations in the choice of foes; Sparta remained expansionist. As shown in *Case 47*, the Dorian ethnic mystique justified aggression by a Dorian superiority in arms, while the Achaean mystique sought to give a mythico-legal basis to Spartan expansionism.

In the case of Sparta, much of the mystique of its ethnic identity was manufactured by outsiders, though the Spartans gladly went along with it.

The Spartans did originate a mystique of superiority, what Ollier (*29*) calls the "romance of Sparta," regarding the antiquity and stability of Sparta's aristocratic constitution. But the "romance of Sparta" was fully elaborated only by pro-Spartan outsiders, the Spartans themselves being too brutishly uneducated to do it. The real "romance of Sparta" was written by three Athenians, all of them disciples of Socrates: the ghastly oligarch and traitor Critias, the bright but naive Xenophon, and Plato, who valued systems more than men and deemed abstractions more real than reality.

I must add that much of the mystique of Spartan ethnic identity rested on a misconception assiduously fostered by Spartans. Its "Lycurgan" constitution was almost certainly less ancient than claimed. But it may well have been the first revolutionary constitution of Greece, because Sparta had earlier and greater inner troubles than the other Greek city-states (*19*). Also, the stability of its institutions—on which the ethnic identity of the "real" Spartans largely depended—was achieved at the appalling cost of turning every free Spartan into a military slave of the state, for Sparta was sitting on a volcano (7). Other states refused to pay so high a price for stability, especially since the continuity of *their* ethnic identity did not depend on it. They had occasional civil disorders, but of a different nature. In Athens, for example, the Athenian aristocrats clashed with the Athenian democrats. But whoever won was an Athenian. By contrast, in Sparta the overthrow of the free Spartans by the Helots would have impaired and changed Spartan ethnic identity and destroyed the city-state. Solon's law could afford to disenfranchise an Athenian who did not take sides in civil strife (*33*, 20), but the laws of Lycurgus could not afford this.

THE FUNCTIONALITY AND DYSFUNCTIONALITY OF GROUP IDENTITIES

Marcel Mauss (*28*) has shown that even though every person is aware of his own identity ("selfhood") many primitive societies do not implement his distinctiveness socially. Sometimes the individual is in some respects functionally interchangeable with other individuals, and he may freely acknowledge this fact (*3*).

Case 51: A Sedang man married two cousins, who were also best friends, and therefore called each other by the same (invented) name. One day I asked one of them if she was jealous when her husband cohabited with her co-wife and cousin. She replied: "Why should I? She is the same person as I" [in this respect]. At the same time, this woman knew herself to be a unique and strong personality, who knowingly repudiated many Sedang attitudes and beliefs.

It is convenient to approach the social implementation of individuality from the vantage point of types of relationships. Parsons has outlined three such types (*30*): (1) *The functionally specific* (e.g., buyer and seller). All that is not explicitly included is excluded. The demand must be justified. This type of relationship is highly segmental and predominates in complex societies. (2) *The functionally diffuse* (e.g., husband and wife). All that is not explicitly excluded from it is deemed to be included. Not the demand, but the refusal must be justified. (3) *The functionally cumulative* (e.g., employer-lover and secretary-mistress). Such relations tend to cause conflict (*12*, chap. 9). Parsons' scheme omits what I consider to be the type of relationship that predominates in primitive societies: *The functionally multiple.* Abraham, for example, was tribal chief, general, priest, and *pater familias,* and could not have been any one of these without being all the others as well.

But the predominance of functionally multiple relationships in some primitive societies does not necessarily represent an extensive social implementation of a person's uniqueness, for a single attribute may enable a person to accede to many a status in which his relations are functionally multiple. In sororal polygyny, it suffices to be a married woman's sister in order to become a wife, though in that capacity the woman's social relations will certainly be functionally multiple, including sexual partner, mother, and cook. In order to become king, one need only be a king's oldest son. The proclamation: "*Le Roi est mort, vive le Roi!*" affirms the functional interchangeability of the defunct king and his successor.

It is precisely at the top and bottom of the social scale that people are, on the one hand, functionally most interchangeable and at the same time possess—at least in principle—the highest degree of freedom to select from the potential range of behavior those aspects which they choose to actualize at any moment. The law of ancient Persia was that the king was not subject to the law (*20,* 3.31). Under the *ancien regime,* the law was in theory the king's untrammelled will: "*Le Roi le veut;*" "*tel est Notre plaisir.*" Even more relevant is Dollard's (*16*) observation that the Southern police often overlooked a Negro's misconduct, though they would have arrested a white for similar behavior.

Evidently, the social recognition and implementation of personal identity resulted from the disintegration of functionally multiple relationships into their components. This appears to have accompanied what Durkheim called "social polysegmentation," which permitted a woman, for example, to become A's wife, B's mistress, and C's cook. Historically, the socially implemented individual identity of A seems to have emerged from the recognition that a person could have simultaneously plural class identities with respect to B, and even that each of his class identities (memberships) could be relevant only with regard to a different person and/or in different contexts. At the same time, a number of conditions which a person had to satisfy in order to be assigned to any particular class tended to increase. Though Louis XIV was in principle still commander-in-chief, in practice he entrusted the command of his armies in the field to great generals.

One also observes that in many instances A's membership in class X gains added dimensions by his membership in classes Y and Z, or, conversely, his non-membership in classes M and N. Thus Conde's status as a (Bourbon) Serene Highness greatly increased his authority as a brilliant general. On the other hand, a ruined nobleman of Normandy who wished to restore his fortune by engaging in commerce could temporarily place his nobility "in escrow" with the parliament of his province.

But the social recognition of A's multiple class memberships can also entail the recognition that he belongs to some class cutting across ethnic lines. Thus a Mohave of the Hipa patrilineal clan would be committing incest if he married a Yuma woman belonging to the same clan. Such multiple class memberships can also lead to the formation of outlooks or character traits cutting across ethnic barriers. Thus some Plains Indian songs and *Fragment 10* of the Spartan poet Tyrtaeus (*45*) affirm that the corpse of a young man fallen in battle is a beautiful and inspiring sight.

Case 52: A Spartan's "Spartan-ness" compelled him to implement intensively and exclusively the segment of behavior related to military prowess. Sparta seems to have produced no intellectuals between the time of Alcman and Tyrtaeus (fifth century B.C.) and the unimportant hellenistic antiquarian Sosibius (third century B.C.). The law prohibiting gainful occupations also caused Sparta to enter the Peloponnesian War with only a negligible amount in the treasury (*44,* 1.130, etc.). In short, the Spartan's Spartan-ness tended to exclude entirely the implementation of many of his potentialities and to subordinate to his Spartan-ness even those of his potentialities which were deemed compatible with his being a Spartan: he had the right to be a husband and father, but his family life was reduced to a minimum, to give him more time to be a Spartan. By contrast, the Athenian's Athenian-ness also demanded that he be brave, but he was free to and expected to express other aspects of Athenian ethnic identity as well. Sophocles was an industrialist, general and statesman, as well as a dramatic poet. He was, moreover, entitled to a genuine private life, to a meaningful social and personal identity. The flexibility of the Athenian's ethnic identity was probably due to the early establishment of a true unity and equality among the inhabitants of Attica. Attic "synoecismus" contrasts greatly with the basic disunity of the Spartan state, inhabited by "true" Spartans, Perioecians ("dwellers about") and Helots—not to speak of a variety of intermediate layers—Partheniae, Neodamodae, and so on—all with very unequal rights. The constant conflicts of these groups were both Sparta's *raison d'etre* and curse. (7).

Of course, in selecting for development only certain aspects of his total repertoire, man theoretically impoverishes and constricts himself. But in practice this loss is more than compensated for by a greater and more satisfying expertness in those aspects selected for development (*12,* chap. 2). Moreover, this selectiveness also has valuable psychological and social consequences. Linton (*27*) hinted long ago that the flexibility of man's instincts is so great that they are unable to organize effectively and to render predictable his behavior and personality sufficiently to make life in society possible. In order to organize his personality and render it predictable, man needs to provide himself with an armor of habits and customs.

I now specify that what in one perspective is a necessarily selective custom is in another perspective the selection, for consistent expression, of certain aspects of man's total potential repertoire. In still another perspective, the selection of certain of these aspects for a consistent behavioral expression entails assigning to A a whole series of class memberships, a series of *class identities,* one of which is his ethnic identity.

But, bearing in mind that A's individuality can be made totally unique by enumerating all his class identities, by assembling an unduplicable accumulation of specifiably imprecise informations about him, it becomes apparent that this selectiveness as to the aspects of the repertoire which A manifests makes him unique, as well as exceptionally creative and spontaneous. In short, A becomes unique by his distinctive selection of certain aspects of his potential repertoire, not duplicated by anyone else. Since the selection of certain of these aspects can, in another perspective, be viewed as the self-ascription of a series of class memberships (class identities), A's unique identity can be determined by an enumeration of all his class identities—or at least of a sufficient number of his class identities to make it impossible for any other person to belong also to all these classes.

When an individual has a sufficient number of sufficiently varied class identities, each of them becomes a tool and their totality becomes a kind of "tool box," which both actualize and implement socially his unique pattern of personality.

But when one of A's class identities becomes hypercathected to the point of severely conflicting with, or else totally subordinating to it, all the rest of A's class identities, singularly dysfunctional manifestations of class identity begin to appear. One conflict can arise when what is deemed to be the principal class identity is actually less effective in certain circumstances than are other class identities.

Case 53: The Marseillaise appeals to all *enfants* of only *la Patrie*; a Marxist slogan urges only *workers* of the world to unite. Yet, in order to encourage the Soviet armies to resist the Nazi armies to the utmost, Stalin had to appeal to ethnic identity and represent the struggle as taking place between Russians and Germans.

Turning specifically to ethnic identity, when a hypercathected ethnic identity overrides all other class identities, it ceases to be a tool and becomes, as was shown for Sparta (*Case 52*), a straitjacket. Indeed, the achievement of a collective distinctiveness by means of a hypercathected ethnic identity can, as a simple example will show, lead to an obliteration of individual distinctiveness.

Case 54: The Spartan hoplite wore a red cloak, which distinguished him from all other heavily armed infantrymen. But the redness of his cloak had another function: if he was wounded, the blood he shed did not show on the cloak (*35,* 24; *48,* 2.3). Hence the wounded Spartan individual's special condition could neither encourage the foe, nor elicit his compassion (Homer, *Iliad* 12.390ff.). Glaucus, wounded, withdraws from the battle, so that his wounded state will not encourage the foe (*21*).

In short, in implementing one's hypercathected ethnic identity, one increasingly minimizes and even negates one's individual identity. Yet, man's functionally relevant dissimilarity from all others is what makes him human: similar to others precisely through his high degree of differentiation. It is this which permits him to claim a human identity.

A hypercathected ethnic identity's implementation can also become onerous to the point of becoming dysfunctional.

Case 55: A Roman magistrate was sometimes compelled by his Roman ethnic identity to sentence his own son to death—and to do so with a stiff upper lip. By contrast, Pericles could afford to plead in tears with the Athenian assembly to secure the acquittal of his mistress, Aspasia (*31,* 32).

Case 56: The cost at which the Jews preserved their ethnico-religious identity need hardly be recalled. Under Antiochus Epiphanes it was at the risk of their lives that they circumcised their sons.

In short, it may be argued that a hypercathecting of one's ethnic identity leads, in effect, to a drastic reduction of one's relevant class identities and thus to the annihilation of the individual's real identity. The same occurs when only one of a person's class identities is deemed relevant. Under the Nazis the Jews were gradually stripped of all their relevant class identities, save only their Jewish identity, and in the process were denied a personal identity.

It is dysfunctional, indeed catastrophic, to reduce another person to such one-dimensionality. But the contemporary scene abounds in examples of persons stripping themselves of all their potentially meaningful class identities, ceasing to be anything but X's, where X denotes a real or spurious *ethnos.* This process is more impoverishing than ever today, when one's ethnic identity can structure only increasingly limited aspects of one's total potential repertoire. Hence, the moment A insists on being only and ostentatiously an X, 24 hours a day, all those aspects of his behavior which cannot be correlated with his ethnic identity are deprived of any organizing and stabilizing framework. His behavior therefore tends to become increasingly chaotic, particularly when he operates as a member of an actual group.

As a result, there tends to appear, side by side with what little structuring of his behavior his ethnic identity ("being an X") provides—even when it is asserted mainly dissociatively ("not being a Y")—a logically untenable and operationally fraudulent incorporation into the ethnic identity of ideologies based on principles which are, in essence, not only non-ethnic, but outright anti-ethnic. It is, and must be, possible to be an American without being a capitalist, a Russian without being a communist and a Jew without being orthodox. In this latter connection, I note a paradox. Israeli law holds that a gentile can become a Jew only by becoming a convert to orthodox Judaism. But a person born of a Jewish and possibly non-orthodox mother is a Jew even if he is an atheist.

Viewing things from another angle, ethnic identity can be functional only if its scope is substantially expanded and if it is appreciably decathected. It must not be permitted to engulf, nor to become parasitical upon, one's other class identities, whose unduplicable accumulation is, as pointed out earlier, the very basis of an authentic identity.

I now come to a point that is crucial logically as well as in practice. Even though ethnic identity (and practically every other class identity) is logically and historically the product of the assertion that "A is an X because he is not a Y," and of the differentiating implementation of this distinctiveness, it is truly functional only if it involves the uninvidious appreciation of "B is a Y by being a non-X." The currently fashionable slogan, "black is beautiful," for example, can be true and functional only if it subsumes that "white is also beautiful," albeit in a different way. The reverse is needless to say, also true (*9*).

Any *ethnos* incapable of recognizing this elementary fact condemns itself dissociatively to a slow drift, as a closed system, toward total meaninglessness, and thereby brings itself—and mankind—to a standstill, and gradually annihilates the individual claiming exclusively such a *purely dissociative* ethnic identity by reducing him to one-dimensionality.

I was not quite twenty years old, and had not as yet taken an interest in the human sciences when, in an open letter to a famous German regional periodical, the now extinct *Böttcherstrasse,* I affirmed that human civilization depended on the diversity of cultures and ethnic identities. I reached this conclusion solely on the basis of my early studies in theoretical physics, for the second law of thermodynamics teaches that a totally homogenous closed system ceases to produce externally perceptible work. As Bertrand Russell expressed this law, the law of entropy, in one of his more popular books: "Things left to themselves tend to get into a mess." That mess mankind cannot afford.

I therefore hold that an insistent and even obsessive stressing of and clinging to one's ethnic (or any other "class") identity reveals a flaw in one's self-conception as a unique multidimensional entity. The Nazi SS member who pleaded that in performing atrocities he only obeyed commands implicitly affirmed that his SS status took precedence over all his other group identities, including his membership in the human estate. Sane and mature persons do not hypercathect their ethnic identity or any other class identity. An overriding emphasis on one of a person's several "class" identities, such as ethnic identity, simply seeks to shore up a flawed self and an uncertain awareness of one's identity as a person. The current tendency to stress one's ethnic or class identity, its use as a crutch, is *prima facie* evidence of the impending collapse of the only valid sense of identity: one's differentness, which is replaced by the most archaic pseudo-identity imaginable. I do not think that the "identity crisis" of our age can be resolved by recourse to the artificial props of collective identities: of ethnic, class, religious, occupational or any other "assistant identity." I have said elsewhere that this can lead only to a renunciation of identity, in order to fend off what is apprehended as a danger of total annihilation (*10*). I consider the evolving of any massive and dominant "class" identity as a first step toward such a "protective" renunciation of true identity. If one is nothing but a Spartan, a capitalist, a proletarian, or a Buddhist, one is next door to being nothing and therefore even to not being at all.

REFERENCES

1. Bonaparte, Marie. "Notes on Excision." In *Psychoanalysis and the Social Sciences*, edited by G. Róheim, Vol. 2, pp. 67-83, 1950.
2. Bryk, Felix. *Dark Rapture.* New York, 1939.
3. Devereux, G. "Social Structure and the Economy of Affective Bonds." In *Psychoanalytic Review*, 29:303-314, 1942.
4. Devereux, G. "Mohave Indian Obstetrics." *American Imago.* 5:95-138, 1948.
5. Devereux, G. *Therapeutic Education.* New York, 1956.
6. Devereux, G. "The Significance of the External Female Genitalia and of Female Orgasm for the Male." *Journal of the American Psychoanalytic Association.* 6:278-286, 1958.
7. Devereux, G. "La Psychanalyse et l'Histoire: Une Application à l'Histoire de Sparte." *Annales: Economies, Sociétés, Civilisations.* 20:18-44, 1965.
8. Devereux, G. "Two Types of Modal Personality Models." In *Studying Personality Cross-Culturally,* edited by B. Kaplan. Evanston, Ill.: 1961. Devereux, G. "Transference, Screen Memory and the Temporal Ego." *Journal of Nervous and Mental Disease.* 143:318-323, 1966.
9. Devereux, G. *From Anxiety to Method in the Behavioral Sciences.* Paris and The Hague, 1967.
10. Devereux, G. "Le Renonciation à l'Identité: Défense contre l'Anéantissement." *Revue Francaise de Psychanalyse.* 31:101-142, 1967.
11. Devereux, G. *Mohave Ethnopsychiatry.* 2nd ed. Washington, D.C., 1969.

12. Devereux, G. *Essais d'Ethnopsychiatrie Generale.* Paris, 1970 (2nd ed. 1973).
13. Devereux, G. *Ethnopsychoanalyse Complémentariste.* Paris, 1972.
14. Devereux, G. "Quelques Traces de la Succession par Ultimogeniture en Scythie." In *Inter-Nord* 12:262-270, 1972.
15. Dodds, E. R. (Introduction to) *Euripides: Bacchae*. 2nd ed. Oxford, 1960.
16. Dollard, John. *Caste and Class in a Southern Town.* New Haven, 1937.
17. Euripides. *Andromache.*
18. Euripides. *Hecuba.*
19. Forrest, W. G. *A History of Sparta.* London, 1968.
20. Herodotus. *The Histories.*
21. Homer. *The Iliad.*
22. Kenyatta, Jomo. *Facing Mount Kenya.* London, 1938.
23. Kroeber, A. L. "Stimulus Diffusion." In *The Nature of Culture*, pp. 344-357. Chicago, 1952.
24. Kroeber, A. L. "Cultural Intensity and Climax." In *The Nature of Culture*, pp. 337-343. Chicago, 1952.
25. Lenzen, V. F. "Individuality in Atomism." In *The Problem of the Individual.* Vol. 20, pp. 31-52. University of California Publications in Philosophy, 1937.
26. Linton, Ralph. *The Study of Man.* New York, 1936.
27. Linton, Ralph. "Culture, Society and the Individual." *Journal of Abnormal and Social Psychology.* 33:425-436, 1938.
28. Mauss, Marcel. "Une Categorie de l'Esprit Humain: La Notion de Personne, Celle de 'Moi'." In *Sociologie et Anthropologie*, pp. 336-362. Paris, 1950.
29. Ollier, F. *Le Mirage Spartiate.* (2 vols.) Paris, 1933.
30. Parsons, Talcott. "The Professions and Social Structure." *Social Forces.* 17:457-467, 1939.
31. Plutarch. *The Life of Lycurgus.*
32. Plutarch. *The Life of Pericles.*
33. Plutarch. *The Life of Solon.*
34. Plutarch. *On the Bravery of Women.*
35. Plutarch. *The Institutions of the Laconians.*
36. Plutarch. *The Sayings of Kings and Commanders.*
37. Plutarch. *The Sayings of Spartans.*
38. Plutarch. *The Sayings of Spartan Women.*
39. Russell, Bertrand. *Introduction to Mathematical Philosophy.* London, 1919.
40. Schapera, I. *The Khoisan Peoples of South Africa.* London, 1930.
41. Sophocles. *Ajax.*
42. Sophocles. *Philoctetes.*
43. Strabo. *Geography.*
44. Thucydides. *The Peloponnesian War.*
45. Tyrtaeus. *Fragment 10.* (Edmunds ed.)

46. Vajda, G. "Juifs et Musulmans selon le Hadit." *Journal Asiatique.* 229:57-127, 1937.

47. Whitehead, A. N., and Russell, Bertrand. *Principia Mathematica I.* Cambridge, 1925.

48. Xenophon. *The Constitution of the Lacedaemonians.*

Bazar Behavior: Social Identity and Social Interaction in Urban India*

GERALD BERREMAN

Say "Hindu" if you have in mind a human type common to the whole continent; otherwise, according as you want to refer to this or that group, say "Bengali, Punjabi, Hindustani, Marathi, Tamil, Sikh, Muslim," and so on. As to the word "Indian," it is only a geographical definition, and a very loose one at that. —Nirad Chaudhuri (*25*, p. 34)

The first year we were butchers, the next Sheikhs. This year, if prices fall, we shall become Sayids. —Indian proverb

3

Nearly all anthropological studies say something about ethnic identity, if only to designate the people studied and to distinguish them from their neighbors. In recent years, special attention has been directed to problems of ethnic identity in culturally plural societies, including urban ones, and in situations of rapid cultural change and social mobility. Some scholars have studied dynamic aspects of identity—how people manipulate their social identities and the symbols thereof in response to the circumstances in which they find themselves, the impressions they seek to convey, or the goals to which they aspire (*12, 14, 31, 74*). Ethnic identity is a matter of shared self-perception, the communication of that perception to others and, perhaps most crucially, the response it elicits from others in the form of social interaction (*76*, p. 572; *63*, p. 167). Ethnicity, like all aspects of social identity, is manifest both as that which is subjectively claimed and as that which is socially accorded (*48*). These may differ conspicuously, creating a situation of cognitive dissonance and consequent efforts at rectification (*34*). Both may vary from person to person, from group to group, from situation to

* A similar, somewhat abbreviated version of this article appeared under the title "Social Categories and Social Interaction in Urban India," in *American Anthropologist* 74(1972):567-86.

situation, and may be rendered differently to, and responded to differently by, different audiences. Ethnic identity, like all aspects of social identity, may be recognized and expressed in significant attributes and in significant interaction. We misunderstand ethnic identity unless all these aspects are taken into account. Notable efforts in this direction have been made by Marriott (*58*), P. Mahar (*55*), and Sebring (*74*) in India, by Leach (*53*) and Moerman (*61, 62*) with reference to Southeast Asian peasants, and by Silverman (*80*) who has studied social strata (not ethnic identity) in rural Italy with these factors in mind. Rather than reviewing further the literature on the subject, I will move directly to some relevant work of my own, focusing on my recent research in a North Indian city.

The context in which this research was undertaken is significant to an understanding of the problems I defined for study, my assumptions, my methods and my modes of analysis. Therefore I will briefly describe that context. Ten years prior to the research reported here, I had done research in an Indian mountain village and its region, concentrating largely on caste organization and its penetration into all spheres of life (*13*). There the caste system was a highly structured form of birth-ascribed social stratification, social separation, and cultural pluralism entailing institutionalized inequality enforced by economic controls and political power as well as by tradition. Castes were culturally distinct, though less so than in many regions of India, for reasons I tried to analyze (*11*). Cultural differences between castes were both a consequence and a symbol of social separation and inequality. The system gave the appearance of relative stability because power and privilege were well entrenched, largely as a result of the concentration of land in the hands of dominant groups and the fact that livelihood and other advantages flow from land ownership. "Status summation" as Barth (*7*, p. 144ff.) has termed the high degree of congruence in status conferred by the various roles an individual plays in a caste system (ritual, economic, political, social) was evident. Nevertheless, change was occurring and the potential for rapid and drastic change was present, as it is in all caste systems (*19*). Status-emulation is a widespread manifestation of mobility-striving in rural India (*29, 69, 70, 78*), and it was present among the lower castes in the region I studied. It occurred not only as "Sanskritization" (*85, 87*)—emulation of the esteemed rituals and traditions of high caste Hindus by those of low caste—but also, in the mountainous region of my research, as the appearance among all castes of what I termed "plainsward mobility"—emulation of the cultural forms of peoples of the adjacent plains. The potential for more drastic change lay in the possibility of changes in the structure of power and opportunities through education, universal adult franchise, land reform, new and diversified sources of livelihood, an equalitarian, democratic, socialist ideology, civil rights legislation, and the like, offering the possibility of changes within the system and alternatives to the system. If depressed castes could evade the stranglehold of their caste superiors, it was apparent that they were ready and eager to throw off their disadvantaged position in society. Research in the village ten years later shows that a few individuals of the privileged castes have succeeded in escaping the constraints of traditional peasant life through new, secular avenues outside of the village (education and urban employment, primarily), while those few of low caste who have escaped their status have done so through refuge in unusual, difficult, but traditional statuses which insulate them from the consequences of their caste. Or they have simply moved away to low-caste villages. Of two young men who escaped many of the consequences of their untouchability without leaving, one became a religious devotee and the other became defined as mentally deranged and hence unaccountable for his behavior. Both instances seemed to be at least partially intentional efforts at escape. Sanskritization attempts have not enhanced their status, for they have not the power to back them up, which is essential if they are to succeed. There have not been the fundamental political and economic changes which would permit more sweeping social changes or mobility by low castes out of the traditional system.

This research led me to look further into caste as a system of social stratification and ethnic pluralism whose principles and effects could be found outside of Hindu India. I came ultimately to a cross-cultural view not far removed from that of "ethnic stratification" (*76, 20*). Like many contemporary students of Indian society, I believed that traditional concepts of caste in India were so narrowly drawn that they were often inapplicable even to many facets of ethnic stratification *within* Hindu India. In any case they were so heavily indebted to ideal depictions that they virtually excluded much daily behavior, its cognitive bases and its meaning to those who live it. I felt that many contemporary studies of caste ranking in India have imposed an artificially one-dimensional quality on that complex phenomenon (*15, 35*). These problems and shortcomings are even more apparent when one considers caste in the urban setting in India. There it is questionable whether caste is the paramount focus of identity. A variety of non-caste social categories obtrude, secular values are apparent, alternatives to caste-based social mechanisms are at hand, and anonymity and mobility make evasion and escape a more realistic possibility than in the countryside. A view of caste which might be adequate to describe most social relations in a peasant village is likely to be inadequate to the urban scene. Yet any adequate theory or description of caste must encompass both.

It was with these reservations in mind that I undertook the research to be described here. It comprised a study of social categories and interaction in

1968-69 in Dehra Dun, a modern, ethnically heterogeneous North Indian city of 165,000 people. Dehra Dun lies near the western boundary of the state of Uttar Pradesh, adjacent to Haryana (formerly part of the Punjab), and at the foot of the Himalayas where mountain culture meets plains culture. It serves as marketplace and administrative center for a large rural hinterland. As the headquarters for several governmental organizations (notably the Oil and Natural Gas Commission, with 5000 employees, and the Survey of India), it has in its population civil service employees drawn from many parts of India. As a center of primary and secondary education, and as the site of the Indian Military Academy and the home base of several military units, it is temporary home to students and military personnel from throughout India and Nepal. Many who were educated or stationed there return to retire. Dehra Dun is also the location of a large number of Tibetan refugees. Half of its population is composed of refugees from what is now West Pakistan (many of them Sikhs), whereas prior to the partition of India and Pakistan, half of the city's population was Muslim (now only 5 percent of the population is Muslim, most of the rest having emigrated to Pakistan). The animosity between Hindus and Muslims was exacerbated by the traumatic nature of their conflict in Dehra Dun and enroute to Dehra Dun at the time of partition, and the experiences of the refugees in Pakistan. Chibbar (*26*) has carried out a brief study of the "middle class" in Dehra Dun, and Bhatt has studied the Chamars (*22*). I wanted to look into how social identity is defined and acted upon in the highly differentiated, desperately competitive and poverty-stricken plural society of urban India. I also hoped to throw some light on the nature and functioning of caste organization, pluralism, ethnic relations, especially with respect to conflict resolution and accommodation in a plural and rigidly stratified society.

Because of my skepticism about the applicability of traditional models of Indian social organization to this situation, I wanted to work inductively, to find how the people define their social world, including themselves, and how they act within it. I adopted a symbolic interactionist perspective, using detailed observation and inquiry regarding what people do in face-to-face interaction, to discover how they choose among alternative behaviors in terms of the meanings that specific attributes, actions and social situations have for them and for those with whom they interact (*23*). My approach was also cognitive in that I was interested in how people viewed their social world, and in the principles upon which they organized its constituent elements, defined systems of relevance and made choices. This approach coincides in part with that of the "componential" or "formal" analysts—the "ethnoscientists" in American anthropology (*44, 17*). My inquiries were directed primarily at discovering the subjective experience of social identity in the society, the variations and manipulations therein, and the relationship of that experience to interpersonal (reciprocal) behavior and the decisions which underlie that behavior.

The research was based upon four fundamental questions: (1) What are the social categories—the social identities—of people comprising the society as defined by themselves? (2) What characteristics are attributed to members of these social categories; in other words, what stereotypes or empirical generalizations are expressed about them? (3) By what cues and in what circumstances do people identify individuals as belonging to a particular social category? (4) How are the above three questions related to interpersonal behavior? That is, given that certain categories of people are recognized and that they are regarded as having significant shared characteristics, how do these facts affect how people behave in one another's presence (or behind their backs)?

I treated the last of these as the crucial question to which the others were necessarily preliminary. To answer it is to get directly at social behavior, its context and meaning, and therefore to throw light on interpersonal and interethnic relations in this relatively large-scale urban environment, characterized by social and cultural pluralism and rigid stratification.

In order to answer the four questions, I observed and talked to people in many situations and in many walks of life. As I learned the social categories they recognized and employed, I tried to sample from them all in various situations. I worked primarily in public places (*42*), where most distinctively urban interaction takes place. I began in the bazar, where urbanites of many groups and statuses interact. It is also the commercial center for people from an extensive rural hinterland comprising three major linguistic and culture areas and representing several religions and numerous castes. I began my work by sitting in teashops, retail stores, barber shops and the like, talking with the proprietors and their customers. Later I moved to other settings—to wholesale markets, residential areas, craftsmen's workshops, small factories, government offices, hospitals, recreation areas, public transportation depots, religious centers and events, the stalls of sidewalk vendors—wherever I could interact with people naturally or in interview situations. I talked with businessmen, laborers, students, gypsies and with such occupational specialists as letter-writers and itinerant dentists who deal with a wide range of people.

SOCIAL CATEGORIES AND ETHNIC IDENTITY

My initial question was, what kinds of people come here? (or do business here, pass by here, work here, live here, etc.). I soon learned that social categories could be elicited to the exclusion of individual social types by asking "Who all comes here?" (*kaun kaun* . . .) rather than literally "What kinds of people come here?" (*kis kisim kē* . . .). In the early stages especially, I was interested in terms employed which defined the general categories—the domains—which respondents had in mind when giving specific answers, as well as the specific answers themselves. That is, I was interested in words such as the Urdu *quōm* (nation, race, tribe—almost literally "ethnic group"), the Hindi *jātī* ("descent," which carries much the same connotation) and *nāshtā* (belief or creed), as well as terms for specific named categories of varying degrees of inclusiveness. To elicit the latter, I asked such questions as "Who is he?" and "What kind of person was that?" I also listened for unsolicited terms of address and reference. In all of this work I used the method of contrastive analysis of terms and behaviors as prescribed by componential analysts: "A word whose meaning is the object of investigation designates some conceptual category within a set of complimentary categories that partition a larger conceptual domain. . . . We learn what the category . . . is by contrasting it with the other categories" and noting the crucial differences (*44*, p. 331). The aim of such analysis is to derive a paradigm of terms corresponding to that used by people in the society, and to infer the rules by which these terms are applied in daily life. This presumably provides a window into the cognitive world of those studied, and affords insight into the bases of their behavior and the choices which underlie it.

As I collected the data, I kept detailed notes on the context of the various terms: who used them, with reference to whom, and in what situations. Where possible, I recorded further contextual material on the background of the individual who used the term, including his ethnic identity, where he came from, his native language, where he had been, his education, his occupation, and so on. I also attended to any explanation or elaboration on the term's use that he or others might provide and noted the reaction of the one to whom it was applied, if possible. These data proved invaluable because the terms used varied greatly according to just these kinds of factors.

In this manner I accumulated a considerable number of terms for social identities of varying degrees of specificity, depending upon a wide range of criteria. The terms are so numerous, and the analysis is so incomplete, that I cannot list them all. A single interview or observation sequence might provide a small sample such as the following, covering most of the major social dimensions but few of the specific categories: Punjabi, Muslim, Kūmhār (potter caste), untouchable, Khatri (caste), Baniya (Vaisya merchant), Vaisya (caste category), Agarwāl (a Vaisya caste), Garg (an Agarwal sib), Shīā (a Muslim sect), Pathān (a Muslim "tribe"), villager, Vaishnavite (a Hindu sect), Pahārī (mountain people), *refūjī* ("refugee" – from West Pakistan), Sikh, *bābū lōg* (white-collar workers), "eating-drinking people" (well-to-do), "man from Delhi," Anglo-Indian, Chamār (leather-worker caste), Shudra (artisan caste category), "small castes" (low castes), Nepali. In other words, a variety of terms were used to describe people by referring to various aspects of their identities. These terms can be analyzed according to the components which are common to each category and those which distinguish constituent subcategories, although this cannot be done fully or consistently without detailed reference to behavioral and situational context. Thus the terms listed above fall into such categories as: (1) *Religious groups:* Muslim and Sikh as contrasted with Hindu, Christian, Jain, Parsi, for example; (2) *Regional-linguistic-national-racial groups:* Punjabi and Pahari as contrasted with Hindiwala (person of Hindi-speaking area), Madrasi (South Indian, sometimes including people from western India: Marathi and Gujarati), Bengali, Anglo-Indian, Englishman, Tibetan, Nepali; (3) *Caste-categories:* "high castes" (comprising Brahman, Kshatriya, Vaisya categories—the "twiceborn"—usually); "small castes" (comprising roughly the Shudra category of artisans); "low castes" (comprising, roughly, untouchables).

Each of these major categories is composed of subsets of differentiated and often contrasting categories, not all of which can be accurately presented in the following two-dimensional outline:

I Religious groups (*dharam*) are subdivided as follows:

- A Muslims
  - (1) sects (*firkā*): Shīā, Sūnnī, Wāhābī, Kādiyānī;
  - (2) tribes (*quōm*): Pathān, Mōgul, Sheikh, Sayid, Rājpūt, Gūjar, etc., and low status occupations (*zāt,* such as butcher, barber, weaver), similar to the lower Hindu castes and contrastive with tribe (cf. Karim, 1956: 111-160);
- B Hindus
  - (1) sects by primary deity or mode of worship (Shaivite, Vaishnavite), and sects by philosophical and textual tradition (Sanatham Dharam [traditional], Arya Samaj [reform]);
  - (2) caste divisions can be viewed from this perspective also;
- C Sikhs, Jains, Christians, Parsis and others can be similarly subdivided.

II Regional-linguistic groups are subdivided by locality and dialect so that, for example, Hindiwālā includes Purbīā (people from eastern Uttar Pradesh) and, as remoteness decreases, "man from Delhi," "man of Agra," "man of Meerut," and so on. *Refūjī* (refugee) seems also to be a term of this order.

III Caste categories, although ideally limited to Hindus, often in fact are applied to members of other religious groups with or without a religious designation appended.

Within caste categories are various specific castes (*jati*: named, birth-ascribed, ranked groups). Terms for these groups, too, are often applied outside the Hindu fold, either on the basis of pre-conversion ancestral status or (in the case of the lower-ranked groups) on the basis of occupation. (Names of some castes or caste-like groups are applied only to non-Hindus.) For example, from the myriad castes and their subdivisions, we can pick the following for illustration: *Kshatriya* category (*varna*) includes Rajput and Khatri castes (but note that some non-Khatri informants would assign the latter to the lower *Vaisya* category). Within each of these castes are numerous phratries (groups with putatively common patrilineal ancestry, in which endogamy is usually preferred). Thus, Khatri are comprised of Arora, Khukran, Banjahi, etc. The phratries are subdivided again into sibs (closer relatives, among whom exogamy is enforced). Arora, for example, are divided into many sibs including Kumar, Gulhati, Madan, Dhingra, Matta, and Sachdeva.

In addition, any of the above terms may be regionally or subregionally designated (Amballa Khatri, Lahore Arora). Among the lower castes, subdivisions may be made on different principles, such as on traditional occupational subspecialty or on region of origin rather than phratry. Also, the caste categories at these levels may be far broader in scope, less specific in content, and less agreed upon in inclusiveness and rank than among the high castes. Untouchables include leatherworkers, sweepers and, depending upon the informant and circumstances, anywhere from a dozen other castes to no other castes. Leatherworkers, for example, are divided into two distinct groups in Dehra Dun (although the division is unknown to higher castes): the *Jatiya* from Gwalior and the *Raidasi* from Bijnore (*22*). Non-Hindu groups generally claim to have no caste-like divisions (the Muslim sub-divisions listed above are claimed to be non-ranked), but all do. Even the equalitarian Sikhs have, for example, in addition to sects, several caste-like categories including the very low status *Bhātrā* (an almost gypsy-like group) and *Mazbhī,* essentially the untouchable category.

In addition to these obviously ethnic categories and sub-categories—obvious in that they suggest common ancestry, common status, common culture and their concomitants—are terms that appear in parallel linguistic and social context without implying ethnicity as social scientists understand the concept. These terms designate social class, life-style, or occupational status, e.g. babu log, student, soldier, "eating-drinking person," laboring person, beggar, villager, official. Subdivisions are often made in terms of the specifics: particular occupation or office, role within the category, degree of wealth or poverty, and so forth.

These are significant social categories and hence refer to social identities. Their character is objectively different from ethnic groups, however, for cultural homogeneity is likely to be less than in ethnic groups, and ancestry irrelevant. Membership in ethnic groups is ascribed; in these categories it is acquired or imposed. People are assigned their class status because they display its attributes and behaviors; conversely, people display the attributes and behaviors of their caste or ethnic group because they are members of it. In the cognitive and behavioral world of the urban Indians I worked with, however, this analytical distinction is not made in practice (it *is* recognized when pointed out). I therefore deal with these terms together with the ethnic terms, as social categories.

Also, since my informants did not consistently separate corporate groups (castes and religions) from non-corporate categories (regions, languages, classes), I did not do so in this study. I tried to follow their taxonomies, not my own.

Terms for social types and personality types—heroes, villains and fools (*52*), liars, men of god, charlatans, etc.—were also easily elicited and frequently occurred spontaneously in conversation. These, however, were *not* used in contexts parallel to those I am discussing here—social categories. Urban Indians thus distinguished clearly in usage between social categories and individual social types. I have followed their distinction and have chosen to confine my analysis to the former except where a social type is relevant as a putative characteristic of a social category (see below).

The terminological categories I discuss are real to those who use them. They come continually into play in conversation and behavior. The terms themselves were collected from many people in many situations. I acquired a great many; I doubtless overlooked some. They can be organized and charted into an inclusive or maximal terminology (*74*, p. 196ff.), and I am in the process of doing so. But the total terminology would be known to no one person, its contrasts and categories would fail to find agreement among many, and there would be numerous points at which no clearcut relationship between terms could be drawn—only the contexts of use could show this relationship. Thus, "Muslim" is often contrasted with "Punjabi" or "Purbia," although it is a religious designation while they are regional-linguistic designations. An Anglo-Indian woman contrasted Hindu, Sikh and Punjabi, and was unaware of the religion of "Punjabi." More important, this was irrelevant to her. Recently an Indian sociologist wrote a book on caste and cited Aroras as a caste contrasting with Khatris, whereas all of my informants and other sources cite Arora as a phratry within Khatri (*26*, p. 6). The Khatri caste itself was not consistently identified as to its *varna* (caste category) status. An inclusive chart of terminology is thus perhaps useful for analytical purposes only in that it identifies the widest range of categories available to people in this city for describing themselves and their fellows.

In working out the terminological system a very complex picture emerges. First, there is a wide variety of terms which may apply to the same individual. Thus, to take a simple case, a man might well be identifiable as (1) a Punjabi, (2) Muslim of (3) Teli (oil-presser) caste who is (4) an urbanite working in (5) a white-collar job—five designations which are usually non-contrastive. Another individual might be (1) a Purbia (that is, from eastern Uttar Pradesh), (2) Hindu of (3) Kumhar (potter) caste who is (4) a villager working as (5) a laborer. The latter five terms are also non-contrastive with one another and each is usually contrastive with the correspondingly numbered term in the preceding five. All five contrast pairs can vary more or less independently, although there are correlations among some of them and a few combinations are unlikely. Other terms can be added within each of these contrast sets (other regions, other religions, other castes, other life-styles and other occupations), while subcategories could be designated within many of these terms (sects within Islam, phratries and sibs within castes, localities within regions) and supercategories could be designated for some (caste categories, more inclusive cultural-linguistic regions, and so on). Clearly, social identity cannot be understood without understanding the variation in peoples' knowledge of and use of the categorical terms, and the individual and circumstantial sources of that variation. These matters, of necessity, became a major focus of the research.

The number and specificity of terms which could be applied to an individual, and which ones would be applied in a particular instance, varied from one informant to another. The total range of terms available and appropriate for an individual was never socially and situationally possible. Individual variation in the use of terminology proved to be largely a function of one's own social identity relative to those of whom he spoke or with whom he interacted. This is partly a matter of knowledge, which in turn is a matter of subculture, social distance and social relevance. For example, most Muslims could tell me consistently and in detail about several subcategories of Muslims: the sects, tribes and caste-like occupational categories and their characteristics. Few Hindus could give even a minimally coherent picture. Muslims, on the other hand, had a fairly clear picture of Hindu social categories, though not as clear as Hindus. Similarly, all Chamārs (untouchable leather-workers) distinguished two endogamous and culturally distinct castes among themselves. No one of any other group made this distinction or even knew of it when it was suggested to them. "Leather-workers are all alike," they said. For them, Chamar was a caste; for leatherworkers it was a caste category. The Chamars, on the other hand, knew a good deal about the culture and social organization of their caste superiors.

Generally, upwardly mobile individuals and groups defined those they regarded as competitors for status differently than did people who were content with or resigned to their social position. The audience to statements about social identity seemed to heavily influence the nature of those statements. Thus behind-the-back statements were different from face-to-face ones; statements before peers were different from statements before social superiors; statements before strangers were different from statements before acquaintances; statements in haste or anger were different from considered statements; statements to unidentified individuals were often cautious, those to misidentified individuals were often regretted.

In a chart of all of the terms collected and their relationships, one could demonstrate with a series of overlays how people in different social positions differentially view the categories which comprise their social environment (*79* p. 186ff.). In a preliminary attempt I find, not surprisingly, that people are most detailed and consistent in the use of terms for their own groups and less so for those socially adjacent. They become vaguer as social distance increases, especially downward distance, or toward greater social stigma or more alien identity. That is, people are most knowledgeable about those in their own and nearby groups. They are more knowledgeable about those superior to themselves in status and power than about those inferior. People know well those who dominate them, but know little about those they dominate. As I have suggested above, untouchables know a great deal about Brahmins; Brahmins know little about untouchables. Muslims know a great deal about Hindus; Hindus know little about Muslims. And this applies not only to terminology and social structure, but to general ethnographic knowledge. There are good functional reasons for this. Those of lower or stigmatized status have both the opportunity (as people who perform services for others) and the need to know their powerful superiors, and these are not reciprocal. There is cross-cultural confirmation, especially in studies of American society. Waller noted thirty years ago, that "it is usually the subordinated member of any pair who tends to develop insight into the other" (*92,* p. 356). This is true of groups as well as individuals.

In the case of regional designations, the specificity of terminology is a function of physical, social and cultural proximity. For example, all South Indians are called "Madrasi" by most local informants although they come from widely divergent cultures and areas. In fact, as I have indicated, some informants identified people of Maharashtra and Gujarat, who come from western India and share the Indo-Aryan culture of the North rather than the Dravidian culture of the South, as "Madrasi," and refused to alter the identification even when these facts were pointed out. Within a radius of 200 miles of Dehra Dun, on the adjacent and culturally similar plains, the distinctions are refined, with people designated by subregion or city. The culturally and linguistically distinct mountain people, even from only a few miles away, are relatively undifferentiated by Dehra Dun informants even though among themselves the distinctions are many and minute (*11, 13*). Within the 60-mile long Dehra Dun valley, with the city in the center, distinctions are made between the eastern and western ends, and within the city people are (or can be) designated by neighborhoods.

Situational differences in the use of terminology are more complex. An outsider can learn quite quickly to make conventionally accurate assessments of a wide range of social identities. Learning which ones are relevant in a given situation is more difficult, for a number of alternatives are always open. Familiar situations elicit varying terminologies. A man of merchant caste who is fastidious about matters of ritual purity and pollution will discuss an impending wedding with detailed reference to the caste, subcaste, sib and family affiliations of the participants, the caste and religion of those who will be hired to provide services, the region and social class of guests. A wide range of statuses will be important to him. In his drygoods shop, however, he will categorize customers only in ways relevant to the customer role, relying on stereotypes about the honesty, tightfistedness, propensity to bargain, and buying preferences of various social categories he encounters. Evidently "everyone's money is green" (in the Indian case, more often blue). He simply notes who is likely to spend it, how readily and for what. If, however, someone crosses him or taxes his patience, he may hurl an ethnic slur at the low status customer ("dirty Chamar," "lying Muslim," "hillbilly") or mutter one under his breath after the departure of a high status one ("stupid Sikh," "greedy Baniya," "arrogant Bengali"). A teashop proprietor, on the other hand, will look at potential customers in terms of religion and major caste categories because he has to attend to his customers' notions of ritual purity and the jeopardy in which inter-dining puts them. A barber will attend to certain categories of class, religion and region in order to assure that he can please his customers in the hair styles they prefer and expect. Customers behave in complementary fashion. It is clear that these relations are not defined by the "whole persons" involved—by the sum of the statuses of the participants—but by those aspects of the social selves which are relevant in the situation. The relations outside of one's own ethnic group are impersonal and fragmented; they are what sociologists have often termed "secondary relationships." They contrast with the personal, holistic, "primary" relationships in the family, the village and other traditional settings where all of one's statuses are known, relevant and likely to be responded to (*33*). Such relationships are found in the city only within the ethnic group or neighborhood, if at all.

Terminologically, then, several sets of social categories are employed simultaneously, alternatively or in various mixtures, depending upon who is speaking and on the situation in which he is speaking, as he defines it. There is no "correct" or "complete" taxonomy of social categories. One man's contrasting terms often prove to be another man's interchangeable terminological variations. For some people and in some circumstances untouchables contrast with Hindus; for others they are a subcategory of Hindus. For some, "untouchable" includes all Shudra castes; for others it includes only leather-workers and sweepers, while for still others it includes three, four or more castes in addition to these. It may or may not be congruent with "low caste." For no one does it include his own caste. For some, "little castes" means Shudra castes; for others it means Shudras and untouchables; for still others it means "castes lower than us." For some, Purbia (people of eastern Uttar Pradesh) is a subcategory of laborer or a synonym for laborer; for others it is a purely regional term. Some apply it across religious and caste lines; others reserve it for low caste (or lower class) Hindus of the region. For some Jain and even Sikh are subcategories of Hindu; for others, including themselves, they contrast with Hindu (and some regard Jains as a subgroup of the Vaisya caste category). Innumerable additional examples could be given. Different experience, aspirations, audiences, and definitions of the situation all lead to different designations and interpretations of ethnic identity.

There is order in the use of terminology, but it is order explicable only by reference to social, cultural, personal and situational context, and is not derivable from the terminological system itself or from the relationship of terms to their referents out of context.

STEREOTYPES AND INDICATORS

The second and third questions addressed in my research: inquiry into stereotypes and the indicators by which people are identified as members of social categories, are relatively straightforward matters upon which I obtained a great deal of data, but which seem not to require extensive discussion here. Stereotypes were many and relatively consistent with terminology. There is no term of social identity which is not richly characterized in stereotypic metaphor and simile. These were discovered through inquiry, spontaneous comments, folklore, epithets, and a wide variety of similar sources. They cover character traits, mental and physical prowess, physical appearance, habits and proclivities. Anant has recently presented the results of social-psychological research on caste, religious and regional stereotypes in North India, giving tabulated results of extensive surveys utilizing 88 stereotypic traits (*2, 3, 4, 67, 81*). These are consistent with my qualitative materials.

Indicators were also many and relatively closely correlated with terminology. They were discovered through inquiry, observation and interaction, "natural experiments," photograph identification, characterizations in mass media, and the like. Readily apparent but often subtle indicators of identity that were most used and most diagnostic in casual interaction were speech, dress and adornment, manners, life style, and physiognomy, in roughly that order (*73*). They ranged from conspicuous indicators (the traditional Muslim woman's all-concealing *burkhā*, contrasted to the stylishly worn middle class Hindu woman's sari), to subtle ones (the regional and subregional differences in mode of wearing the sari), and to unverifiable stereotypes (including many of the alleged physical differences among groups, such as the "loose skin" of Paharis). Distinctive cultural and social structural attributes also symbolize identity (ceremonies, myths, systems of kinship, social organization, traditional occupations, dietary preferences). Some of these are not readily apparent but are nonetheless important as symbols of identity and foci of self-esteem. Muslims are proud of their cross-cousin marriage, polygyny, standards of meat preparation, prohibition on pork, prohibition on graven images, and on portraits and music in mosques, while Hindus are repelled or amused by them. Muslims are repelled or amused by Hindu deities, ceremonies, cow worship, eating habits and marriage customs. Mountain people are proud of their bride-price marriage; plains people are proud of their dowry marriage. And so it goes.

Interaction is also a key indicator of ethnic identity. People of common status tend to interact more freely and intimately with one another than with those outside. The caste, for example, is the maximum unit of status-equal interaction in many contexts and especially in those which are intimate or ritual in nature. Those of common ethnic status are likely to live, eat, work, converse, worship, and marry together. Even those sharing only common language interact in casual conversation more freely than with others, while common regional origin may bring people together in ethnic restaurants or at ethnic celebrations. The identity of a person is often discovered by the company he keeps.

People put as much effort into expressing the desired symbols of identity to others and trying to get the desired response, as they do in discerning such symbols in others. Conventional cues obvious to the initiate are often subtle to the stranger. Teashops, for example, conventionally indicate the religion of their proprietors by the cooking utensils prominently displayed: stainless steel or aluminum for Muslims; brass for Hindus. Each group rationalizes the superiority of its utensils in terms of beauty and cleanliness. "Mutually antagonistic symbolic degradation" is a prominent feature of Hindu-Muslim relations (and of relations between several other pairs of competing ethnic groups, especially Hindu-Christian, adjacent linguistic-cultural groups and competing castes). Thus the utensils of Hindu and Muslim teashops were used by each group not only for purposes of identification, but to verify favorable self-images and unfavorable images of the other (in this case, cleanliness-slovenliness). The Hindu and Muslim methods of slaughtering animals were used by each group to verify the cruelty, immorality and crudity of the other. In general, competing groups engaged in what might appropriately be called mutual status degradation, implicit in which was status affirmation of one's own group.

A stark reminder that the question of indicators is not academic appeared in a news item from Ahmedabad, reported in the *San Francisco Chronicle*, on October 1, 1969. Describing the Hindu-Muslim riots there in which 1000 are reported to have died, the article noted that "since would-be killers identify their victims through dissimilar Hindu and Moslem ways of dressing, many Ahmedabadis have started wearing Western clothes as a measure of safety." Fortunately, ethnic identification and interaction are not often so violent; unfortunately, they *are* often crucial to the well-being of those involved.

INTERACTION

The fourth and most important question addressed in the research was that of the relation of behavior to the categories expressed in terminology, to associated stereotypes and to other aspects of the social situation. I focused on people's responses to others, but was also alert to management of the self in conveying a desired impression and eliciting a desired response (*41, 43, 12*). My aim was to find out how people act in terms of the identities available to them and confronted by them.

In this phase of the research, I wanted to rely primarily on observation, to see and hear behavior that was conditioned by cognitive assessments of social identity. I listened, for example, to the drivers of horse-drawn vehicles as they shouted to clear the path of pedestrians. I was rewarded not only with an enriched vocabulary of threats and epithets, but with modes of address corresponding to the drivers' judgments of the social identity of the people they were addressing, ranging from the deferential request that the well-to-do Brahmin save himself, to the insulting threat directed at the country bumpkin. I saw teashop keepers send Muslim and untouchable potential customers on their way or, more often, require them to wash their own utensils after use. I saw passengers move away from undesirable seat partners on public buses. I saw and heard people deferred to, abused, flattered, patronized, welcomed, and avoided in contexts where it was apparent (and often explicitly verified) that this was a consequence of their ethnic identity. This was ethnic identity, social hierarchy and social separation in action. I also saw votes courted on ethnic appeals, and abrupt repudiation of that appeal if misidentification of ethnic identity occurred or if the appeal was regarded as spurious.

A wide range of data on behavior was obtained indirectly, by talking extensively with people about inter-ethnic experiences. One could observe for days before seeing behavior identifiable as ethnically conditioned, but cooperative individuals could recall instances from a lifetime of experience and observation.

Symbols of identity and in fact identity itself can be and are manipulated in order to maximize the rewards or minimize the sanctions which adhere to them in the rigid social inequality of India's plural and stratified society (*49, 87*). Sanskritization is a well-documented method of identity manipulation, as is Islamicization and analogous processes of status emulation among members of ethnic groups attempting mobility, revitalization or solidarity. Westernization is another, and individual, means to status enhancement and material advantages. Recourse to deviant status (as exemplified in the abovementioned cases of low-caste villagers' retreat into religion and putative insanity) is another form of individual mobility.

Most indicators of ethnic identity are under some degree of individual and group control. Skin color, physiognomy and other unalterable features are of relatively minor importance. Hence, identity is to a significant extent a matter of choice in the relatively anonymous and momentary arena of much urban interaction. The indicators are assumed to be intrinsic to groups or categories; in fact they are often manipulated. The effectiveness of their manipulation is largely a function of the credibility of the assumption that they cannot or will not be—that indicators in fact indicate the ethnic identity of those who display them.

In the manipulation of identity, people make use of the currency that is available to them in the marketplace of public esteem, advantage and other rewards. Thus, in the city, students, white-collar workers and other employed non-menials can often maximize their status through obscuring ethnic ties and adopting Western clothes and manners, and they often attempt to do so. These are the people hardest to distinguish ethnically, and whose ethnic identity is least relevant in most of their social relations. Among people in menial or traditional occupations and those who have retained strong rural ties, status enhancement may be most attainable and relevant through Sanskritization—conformity to a high-status traditional ideal of behavior. To some who regard themselves as discriminated against but who are numerous or well-organized and cognizant of common interest, organization into caste associations (*71*), into ethnic nationalist movements (*65, 40*), into political action groups, into unions and the like is most advantageous. Every conceivable urban occupation and small business category from coolies to drygoods merchants is organized into an association in Dehra Dun, as is every regional group represented in town. The effectiveness of the organizations varies widely. For those of high status, fraternal groups, professional associations and chambers of commerce may be avenues to status enhancement or status protection. To the most marginal, the tradition of marginality itself may pay off, as in the case of itinerant blacksmiths, resident puppeteers, basketmakers, utensil sellers, certain groups of beggars, and animal trainers, all of whom live on the physical and social periphery of the city and who are tolerated and rewarded (however grudgingly) partly because of their traditionally esoteric cultural characteristics which often derive from a distant homeland or a glorious or mysterious past. For them, no other avenue to social survival and enhancement is realistically available, so they emphasize their group identity and uniqueness through dress, manner and style of life, as do gypsy fortunetellers in American society. In all of these cases, corporate groups are formed and utilized to promote self interest. That tradition runs deep, and as circumstances change, it surfaces in many guises.

Identity manipulation, though possible, is not easy, because most indicators are not easily dissimulated, especially in intense or extended interaction. As a mountain villager lamented, "We don't know how to dress or act in town. There even a poor untouchable puts on a shirt and pajama and looks respectable, but we can't look like that. Even if we spend Rs. 200 on the finest cloth and have the best clothes made, we still look like fools in town" (*13,* p. 307). Moreover, in the most crucial circumstances, ethnic credentials are sure to be closely checked through acquaintances, kinsmen and one's natal village. This is a deterrent to ambitious plans for "passing."

There is a traditional kind of entertainer (*bahurupiya*, or "one of many disguises") who travels among Indian towns and cities making his living from the amusement he affords others by skillfully simulating various identities (policeman, meter-reader, fakir, sadhu, transvestite, Anglo-Indian, rich man, blind woman) and fooling shopkeepers and others in repeated interaction in many guises and on successive days. Few could get away with it—it is an art at least as difficult as that of the juggler, who does easily what others find impossible. His remuneration is a gauge of his skill, revealed only when, after a series of successful encounters over a period of several days, he reveals himself to those whom he has fooled. This is identity manipulation made into entertainment and into a profession.

Identity manipulation is often expressed as casual, situational or instrumental impression management (*41, 42, 12*). I saw many examples: young village men affected western dress in town; high caste Bengali men changed from regional to western dress depending upon the social situation; politicians adopted the dress identified with Congress Party leaders or the dress of the ethnic community whose votes they sought; applicants for waiters' jobs in high-class or high-caste restaurants concealed low caste status by their manner and the temporary adoption of high caste names, while Muslims did the same. It is proverbial that mountain men who emigrate to seek work in homes and hotels in the cities are largely of low caste, while mountain men who have obtained work as servants in such places invariably claim to be of high caste. Speech patterns are manipulated much as are manners and patterns of dress, and for the same purposes—but perhaps with more difficulty or less success (*46*).

RELATIONSHIPS BETWEEN ASPECTS OF IDENTITY

In general I found that stereotypes and indicators of ethnic identity were closely related to terminology. Once these three kinds of data were known in an ethnographic sense, there were few instances in which they did not correspond in the expected manner. One could predict with fair accuracy from any one of the three to the other two.

Interpersonal and intergroup behavior, however, was *not* closely related to terminology and its correlates. As sociologists of race relations in America have repeatedly demonstrated, people often do not act as their attitudes suggest or even as they say they would when confronted by an individual of a despised or honored or feared group. They behave as the situation demands or makes most comfortable rather than as consistency with belief would seem to dictate. Ethnic identity is relevant to, but far from determinative of, behavior; people act in context, not in the abstract. The structure of interpersonal and intergroup behavior, then, lies in the interplay of situational and motivational factors underlying choices among alternative behaviors, with cognitively distinguishable and terminologically specifiable identities relevant, but not determinative.

Behavior proved to be less specific than terminology: people knew many more social distinctions than they acted upon in any given situation. They tended to assimilate terminological categories into broader behavioral categories and to apply them as the purpose and context of the interaction dictated.

Rough analysis suggests that the most common behavioral categories in impersonal, short-term, face-to-face interaction were: superiors (those honored, feared or obeyed), equals (often far broader, as a category, than the caste system would suggest, and often with far more suppressed reservations and anxieties on the part of participants than their behavior would reveal), inferiors (those disparaged, dominated or shunned), aliens (those regarded warily and avoided), and non-entities (those irrelevant, unimportant or inexplicable, hence ignored). To which of these broad categories a member of a group would be behaviorally assigned often varied with the situation. A poor Brahmin, treated as superior in a ritual context might be treated as an equal in a western setting, and as an inferior in a business transaction. An untouchable sweeper or low caste tailor might be treated as a non-entity when performing his job in a high caste home.

Certain social categories, especially those that were stigmatized or alien, consistently obscured or took precedence over others in their influence on behavior. To Hindus, being Christian or Muslim was more relevant than being Punjabi or Purbia, usually; being untouchable took precedence over being Hindu and over being Punjabi or Purbia; being a villager, a hillbilly or a laborer took precedence over being Brahmin or Rajput. The most consistent exception seemed to be that middle-class status, particularly at the upper end of the scale, often took precedence over virtually all else, including over religion, region and even caste. This was less true, however, in narrowly ritual, patently traditional or intimately familial contexts, of which the epitome in all respects is marriage. The exceptions in these traditional spheres are most conspicuous as they are manifest in areas that might elsewhere be regarded as beyond the sphere of traditional corporate-group responsibility: in employment (where it takes the form of nepotism [75]), credit transactions, legal testimony, and bureaucratic functions. Most of my informants regarded these as extensions of familial, caste and ethnic functions, where "primordial sentiments" of group identity, loyalty and commitment are regarded as morally primary.

The situation described here seems to be generally true of contemporary life in urban India as secularization, political participation and westernization increase, as new criteria of social identity assume importance, and as new avenues to power and privilege become available.

CONCLUSIONS

As highly structured as Indian society is in terms of traditional corporate groups (notably castes), and as often as they appear or reappear in urban situations, these are only part of the basis for urban social interaction. Their traditional functions seem to be diminishing in importance (*21,* pp. 30-56; *79,* p. 127ff.). In urban society, other named and readily distinguishable social categories are becoming at least equally important. But even knowing all of these does not afford an adequate understanding of urban social interaction and urban social structure, for such interaction depends upon and is composed of complex behavioral choices within the structural framework and its associated values. These choices are based largely on implicit rules which take into account a variety of situations, goal-orientations, matters of personal and temporal circumstance, the immediate and ultimate audiences to behavior, the actors' own definitions of the social situation, their respective roles in it, and its probable outcome.

The terminological system of social categories reveals some important parameters within which the choices are made, but it by no means reflects them all. To understand urban society one must also know the context of their use, the behavioral alternatives available and the criteria for choice among them.

These are the most general conclusions of this research. Although the analysis of data is not complete, they may be usefully elaborated upon. In the following pages, some of their implications will be pointed out and speculated upon.

To discover the significant social categories in urban India, it is necessary to find out what people say and how they act with reference to one another. Terminology, its meaning and use, is important in this regard. The discovery and description of social categories requires attention to the subtle as well as the conspicuous aspects of social behavior, to verbal and non-verbal communication, to social situations including their participants and the participants' identities—in short, to the total context of interpersonal behavior and how it is perceived by its participants. This can only be derived by intensive participant observation, extensive interviewing, and the willingness to secure information and insights wherever and however they appear. This is as true in seeking to learn the terminological system of social categories as it is in the investigation of their stereotypes, and in the identification of characteristics and interaction. The methods used in the research reported here have been briefly described in earlier sections. As a result of my experience I agree with Perchonock and Werner (*66,* p. 238) when, after pursuing their componential analysis of Navajo classifications, they concluded that "every statement uttered by informants [and, I would add, every bit of social behavior] is worthy of consideration and analysis." This conclusion is not surprising in ethnography; indeed, it is axiomatic in participant observation, the traditional method of ethnography. It becomes significant in the context of "the new ethnography" (as componential analysis has been called by some of its practitioners) where it has been largely ignored, only to be recently rediscovered (*17*). Analysis of terminological systems is a useful and necessary tool, as the formal analysts have emphasized, but without behavioral, interactional and contextual analysis it remains, as Perchonock and Werner suggest, "simply a process of description and enumeration." It is especially sterile and likely to be both fragmentary and misleading when it deals with terminology which is complex, acutely relevant to behavior, and when that behavior is heavily laden with vested interest and affect, as is the case with social categories in urban India. In short, it is inadequate precisely where understanding is most crucial. Similar sterility results from a purely social-structural approach or a purely cultural description, as too many accounts of caste in India demonstrate. Inquiry into the subjective meaning of behavior in social context seems to be the best means for deepening our understanding of inter-ethnic relations in the societies of most contemporary nations, just as in this instance it has contributed greatly to our comprehension of ethnic group relations and social categories in India's pluralistic, urban society.

This research suggests some inferences about the nature of urban society and ethnic relations in India and about the way in which they contrast with the better-known and more thoroughly researched rural situation.

Rural-Urban Contrast

A comparison of my data on social categories, ethnic identity and social behavior in village and city demonstrates some contrasts between villagers and urbanites with respect to social organization and to the kinds of knowledge of them. These contrasts correspond roughly to the *Gemeinschaft* and *Gesellschaft* contrast of Tönnies (*88*) and the folk-urban continuum of Redfield (*68*).

The village is composed of people whose statuses are largely a function of their membership in corporate groups (families, sibs, castes). They tend to remain in their "home territory," the familiar setting of the village and its local region. Religious diversity is often absent, and where this is not the case, it is handled in traditional fashion, very often on the model of caste differences. Villagers interact in terms of their total identities on a personal basis with others who know them well. Status summation is the rule: well-to-do people are powerful people of high ritual and social status; poor people are relatively powerless and of low status (with the exception of some religious roles where poverty is defined as consistent with or even necessary to high ritual status). As a consequence, a novel interactional situation is relatively rare, as is status incongruity and important interaction with strangers. In the city, on the other hand, ethnic diversity is great. A large proportion of one's interaction is outside the "home territory" of one's neighborhood, and is with strangers or casual acquaintances. Even those who are not strangers often know little about one another and see one another in limited, stereotyped situations. Therefore, much interaction occurs in contexts where only specific statuses (parts of the social identity) are relevant or even known, and the elements of individual status (ethnic, ritual, economic, occupational, political statuses) are not as highly correlated as in the village. People therefore have to figure out how to interact on the basis of minimal information in highly specific, impersonal situations rather than on the basis of thorough knowledge, consistent statuses and generalized relevance.

City people usually know very little about internal structure of the corporate groups to which their fellow city-dwellers belong. This does not mean that the city is socially unstructured or even less structured than the village, but that its structure is less conspicuous, lying largely in the regularity of behavioral responses to those subtle cues about social identity (and its situational relevance) which are extracted from face-to-face yet impersonal and often fleeting interaction. This is reflected in the stereotypic differences between the social knowledge and skills of the country bumpkin and the city slicker, each of whom is a laughingstock in the other's milieu, where his hard-won social knowledge and skills are inappropriate and irrelevant. Both survive socially by reacting to the social identities of others, but the expression, definition and recognition of those identities and the appropriate responses are quite different. The villager is well-versed on corporate groups, the individuals who comprise them, their characteristics and the traditional social, economic, political and ritual interrelations among them; the urbanite is well-versed in the identification of a wide variety of strangers as representatives of both corporate and non-corporate social categories. He knows their stereotypically defined characteristics, the varieties of situations and the social information necessary for interaction with them, and methods of defining and delimiting interaction in the impersonal, instrumental world of urban interaction. He knows also when situations are *not* impersonal and instrumental, and how to act accordingly and appropriately. Urban residential neighborhoods are often relatively stable and ethnically homogeneous, so that interaction approximates that in the village. Indian cities have for these reasons often been described as agglomerations of villages. What I have noted above about urban interaction applies, therefore, to the work-a-day world of the city—the bazar and other public places. It is less applicable to interaction within residential neighborhoods, and relatively private settings.

In the urban situation, where status summation is less and is less relevant than in the village, and where livelihood is not dependent on high-caste landowners, power and privilege are not tied so closely or necessarily to traditional ritual status. People of low ritual status who have essential services to offer may be able to organize themselves, for they are in a position to exercise political and economic influence and to acquire or demand social amenities. Thus, the sweepers of Dehra Dun, one of the most despised groups in the society, have been able to organize and surpass other low-status groups in security of employment, standard of living, and morale, because they are the exclusive practitioners of an essential service: providing the city's sewage and street cleaning systems. They are also a significant political bloc and a self-confident people. This is a distinct contrast to the situation of their caste-fellows in surrounding villages, whose untouchability and dependence upon farming castes of high status insures deprivation and discrimination. The position of urban sweepers also contrasts sharply to that of the Chamars in Dehra Dun. The latter are unorganized, impoverished, almost powerless, and despondent. Their despised status is compounded by technological displacement (commercial shoes are replacing their hand-crafted ones). Only those individuals who have escaped to non-traditional, non-menial occupations (and they are few) have escaped the full consequences of their untouchability.

Ethnic Identity, Social Relations and Change

Despite ethnic heterogeneity, impersonal interaction, the dependence of ethnic ascription and response on the specific context, and the prevalence of impression management, urban residents of Dehra Dun cannot, and do not for the most part, change their ethnic identity. In this respect they are unlike the Kachin described by Leach (*53*). Instead, they manipulate aspects of it, bringing to the fore that which the situation or their goals require. Just as caste is a matter of birth, religion, region and language are matters of birth or early socialization in most cases. Class status and even occupation are not easily altered, because of the limited opportunities in this relatively closed society. Thus in a world where status manipulation and impression management are frequent, status change is infrequent.

This structural rigidity is reflected in terminology where *jati* ("descent group") or *quom* ("tribe, ethnic group") may refer to religion, region, or language as well as to caste. Beteille has discussed this matter explicitly, concluding that "the word *jati* may thus be applied to units based on race, language and religion as well as to castes in the narrower sense of the term. How easily these different kinds of identity are confused can best be illustrated by a common remark I used to hear in Bengal where I grew up. It would be said of a person: 'He is not a Bengali, he is a Muslim (or Christian)' " (*21*, p. 48). The system is based on an assumption of status stability for which caste is the model.

It is possible to change religious identity by conversion to Christianity, Sikhism, or the reformist Arya Samaj sect by marriage; (a woman may marry and become a Jain or Sikh), or by upbringing (a Hindu family may vow that if a son be granted them by the deity, he will be raised as a Sikh). But these are unusual and virtually irrevocable shifts. Interesting in this regard are the recent and numerous court cases in which low caste converts to Christianity or Buddhism, whose conversion had been denied recognition by dominant groups and who had been accorded none of the advantages implied in their conversion, have claimed the benefits of recently adopted civil rights legislation for low caste people. Such legislation grants members of low castes preferential economic, educational and political treatment. The converts' claim is made on the basis of the pre-conversion status, but privileged castes have contested the claims on grounds that the former status was relinquished by the claimants upon conversion and with it was relinquished any right to make claims contingent upon that status. Thus the paradoxical situation emerges wherein converts are claiming the relevance of a formerly repudiated status, while dominant groups are claiming relevance of a status-claim they had refused to honor. Judicial decisions rendered tend to grant priority to de facto status rather than claimed status (*37, 38*). *Within* broad status category, shifts may be made in response to changes in prosperity, education or other circumstances, not unlike the shifts Leach describes for the Kachin. This is the message implicit in the ironic proverb about Muslims quoted at the beginning of this paper (*24*, p. 184). The proverb is: "The first year we were butchers, the next Sheikhs. This year, if prices fall, we shall become Sayids." Its irony lies not only in the fact that status claims reflect financial fortunes, but in the fact that Sayids are accorded the highest status of the three groups mentioned on the basis of religious merit rather than wealth. The family began as low-status butchers, then, presumably with prosperity, rose to claim Sheikh status. Now, if prices fall, they will apparently cover declining fortunes with a claim to even higher status. Such shifts are claimed far more often than they are accorded by other groups in the society. Across major boundaries (Hindu-Christian; touchable-untouchable; tribal-non-tribal), the likelihood of successful shifts decreases drastically.

The comment by Beteille quoted above points up the fact that although changes in identity are difficult and unusual, it is usual and expectable that people will be called upon to make choices among alternative and complementary statuses in various circumstances, especially where status summation is imperfect, as it characteristically is in the city. People expend considerable effort trying to assure that the statuses they regard as appropriate for themselves are conveyed in particular contexts, and they expend considerable energy in trying to discern and respond to relevant and appropriate identities of others. This is where knowledge of the meanings attached to attributes and behaviors in various social contexts is crucial to successful interaction, and where the manipulation of these meanings is crucial to identity maintenance. This is the crux of urban social organization.

Rank, Power and Conflict

The ethnic categories of Dehra Dun are objectively distinguishable; that is, they are cultural and social entities. More importantly, they are perceived as such by their own members and by others in the society. Ethnic awareness (cultural consciousness) is partly consciousness of the common and distinctive interests of the group vis-a-vis other groups in the society. Ethnic identity is thus a natural basis for the mobilization of people for shared goals.

The distinctiveness of ethnic groups in India tends to be translated into social ranking—into differential social valuation and differential access to goods, services, and other rewards in society. That is, ethnic identity makes a very tangible difference in one's life chances. This is ethnic stratification. It is epitomized in caste (*16*), but carries over into most sets of social categories. Stratification or ranking is a common way of organizing the relationships of constituent groups in a pluralistic society, as I have noted elsewhere (*19*). It is especially characteristic of India, where hierarchy is a deeply pervasive and contagious feature of society and culture (*64*). There privilege is zealously sought and jealously guarded, and ethnic groups are the locus of privilege or its denial. Conflict, open or covert, is inherent in such systems.

The prevalence and pervasiveness of ranking should not lead one to the assumption that *all* ethnic groups are consistently and unambiguously ranked relative to one another. In Dehra Dun they are not, even within the same set of contrasting social categories. Thus Sikhs are not consistently ranked relative to Hindus, and Punjabis are not consistently ranked relative to Bengalis. Also, as I have indicated, a person may choose to convey that aspect of his identity that is most advantageous from among several available to him in any given situation. Individuals of any group may attempt to move into the semi-western middle class, where ethnic identity diminishes in its day-to-day relevance and status and rewards are to an increasing degree (although not altogether) independent of ethnicity. Here one must be careful not to confuse the casual but frequent relations of customer-proprietor, official-applicant, student-student, etc., with the important ones of employee-employer, debtor-creditor, etc., for in the latter instances entailing long-term relationships and fateful consequences, ethnic, familial and other ties play crucial roles, as they do in religion and marriage. The reason seems to be that these are relationships fundamental to the welfare of individuals, and individual welfare continues to be regarded as the responsibility of and a reflection upon the group with which he is identified, even in the upper and middle class. A sophisticated man may mingle freely with people of other groups, but he must see to the welfare of his family, his caste-fellows, his co-religionists and co-nationals before committing himself to others. Primordial attachments will out, even over school ties and life-styles (*40*).

Wallace (*91,* p. 41) has contended that "The [cultural] relationship is based not on sharing, but on a complementarity of cognitions and motives." People get along with one another not so much because they agree or act from the same motives or in the same ways, but because they are able to predict one another's behavior and, as a consequence, accommodate to it and articulate their own behavior with it. This is demonstrated clearly in my research. Urban society in India is based not primarily on value consensus, but on insight into the nature of the social world, and that has to do largely with understanding the characteristics of groups, the relationship of groups to privileges, the power which confers those privileges, and the sanctions which enforce them. On the individual level this means knowing the relevant social identities, recognizing them in those one meets, knowing what such people expect, what they are capable of, how they can be expected to act and react in particular circumstances. To the extent that social stability exists, it is largely a consequence of balances of power and rewards, rather than a result of consensus on the desirability of the system. On the individual level it is based on realistic assessments by people of one another. No stigmatized, oppressed or even relatively deprived ethnic group or social category that I have encountered accepts its status as legitimate. But many and probably most people in such statuses accept that status as fact and accommodate to it while cherishing a hope or nursing a plan to alter it. No such group accepts the explanations justifying its status, no matter how convincingly portrayed in religious or philosophical terms. Such portrayals are purveyed and believed by beneficiaries of the system, not by those who suffer from it (*19*). Consensus on these matters is simply non-existent. That this is the case is amply attested by India's long history of social mobility movements even in the most unlikely circumstances (I know of no low caste in India whose members do not cherish a claim to higher status), its history of social conflict, and the recurrence of social movements and religions advertising themselves as caste-free, appealing alike to the deprived and the socially conscious (for example, Jainism, Buddhism, Islam, Christianity, Sikhism, neo-Buddhism, Arya Samaj, and a wide variety of movements advocating status enhancement or emancipation for low castes). Indian society is one whose institutionalized inequality, rigid as it is, has generated a long, sad history of resistance against overwhelming odds. Fragmentation of the society into small, competing social cells and concentration of the sources of power and wealth have been the major factors enabling the system to continue, by minimizing the likelihood of concerted or successful remedial action among the oppressed.

Consensus

While inter-ethnic relations in India cannot be understood in terms of consensus, and while a model based on power, conflict and pragmatic appraisals thereof is essential, neither can it be understood without reference to consensus. This statement is less enigmatic than it may sound, for the consensus is not of the kind that is usually cited. It is not consensus on values and goals, on the legitimacy and desirability of social forms and relations or on cultural content. Instead it is an underlying consensus on the nature of the system and of the power relations which maintain it. In the welter of conflicting traditions, values and interests, the necessary consensus—that which makes successful interaction possible—is consensus on who has the power, how and under what circumstances and for what purposes it will be used. On the interpersonal level this means agreement on the nature and identifying characteristics of the various social categories of which the society is composed, and how their members behave in various circumstances, and with what resources. It is when this minimal but crucial consensus breaks down that conflict is likely to become overt and the ever-present potential for drastic change becomes manifest (*19, 14*). When suppressed groups decide that they no longer can be or will be held down—that they have the means to alter their situation, that others cannot or will not effectively maintain the status quo, or that the cost of trying to change it is less than the cost of enduring it—then they move to throw off the suppression. When privileged groups come to the same understanding, they move to preclude the perceived threat. The precipitating change may be the acquisition by low status groups of economic, political or supernatural power (land reform, wage-labor, unionization, universal franchise, direct political representation, civil rights legislation and its enforcement, education, appearance of a powerful religious or political leader or movement or some other powerful advocate of the cause of the oppressed, or the appearance of a compelling ideology of change). It may also occur through the emergence of group self-esteem as a result of any of these or other changes. The consequence is likely to be willingness to assert whatever power is available to the group.

The traditional mechanism for handling such threats to the status quo and the interests of those who benefit from it, has been to attempt to prevent the opportunity for depressed groups to effectively assert their claims by denying them independent income, political influence, education and the like. If prevention is unsuccessful, punishment is tried, often of the most brutal sort. If this does not deter them and if all else fails, the assertive group will usually be promoted within the system rather than risk breakdown of the system. Thus, in instances of successful Sanskritization, a powerful Shudra caste or a tribal group, whose members will not acquiesce to the status accorded them and who are able to back up their claims with power, are finally recognized as people of legitimate but hitherto undiscovered or unrecognized Kshatriya ancestry. The claim is futile without the power to back it up. Integrity of the system is assured by rationalizing the granting of claims to higher status and privilege only on evidence that can be proclaimed legitimate in traditional terms (not simply as a result of forceful demands), and only by granting them to groups rather than individuals, thereby insuring that descent remains the basis for status. Again, caste is the archetype for this kind of mobility in India, but the analysis holds to a large extent for other ethnic groupings as well. Well-to-do Muslims, for example, are often said to deserve their high status on the basis of pre-conversion Rajput descent or elite foreign ancestry. Poor Muslims are generally presumed to be descendents of low caste converts and are treated accordingly (*50,* p. 120ff.). Landholding segments of a tribe may be incorporated into the Hindu rank system at a high level, while their landless fellows are incorporated at the lowest level, as occurred in the cases of both the Raj and the Gonds of Central India. (*36, 32*).

Pluralism, Chauvinism and the Future

The fact of cultural differences within a society is an expression of social relations, as Leach has noted for the Kachin (*53,* p. 17), as well as a factor influencing the nature of those relations. That a man is a Sikh ensures that Hindus, Muslims, and Sikhs will assume certain things about his character, his abilities, his motives, and his habits, and will in various situations act differently toward him than toward non-Sikhs. The same is true of all ethnic groups. At the same time, those identities are sources of self-esteem and mutual esteem among those who hold them, even if they are denigrated by others. They define social entities whose members can be counted upon to have common values, goals and interests, whose behavior can be predicted, who can be trusted, and who can therefore be called upon and mobilized for individual and group welfare. These assumptions cannot be made about those of alien ethnic identity; they can be made to varying degrees and in specifiable circumstances about those who share some aspects of one's own identity.

It is in these facts that much of the dynamics of India's plural society can be understood. Through comprehension and skillful manipulation of their social identity individuals are successful in negotiating their society.

Indian society is one of many in which secularization, urbanization, westernization and industrialization are powerful forces. It is one in which the legacy of colonialism is strongly felt and in which power, whether conferred via colonialism or indigenously derived, largely determines who prospers and who suffers. It is also a society in which cultural distinctiveness translated into ethnic identity is a major factor in determining the quality of life the society makes available to individuals and groups. Consciousness of ethnic identity and the common interests it implies is important in determining the directions of change and the channels it follows. Except among some of the numerically small middle and upper classes, there is no headlong rush among Indians even in cities to emulate Western society, beyond the desire for certain material goods and the basic rewards of a secure life and livelihood which are increasingly thought to require some Western technology and Western institutions. Ethnic pride—self-esteem and confidence based on that which is closely identified with one's group and hence one's self—is a major value, and one Western influence has not greatly altered. Communal values are championed at least as often as they are suppressed. Hindu nationalism is almost as prominent as secularism in contemporary political rhetoric, and far more prominent in daily life. Demands for ethnically based states, often based on the constitutionally sanctioned criterion of common language, are proliferating and are as frequent as pleas for national unity. Ethnic solidarity is as often sought as national integrations (*65*). These sentiments are evident in interpersonal and intergroup relations, whether as solidarity or conflict, loyalty or prejudice, chauvinism or discrimination, and are expressed in behavior ranging from riots to votes, and from etiquette to oppression.

The lines along which people mobilize for action are traditional and modern, religious and secular, caste and class. As the society changes, new identities emerge, and new identities entail new bonds and new schisms, some replacing the old, some supplementing the old. Pluralism in ethnic identity and interests seems to persist, in any case. This is a primary domestic problem for India as a national entity and for individual Indians. From it flows much of the inequity and conflict of daily existence. The outcome depends upon the ability of the nation to encompass its cultural diversity, respect its heterogeneous peoples, traditions and values, drastically diminish the disparity in economic and political rewards between them, and enhance social justice. If these things are not quickly, effectively and thoroughly accomplished on a massive scale within the present institutional framework—as seems unlikely—alternatives will surely be sought elsewhere, for the status quo cannot long persist. It will either be maintained in some form by increased force from above, or it will be rejected and replaced by drastic changes initiated from below. Either would be painful and humanly costly. But for many people the status quo is already both, and they would not regret its disappearance. Most thoughtful informants in Dehra Dun regardless of status or ethnic identity, agreed upon this, and it worried them deeply. That drastic change has not happened yet is most likely a result of the inhibiting effect of the poverty, powerlessness and hopelessness of most of India's people—of those who would benefit most from change. Slight improvements may well lead to a redefinition of their chances in society, to the emergence of hope, determination and consequent demands and action for change. Availability to these people of education, mass media, and political participation, together with conspicuous consumption of luxury goods by the well-to-do, and callous disregard for the needs and desires of the poor by many of the well-to-do, accelerate the likelihood of change by enhancing their awareness of alternatives, providing an understanding of the means to change and increasing accessibility to those means. Urban India is the arena in which these changes are taking place most rapidly. There the social structure is loose enough to allow experimentation with various alliances and social structures which have been elsewhere inhibited by the rigidity of traditional, rural social organization and the unitary relationship between that social organization and the distribution of power. Effective mechanisms for change may result, carried out by newly mobilized interest groups growing out of significant urban social categories.

As people thread their way through the intricate networks of urban social structure, they are able to choose paths which accommodate their needs, reward their aspirations, and justify their humanity. People travel these paths in groups more often than alone. Future trends in Indian social, economic and political organization will be largely determined by which paths are followed and which reward their followers. It is in this respect that the analysis of urban Indian social organization takes on an acutely practical significance, and that the role of ethnic identity, its maintenance and manipulation, assumes critical importance. Similar processes can be seen at work in ethnically plural, rigidly separated and sharply stratified societies in many parts of the world, including the United States.

REFERENCES

1. Aberle, Kathleen Gough. "Criteria of Caste Ranking in South India." *Man in India*. 39:115-126, 1959.

2. Anant, Santokh S. "Self- and Mutual-Perception of Salient Personality Traits of Different Caste Groups." *Journal of Cross-Cultural Psychology.* 1(1):41-52, 1970.

3. Anant, Santokh S. "Stereotypes of Hindus About Different Religious Groups in India." *Man in India.* 52:123-130, 1972.

4. Anant, Santokh S. "Provincial and Regional Stereotypes in India." Ms. *forthcoming* (probably in *Man in India*).

5. Bailey, F. G. *Caste and the Economic Frontier.* Manchester: Manchester University Press, 1957.

6. Bailey, F. G. "Closed Social Stratification in India." *Archives of European Sociology.* 4:107-124, 1963.

7. Barth, Fredrik. "The System of Social Stratification in Swat, North Pakistan." In *Aspects of Caste in South India, Ceylon and Northwest Pakistan,* edited by E. R. Leach. Cambridge Papers in Social Anthropology, 2:113-146, 1960.

8. Barth, Fredrik. "Ethnic Processes on the Pathan-Baluch Boundary." *Indo-Iranica,* pp. 13-20. Wiesbaden: Otto Harrassowitz, 1964.

9. Barth, Fredrik. *Ethnic Groups and Boundaries,* edited by F. Barth. Boston: Little, Brown, 1969.

10. Berreman, Gerald D. "Caste in India and the United States." *American Journal of Sociology.* 66:120-127, 1960.

11. Berreman, Gerald D. "Cultural Variability and Drift in the Himalayan Hills." *American Anthropologist.* 62:774-794, 1960.

12. Berreman, Gerald D. *Behind Many Masks: Ethnography and Impression Management in a Himalayan Village.* Ithaca, N.Y.: Society for Applied Anthropology (Monograph No. 4), 1962.

13. Berreman, Gerald D. *Hindus of the Himalayas: Ethnography and Change.* Berkeley: University of California Press, 1972.

14. Berreman, Gerald D. "Aleut Reference Group Alienation, Mobility and Acculturation." *American Anthropologist.* 66:231-250, 1964.

15. Berreman, Gerald D. "The Study of Caste Ranking in India." *Southwestern Journal of Anthropology.* 21:115-129, 1965.

16. Berreman, Gerald D. "Caste in Cross-Cultural Perspective." In *Japan's Invisible Race: Caste in Culture and Personality,* edited by G. DeVos and H. Wagatsuma, pp. 275-324. Berkeley: University of California Press, 1966. See also Berreman, Gerald D. *Caste in the Modern World.* Morristown, N.J.: General Learning Press, 1973.

17. Berreman, Gerald D. "Anemic and Emetic Analyses in Social Anthropology." *American Anthropologist.* 68:346-354, 1966.

18. Berreman, Gerald D. "Stratification, Pluralism and Interaction: A Comparative Analysis of Caste." In *Caste and Race: Comparative Approaches,* edited by A. de Reuck and J. Knight, pp. 45-73. Boston: Little, Brown, 1967.

19. Berreman, Gerald D. "Caste as Social Process." *Southwestern Journal of Anthropology.* 23:351-370, 1967. See also Berreman, Gerald D. "Self, Situation and Escape from Stigmatized Ethnic Identity." In *Yearbook of the Ethnographic Museum,* pp. 11-25. Oslo: Universitetsforlaget, 1973.

20. Berreman, Gerald D. "Caste: The Concept of Caste." In *International Encyclopedia of the Social Sciences,* Vol. 2, edited by D. Sills, pp. 333-339. New York: Macmillan and Free Press, 1968. See also Berreman, Gerald D. "Race, Caste and Other Invidious Distinctions in Social Stratification." *Race.* 8:385-414, 1972.

21. Béteille, André. *Castes: Old and New; Essays in Social Structure and Social Stratification.* Bombay: Asia Publishing House, 1969.

22. Bhatt, G. S. "Urban Impact and the Trends of Intra-Caste Solidarity and Dissociability as Measures of Status Mobility Among the Chamar." Paper presented at the Indian Sociological Conference, Saugar, India, 1960.

23. Blumer, Herbert. *Symbolic Interactionism.* Englewood Cliffs, N.J.: Prentice-Hall, 1969.

24. Blunt, E. A. H. *The Caste System of Northern India.* London: Oxford University Press, 1931.

25. Chaudhuri, Nirad D. *The Continent of Circe.* London: Chatto and Windus, 1967.

26. Chibbar, Y. P. *From Caste to Class: A Study of the Indian Middle Classes.* New Delhi: Associated Publishing House, 1968.

27. Cicourel, Aaron V. *Method and Measurement in Sociology.* New York: Free Press of Glencoe, 1964.

28. Cicourel, Aaron V. "Preliminary Issues of Theory and Method." In *The Social Organization of Juvenile Justice,* pp. 1-21. New York: John Wiley, 1968.

29. Cohn, B. S. "The Changing Status of a Depressed Caste." In *Village India,* edited by McKim, Marriott, pp. 53-77. Chicago: University of Chicago Press, 1955.

30. de Reuck, Anthony, and Knight, J., eds. *Caste and Race: Comparative Approaches.* Boston: Little, Brown, 1967.

31. De Vos, George, and Wagatsuma, H., eds. *Japan's Invisible Race.* Berkeley: University of California Press, 1967.

32. Dube, S. C. "A Deccan Village." In *India's Villages,* pp. 180-191. West Bengal Govt. Press, 1955.

33. Faris, Ellsworth. "The Primary Group, Essence and Accident." *American Journal of Sociology.* 38:41-50, 1932.

34. Festinger, Leon. *A Theory of Cognitive Dissonance.* Evanston: Row Peterson, 1957.

35. Freed, Stanley A. "An Objective Method for Determining the Collective Caste Hierarchy of an Indian Village." *American Anthropologist.* 65:879-891, 1963.

36. Fuchs, Stephen. *The Gond and Bhumia of Eastern Mandla.* Bombay: Asia Publishing House, 1960.

37. Galanter, Marc. "Changing Legal Conceptions of Caste." In *Structure and Change in Indian Society,* edited by M. Singer and B. Cohn, pp. 299-336. Chicago: Aldine Press, 1968.

38. Galanter, Marc. "Untouchability and the Law." *Economic and Political Weekly* (Bombay). January 1969:131-170.

39. Garfinkel, Harold. *Studies in Ethnomethodology.* Englewood Cliffs, N.J.: Prentice-Hall, 1967.

40. Geertz, Clifford. "The Integrative Revolution: Primordial Sentiments and Civil Politics in the New States." In *Old Societies and New States,* edited by C. Geertz, pp. 105-157. New York: The Free Press of Glencoe, 1963.

41. Goffman, Erving. *Presentation of Self in Everyday Life.* New York: Doubleday, 1959.

42. Goffman, Erving. *Behavior in Public Places.* New York: Free Press of Glencoe, 1963.

43. Goffman, Erving. *Interaction Ritual: Essays on Face-to-Face Behavior.* Garden City, N.Y.: Doubleday (Anchor Book), 1967.

44. Goodenough, Ward. "Frontiers of Cultural Anthropology: Social Organization." *Proceedings of the American Philosophical Society.* 113 (No. 5): 329-335, 1969.

45. Gould, Harold. "Castes, Outcastes and the Sociology of Stratification." *International Journal of Comparative Sociology.* (India: Karnatak University.) 1:220-238, 1960.

46. Gumperz, John J. "Hindi-Punjabi Code-Switching in Delhi." *Proceedings of the Ninth International Congress of Linguists.* The Hague: Mouton, 1962.

47. Gumperz, John J. "Linguistic and Social Interaction in Two Communities," *American Anthropologist.* 66(2):137-153, 1964.

48. Hyman, Herbert. *The Psychology of Status.* Archives of Psychology, No. 269. New York, 1942.

49. Isaacs, Harold. *India's Ex-Untouchables.* New York: John Day, 1964. See also Mahar, J. M., ed. *The Untouchables in Contemporary India.* Tucson: University of Arizona Press, 1972.

50. Karim, A. K. Nazmul. *Changing Society in India and Pakistan.* Dacca, Pakistan: Oxford University Press, 1956.

51. Kay, Paul. "Some Theoretical Implications of Ethnographic Semantics." Working Paper No. 24, Language-Behavior Research Laboratory, University of California, Berkeley, 1969.

52. Klapp, Orrin E. *Heroes, Villains, and Fools.* Englewood Cliffs, N.J.: Prentice-Hall, 1962.

53. Leach, Edmund. *Political Systems of Highland Burma.* 2nd ed. Boston: Beacon Press, 1965.

54. Lynch, Owen. *The Politics of Untouchability.* New York: Columbia University Press, 1969.

55. Mahar, Pauline Moller (Kolenda). "A Multiple Scaling Technique for Caste Ranking." *Man in India.* 39:115-126, 1959.

56. Mandelbaum, David G. *Society in India.* Berkeley: University of California Press, 1970.

57. Maquet, Jacques. *The Premise of Inequality in Ruanda.* London: Oxford University Press, 1961.

58. Marriott, McKim. "Interactional and Attributional Theories of Caste Ranking." *Man in India.* 39:92-107, 1959.

59. Marriott, McKim. "Multiple Reference in Indian Caste Systems." In *Social Mobility in the Caste System of India,* edited by J. Silverberg, pp. 103-114. Comparative Studies in Society and History, Supplement III. The Hague: Mouton, 1968.

60. Mayer, Adrian. "Some Hierarchical Aspects of Caste." *Southwestern Journal of Anthropology.* 12:117-144, 1956.

61. Moerman, Michael. "Ethnic Identification in a Complex Civilization: Who are the Lue?" *American Anthropologist.* 67(Part 1):1215-1230, 1965.

62. Moerman, Michael. "Being Lue: Uses and Abuses of Ethnic Identification." In *Essays on the Problem of Tribe,* pp. 153-169. Seattle: University of Washington Press, 1967.

63. Morris, H. S. "Ethnic Groups." In *International Encyclopedia of the Social Sciences,* edited by D. L. Sills, Vol. 5, pp. 167-172. New York: The Free Press, 1968.

64. Opler, Morris E. "The Themal Approach in Cultural Anthropology and Its Application to North Indian Data." *Southwestern Journal of Anthropology.* 24:215-227, 1968.

65. Orans, Martin. *The Santal: A Tribe in Search of a Great Tradition.* Detroit: Wayne University Press, 1965.

66. Perchonock, Norma and Werner, Oswald. "Navaho Systems of Classification: Some Implications for Ethnoscience." *Ethnology.* 8:229-242, 1969.

67. Rath, R. and Sircar, N. D. "The Mental Pictures of Six Hindu Caste Groups About Each Other as Reflected in Verbal Stereotypes." *Journal of Social Psychology.* 51:277-293, 1960.

68. Redfield, Robert. "The Folk Society." *American Journal of Sociology.* 52:293-308, 1947.

69. Rowe, William L. "The New Chauhans: A Caste Mobility Movement in North India." In *Social Mobility in the Caste System in India,* edited by James Silverberg, pp. 66-77. The Hague: Mouton, 1968.

70. Rowe, William L. "Mobility in the Nineteenth-Century Caste System." In *Structure and Change in Indian Society,* edited by M. Singer and B. S. Cohn, pp. 201-207. Chicago: Aldine, 1968.

71. Rudolph, Lloyd I. and Susan H. "The Political Role of India's Caste Associations." *Pacific Affairs.* 33:5-22, 1960.

72. Schutz, Alfred. *Collected Papers, I: The Problem of Social Reality,* edited by M. Natanson. The Hague: M. Nijhoff, 1962.

73. Sebring, James M. "Caste Indicators and Caste Identification of Strangers." *Human Organization.* 28:199-207, 1969.

74. Sebring, James M. "Caste Ranking and Caste Interaction in a North India Village." Ph.D. Dissertation, University of California, Berkeley. 1968.

75. Sharma, K. N. "Resource Networks and Resource Groups in the Social Structure. *The Eastern Anthropologist.* 22(1):13-27, 1969.

76. Shibutani, Tamatsu and Kwan, Kian M. *Ethnic Stratification.* New York: Macmillan, 1965.

77. Silverberg, James. "Caste-Ascribed Status Versus Caste-Irrelevant Roles." *Man in India.* 39:148-162, 1959.

78. Silverberg, James. "Colloquium and Interpretive Conclusions." In *Social Mobility in the Caste System of India*, edited by J. Silverberg, pp. 115-138. (Comparative Studies in Society and History, Supplement III.) The Hague: Mouton, 1968.

79. Silverberg, James, ed. *Social Mobility in the Caste System of India.* (Comparative Studies in Society and History, Supplement III.) The Hague: Mouton, 1968.

80. Silverman, Sydel F. "An Ethnographic Approach to Social Stratification: Prestige in a Central Italian Community." *American Anthropologist.* 68:899-921, 1966.

81. Sinha, G. S. and Sinha, R. C. "Exploration in Caste Stereotypes." *Social Forces.* 46:42-47, 1967.

82. Sinha, Surajit. "Bhumij-Kshatriya Social Movement in South Manbhum." *Bulletin of the Department of Anthropology.* (Calcutta) 8(2):9-32, 1959.

83. Sinha, Surajit. "State Formation and Rajput Myth in Tribal Central India." *Man in India.* 42:35-80, 1962.

84. Smith, Michael G. *The Plural Society in the British West Indies.* Berkeley: University of California Press, 1965.

85. Srinivas, M. N. "A Note on Sanskritization and Westernization." *Far Eastern Quarterly.* 15:481-496, 1956.

86. Srinivas, M. N. *Caste in Modern India and Other Essays.* Bombay: Asia Publishing House, 1962.

87. Srinivas, M. N. *Social Change in Modern India.* Berkeley: University of California Press, 1966.

88. Tonnies, Ferdinand. *Fundamental Concepts of Sociology,* edited and translated by C. P. Loomis. New York: American Book Co. (First ed., 1887: *Gemeinschaft und Gesellschaft.*) 1940.

89. van den Berghe, Pierre. *Caneville: The Social Structure of a South African Town.* Middletown, Connecticut: Wesleyan University Press, 1964.

90. van den Berghe, Pierre. *Race and Racism: A Comparative Perspective.* New York: John Wiley, 1967.

91. Wallace, Anthony F. C. *Culture and Personality.* New York: Random House, 1961.

92. Waller, Willard. *The Family: A Dynamic Interpretation.* New York: Dryden Press, 1938.

Cultural Totemism: Ethnic Identity Primitive and Modern

THEODORE SCHWARTZ

4

The point of departure for this paper is my conception of cultural totemism, which can be shown to embrace a broad range of processes that contribute to the identity of individuals and groups. Students of culture from Tylor *(25)* to Lévi-Strauss (in his recent reconsideration of totemism [*8*]) have understood its bearing on the problem of identity. In the classic anthropological sense, totemism linked men into groups under the emblem of a common totemic species (animal or plant usually, but sometimes also objects, places, and natural pehnomena) and set them apart from groups claiming common substance or origin under other species.

It is true that Lévi-Strauss declared totemism an illusion on the ground that no single set of attributes would fit all cultures that hold a belief in some special relationship between individuals or groups and natural species. Beliefs concerning descent from the totem; taboo on killing, eating, or using the totem; a "ritual" attitude toward the totem considered as sacred; a rule of exogamy imposed on all having the same totem—such traits, as Goldenweiser noted (*4*), did not invariably constitute a complex but could occur separately and in quite different combinations in those cultures where they occurred at all.

Illusion or not, totemism remains the theme of much of Lévi-Strauss' recent work. He maintains, as others (*3*) had maintained, that totemism constitutes a system of classification of human groups, with natural species providing a set of convenient labels. But for Lévi-Strauss it is more than this: it is also the perceptible similarities and differences of one natural species contrasted with another. Not only could species be used as arbitrary labels, they could be used to represent the relations among human groups. He sees the natural species as suggesting a mode of thought to man: ". . . natural species are chosen not because they are 'good to eat' but because they are 'good to think' " (*8*).

It can be argued, as Durkheim's school maintained, that the social order is primary, that the assemblage of totems is either arbitrary or reflects social order through attributes and dimensions of contrast chosen from many possible ones to reflect the changing relations between social groups. The reader may find the Lévi-Straussian interpretation disappointing, and ask, "Is that all totemism is?" His interpretation amounts to an intellectual reductionism of a phenomenon that seems to be more than a calculus of categories. Totemism *is* that, to be sure, but it is apparently also a religion, a world view, a theory of origins, a theory of the relation of man to nature.

Durkheim thought that man at a primitive stage of cultural development could not have arrived at a complex system of categories without an external model. For Durkheim, that model was the social order itself. And even though Lévi-Strauss sees himself not disparaging but defending the intellectual capabilities of "savage" man, newly emergent but still near to nature, he, too, seems to argue that the mode of thought must be derived from an external model—the relations among natural species. I would maintain that the social order or the natural species are domains to which the human intellect (the culturally implemented intelligence) is applied. The "mode" is man's. The model is a human construction, but it is under the adaptive constraints of an external reality. A model of one domain may be mapped onto another. In suggesting a cultural totemism, I wish to *add,* not substitute, another domain—that of the perceived similarities and differences among human cultures themselves, the ethnic groupings conceived of by men as if those groupings were species.

Man generally discovered (as anthropologists did much later) that cultures, too, are "good to think." There would be sufficient interest in considering culture as one among the many domains to which man in all societies, primitive and modern, turns his mind. But the phrase "cultural totemism" may suggest even more than simply the comparison between thinking about culture and thinking about natural species.

De Vos has commented that "ethnicity is like religion, people seem to need it." I would speculate that in order for people to "have ethnicity" they must have at least two (and usually more) ethnic groups. The same may be true for religion, where the point may be as much to differentiate oneself from others (infidels or sectaries) through the object or manner of one's worship, as it is to worship at all. If this were true, then religion would be (among other things, of course) an "ethnognomonic trait" illustrative of what I mean by cultural totemism. That is, it would be a cultural trait characteristic of one group in contrast to others, at once emblematic of the group's solidarity and of the group's contrasting identity and relation to the groups within its ambit of comparison.

Religion is only one among the features of an identified or self-identifying group that could be taken by members of that set of ethnic groups as ethnognomonic. Other likely candidates are variations in physical appearance, language, hairdo and body ornamentation, costume, the shapes of artifacts such as houses and weapons, and ecological type such as farmer, fisherman, or pastoralist. Not surprisingly, a classification based on such traits might not be that different from the classification an anthropologist would arrive at. Anthropologists do purposively and methodically what men have always done intuitively, often consciously. They perceive a degree of order and predictability as well as similarities and differences in the behavior of other persons, and they characterize or represent this behavior to themselves in various ways. Their formulations are construals molded to their interests under the constraints of an external reality. Such cultural construals are fairly adequate for their purposes, being neither wholly objective nor wholly capricious. To such fields as ethnobotany or ethnoichthyology, then, we could add ethno-ethnography and ethnolinguistics (in the sense of folk taxonomy and characterization of languages and cultures). They constitute part of what one might call the self-reflexive portion of a culture.

After describing the field experiences that suggested this analogy between totemism and ethnicity and the idea of a totemism of cultural differences, I will discuss some of the ways in which cultural totemism operates as a component of individual and group identity. I must admit that, having been raised on the classical ethnographies in graduate school, I was thrilled to find, during my first field work in 1953 in the Admiralty Islands (Manus) of Melanesia, people who told me

> I am a descendant of the crocodile. I must not kill the crocodile of a particular river where my ancestor came from nor eat the meat of any crocodile. If I do I will get sores, my teeth will fall out and I will age quickly. My wife is descended from the *chauka* bird and our children will inherit her taboo. They and their children will have to watch out for mine too, but after that it will have no effect. I must be careful also to burn no wood of this tree called "crocodile." I think it is all right for me to marry a woman with the crocodile taboo though some say it is not, but if I did, we

> would check very carefully to be sure we are not closely related. If I went to another village [back in the days of inter-tribal warfare], I could ask if there was a child of crocodile in the village. He would protect me, feed and house me and assure my safe departure even if he was a complete stranger to me and we could trace no other relationship.

This is a condensation of the general formulation of totemism among the people of the interior and fringe islands of the Admiralties. The Manus of Melanesia, fishing people who formerly lived over the lagoons and the in-reef waters, have the food taboos. Their taboos are similarly inherited but they are without the rationale and elaboration of the other groups. The Manus do tie into the totemic system through a certain small percentage of cross-ethnic marriages with mainland and island women. They formerly exploited these ties, utilizing the privilege of supposedly safe conduct to make "roads" for trade. In view of my Admiralty Island experience and in spite of the deficient totemic package of the Manus seafaring people, I find it difficult to view totemism as an illusion.

Ethnic Interpenetration and Separation in the Admiralties

Totemism was only one of the systems segmenting the population of the entire archipelago in various interlacing ways. In a previous article (*21*) I attempted to break away from the more usual anthropological practice of taking "cultures" one at a time, often as represented in a single village at a single point in time. There were at least twenty locally recognized linguistic groups in the Admiralty Islands, each associated with cultural differences other than language. I believed that I was dealing with a single area-wide culture of the Admiralty Islands, the components of which were the many mutually identifying ethnic groups. I distinguished this kind of "areal culture" from the more familiar "culture area." The cultures making up a culture area need only be historically related. In an areal culture such as that of the Admiralties, direct and indirect interaction links all groups, making events in any part relevant to the whole. The area was tied together through networks of trade and markets, ceremonial exchange, totemic relations, marriage and warfare.

The languages were related and structurally similar. But they were at the least as different from one another as, say, Spanish and Portuguese and at the most, as different as Portuguese and Italian. No lingua franca had developed—rather, polylingualism was prevalent. Many adults spoke the languages of all groups with whom they had regular contact. Minimally, each could speak his own language to the other, having learned to understand neighboring languages. Cross-ethnic marriages were relatively more common (under polygyny) in families of relatively higher prestige. It could happen that one's parents spoke different languages. The grandparents of one important man each spoke a different language.

Language merely illustrates the more general point that difference within the areal culture was not based on separation or communicational gaps. I began my areal study puzzled about the proliferation of languages and "cultures" in spite of propinquity in the whole of Melanesia, in contrast to some other parts of the world, such as Polynesia. I began to see that there were mechanisms that maintained, if not proliferated and amplified, "ethnic" differences. There were cultural attitudes or sets toward the perception and emblematic use of cultural differences (including language, of course) that were characteristically Melanesian, although I have no doubt they could be extensively demonstrated elsewhere.

The area that I am depicting is organized as a stateless society. Headmanship, for example, did not formally extend beyond the village, although a "big man" may have been influential within the aura of his renown. The area is well characterized (prior to European administration) as politically atomistic with extreme local particularism. Even villages, the maximum effective public of a "big man" (aside from his diffuse network of cooperating affines and allies) were unstable, often splitting along clan lines. It could be reconstituted from clans and village fragments which had been autonomous for a time. The clans themselves split along lineage lines, not automatically on the basis of size alone but with the occurrence of rival aspirants to leadership. Many were motivated to strive for independent status as "big man." To have a "name" required that one have a "place" and public of one's own, however small, if one's feats of warfare and exchange were not to redound to the credit of another.

I stress the pre-state level of Melanesian cultures because it might be thought that ethnicity and its implied problematics of identity could exist only in complex, pluralistic societies that unite different ethnic groups on a territorial basis under state control—in contrast to the supposedly more primitive "isolated" cultures. Much of the primitive world must have been like Melanesia before the establishment of large-scale states. Each group experienced its social environment as a mosaic of groups manifesting, even consciously "instancing" to use Devereux's term (*2*), certain similarities and differences. They were different, not out of lack of awareness of the behavior patterns of others but in spite of and by means of such awareness. I am not attempting to nullify the effect of geographic barriers and sheer distance. Rather, I am asserting that interaction and communication generating difference and similarity must always have depended greatly on cultural definitional boundaries. The "speciation" of cultures is largely a cultural process.

The Manus, who were the most widely dispersed and largest linguistic-ethnic group of the Admiralties, intermarried and maintained a high degree of linguistic and cultural commonality. At the same time they maintained their differences from the bush villages within a mile or two of them, while they engaged in trade, markets, ceremonials, and war with these bush neighbors. On the other hand, the Manus, like all other linguistic-ethnic groups in the Admiralties, illustrate the difference-amplifying effect of formally recognizing incipient cultural differences that would seem very small to the outsider, while overlooking (in some contexts) massive commonality.

The Manus see themselves as divided into two main named dialect groups on the basis of a single phoneme shift */r/* to */l/*. They also recognize a considerable number of differences in vocabulary based on substitute terms rather than on sound shifts. In all cases my informants could state, "We say this, but they say that," specifying the corresponding terms. To a remarkable extent, people of all ethnic groups could demonstrate their knowledge of linguistic and cultural differences for many or all of the recognized Admiralty Island groups. I found that languages and at times the collectivity of their speakers were referred to by one or more of four common words that occurred frequently in speech. These were the demonstrative pronoun meaning "this" "here," "today" or "now" (sometimes the same as "this"), the word for "brother," and the word for "speech" or "language." Thus the Manus were often referred to as "the *titan*" ("that") or as "the *ndrasi*" ("brother"), or as speakers of the "*angan*" ("language"). These terms contrast with *ario* or *mepo* ("this," "today"), or *nali* ("brother") or *nongan* ("language") by which their closest mainland neighbors were known. This minimal lexicographic list serves to set apart the languages of the Admiralties while giving some indication of the degree of relationship between them. On the cultural level the picture is at once more complex and in some ways simpler.

All Admiralty Island groups divide the peoples of the area into three gross ecological types that correspond to the most fundamental cultural differences. These are the Manus, the fishing, trading, lagoon-dwelling people with whom Margaret Mead's and Reo Fortune's studies are largely concerned (*12, 6*), the Usiai (gardening, non-seafaring peoples of the interior of the mainland), and the Matankor (of the fringing islands, practicing mixed fishing and gardening and noted for specialized manufactures). Without exception, all ethnic groups were entirely contained within one or another of these ecological types. The Manus are a single ethnic group, whereas the Usiai and Matankor are subdivided ethnically. The major difference between high, large-island Matankor and low-island Matankor is not part of the native set of categories. Intra-ethnic relations are always intra-ecological. The most economically important cross-ethnic relations are those which are cross-ecological. Cross-ethnic relations within the same ecological grouping tend to resemble intra-ethnic relations in that the exchange is between groups commanding similar resources. This arrangement has important consequences for the structure of the areal cultures (*21*).

Not all culture traits serve as ethnognomonic features. Some basic institutions and modes of organization—for example, village social and political organization, and ways of thinking about marriage and ceremonial exchange—are uniform throughout the Admiralties. Other traits—myths, for example—circulate freely throughout the Admiralty Islands. They are usually told as having been brought in from somewhere else within the archipelago. "Original" provenience is usually impossible to establish. On the other hand, manufactured objects such as pots, carved beads, lime spatulas and gourds, basketry, and spears are completely characteristic of particular ethnic groups. Furthermore, to the connoisseur they are characteristic of their village of origin, and often their maker. Song styles can be broadly grouped according to the three ecological types but further subdivisions are possible (although the Usiai ethnic groups tend to fall together on this and a number of other features). Songs can be readily assigned to particular ethnic groups among the Matankor without using language as the indicator. Their songs are as distinctive as bird calls. Distinctiveness may be one of their functions, whatever else they also convey. Dance styles, in contrast, tended to be much the same throughout the Admiralties until the effect of recent outside influences that now produce "native" dances that have little to do with traditional Admiralty Island forms.

Village particularism, schismatic leadership, and the competitive prestige motive make for patterns of diffusion of other major traits, such as ritual innovations, that tend to cut across and weaken the ethnic groupings. Diffusion of such innovations and their further elaboration takes place within the entrepreneurial framework of aspirant leadership. The competition for reputation is undertaken especially with reference to other leaders of one's own ethnic group. This means that because one leader becomes associated with a given innovation, some of the other leaders of the same ethnic group will not adopt it. They will assert the superiority of previous forms or they will create or import a competitive innovation. Such innovations may be minor, perhaps a change in the design of the men's house or of canoe prows, or they may involve a major block of culture, such as a new form of ceremonial in affinal exchange with associated paraphernalia and perhaps a mythological rationale. The spread of the cargo cults that I have described elsewhere was affected by this pattern of competitive diffusion (*20*).

However, to say that the ethnic group was weakened by such cross-cutting diffusion might give the impression that they were otherwise cohesive. They were not. The ethnic groups were the largest grouping of people who shared a presumed common origin, blood, or substance and who were marked by common language and an assemblage of culture traits that were their "property." Ethnic groups often had myths of origin that accounted for their descent from particular persons in a specified place and for the present location of their members. At present this "accounting" is generally fragmentary, vague, and seemingly unimportant to the members of the ethnic group. The myths characteristically take account of no group on the island other than their own. Even the few hundred people of the two neighboring islands of Hus and Andra off the north coast, although obviously closely related, look upon themselves as separate ethnic groups and take no account of each other's existence in their origin myths. The larger, multiple-village ethnic groups seemed to have no social or political function as such, other than endogamy and exophagy.

By exophagy ("eating out") I mean the prohibition on eating a member of one's own ethnic group who is killed or taken in warfare. The prohibition resembles the totemic taboos prohibiting one from eating one's own substance. Cannibalism but not auto-cannibalism was practiced by all groups except the Manus, who traded any bodies that came their way to members of other ethnic groups. Although warfare was not infrequent within ethnic groups, exophagy may have prevented vendettas leading to decimation. To return a body to the enemy was an act of peace; to eat him was the gravest insult.

Ethnicity and Endogamy

Ethnic endogamy did not operate on the basis of any explicit rule but followed established customs. Marriages were investments between sponsors or financiers of the marriage who were preferably in a relation that could be classed as that of cross-cousins. The sponsors should be matched in status and able to meet their exchange partner's show of wealth in a long series of transactions that would exceed their own lifespans. I do not wish to elaborate the relevant ethnography here more than is necessary (*12*). Obviously, ethnic matching in such complex interactions makes for trust and reliability. I have mentioned that cross-ethnic marriages were more prevalent in families of highest status, who both competed and cooperated across ethnic lines, dependent on each other as trade and exchange partners in the sharp ecological complementarity of the Admiralties. In warfare and reputation they required each other as worthy adversaries.

Another factor that reinforced ethnic endogamy was fear of the magic and sorcery of "foreigners." Any stay among other ethnic groups in their own place must have been an uneasy one. The primary circle of trust was one's lineage. Trust within the ethnic group as a whole was weaker than the lineage but much greater than between ethnic groups. Under colonialism and, as mobility of Melanesians within the Territory grows, more and more people spend time away at work or at school among foreign natives. There is some evidence that the attribution of serious illness to sorcery is increasing in response to the levels of anxiety occasioned by this dispersion (*17*). Away from the Admiralties, any Admiralty Islander is a relatively welcome associate, as if all are "Manus"—a single ethnic group when viewed from this new level of contrast. Where possible, however, urban associations are with others of one's own ethnic group.

In Admiralty Island cultures, the female is the exogam. She must leave her lineage and clan to live among those who, as persons suitable for marriage, are by definition people of a different substance. They are people whom she has been taught to avoid and before whom she feels shame, but at least they speak her language. Even without cross-ethnic marriage she would be regarded with some distrust, as representing or even spying for her brother's clan or village. Distrust is endemic and pervades the ethnic group as well, but it is exacerbated in cross-ethnic relations (*22*).

Another contributing factor to endogamy is the effect of respect and disparagement between ethnic groups. In some ways, all groups felt superior. The Usiai disparaged the landlessness of the Manus who "lived like fish" and were dependent upon the Usiai for all cultivated foods. Although the Usiai collectively outnumbered the Manus, the Manus despised them as "landlubbers" who worked in dirt, had skin diseases, and "lived like animals," even making their house floors of bare dirt.

Manus men occasionally married Usiai, gaining a woman who would live among them, bringing her kinship ties with her in a relation in which the Manus, on the groom's side, could give valuables in exchange for the consumables they desired. I have mentioned the totemic connections gained through the woman. A Manus woman, however, would be demeaned and in danger living among the Usiai. The Usiai, on their part, displayed the adaptations of an entrapped, disparaged minority even though they were in fact the majority. They were both hostile to and respectful of the Manus. They internalized the Manus disparagement. The coastal strip became a no-man's-land where markets could be held at river mouths, but where trade always tempted ambush by one side or the other. The Matankor were intermediate in the scale of respect. The Manus generally disparaged them as little better than Usiai and made their ventures away from their immediate coasts high-risk operations.

During the period of continuous colonial domination (since the establishment of the German colony in 1884), the Manus continued to dominate. The Admiralties were eventually pacified by about 1912, ending the marauding of the Manus. But the Manus became the favorites of the Europeans, although they were considered to be "cheeky" types. They were quite open to change as a result of culture contact, although in their seeming openness they were being and preserving themselves. They became an over-represented group in ship's crews, in the native constabulary, and later in the new, English-educated civil service. During this period, which lasted into the 1950s, they served as the mediating model of acculturation for the Usiai. They formed the core of the Paliau Movement (*20*), although its leader Paliau was a Matankor only weakly supported by his own ethnic group on Baluan Island. Manus dominance began to decline thereafter, partly because of the Paliau Movement which they supported. With the end of native internal warfare, villages began moving from their less accessible defensive locations to the beaches, and gardening peoples walked inland as often as necessary to attend their gardens. They began to use sea-going canoes although they generally did not move beyond the shallow, safer waters within the reefs. To the extent that cash-cropping, native plantations, and agricultural programs became important, the Manus—still effectively landless—were left out. The Manus were successful in converting their ethnic self-confidence into scholastic achievement, but Usiai and Matankor children raised entirely within the postwar contact culture in beach villages are now doing as well.

The Paliau Movement represented a turning point in the totemic perception which emphasizes difference. Paliau belittled differences. He saw through to the basic institutional similarity of Admiralty Island and, more generally, of all Melanesian cultures. He called for the end of all major lines of division within native society. He set himself against the ecological split and tried to bring Usiai and Manus to practice mixed economies. This met with little success among the Manus, except for their recent acquisition of European coconut plantations. He was especially concerned about ending the sharp ethnic separation of the Admiralty Islands people. He promoted the move to the beach and in many locations brought villages of diverse ethnic membership together to form larger, composite villages.

In spite of "integration," my 1967 survey showed that the relations of Manus to Usiai and Matankor remained much as before. In Bunai village, where since 1948 various Manus villages had united with five main Usiai villages, twenty years had produced only three intermarriages between Manus and Usiai, two of which were explained away by physical or moral defects of the Manus bride.

Ethnicity was and remains an important component of the identity of individuals and groups in spite of the informality of the ethnic group, its few social and political functions, and its relative lack of economic importance due to the iso-ecological position of villages of the same ethnic group. What I have called "ethnic groups" would sometimes be called "tribes" (*19*). The term "tribe," however, already seems to be extended too far from its established traditional sense to be applicable to these politically and socially unorganized groupings based on presumed common descent, blood, and culture. Under the influence of new and broader forms of political leadership within the imposed and assimilated state, some of the ethnic groups may become tribal in the more prevalent political sense. "Tribalism" of the sort described in Africa is a spectre much feared in Melanesia as independence approaches. Hostility and distrust remain. Here and there violent encounters occur. The rubric of ethnic relations serves us better if it is free of the connotations of the "tribe."

Melanesian Ethnicity and Cultural Totemism

Thus the existence of ethnic groups and ethnic relations are an important part of the areal society and culture comprising the whole of the Admiralty Islands. The differentiation and maintenance of difference among these group depends on self- and mutual-definition. That is, the groups are distinguished by selected ethnognomonic traits emblematic of the separate identity and community of substance of each group.

In the course of my studies of the Admiralty Islanders (*20, 21*) I found among them an attitude toward culture which made them hypersensitive to selected cultural and linguistic differences but relatively blind to the similarities between groups thus defined as different. This subgrouping of a society in terms of diagnostic cultural traits I have termed "cultural totemism," comparing it with the coding of social structure in terms of natural species, the attribute relations among which provide an analog for the relations among social groups..Culture provides its own analog.

Social structure is a cultural artifact like anything else to which man imparts form, selects, and categorizes. Cultural differences reflect the social differentiation and grouping which they are used to map and label. But the relation is not merely one of passive reflection. The totemic attitude, natural or cultural I would assert experimentally, *promotes* differentiation and fragmentation of a certain order characteristic of Melanesia, and perhaps of many primitive societies.

The totemic attitude, which I perceived in 1963 and later related to totemism (1968), I believed to be an explanation for the proliferation of languages and cultures in Melanesia, and specifically in the Admiralties. This attitude cannot be left unexplained as if it were a prime mover rather than a link in a nexus of intercausality. I suggested that it derives historically from the original multi-ethnicity of Melanesia, resulting from migration and settlement patterns that brought already differentiated Austronesian- and non-Austronesian-speaking peoples into contact. Diversity became a way of life, an adaptation to this ethnic mosaic. The overall system of areal integration combines political atomism with economic-ceremonial integration. Fragmentation provides more people with the opportunity to be big men to numerous small publics. Yet leadership which promotes political fragmentation must manifest itself in exchange and network building, reintegrating the fragments in a nonpolitical mode. The participant in such a system is attuned to relatively small group differences.

As a kind of consciousness of culture, cultural totemism apparently amplifies differences. Natural totemism would not seem to have this effect. To seize upon incipient differences for their emblematic value appears to cause, as much as to reflect, social differentiation. Such differences, overly attended, can define the lines of further differentiation.

Under cultural totemism, anything that is recognized as culturally distinctive is regarded as the property of a group (or individual). It is a property in the dual sense of an attribute and of a possession or a patent. Thus, in spite of mutual knowledge of each other's manufactures and special practices, these properties cannot simply be imitated, without securing the right to them through kinship, marriage, or some form of purchase or licensing. Diffusion is not automatic on exposure, as we sometimes imagine. At best we have thought of selection on the part of the recipient. For the cultures in question here, the owner of cultural property has rights of control over its diffusion. I am aware of instances of native warfare over violations of such rights as a way of ornamenting a canoe prow. Cultural totemism would have the effect of defining new social divisions, of amplifying differences, and of maintaining difference in the face of contiguity and communication. Cultural totemism is not only a form of ethnic recognition and categorization, it is an ethnicizing process—a mechanism of cultural speciation.

Further reflection subsequent to my 1963 paper (*21*) led to some revision of the above emphasis on the amplification of differences. Is the recognition of incipient difference the start of a schizmogenic process (*1*)? Does the difference, once noted, act like the beginning of a furrow on a rain-washed embankment which, as it continues to deepen, channels an increasing volume of water that works to deepen it even more? If so, why are the differences kept within the recognizable outlines of Admiralty Island cultures? They are limited, of course, by the general evolutionary level of these cultures on a given technological base, but this base has supported far greater diversity than is manifested in the Admiralties. The very isolation of selected traits by people "interested" in finding and maintaining such differences allows the massive similarity of all else to go unnoticed. This aspect of cultural totemism has implications as important to the general understanding of ethnicity as the difference-amplifying aspects. Anthropologists also alternate between these aspects of our own cultural totemism. At times we are intent on differences, which have great value to us in expanding our awareness of the range of possibilities in human cultures. They may also, perhaps, reward us with a differentiated "property" that becomes our particular stock in trade. At other times we allow ourselves to perceive the commonalities that, on a given level or type of culture, extensively underlie the differences. There would seem to be good bases in information theory for the behavioral tendency to perceive and react to differences as stimuli. Their magnitude need not be great. They may be the "just perceptible differences" of psychophysical research fame. Information requires difference: more accurately, information is *about* difference. The sameness of difference-manifesting objects is of indefinite extent, hence not determinately describable until we shift to a higher level of contrast at which this former sameness then becomes one side of a difference.

On their own level, Admiralty Island cultures could keep generating differences that are usable for social differentiation without the area really becoming much more culturally varied. In this light the totemism analogy becomes striking. The differences are real, but most often (outside of the ecotypic division) are instancings of ethnicity having an identificational, bounding function. Much more in culture might be of this order than we think. Sectarian distinctions that seem very important to insiders, dividing them into passionate factions, may to outsiders seem like the merest variations on a theme. The similarities revealed by external contrast are, perhaps, the more remarkable. As I argued earlier, similar basic institutional designs prevail throughout the Admiralty Islands, and some of them throughout Melanesia, in spite of the dramatic contrasts of ecological areas and the different historical provenience of peoples.

The above discussion would seem to raise the question, "How great is a difference?" which sounds a bit like the children's conundrum, "How long is a piece of string?" Obviously, once the difference and the objects in the implicit comparison are specified, the anthropologist can answer this question in many ways. He might ask, "How many people are affected?" Or "How much system accommodation does the difference set in motion?" Or "How much would communication by people on either side of the difference be affected?" Much but not all can be learned by ascertaining the insider's construction of the matter. Regarding languages, it is clear to the Manus that some are more distant from their own than others and therefore more difficult – or "dear" (costly) as they sometimes put it in Pidgin English – to learn. Such inquiries reveal that even where the differences between groups are many, only a few need be taken into account, and these need not be the etically (descriptively) major ones. The brief lexicographic list of language designations is a case in point. Another, for example, is the difference in carving styles among the Matankor. It is enough to say, "This is a carving from Pak Island. They make noses that way." This ignores as unnecessary, for ethnic assignment, the many other differences perceptible to the outsider whose comparisons among the objects of Admiralty Island cultures are affected by innumerable external contrasts that he has registered in past experience. The outsider's interests are not confined to ethnic assignment alone but to the overall characterization of style. The insider's is largely the cultural totemic view.

It has perhaps been formative of the distinctive Manus ethnic culture and ethnic "personality" (in Devereux's sense) that the Manus alone, of all Admiralty Island ethnic groups, are set off from others at the level of their ecotype, which they alone occupy. By contrast, all the Usiai ethnic groups within the Admiralty Islands comprise a single ecotype, as do the Matankor ethnic groups, so that they must distinguish themselves from each other at a different level of ethnognomonic detail.

Ethnic Groupings in Relation to Other Groupings

Thus far I have described the segmentation of the Admiralty Island areal culture at the ethnic level. The actual situation is more complex. The ethnoethnography contains multiple, hierarchic, cross-cutting taxonomies which must be taken into account for a more complete picture of the overall identificational matrix. Natural and cultural totemism are two such cross-cutting taxonomies. As an initial crude approximation I could characterize cultural totemism (membership in the ethnic group and its subdivisions) as patrilineal, and natural totemism as matrilineal. Given the combination of the two I could speak of dual descent, but either the unilineal or the duolineal characterization would somewhat exaggerate the difference between Admiralty Island and other primitive cultures.

All unilineal societies pay some attention to relations with the descendants of their exogamic members—such as, in the Admiralties, the women who marry out and their descendants. Lifelong exchange with one's affinal allies follows the path of the out-marrying women. Their children are the cross-cousins and future exchange partners of the men who remain in the village or clan. The grandchildren of the exogam will again seek wives from their grandmother's clan. The progeny through the outmarrying sex are regarded as having residual rights in the patrimony of the clan. They are potential recruits to the clan, should its numbers dwindle. Therefore, whether one speaks of dual descent or of complementary filiation (*5*), the unilineal idea, applied flexibly to local group composition, is always accompanied by a more or less formal accounting for relations through the opposite sex. This accounting is formally marked in the Admiralty Islands in various ways, including the lines of descent that make up the natural totemism. (It is also marked by the Crow-type kinship terminology which, as argued in Schwartz [*21*], reflects not some culminative development of unilineality but rather an emphasis on the cross-cutting ties centering on the solidarity of siblings of opposite sex and the continued relation of their progenies.)

The natural totems and associated taboos comprise a flat taxonomy. They do not divide into sub-totems. They do not map a hierarchic structure comparable to that of the patrilineally organized, co-residential or co-territorial ethnic groups, villages, clans, and lineages. The tree formed by these entities is not simply a downward-radiating genealogy, real or assumed, but has different bases for membership on each level. The ethnic group is assumed to be a community of substance, even though members are aware at times that members of other ethnic groups have been assimilated, for example, as captives. One Matankor village is now largely descended from an Usiai taken captive several generations ago, with no apparent cultural or linguistic effect and no sense of ethnic discontinuity.

Full membership in the ethnic group is patrilineal in native theory. The child of a woman of the ethnic group is said to be a "lateral," to supply a gloss for native terms which they translate as "half-caste" in Pidgin English. Inquiry evokes the names and territories of quite a few ethnic groups of which it is said only half-castes remain. The same conception applies at the clan and lineage levels.

Clan membership is also patrilineal in the above sense, but clans are subject to splits along lineage lines. In such cases the clan name is often retained by one of the products of fission, together with a clan location and territory. A clan is thought of as a "place." It has a location in a village and territorial resources, land, fishing areas, sago swamps, reefs, and cultural properties such as types of fish nets or particular ceremonials. Clans consist of one or more patrilineages. In all other groupings, lineages are the unit of composition most firmly rooted in genealogical relations, either known or stated as if known. They are named for the nodal ancestor from whom they trace descent. The level of mutual trust is strongest within the lineage, in consonance with the assumption of the closest community of substance. One or more lineages can become clans by splitting off and becoming associated with a place of their own. Many clans, however, are quite old and consist of lineages that cannot trace their relations to one another. They assume that such relations exist and that the lineages of a clan have always been associated with one another.

Villages may split and recombine along clan or sub-clan (that is, lineage) lines. The political association that a village represents may be disrupted by quarrels or by rivalry. The split can be violent or merely one of spatial separation. At times a move of even a few hundred yards will serve the purpose. The lineage and the ethnic group thus resemble one another in contrast to the clan and village. They are not directly territorial. The ethnic group is associated with a territory over which its members are spread, but it is the clans and villages that hold and defend the territory. Both lineage and ethnic group are communities of substance like the natural totemic lines, in contrast to the clan and village, particularly the latter, which are political associations. The village is a purely political, unstable assemblage of a selection of clans from within the pool bounded by the ethnic group.

An ethnic group, like a lineage, stresses substance rather than place. Like totemism, such groups are useful for broad or fictive association on a scale for which political organizational means does not exist. Village and clan membership, by contrast, implied a kind of citizenship in a microstate. Clan and, to a greater extent, village cohesion was consensual, dependent on the current prestige and vigor of their leaders and always limited by the potential exercise of the sanction of withdrawal or separation. It is often asserted that the assumption of common substance is the basis for food taboos (including ethnic exophagy), as well as lineage, clan, and broader rules of exogamy. But this assumption must also be one of the bases of ethnic endogamy, even though the latter is a result rather than a rule and lacks the kinds of sanctions attached to incest or totemic taboo violation. Lineage and its extensions seem to define an inner circle, whereas ethnicity defines an outer circle. Within the inner circle, incest is prohibited. But between the inner and outer circle there is an area of relatively safe incest in the sense of copulation with one defined as of the same blood or substance. Any excursion beyond the outer circle is at the venturer's risk in much the same degree as inter-ethnic trade or warfare.

One effect of colonial administration and of the models of the new amalgamated communities has been to inhibit but not eliminate the processes of split and merger. Ethnic groups tend to be represented in fewer separate communities. In some cases they have coalesced into a single community. Some leaders of the Manus group have had the fantasy of reversing the Manus diaspora, which they trace back in myth to a single founder village. They dream of bringing all of the ten or so current Manus villages together into a single Manus town based on the acquisition of a sufficiently large European plantation. Certain ethnic groups may yet become politically coordinated in the context of modern political action.

Ethnic Traits as Emblematic Property

Ethnic group, village, clan, lineage, nad individuals comprise a hierarchy of material and nonmaterial property-bearing entities. Admiralty Islanders have terms such as the Manus word *kaye* which, applied to any of these levels, means any and all of the following: way, manner, kind, fashion (the actual Pidgin English gloss), property or attribute, and inherent characteristic of that object. The *kaye* was conceived of as inherent but not in the same way as a physical property such as skin color. For such attributes the person is taken as an object and I have never heard *kaye* applied to objects. A ceremony, a way of fighting, a trait of touchiness about status, a style of canoe construction or a love of canoe racing, an individual's lack of generosity—any of these and all collectively would be referred to as the *kaye* of that individual or group. Statements using the term are often comments intended as explanations: they are behaving in a certain way because it is their *kaye*—"That's the way they are." Although the conception is different, it tends to cover what we mean by culture, when applied to groups, or personality, when applied to individuals.

If one asked, what are the *kaye* of a particular ethnic group, village, clan or lineage, one would elicit not an exhaustive characterization, of course, but a brief set of group properties or distinctive traits, not necessarily selected for contrast on the same attribute dimensions as those mentioned for other groups. It is assumed that all groups will manifest some behaviors by which one can identify them. These are the behaviors by which they express their group membership. Many other behaviors, if they are distinctive of the person or group to which they are attributed, will be recognized as *kaye*, but they will not be the ethnognomonic traits that come most readily to the informant's mind. The extension of cultural totemism to individuals, in the same terms and conventions of discourse, as apply to groups, is logically consistent for the Admiralty Islander and parallels my own preferences in modeling the relation of culture and personality (*22, 23*).

The totemic attitude is still with us. As Lévi-Strauss argues, it is not a distinguishing characteristic separating primitive from modern or civilized man. Linton's parable of the Rainbow Brigade in World War I beautifully illustrates the assimilation of the primitive into the modern. Totemism is a mode of human thought that has certain effects, and perhaps shortcomings, that are important to human conceptions of ethnicity and the behavioral implications of these conceptions. These effects were discussed in relation to the possible difference-amplifying effects of according emblematic significance to seemingly slight or incipient cultural differences. At the same time it became noticeable that what was being multiplied was not the degree of difference or overall cultural variation among all groups of this interactive areal culture, but only the number of distinctive groups. This increase in groups means that the number of domains increased within which entrepreneurs could separately reckon their own prestige. *Since similarities pass unnoticed when attention is focused on the emblematic differences, it would be possible for cultural diversity to diminish even while ethnic diversity increases.*

Figure 1 illustrates the totemic attitude and its effect. This attitude clearly leads to the use of only one of the diagonals in selective perception and neglects or overlooks the other. In differentiating groups from one another by a set of distinctive traits, it emphasizes the similarity or solidarity within each of the distinguished groups and the dissimilarity between the groups. As De Vos felicitously expressed it in speaking of ethnicity, "It takes care of belonging and distantiation at the same time." What is ignored are the variations within each group and the similarities between them. Also ignored are all similarities and differences on noncriterial traits.

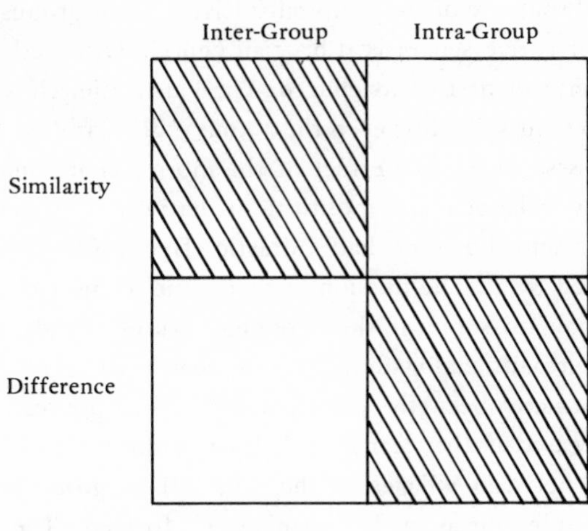

Figure 1

The totemic attitude involves the perceptual speciation of all known mankind. The premises of natural totemism seem to enjoy a primacy that goes beyond its value of totemism as a classificatory analogy. Groupings based on any criteria—genealogical, cultural, territorial—either assume a set of species-like qualities or remain weak, conflictful, and schismatic assemblages. Upon this mosaic of little "species" men further impose their rankings of respect and disparagement which become embodied in patterns of domination and counterdreams of revindication.

Christian Conversion and Religious Ethnicity

The tendency to convert groups not based on genealogy and not initially taken as ethnic into quasi-ethnic "species" may be illustrated by the effect of the conversion of Admiralty Islanders to the various Christian missions. The process began in the 1880s and was largely completed in the 1930s when the Manus became Catholic en masse. The Usiai and Matankor had been split into several groups by Catholic, Lutheran Evangelical, and Seventh Day Adventist missionaries. The conversion of the Manus to a single sect both reflects and reinforces their ethnic unity and seems in consequence to have had little effect on their internal relations. Other small ethnic groups went to one or another of the sects, while many were split between two or more. The Seventh Day Adventists sometimes were able to gain converts from other missions, dividing some ethnic groups. In the 1940s, the Paliau Movement led to a break between its adherents and the Catholic and Protestant missions to which they had belonged, although the Seventh Day Adventists seem to be immune to such defections. Once again the Manus, though the largest and most dispersed spatially of the Admiralty Island ethnic groups, went en masse into the Paliau native separatist Christian church. Other ethnic groups were divided by recruitment to this church. The Paliau Church was split episodically by splinter cults dividing even the Manus ethnic group.

I cannot assess as yet the effect of the more recent segmentation of the Admiralties by religious and political affiliations. The initial pattern of mission recruitment, however, had a drastic effect on the ethnic groups that were partitioned by it. The mission sects became themselves similar to ethnic groups and took on some of the totemic features already discussed. They soon became virtually endogamous. Where nearby villages of the same ethnic groups had formerly been the principal sources of spouses for one another, this relation ceased if they came to belong to different missions. Marriages predominated between villages of the same ethnic group and mission, but many cross-ethnic, intrasect marriages were formed. The Paliau Church, sometimes known as the Baluan Church, began to have the same effect. Each group had its own taboos and new ethnognomonic traits.

Members of other sects looked with awe upon the transformation of behavior effected by Seventh Day Adventists and their considerable success in tabooing the most highly valued oral pleasures: betel nut, tobacco, pork, and alcohol (recently become available to natives). The distinctive Sabbath day and the use of English as a liturgical language all heightened the sense of belonging among Seventh Day Adventist converts and their sense of distance from non-Adventist groups. Their belief in an imminent apocalypse also helps account for the strength of their new "ethnicity" and the commitment that made them immune (until 1967, at any rate) to the attractions of other cults.

The other missions, churches and cults were less impermeable during the period under observation, but at their height they showed similar characteristics. The members, encouraged by their leaders, have come to think of themselves as different or new kinds of men. They wear the new (or relatively recent) identities conspicuously. During periods of strong group feeling they have tended to act as political blocs, putting forward their own candidates in Territory-wide and local elections. Since some church groups require the non-member spouse to join the church, endogamy results partly from rules. In most church groups, however, it operates like that of the old ethnic groups, informally as an effect of attribute clustering, preference and the operation of community pressures, as well as the effect of network involution on the likelihood of inside and outside contacts of potential sponsors and spouses. The heterogeneous members of the new sects seemingly could not claim common origin, yet they do develop an identification with the origin myths of their sect as well as with its unique correctness and the special benefits promised to them as the elect. They feel tied as well to the countries of origin of their sects. It is another source of strength for the Seventh Day Adventists that their sect is of American origin, given the prestige of America, which had an enormous military base in the Admiralties in World War II. I found their members to have the impression that most Americans are Seventh Day Adventists, even though the other sects are also represented by American priests and missionaries who have largely replaced the earlier German ones.

Although they are in many ways deeply separated from one another by their different religious memberships, converts are linked, albeit somewhat remotely, to organizations of worldwide scope. On the local scene, however, I believe my comparison of the sects to the old ethnic groups is justified.

In the towns, at boarding schools and work centers, and in the civil service, individuals of ethnic groups derived from all parts of the mainland and islands of the Territory of Papua and New Guinea now intermingle. And there is now a higher level of contrast in which Admiralty natives are classed together as a unit, in comparison with other equally broad groups whose ethnic differentiation becomes irrelevant at a distance. In the towns, attribute clustering takes place to the greatest possible extent. The more specific the shared attributes, the more likely an intimate association. Manus in Rabaul, for example, will first associate with their own kin if any are present, second with members of their own village, third with other Manus, and fourth with other Admiralty Islanders of their own locality, religious background, and so on through a series of increasingly general attributes. The ethnic enclaves or networks of ethnic associations in towns are not merely indifferently ethnic but ethnolocal. African urban studies indicate the same pattern. For example, a

Yoruba's ties in town are not with just any Yoruba, but primarily to those of his home locality (*15*). Jacobson indicates this is more true of nonelite than of elite urban workers (*17*).

Sexual Attraction and Ethnic Contrast in Pluralistic Situations

In Melanesia this picture of ethnic clustering may hold somewhat more strongly for ties with persons of the same sex in towns, schools, and work centers, than for persons of opposite sex. Admiralty Island parents are disturbed at the frequency with which their sons and daughters marry or become romantically and biologically involved with young women and men of the most diverse origins—New Guineans, Trobrianders, Solomon Islanders —when they are away from parental supervision. Many cross-cultural marriages are occurring. The greatest concern of the Admiralty Island parents is that a daughter will go to live with strangers and be subject to dangers that this entails beyond the reach of their protection. Romantic sexual attraction not only does not respect ethnic lines, it may be stimulated by the very distantiation that ethnic contrasts guarantee, since it may depend to some extent on the contrast, on mystery, on the assumption of an informational gradient.

Within the ethnic group the incest taboo provides a line between the familiar and the sufficiently distant insider. Our thinking about incest usually focuses on it as a prohibition that compels men to marry out, as if without it their "natural tendency" would be to couple with whomever were closest at hand. The incest taboo could be seen as a guarantee of a marriage that is sufficiently distant by definition for an adequate initial potentiation before it too becomes affectively and institutionally "familiar." To the extent that the mating is distant (but still "inside") it is approved. To the extent that such a mating is approved, it becomes less distant. If there is anything to this speculation, why would incest taboos have to be stringently sanctioned if attractiveness is lessened with familiarity? For one thing, the effect on intrafamilial attraction may not be wholly nullified. An attraction may exist at one stage of life which in the presence of the incest taboo would be repressed later or redirected as part of the basis for the potentiation by distance. But aside from that, I might hypothesize that a taboo requires enforcement because it exists. The incest taboo itself provides distance to a disapproved coupling which counteracts, to some extent, the effect of familiarity. In sum, with respect to sexual attraction, close "familiar" relations are less potent sexually but are made more so by their distantiating illegitimacy. Permissible, enjoined, or prescribed relations are by definition sufficiently distant but made less so by their legitimacy and institutionalized "familial" status. Under past circumstances as well as the present situation of a mingled ethnic setting, the cross-ethnic liaison between young people is still more distant, less incestuous, in that the partner is unlike one's familiars in more ways. In addition, such a liaison is formally legal but disapproved by one's home community and family. The resultant marriages usually gain approval after the fact, but they are regarded as potentially unstable and dangerous.

Conclusions: Cultural Totemism and Identity

I have taken the concept of totemism as the starting point of this paper and have attempted, by way of the notion of cultural totemism, to extend it to ethnic relations in a primitive areal culture. I have argued that ethnicity is decidedly relevant to primitive societies when they are taken not as isolates, either culturally or socially, but as we usually find them, part of a complex of communities. In these stateless societies the boundaries between ethnic groups are neither political nor necessarily "natural" boundaries but are instead defined within the areal culture. These definitions are subject to both gradual and relatively sudden changes, even within the relative stability and relatively slower rate of change that characterizes societies at the pre-urban, pre-industrial level. Nor are such changes simply the result of passive drift of cultural differentiation. Human beings themselves cannot help but treat human behavior as they do all other phenomena. They form constructs of the phenomenal field that are derived from it and imposed upon it. In this case, the constructs of the field of cultural variation and similarity form a part of the system of constructs orienting the very behavior that is being perceived.

I have asserted that this perception is selective, attending most sensitively to certain key differences, and I have described schematically what I have called the totemic attitude or mode of perception. Implicit in the totemic mode is that the resulting social segregates are conceived of as species, each united in substance and origin, each manifesting its species-specific behavior. The fact of inter-ethnic marriage and assimilation of persons and behavioral properties is not missed, but the analogy to a species remains, enhanced by ethnic endogamy and myths of origin and continuity. For the Admiralty Islands, I have compared the cross-cutting relations of natural and cultural totemism.

Totemism, even in this extended sense, remains a matter of classification, as so many have established. But as others have sensed, it is more than this. The classification is a means of reciprocal identification of individuals and groups. It provides both a key and a model, perhaps corresponding with Devereux's ethnic identity and ethnic personality, or again to a status system and a role system. Any status system is not merely a set of labels corresponding to a set of relative social positions. It must also specify how individuals or groups are to be assigned to these statuses by providing a set of qualifying attributes. We often believe we can decide on the position assignments without necessarily considering what behaviors will be expected of the persons occupying such positions. We cannot always find exclusively nonbehavioral criteria. Furthermore, non-behavioral criteria, other than marked racial or sex differences, are not visible, not supportive of the species analogy. Cultural totemism applies where certain particularly attended behavioral differences are the bases for the assignment or validation of ethnic status. Manifesting or, as Devereux puts it, "instancing" the role, validates the status. Such instancing, singly or collectively, is very much the concern of members of the mosaic of ethnic groups that I have described. One proves as much to oneself as to others who one is, or one seeks to discover who one is, by displaying various behaviors—trying on identities.

In what I have described, as well as in the details of individual behavioral stances which I could not deal with here, I am asserting that there is evidence that identity is always problematic and consequently dynamic, not only in modern, rapidly changing societies but in primitive societies as well. It becomes problematic in new ways under culture contact, domination, and acculturation, but it is not created anew. Much of culture and personality is adaptive to the problem of identity, which is never completely resolved in a given culture or personality. The individual or group seems always to confront the question of their identity—of what that identity implies and of what they must do to validate their own and others' sense of that identity. Against what counter-assertion is directed the assertion of identity in myth, in ritual and religion generally, in institutions, in the flow of behavior itself? Why is all this necessary? What is the problem? Perhaps all we need posit to begin to answer this question is the existence of more than one individual and, beyond this, more than one distinguished group of people. We would then have to explore the individual and cultural ontogeny of how identities are established and maintained. Much of psychoanalysis is concerned with this question, most explicitly the work of Erikson.

Any status is a part of identity, and for most societies ethnic status (like sexual status but perhaps with an even greater priority) is one of the bases upon which identities are constructed. It establishes a relative ranking for all other statuses that are added on for the individual or group vis-à-vis the corresponding statuses of others. Thus it would follow that if white is higher than black, a white doctor is higher than a black doctor. But ethnic statuses are often so displaced in rank that the lowest-ranked secondary statuses of one are above the highest-ranked of the other. Probably the weight of ethnic status as a component of identity is correlated to the degree of status ranking on that basis. Where it is not so used (as within a given ethnic group), sex or occupation or age may act as the basal status that calibrates the relative standing of the rest and upon which identity is constructed. Under such circumstances sex, occupation, age or other statuses may be ethnicized, cleaving the social spectrum into groups of persons manifesting the emblematic traits of sexual, class, age grade or generational identities.

The weighting of a basal status in the construction of identities depends on their use in ranking individuals and groups in institutionalized patterns of dominance. A basal status such as ethnicity would become even more salient when ranking becomes unstable. In an assimilating environment, ethnicity itself is thrown into question as a significant basis of identity and some alternative basis such as class or nationalism is asserted (and may take on ethnoid or specioid characteristics as a result). Ethnicity is most prominent when the rank order rather than the ethnic basis is under attack. Where ethnicity and rank are fused, the relative movement of any one person sets all into movement. The relativity of such a basal status system is highly problematic unless it is based on an overwhelming domination, which even then will not stifle all fears of revindicative movement from below. In the Admiralty Islands, the two situations combine. The Usiai can rise in relative status through assimilation without asserting Usiai ethnicity, which was always plural rather than a strong collective identity. The Manus, on the other hand, have no power to prevent the Usiai from overcoming their pre-contact inferiority and they are, partly by the very strength of their own singular ethnicity, less able to assimilate because they lack the land base with which to do so. For them, the reference group is European; for the Usiai, it is both Manus and European.

As culture change has accelerated, time makes an increasing difference in defining the identity of individuals. They are grouped by the totemic perception in time and change as they once were in space. It is increasingly true that cultures are bounded more in time than in space. The result differs greatly from the age grading which has been a feature of all cultures to some extent. Although one now becomes a member of the adult age grade, it is part of a culture that differs from that to which one's father belonged. Somewhere one's identity becomes anchored in time as part of a generation in the cultural sense. But this generation does not extend throughout the lifetime of the individual. His generation is attached to a certain period of his life—in America, late adolescence and young adulthood, perhaps—the age at which one has one's war, learns the songs and dance styles that are especially his, receives his most formative occupational training, and so on. One survives through the successive generations of others in more or less useful ways.

This longitudinal effect of cultural acceleration creates a new kind of plurality of identities which are, like geographically separated ethnic groups, sharply set apart by the totemic perception. Our societies are pluralistic with respect to these time-limited cultures as well as with respect to the older types of culturally differentiated segments. And with this new multiplicity, identity becomes all the more problematic. Riesman, Mead and Toffler (*16, 13, 24*) have done interesting explorations in these time-limited cultures and in the problem of identification when one lacks exact precedents in identity but must extrapolate to something new. Many have written about peer group modeling as one response to this situation.

The problem of finding an identity without precedent is not completely solved by adopting a contemporary precedent. The signs of search seem even more evident and more frustrating than ever before. Migrants of identity wander the land, trying on this or that identity, never sure, and perhaps under the circumstances unable to attain familiar forms of authenticity of identity. To terminate any search requires that, whatever one is seeking, one must recognize it when it is found. It must also be acceptable, if the masquerade is to be ended. The search for another or a new identity is almost a contradiction in terms.

My further research among the people of the Admiralty Islands will be particularly concerned with where they find themselves in time and change, with the state of their present self-recognition, and with the conception of themselves and of their elders formed by the young, who have been raised and educated wholly within the post-World War II contact culture and who are taking their places as mature adults. What do the old bases of identity now mean to them? What has been the fate of the old ethnicity? How "modern" have they become? Although identity has always been problematic in primitive and modern cultures alike, we may yet find that there has been a change, from the question "Who am I?" to "Who am I really?"

REFERENCES

1. Bateson, Gregory. *Naven.* Cambridge, England, 1936.
2. Devereux, George. "Ethnic Identity: Its Logical Foundations and Its Dysfunctions." Chapter 2 in this volume.
3. Durkheim, Emile, and Mauss, Marcel. *Primitive Classification,* translated and edited by Rodney Needham. Chicago: University of Chicago Press, 1963.
4. Goldenweiser, Alexander. *Anthropology.* New York: Crofts, 1937.
5. Fortes, Meyer, ed. *Social Structure: Studies Presented to A. R. Radcliffe-Brown and D. Forde.* Oxford, 1949.
6. Fortune, Reo F. *Manus Religion.* Philadelphia: American Philosophical Society, 1935.

7. Jacobson, David. *Itinerant Townsmen: Friendship and Social Order in Urban Uganda.* Menlo Park, California: Cummings, 1973.

8. Levi-Strauss, Claude. *Le totemisme aujourd'hui.* Paris: Presses Universitaires, 1962.

9. Linton, Ralph. *The Cultural Background of Personality.* 1942.

10. Linton, Ralph. "Nativistic Movements." *American Anthropology* (new ser.) 45(2):230-240, 1943.

11. Mead, Margaret. *Growing Up in New Guinea.* New York, 1930.

12. Mead, Margaret. "Kinship in the Admiralty Islands." Anthropological Papers of the American Museum of Natural History, Vol. 34, Part 2, 1934.

13. Mead, Margaret. *New Lives for Old.* New York, 1956.

14. Mead, Margaret. *Culture and Commitment: A Study of the Generation Gap.* New York: Natural History Press, 1970.

15. Plotnikov, Leonard. *Strangers in the City.* Pittsburgh: University of Pittsburgh Press, 1969.

16. Riesman, David. *The Lonely Crowd: A Study of the Changing American Character.* Garden City, N.Y.: Doubleday, 1953.

17. Romanucci-Ross, Lola. "Conflits fonciers a Mokerang, village Matankor des iles de l'Amiraute." *L'Homme* 6(2):32-52, 1966.

18. Romanucci-Ross, Lola. "The Hierarchy of Resort in Curative Practices: The Admiralty Islands, Melanesia." *Journal of Health and Social Behavior* 10(3):201-209, 1969.

19. Sahlins, Marshall. *Tribesmen.* Englewood Cliffs, N.J.: Prentice-Hall, 1968.

20. Schwartz, Theodore. "The Paliau Movement in the Admiralty Islands, 1946-1954." Anthropological Papers of the American Museum of Natural History. New York, 1962.

21. Schwartz, Theodore. "Systems of Areal Integration: Some Considerations Based on the Admiralty Islands of Northern Melanesia." *Anthropological Forum* 1(1):56-97, 1963.

22. Schwartz, Theodore. "Cult and Context: The Paranoid Ethos in Melanesia." *Ethos.* 1(2), 1973.

23. Schwartz, Theodore. "Distributive Models of Culture in Relation to Societal Scale." Burg Wartenstein Symposium no. 55. *Scale and Social Organization.* New York: Wenner-Gren Foundation, 1972.

24. Toffler, Alvin. *Future Shock.* New York: Random House, 1970.

25. Tylor, E. B. *Primitive Culture.* New York: Harper, 1958.

Ethnic Identity and National Character

PART TWO

PART TWO

ETHNIC IDENTITY AND NATIONAL CHARACTER

The four chapters that follow are discussions of ethnic identity as part of national character by anthropologists Geoffrey Gorer, Margaret Mead and Lola Romanucci-Ross, and by an anthropologically oriented psychiatrist, Hsien Rin. As perceptive, self-conscious representatives of their respective ethnic traditions, they have each chosen to discuss a particular theme from the perspective of what it is to be "Chinese," "English," "American," or "Italian."

Rin describes the synthesizing mentality of the Chinese, a quality which allows one to remain Chinese while adapting without too much stress or difficulty to a foreign setting. In adapting to the present, fidelity to a sense of inherited past wisdom remains. He illustrates the Chinese sense of harmony and integrative balance in his description of the pragmatism of the Chinese medical tradition. The Chinese tend not to divide themselves by class, but by family lineage.

In contrast Gorer, in considering the English (who, he points out, are not the "British"), indicates how their absorption with social class position among themselves excludes concern about outsiders as audience. The English identify themselves by contrast with other English who are members of social classes other than their own. Like the Chinese, they maintain a secure sense of social presence which cannot be easily disturbed by the attitudes of outsiders.

The American identity, as sketched by Margaret Mead, begins with a colonial ambivalence about the dispossessed Indian. This ambivalence extends through subsequent American history as an ethical dilemma of separation versus inclusion and ethnic pluralism versus integration. Inhabitants of the United States, Mead contends, are continually changing as they change their appraisals of subsequent waves of immigrants. Ethnic separation becomes a "self-selected mutually rejecting superiority, pitted against the ethic of ethnic assimilation." Mead also draws attention to the second central dilemma to be found in the American identity—a sense of the factual barriers to mobility lodged in a class system which belies an ideological commitment to an ideal of social mobility devoid of class considerations. The American identity is a conflictful one in which inclusiveness versus exclusiveness continues from past into present, creating the dynamic tension that shapes the course of change in American history.

Finally, the Italian identity as discussed by Lola Romanucci-Ross shows that an awareness of regional conflicts over unity and diversity is part of the Italians' consciousness of "Italian" history. Nevertheless, time, not space (in contrast to the Americas), is integral to the shaping of Italian identity. The influence of past Roman cultural ascendency is still felt by contemporary Italians. The fall of the Roman Empire led to a regionalism that was fortified by an original substratum of linguistic separation. The rediscovery of a buried unified classic civilization was not accompanied by political reintegration during the Renaissance. The Italian sense of identity today still reflects psycho-cultural problems about what it means to identify with an ambivalently conceived Italian heritage. Here we find examined, also, the feudal relationship between aristocracy and peasantry in the maintenance and exchange of the cultural heritage of a group. Establishing a stable and viable identity involves the continuing attempt at reconciling in oneself and in one's behavior as a group member, the constantly evolving issues of distrust, defeat and deceit originating in one's past cultural history.

The Synthesizing Mind in Chinese Ethno-Cultural Adjustment

HSIEN RIN

5

It is difficult to consider the Chinese a single cultural group in a discussion of psychocultural adjustment in a changing world. This article will be limited to brief discussions of the subjective meaning of being Chinese, the relationship of the Chinese to their neighbors, how identity was and is maintained in a foreign setting when a territorial base is lacking, special problems of minority Chinese in Southeast Asia and elsewhere, and a brief allusion to the aboriginal minorities in Taiwan.

The main focus will be on what I term the "synthesizing" style of thinking of the Chinese, how they think about self and others and how they look at the world. I will describe the "synthesizing" mind of the Chinese by using my experience in medicine as an example, since it will serve as a paradigm for other uses of the synthesizing view—especially as it pertains to social relations.

Chinese Thoughts About Man, Life and the World

To begin this discussion we must cite the continuing effect of a unifying traditional philosophy, which for the Chinese has been the essence of accumulated ancient wisdom and whose teaching has been transmitted to the vast majority of the Chinese people: Confucianism. Secondly, we raise the question of class differences in Chinese society. Thirdly, the discussion will be extended to consider the Chinese concept of man, the human body, life and the world. Despite changes in political power, China has long and enduring traditions in respect to kinship values, intra-familial decorum, and in aesthetics.

The Chinese people have described themselves in their own literature as cheerful, carefree and good humored; honest, kind, and with a genius for friendship; self-respecting, dignified, composed, discreet, and proud; energetic, secure, and loyal to family, or realistic and shrewd. But outsiders (including anthropologists) have emphasized other dimensions, especially their "orality," which has often been discussed psychoanalytically. Most discussions of Chinese character have focused on the importance of family ties and filial piety, on how one learns obedience and conservatism and how one is obligated to preserve the family name and reputation. Furthermore, a mother's exclusive role in child rearing and the prolongation of breast feeding have been considered key issues in the development of Chinese personality including its "orality." These emphases have unfortunately led to some false overextensions and misapprehensions.

Confucians stressed that the fulfillment of social role expectations is also the fulfillment of the potential of human nature. In Buddhism, the ultimate objective was rebirth in paradise, attained through meditation and serenity. Taoism, aiming at the realization of the three original principles of essence, vital force and spirit, emphasized cultivation of one's nature and development of one's vital force. In Chinese philosophy and religion, the above three doctrines co-exist. When taken together, they constitute a unique theoretical and practical principle idealizing harmony as the ultimate social ideal. Chinese philosophers have attempted to look at life and philosophy in its dynamic totality.

Through two thousand years of historical development of Chinese philosophy, especially by Neo-Confucianists in the twelfth century, most of the doctrinal books were evaluated with a spirit "seeking exhaustively to investigate the reason in all things." Such philosophical tradition, through repeated research, has been transmitted and been woven into daily life and the educational system of the Chinese. Looking at life as a harmonious totality has been the main issue in the Chinese mind.

Since China's first encounter with Western science, tremendous effort has been put into the learning of modern technology. However, the attitude of Chinese in this situation appears to be again uniquely concerned with harmony or synthesis. This outlook continues from that which is well illustrated in the work of ancient Chinese scholars. The best examples of the latter appear in an article by a famous modern Chinese philosopher, Hu Shih (*3*). The article illustrates the synthesizing attitude as applied to the relationship between East and West. Although many scholars contend that the East used doctrines built out of concepts by intuition, whereas Western doctrine tended to be constructed out of concepts by postulation, Hu argues that this bifurcation of East and West is untrue as far as the intellectual history of the East is concerned.

> In the first place, there is no race or culture which admits only concepts by intuition. In making inferences, man must use all his powers of perception, observation, imagination, generalization and postulation, induction and deduction. In that way, man develops his common sense, his stock of empirical knowledge, his wisdom, his civilization and culture . . . To love dispassionate search for the truth, to use human reason critically and without prejudice, to probe deeply without fear and favor . . . these aspects of the scientific spirit and method are found in the intellectual and philosophical history of China.

But Chinese thinkers are not only concerned with ancient traditions. Today, in their research and practice, Chinese intellectuals are also working to integrate the ancient age with the modern, the thought of the West with their Eastern heritage. The synthesizing mind of the Chinese seeks to integrate time and place into one-world. From this, we can understand the attitude of the Chinese individual. He is proud of the glory of ancient China. Consciously or unconsciously he believes he is a dignified descendant of the Yellow Emperor, and he is proud of inheriting blood of "good nature," spirit and talent, and thus he is secure.

An example of this resurgence of interest in Chinese tradition can be found in Taiwan, where a large group of herb doctors maintain that they should rank with Western medicine in the national health program. In this claim, we again could see a synthetic attitude looking at Chinese and Western medicines, with an emphasis on maintaining traditional cultural values. Neither medical system should depreciate the other. Similarity should be appreciated and dissimilarity respected. This is a characteristic view of Chinese culture. Thus, with belief in *Tao* ("the way"), one can get along with the world without conflict. With an open heart, one can reach *ta-t'ung* ("one-world philosophy"). Given numerous facts men gain experience and compile statistics. With repeated experiments men discover laws of nature: facts are eloquent. Why should many people maintain a prejudice, accepting only Chinese medicine or Western medicine? If a Chinese brings a member of his family to a Western doctor, finds treatments ineffectual, and then brings the patient to a Chinese doctor and finds him improved, he would believe in Chinese medicine. Chinese medical practice is based on several thousand years' experience of continuous trial and error. It should not be quickly discarded with the word "unscientific." Mobilizing scientific methods and efforts, modern medicine has still failed to discover a cure for many diseases.

The older theory of Chinese medicine stems from the *I-ching* (Book of changes). It shows us principles of synthesis, of ways of heaven and humanity, and is one of the most important references of Chinese culture and spirit. The *yin-yang* interaction and changes presented in this book conform to dynamic principles. In eternal actions and changes of the universe, the nature of change and changelessness was searched out and interpreted. Those principles were applied in the doctrines of Confucius, Lao Tzu, Chuang Tzu, and Sun Tzu, as well as in medicine.

Chinese and Western medicine proceed from diverse assumptions. The Chinese regard a man as an integrated being, as a microcosm. This world has autonomic functions, and can recover from deviation by proper intervention of balancing drugs. Human physiology regulates itself with the changes in the seasons. Drugs can be applied so that cool remedies balance warm weather and hot remedies balance cool weather. Sudden change provoked in the intra-somatic environment will kill toxic agents or germs. Chinese culture is inclined to the study of human nature and Western culture is inclined to the study of material nature; both are necessary approaches. In the book of the "Doctrine of the Mean," it is proved that, since the truth of the universe relies on the development of the nature of man, one who fully develops his nature will develop the nature of human beings. The one who fully develops the nature of human beings will develop the nature of things, and the one who fully develops the nature of things will develop the nature of the whole universe.

ON SOCIAL CLASS IN CHINA

In the history of China, some democratic forms of society were developed. The thousand-year-old system of competitive examination of scholars stimulated those able to study assiduously. Entry into the class of government officials was open even to the peasantry. A highly intelligent official class was thus continually recruited, and the "cultivation of one's self" made eminently good sense.

The development of the Chinese sense of the individual has its root in the unique concept of one-world. The individual tends to look at groups rather than individuals as independent personalities. To a Chinese a family is much more important than any one of its members. Hungry relatives are helped out of a sense of family loyalty and obligation, rather than out of sympathy with their hunger. The individual is sensitive to the pursuit of harmony in his dealings with and in his management of social intercourse. Human empathy (*jen-chin*) cannot be slighted even if it entails breaking a law. The individual always faces an inclusive outside world. Attention is on inclusion rather than on exclusion in the classification of persons.

Religious practice is largely an individual matter in China. During the past two or three decades in Taiwan new religions have appeared, comprised of large numbers of believers. One which I know of personally is the *Tien Tao Chiao* ("doctrine of the way of Heaven"), which originated in Shantung province in mainland China during the prewar years. Basically, this religion attempts to integrate three religions of Confucianism, Buddhism and Taoism into one set of beliefs. Many even believe that all world religions should be united, and their number appears to be increasing.

I have long felt that the Chinese have paid relatively little attention to social class. Although social change and the occupational revolution took place in the modern era, in Chinese eyes it seems to mean little to divide people into classes. The difference of status among people depends on their degree of prosperity. If one is born in a family of peasantry he is unlucky. If one is reared in a rich family, he is lucky; it is fate. Still, one who wants to be prosperous must study and work hard. Confucius wrote, "With education there will be no classes." Practically, feelings of belonging to his people, including relatives, friends, and colleagues, are of much more importance for a Chinese than belonging to a class.

Up to the present, the majority of Chinese have lived in rural areas, and distinct class differences existed between the peasantry and the gentry, as Fei (*2*) described. The autonomous village emphasized kinship traditions, intra-family roles and decorum, and ancestor worship. In addition, peasant life was ridden with recurrent epidemics and other misfortunes. Fei explains the character formation of the Chinese peasant in these circumstances: "From observing the petty politics of family members he learns to put on a feigned obedience, can become imbued with a sense of futility about all effort, and becomes trivial, resigned, conservative, and cowardly." It was almost impossible for a rural family to leave the peasantry and join the gentry in the town. The gentry, a tight network of families, managed local situations by cooperating with government officials. Fei went on to say, "The gentry is in fact a safety valve in social change. . . . Conservatism was the rule of Chinese society, and China as a culture is singular in human history in respect to its stability and perpetuation." In sum, the Chinese look at people in their life circumstance as a whole, and the structure of their society tends to be homogeneous. In Chinese society there is little tendency to segregate the few minority groups, either economically or geographically. [Communities of

Hakka or Muslims, however, have separately existed for many generations.—ed.]

So far I have outlined some of the reasons for the cultural continuity and the stability of Chinese society. But the synthesizing element of Chinese thought is also evident in more tangible, practical realms. For example, the Chinese learned how to utilize every part of the animal body in cooking. In the present more prosperous age, ox tail, pig's leg, duck head, etc. still represent tasteful foods, so such customs cannot have developed strictly from need. The Chinese look at the body as a whole, regarding every part of the body as functional, even in their cuisine. Also, they consider each part of the animal body as well as various kinds of vegetable and plants to have specific effects on the human body, which again is regarded as an integrated whole consisting of many functions. This idea derives in great part from the tradition of Taoist religion, which has paid special attention to the unity of the human body and has thus led to the development of a refined cuisine and a pharmacopoeia of herbs, dedicated to a fulfillment of balance in human nature.

The Chinese are thought to be "situation-oriented," which makes them seem practical and shrewd. But it is more accurate to say that they take every event related to a situation and view it in relation to the total. They perceive much, talk much and quickly, and keep busy. In a group of more than three people, there are simultaneous conversations, with no regard about interference or interruption. Indeed, for them relations can not be disturbed by "interruptions." It is not necessary to talk only in a one-to-one relation with grammatically complete sentences. In get-togethers, as in restaurants, they are noisy and appear to be cheerful. Topics are random and there is no differentiation of people by status. Service men shout ordered menus to back kitchens. Nobody is disturbed by the noise; it is enjoyed as part of the context. Many matters are discussed without systematic argument, but rather with lively imagination. Chinese in restaurants look cheerful and "oral," involved in the totality of the situation.

For the Chinese, grasping of a total situation is of supreme importance. It makes them capable of adaptation to the most alien of circumstances. Chinese overseas as well as visiting scholars and students all appear to manifest such characteristics. Looking around, seeking human communication, utilizing resources of any kind, they quickly find a way to adapt safely and harmoniously in their totally new circumstance. Many of them are quickly successful. In other words, they do not wait for logical exposition, but they begin immediately to place events into a holistic frame of reference. They tend to grasp any situation as a part of a whole, although in their thought and speech they may seem to be trying mainly to grasp the meaning of a particular situation. Along with Prof. Edward Weinstein, formerly of the Walter Reed Army Institute and the Washington School of Psychiatry, I planned comparative research on the verbal behavior of hysterical patients. We intended to see how a patient expressed violence verbally during a single interview, hypothesizing that the gross hysterical symptoms are pathological symbols of aggression. Professor Weinstein and his colleague found in my first two patient interviews that any detailed comparative analysis involving word counts, parts of speech, etc., could not be carried out, because of the differences in language usage. Not only the psychiatric patients but normal Chinese speak generally in a fragmented style—that is, with many extraneous words inserted into their sentences, with words repeated to attach specific feelings to the whole speech, and with sentences often left without closure. One cannot interpret this style of thought and speech as necessarily pathological. As linguists have noted, the style of the flow of speech cannot be analyzed without taking into account the non-verbalized framework which is a shared part of a total meaning of communication.

In summary, identity is the sharing of traditions and feelings. Those who think, feel, and behave in a similar way gather together and form a social group. One who shares the above-described tradition and view of the self in the world appears to others to be "Chinese," and one who does not share the tradition does not appear to be a Chinese.

THE CHINESE OVERSEAS

Waves of Chinese culture have spread out into surrounding countries from dynasty to dynasty. Tides of Chinese emigration sometimes carried their participants into the Pacific islands or into Southeast Asia. However, it is impossible to know to what extent Chinese have mixed with surrounding races in the course of history. The name "overseas Chinese" was given to those who emigrated, mainly to Southeast Asia, but also in smaller numbers to Japan, the United States and many other countries in more recent times. The migration of the Chinese from Southern China to Southeast Asia started in the fourteenth century, and occurred most intensely during the past two centuries. The migration occurred primarily for economic reasons—the Chinese provided the labor force which the colonialists of Southeast Asia needed for the cultivation of new lands. In time, those Chinese gradually became economically autonomous and congregated into unique residential colonies known as "Chinatowns." During the past half century, another group of Chinese went abroad, consisting of students or scholars, who settled mainly in the United States, Europe, and Japan. I think it is appropriate to discuss in detail these two groups of overseas Chinese in the context of ethnic identity, because they are so different with respect to the motive for migration, status prior to migration, and ways of adjustment to an alien environment. I shall rely mainly on Kawabe's *Southeast Asia* (4) in discussing those who have emigrated for economic reasons and shall present my own observations about overseas Chinese students.

A large number of Southern Chinese went to the Southeast for work. Though they left their wives and children at home and did not wish to lose contact with China, they became reluctant to return to China and to give up property they had gained through hard work. As a result, many built new homes in the Southeast, and came to have two families, one in China and the other in Southeast Asia. This style of life is called *lian-tou chia.* Some emigrants brought their families from China upon achievement of success in business. Some sent money back to their families remaining in China, where post offices dealing with such remittances had been developed. Before long, as they were neglected by the governments in both sites, some became people without citizenship. So-called *pang* groups were established as protective societies by those who remained in Southeast Asia to maintain cooperation among themselves. Examples of *pang* were the native organizations (*shian-pang*) in Fukien, Tsaochow and Canton. The Hakka, a separate caste-like group, had their own *pang.* These organizations contributed to the construction of association buildings, public cemetaries (*vi-tsuo*), schools and hospitals. Another kind of *pang* was an occupational organization called *yieh-pang,* which promoted business cooperation. In their "Chinatowns" temples were built and folk religious objects were brought in from China. Together with native folk beliefs, there were the beliefs of Confucianism, Buddhism and Taoism which comprised the religious life of overseas Chinese society. They continued to speak their original languages and maintain their own culture and cohesiveness, living in several Southeast Asian countries as alien minority groups. In the chaotic days of the last Chin dynasty, during the population expansion, numerous peasants of Southern China sold their petty lands and went south. Western colonialists in Southeast Asia welcomed them, for they constituted a more efficiently utilizable labor force than the natives of the area. In addition, Dutch merchantmen and pirate vessels sailed the coast of Southern China and captured peasants in order to use them as slaves. The impotent Chin Government warned people to evacuate the coastal areas to 30 miles inland, and abandoned those who refused to move, giving them the name *tien-tsao chi-ming.* Chinese emigration continued until 1930. Since the outbreak of World War II there have been no more mass migrations. With the birth of new independent countries in Southeast Asia and as a result also of stringent regulations about immigration, Chinese migration has been terminated altogether.

From 1910 on, nationalist movements developed among overseas Chinese, stimulated by the birth of the new Republic of China. The glory of a new China became a source of pride to overseas Chinese, who sought to share their prosperity with their mother country. Meanwhile, the Nationalist Government of China established the Committee of Overseas Chinese. This organization registered overseas Chinese who once were the *chi-ming* (abandoned people) at Chinese consular offices and clarified their status as overseas citizens. With the revival of Chinese culture, many overseas Chinese schools were opened in order to encourage the younger generation overseas to learn Mandarin.

The colonial societies of Southeast Asia were characterized by ethnic pluralism. An overseas Chinese society was an economic and social layer between the dominant imperialist white society and the native societies. The Chinese became mediators between the two other cultural groups which co-existed, but lacked any real communication. In this way the status of the Chinese as an intermediate group of traders became firmly established, and they soon controlled national economies. Such gains greatly encouraged the Chinese to maintain their own cultural identity. In so doing, however, they could not avoid racial and economic conflicts with native societies with which they, too, lacked communication. These conflicts did not become overt until the period before World War II, when the white strata put more emphasis on the three-tiered social structure for their own purposes of control.

The start of Sarikat Islam in Indonesia in 1929 was the first nationalistic movement which attacked the economic position of the overseas Chinese. Suppression of overseas Chinese reached a peak under the government of Thailand between 1938 and 1944. In 1941, Thailand became the first country to restrict the occupations open to Chinese. Many other countries developed similar regulations after World War II in order to encourage the economic advancement of the native populations. The most recent example is the double nationality problem in Indonesia. According to Chinese law, children of Chinese parents retain their fathers' nationality, thus remaining Chinese even when overseas. However, most countries in Southeast Asia adopted laws regarding the native-born as citizens. Therefore, the native-born Chinese in those particular countries automatically received double citizenship. In 1955, the Indonesian Government allowed the Chinese to choose one of their two nationalities, with the result that 70 percent of them chose Indonesian citizenship. The Chinese reacted to this political and economic suppression by investing their capital in foreign countries, or by assimilating into and cooperating with their adopted country, or by withdrawing. The majority of them chose assimilation, deciding to reside in their adopted countries permanently.

The Chinese concept of "providentialism" and of *mei fa tzu* ("couldn't help it") helped the Chinese to find compromises and to develop a practical wisdom in resolving difficulties encountered. With increasing political pressure, they bought citizenship, or took advantage of their native wives' names for registering property, or transferred property to their native-born children. There was no pressure on these Chinese descendants, because the law applied only to the property of Chinese who retained a foreigner's status in the country. The Chinese also cooperated with government officials, and shared their economic resources, knowledge and experience with the leaders of the new countries, which badly needed financial and technological aid. Nevertheless, tension inevitably developed between the Chinese and the native people. Thus, suppression and assimilation, restriction and integration are all interwoven in the complexity of the present overseas Chinese society. In spite of such changes, the Chinese still tend to adhere to their traditional culture and to maintain their pride in being Chinese. Many of them are fond of using the two words, *ta-t'ung* ("one-world") and *tsuang-tong* ("tradition"). They try to assimilate themselves to the present environment but never forget the traditional spirit of their own culture. Aided by such an outlook on the part of the Chinese, some Southeast Asian societies have been moving toward the integration of different ethnic groups and cultures.

Reviewing the psycho-cultural adjustment of the farflung groups of overseas Chinese is not a simple task and I cannot deny the speculative nature of the following discussion. In it I shall focus on the psychic mechanism of "double identity." Those factors which encouraged the maintenance overseas of Chinese tradition seem to be as follows: 1) a strong economical and psychological interdependence among kin and fellow Chinese; 2) ethnic identity and nostalgia for their homeland and cultural tradition; and 3) fundamental pride in being Chinese and in having a history. The overseas Chinese learned to ameliorate difficult situations with their skills in social strategy and through the utilization of financial resources, since, with the rise of Southeast Asian nationalism, double nationality became problematic for many Chinese.

Working out a double ethnic identity takes several generations. I assume its outcome shall largely be determined by the degree and type of integration between the Chinese and the indigenous populations. A double identity or ethnicity involves assimilating a given dominant cultural milieu into one's self. One becomes an Indonesian or a Malaysian, but one simultaneously remains Chinese deep down. Of course, the change of ethnic identity is affected by the exertion of political force, by the extent to which a given culture is capable of assimilating a Chinese population, by the difference in number between Chinese and native populations, and by the number of first-generation Chinese migrants (with their strong ties to the motherland) who are still alive. For the Chinese, the possibility of a hyphenated identity may effectively increase their willingness to change their ethnic identity.

Over 100 years ago, a merchant named Wang from central China went to a business center in Japan. Through four generations, fathers of the family, who had all married Japanese women, retained their Chinese nationality and their Chinese family name. They taught Mandarin to their children, though all attended formal Japanese schools. The subject of this case history was the eldest daughter of the fourth generation. As a schoolgirl she was terribly frustrated for having a Chinese name at the outbreak of the Sino-Japanese War and later of World War II. She was badly treated by other Japanese girls in school and called bad names. Ignorant of her mother country, China, she developed a strong hostility toward her father, who firmly insisted on retaining the Chinese family name and nationality. Her father praised her younger brother who obediently learned Mandarin at home. Several marriage arrangements were broken because of her family name. Finally a matchmaker introduced a Taiwanese boy who was also disappointed in a love affair with a Japanese girl, whose parents strongly objected to their marriage. The boy, Yang, a university graduate with Japanese citizenship and Chinese blood, was considered a most suitable marriage partner. The couple were married and moved to Taiwan after World War II. The young wife found it completely different from the Japanese culture to which she was accustomed and became confused. Although Yang's relatives were kind to her, she soon suffered from a serious breakdown. Fifteen years later, when the family migrated to Japan she recovered her sanity. There, she seemed to cope adequately with some Chinese patterns of life, including fluency in more than one Chinese dialect. With her knowledge of both Chinese and Japanese cultures, she seemed to be able to tolerate in Japan (but not in China) the co-existence of Chinese and Japanese identities within herself. She was happy to join her Chinese relatives in Japan and often visits other overseas Chinese families there. In this case history, some significant mechanisms of a double ethnic identity are visible. Fathers in the Wang family were firmly loyal to their ancestors and to China, and felt obliged to maintain the core lineage identity of the Chinese through several generations. Mrs. Yang's marriage arrangement resulted, however, in her exposure to a real rather than an idealized Chinese culture. She could not be totally Chinese: the resulting strain was intolerable. Returning to Japan she found adjustment possible by maintaining a double ethnic identity.

Scholars comprise a second type of overseas Chinese. Young, able college graduates have gone abroad, mostly to the United States, "with a dream of chance and prosperity." Few expect when they leave home that they will not return. Many, however, do not, for they find permanent foreign residence has become attractive. I lived once close to a friend of mine who was a successful professor in the United States. He and his family were happy in terms of his career, social relations, economic status and family life. Apparently his feelings of obligation toward his former colleagues and his job in Taiwan had weakened over a period of fifteen years. He is a typical scholar with a "double ethnic identity." He felt extremely guilty, however, about not seeing his old mother at home, knowing he would probably never see her again.

The Department of Psychiatry at Wisconsin University and our Department of Psychiatry in Taipei have been conducting some joint research on the psychosocial adjustment in Chinese overseas students. Professor Milton Miller, then Chairman of the Department at Wisconsin, presented the case of a Chinese girl who arrived at a college in the United States to study history. In the beginning, she avoided other Chinese students or speaking Chinese, in order to improve her English by meeting more Americans. Initially, she seemed to have made a good adjustment in the new environment. When Thanksgiving day came and she was invited to dinner by an American family she was happy and proud, since many other Chinese students had not been invited into American homes. The whole family accepted her warmly, and that night was her first experience in a happy atmosphere since she had left Taiwan. Before she parted, the mother of the family asked her not to hesitate to visit them and promised to call her up again soon. She waited for a telephone call from them day and night for weeks, but no call ever came. She gradually became disappointed and skeptical about American hospitality, and started to think that Americans were superficial, unkind, and untrustworthy. She became angry and depressed about this hypocritical attitude of Americans. A few months later she began to accept contacts with other Chinese students and joined their parties. Her initial attempt to penetrate the American culture had resulted in failure and now she attempted some readjustment. Many of the Chinese students had had similar experiences in their attempts to integrate into a foreign culture. After a period of time they often regress into their own group, taking comfort in a shared identity overseas. Chinese students are thus apt to build up a subculture group within the American society.

Practically all students who have been educated under the modern system in Taiwan finish their college courses and prepare English extensively before they go abroad. They are familiar with the modern style of life and social system. Nevertheless, they often retreat after direct cultural contact. The term "cultural regression" may be applied to this condition. This is clearly seen in their pattern of marriage, which occurs several years after their arrival to the States. For example, a brilliant young male Ph.D. candidate seemed quite different from most other shy Chinese students. He was active, drove a car, and had many American and foreign friends, including girlfriends from America, Europe and the Orient. He was successful in his career during the next ten years, and finally married a girl from Taiwan introduced to him by his parents. Another example is a girl who, when she arrived at a city in the United States, stayed in a dormitory and avoided any calls from Chinese students, intending to adapt herself to American life. Her pattern was similar to that of the first girl reported above. She studied hard, got a job and remained single for eight years. However, she then married her cousin, younger than she, who came to study in the city where she had long resided. Similar patterns of marriage have been common among the Chinese students overseas. They tend to marry native partners, forming "Chinese" families. They try to educate their children simultaneously in Chinese patterns and in American patterns. If they have a chance, they are eager to bring their children back to Taiwan in order for them to get acquainted with Chinese culture. But they still seek to maintain permanent residence in the United States.

Cultural regression is more severe when a person comes to an alien environment from a background of disturbed relations with his own group people. Pathological regression and compensation might lead him to a neurotic or psychotic breakdown. The following are two such cases. As an undergraduate college student, Mr. Chang went to the United States to study engineering. He resided in a dormitory where the majority of students were Americans. He felt inferior and was bothered by the different patterns of behavior observed in other students. He came to feel insecure, apprehensive and gradually began to experience a change in his sense of reality. He did not feel "real," looking at people and at what was happening around him. It never occurred to him to visit other Chinese. He depreciated himself, feeling that he was short and weak as compared with American students, and that his genital organ was shorter than those of other students he observed in the shower room. He felt that Americans were unkind and unfriendly. Paranoia appeared later, as he thought that many Americans were trying to harm him and kill him. He was terribly frightened with this idea and started to show agitation and even violent behavior. He was taken to a state hospital and soon was sent back to Taiwan via steamship. When it set sail at San Francisco, he saw the figure of Jesus up in the sky and imagined that Jesus came to protect him from American persecution. During the weeks on the boat his delusions and vivid hallucinations persisted. He then saw the figure of Buddha in the sky when the boat sailed close to Yokohama.

The second case is that of a college boy who is studying in Taipei as an overseas Chinese student. His family moved to Japan when he was a schoolboy. Introverted and shy as a child, he could not learn Japanese very rapidly. He kept silent most of the time at school, and though he studied hard, was unable to become friends with his Japanese classmates. Moreover, his personality developed inadequately, so that he often lost his temper at home. He hated his parents for many reasons. Once in his middle school days he attempted suicide by taking thirty sleeping pills after a bitter quarrel with his older brother. Although unsuccessful, he continued to be withdrawn. Once in Taipei, he began to feel there was no place he could belong. He did not dislike the world, but the world did not need him, he felt. Pessimistic and nihilistic, he denied his belief in any gods. He depreciated himself and became a depressed insomniac. Prior to his visit to the clinic, he wrote a will, leaving his residence with the idea of committing suicide.

I am fully aware of the fact that these few cases do not illustrate the whole range of adjustment of overseas Chinese, but I have attempted to report some examples of mental breakdown caused by a crisis of ethnic identity. For the average student, life in a new culture might engender tension and strain, feelings of isolation and loneliness, and sometimes hostile feeling. But maintaining relationships with their relatives, friends, and with their ethnic group can provide a safety device and a way of relaxation. Thus cultural regression can be a positive attempt to create a safe atmosphere so as to protect oneself from an identity crisis. Resuming one's ethnic identity becomes a significant way of responding to a situation demanding cultural adjustment. For people like the Chinese, who grow up in a culture in which human interdependence is the core value, the maintenance of ethnic identity assumes great importance, since it overcomes feelings of alienation. One of my friends once said on this point, "Blood calls blood, it is an unavoidable dynamic!"

THE CHINESE IN TAIWAN

The Chinese capacity to adapt differences into a larger, harmonious whole can also be illustrated by a discussion of the Chinese experience in Taiwan. The first migrants to Formosa were the Malayo-Polynesians from Southeast Asia, some 2,000 years ago. These seamen, who maintained their original cultural traditions, were scattered over the island. There is no record available as to how many distinct tribal groups existed, although some anthropologists think there were at least 24. With primitive or semi-primitive skills they cultivated the island.

The Chinese from South China were the second wave of immigrants, particularly from Fukien and later from north Canton in the seventeenth century. Chinese immigration intensified after Tseng Cheng-kong drove the Dutch from the southern part of the island in 1661. The majority of the Chinese, the Fukienese, were called *Holo.* The minority group from Canton were called *Kelan* (Hakka). They resided on hillsides and maintained subordinate status. One record reported that the Cantonese were considered "rough" in the eyes of the other Chinese. Frequent battles were fought between the aborigines and the Chinese. Besides the aboriginal Ami on the east coast and the Yami on Orchid Island directly eastward, nine other aboriginal groups remain in the mountain districts, where historians believe they retreated under Chinese pressure. This is not likely, in my opinion. They are so well settled in their present location that it is hard to believe their present villages have been established only over a few hundred years. Besides these aboriginal tribes, there are minority groups called *Pin-pu* who reside on six hillside areas, with a few hundred people in each settlement. They are hardly distinguishable from the Chinese of the plains, but retain some minor local characteristics of an aboriginal nature. Many aboriginal tribal groups living on the plains must have been absorbed by the Chinese, and probably a few were exterminated, although we have no accurate historical record. We do know that the Chinese assimilated some of the aborigines. On the other hand, *Pin-pu,* which have remained solitary groups, have also largely adopted Chinese culture, and are gradually disappearing. There are now only nine large tribal groups left, protected by their geographical locations. They are called *hwanna* ("savage") by the Taiwanese.

At the end of the first Sino-Japanese War in 1895, Taiwan was ceded to Japan in the Treaty of Shimonoseki. Around 1920, at the beginning of modern commercial development, the population of Taiwan was about three million, including the majority of the *Holo,* about 17 percent of *Hakkas,* and about 200,000 aborigines. During the Japanese occupation aborigines were put in mountain reservations, where trained policemen were sent up to "educate" them. Generally the Japanese segregated the Taiwanese from themselves. The officials classified people according to their ethnic origins for census registration. This continued until toward the end of World War II, when Japan began to try to strengthen the position of Taiwan in Southeast Asia under the slogan "Greater East-Asian mutual prosperity sphere." Starting around 1920, many youngsters from well-to-do Taiwanese families went to Japan to study in high schools and colleges. The number of Taiwanese students in Japan numbered about 30,000 in 1945. Hundreds of those students worked in Japan and married Japanese women, although very few Taiwanese women married Japanese men. College education was also promoted in Taiwan. In spite of Japanese technological developments, the Taiwanese maintained their Chinese tradition. Naturally, some people developed a double ethnic identity, even though many Taiwanese referred to Japanese as "dogs" and to Japanized Taiwanese as "three legs."

After World War II, a third large wave of immigration occurred in Taiwan. About two million mainland Chinese were added to the seven million Taiwanese. After several years of chaos, Taiwan entered a period of rapid modernization and population growth. Symbols of subethnic diversity gradually faded, especially by 1955, and intermarriage between mainland men, who had come without families, and Taiwanese women rapidly increased. Marrying a mainland man was a way to avoid the traditional mother versus daughter-in-law conflict, which is common among Taiwanese families. There are no ethnic contrasts now between *Holo* and *Hakka*, though previously they maintained quite different patterns of family life. In the latter, women worked on the farm and took a greater role in the livelihood than those of the former. Intermarriage between these two groups was difficult. With the present pattern of large-scale intermarriage, the whole population in Taiwan is rapidly moving toward a general Chinese identity.

The Chinese word for "everybody" is *ta-chia,* which means "a great house." When the Chinese get in trouble with each other, they would say *i-chia-jen ma!* ("we are the one-house people!") and try to reach a compromise. After the war, aborigines were no longer called savages, but named *shan-ti t'ung-pao* ("mountain sibs"). A home or family is the fundamental unit to which the Chinese feel close ties, but they identify their country and society with home, and identify their countrymen with family members. Actually, the Chinese pay little attention to the existence of minority groups. They are now trying to integrate many groups into one, so they tend not to make anthropological analyses of the minorities, although the aborigines' costumes and dances are exhibited in public. Many schoolchildren sing and dance in aboriginal styles in television performances. Thus are the romanticized aboriginal minorities incorporated in a general present-day Chinese culture.

A tribal chief of Saisiat, the smallest aborigine group in Taiwan living on the northwest hillside of the island invited me once to a tribal ceremony. The chief told me with dignity that, according to tribal legend, the Saisiat once lived in the plains, so they therefore must once have been a branch of the now prestigious and dominant Chinese. Linguistically and culturally, however, they seem to belong to Malayo-Polynesian stock, despite the chief's attempt to create a mythical origin uniting his tribe with the Chinese. We can assume that under the pressure of the Chinese population, the Saisiat retreated from the plains. Ironically, the ancestors of the tribal chief might well have decided to relocate their people to the present area in order to maintain their separate culture and tradition.

The Atayal are residents of the northern mountain range, with a population of about 50,000. This tribe has been investigated intensively by anthropologists and thus is rather well known. The tribe is divided into three subgroups, with slight differences in language and culture. In the past these tribesmen, with their practice of head hunting, were threats to people of other villages, and also to the Chinese on the plains. In spite of inter-village and inter-tribal tensions, all the Atayal believe in their common descent from ancestors born on the top of *ta-pa-chien-shan,* a mountain in the northwest. This is a case of the usage of uniqueness of tribal genesis to enlarge ethnic identity beyond the village level.

In the summer of 1953, our research team stayed in a village of Ami in a narrow east-coast valley of the island. The Ami are the only aboriginal tribe to remain on the plain and reach a high level of culture, including skill in planting rice. During the time of our research, a cultural clash was beginning to occur between the native Ami and the increasing number of Taiwanese immigrating into this area. Under Taiwanese economic pressure, many Amis lost their rice fields to pay off loans made at high rates of interest. Ami men were quickly absorbed into factories in the city, among a majority of Taiwanese. We observed Ami cases of alcoholic and delinquent behavior arising from this situation of conflict (*7, 8*). Two cases of catatonic schizophrenic male patients revealed the stress of an ethnic identity crisis. One had been educated in a Japanese middle school and became a Chinese herb doctor, but after the war he was rejected by both the Chinese and the aborigines. He was regarded as a Taiwanese by the native village people and was treated as an Ami by the neighbor Taiwanese. After his mental breakdown, Ami people refused to live next to his family. An old Ami woman sprayed salt on him to drive him away. He was treated like a devil in the village and lived in a separate cottage built in a corner of a yard. His mixed identity was not accepted by the surrounding people. He became completely confused and acted out his violence.

Another case was that of a man who worked in a city factory. Feeling that he was being rejected by regular Taiwanese, he began to drink. He was born in a family of mixed Taiwanese blood. He was regarded neither as a village man, nor as a Taiwanese. Acute violent behavior accompanied his mental breakdown. Ten years later, when I visited the village again, I was surprised to see that there was no longer a separate Ami community; the Chinese and Ami were now living together peacefully, ignoring their different origins.

Aborigines are still confined to the mountain reservations in order to protect them from economic exploitation. Other aborigines live in mixed villages and in cities. By now little stigma is attached to them by the majority. Educational and technological backwardness, however, have continuously created hardships for them, hampering their adjustments to rapid social change, although schools, missions, and Christian hospitals have provided continuous support. "Mountain people halls" in large cities also provide free rooms for those who come up to seek jobs. Their magico-religious pattern of belief has been largely transformed by Christian missionaries. In some villages more than three-quarters of the population have converted to Christianity, including the majority of the younger generation, particularly females. This is noticeably different from the Chinese, among whom less than 10 percent have converted to Christianity during the past century. Intermarriage between aborigine women and mainlander men has become common. In sum, the assimilation of minorities into Chinese culture in Taiwan is taking place at a more rapid rate now than at any time in the past three centuries.

CONCLUSION

I have described the synthesizing habits of thought of the Chinese, habits which have constituted their philosophy of life, nurtured throughout their long history. These attitudes have contributed to the maintenance of their ethnic identity, provided a tolerance for a double identity living in foreign cultures, and eased the acceptance of minority ethnic enclaves within Chinese territory. Our rapidly changing world, however, is having considerable effect on family life. In the majority of modern families, differential roles by sex and sibling position receive less emphasis, while parental values now stress self-direction rather than passive obedience of parental commands. Western patterns of aesthetic values also exert tremendous influence. But access to a modern style of life does not mean the abandonment of a traditional value system, for tradition continues to provide a secure feeling of belonging (*6, 1*). The current resurgence of interest in the Chinese heritage can strengthen one's sense of being Chinese without conflicting with modern science and technology. This is an example of the synthesizing capacity of the Chinese.

Thought and behavior patterns of Chinese overseas students represent interesting examples of psychocultural adjustment. I think that the Chinese have a remarkable capacity to incorporate other cultural components into the self and to formulate a double identity, all the while maintaining a deep sense of being Chinese. From the beginning of contact with a new culture, many Chinese students perceive an active penetration into that culture as an important achievement. Most of the overseas Chinese students are multilingual, but fluency in a foreign language can be a measure of level of regression. There are certainly varieties of cultural adjustment and details of ethnic identity that need much further investigation. It is my hope that more discussion of ethnic identity will contribute to international and intercultural understanding.

REFERENCES

1. Chance, N. A.; Rin, H.; and Chu, H. M. "Modernization, Value Identification, and Mental Health: A Cross-Cultural Study." *Anthropologica.* 8:197-216, 1966.
2. Fei, H. "Peasantry and Gentry: An Interpretation of Chinese Social Structure and Its Changes." In *Social Structure and Personality,* edited by Y. A. Cohen. New York: Holt, Rinehart and Winston, 1961.
3. Hu, S. "The Scientific Spirit and Method in Chinese Philosophy." In *The Chinese Mind,* edited by C. A. Moore. Honolulu: East-West Center Press, 1967.
4. Kawabe, T. *Southeast Asia.* World History, Vol. 18. Tokyo: Kawaide Syobō, 1969.
5. Moore, C. A. "The Humanistic Chinese Mind." *The Chinese Mind,* edited by C. A. Moore. Honolulu: East-West Center Press, 1967.
6. Rin, H.; Chu, H. M.; and Lin, T. "Psychophysiological Reactions of a Rural and Suburban Population in Taiwan." *Acta Psychiatrica Scandinavica.* 42:410-473, 1966.
7. Rin, H. "An Investigation into the Incidence and Clinical Symptoms of Mental Disorders Among Formosan Aborigines." *Psychiatria et Neurologia Japonica.* 63:480-500, 1961.
8. Rin, H. "The Alcoholism Problem in Nan-shih Ami People." *Studia Taiwanica.* 2:7-16, 1957.

English Identity Over Time and Empire

GEOFFREY GORER

6

The word "English" rather than "British" in the title outlines the scope of my presentation for, although I have acquired some knowledge of English character through four surveys in the last twenty years (*3, 4, 5, 6*), my knowledge of the Scots is slight and my knowledge of the Welsh and Irish is practically non-existent. In this I think I am a typical Englishman. Indeed, the main argument in this paper is that English identity depends on the relationship with other Englishmen almost exclusively. The relevance of the non-English to English identity is minimal for most of the population, except for the fear of being "swamped" (a point I will take up later). It appears to me, on the other hand, that the Scots, Welsh or Irish sense of identity depends on the presence of the English for self-definition: one is Scots, Welsh, or Irish to the extent that one differs from the English. If the English did not provide this point of reference, the monolingual, English-speaking members of these groups would find great difficulty in identifying themselves. The converse is not true.

I am no historian, but my desultory reading suggests that this self-sufficient aspect of English identity has been dominant since at least the seventeenth century and is well illustrated in many of Shakespeare's histories. In the nineteenth century, after the industrial revolution, English society became much more complex, and the number of internal points of reference increased. But psychologically, England has remained an island:

> "This royal throne of kings, this scepter'd isle,
> . . .
> This fortress built by Nature for herself
> Against infection and the hand of war;
> This happy breed of men, this little world,
> This precious stone set in the silver sea.
> . . .
> This blessed plot, this earth, this realm, this England
> . . . ."
> (Shakespeare: *King Richard II,* Act II)

There have been three frames of reference during most of English history by which an Englishman could place himself in reference to other Englishmen: region, creed and social class. Membership in one of the political parties has been and largely still is determined by one or more of the above frames of reference. Consequently, membership in a political party is a primary frame of reference only for a statistically insignificant minority.

The regions appear to have been the dominant frame of reference during the dynastic wars (the Wars of the Roses) in the fourteenth and fifteenth centuries, and they appear to have played some role in the revolution of the seventeenth century. But since that date their importance as a primary frame of reference has continually diminished. In many ways this is a world-wide phenomenon, if one defines a region as a geographical section of a nation-state which does not differ from the rest of the state in language or dominant creed. Where regions are separated from the rest of the state by language, not merely dialect (as for example, Wales, parts of western Scotland, French-speaking Canada), or by the predominance of a different religious creed (again French-speaking Canada, Northern Ireland), there is a contemporary tendency for such regions to insist on difference and to demand more independence. This is not, however, a phenomenon of contemporary England, even though the rural dialects of some of the regions are mutually incomprehensible, and there is some concentration of Roman Catholics in the Northwest and of Methodists in the Northeast.

Regional identity is apparently strongly maintained in areas where the majority of the population are engaged in agriculture and its ancillary trades and live in small villages. As is well known, England has the smallest proportion of its population engaged in agriculture of any advanced society, and, with the possible exception of Belgium and Holland and Japan, the highest proportion of its population living in cities or "conurbations."

Maintenance of regional identity is also facilitated by poor communications between the regions. Although today we rank well below many other nations with respect to miles of road constructed, in the nineteenth century the English railroad system was incomparable in relation to the area involved. Certainly the railways did much to diminish the sense of regional identity, with the result that today the sense of regional identity is strongest in the sparsely populated areas where it did not pay even the most ardent speculators to build railways, and those which are furthest from London.

As far as my investigations go regional identity is important for about a third of the English population to the extent that a person from these regions who is living outside his home region will feel he is living among strangers (and possibly enemies) and will bring his regional origin into any initial conversation with a strange Englishman. (For an excellent discussion of English regional differences, see Allen [*1*].) These emotionally important regions and the approximate percent of the population residing in them (*6*) are: North (Northumberland, Cumberland, Westmoreland), 6%; Yorkshire, 11%; Northwest (Lancashire and adjoining counties), 13%; Southwest (Somerset, Devon, Cornwall), 8%; and East Anglia (Norfolk, Lincoln, Suffolk, Cambridgeshire), 4%. The remaining 58% of the population live in and around the major conurbations of London and Birmingham, though for purposes of surveys both these areas are subdivided (West Midlands 14%; Southeast Midlands 8%; Greater London 17%; Southeast excepting Great London 19%). But except for the diminishing claim to be a cockney on the part of some working class people born and bred in limited areas of central London ("within sound of Bow Bells"), these densely inhabited areas do not appear to be a source of regional identification.

The five regions listed above each have distinctive dialects which most of the younger people and those adults working in factories, business or the professions can employ as seems opportune. Many of the older people, however, especially those who have worked in agriculture, cannot switch to standard English and are often more or less incomprehensible outside a small area. Although the regions also tend to have varying preferences in food ("regional specialities") and differ to a certain extent in the composition and timing of the meals of the day, I do not think these variations in eating habits are psychologically significant.

All five regions are, or were, distinguished by one or more types of industry or occupation: agriculture in the Southwest and East Anglia, cotton spinning and weaving in the Northwest, wool spinning, weaving and fishing in Yorkshire, coal-mining in Yorkshire and the North.

Occupations may have a connection with the differing psychological characteristics which the members of the different regions believe distinguish them from the rest of the English population. Thus, the fact that cotton--spinning and weaving in the Northwest depend very heavily on feminine skills may have a connection with the region's view of itself as exceptionally warm, friendly and neighborly. Compared with the rest of the English population people in this area tend to stress the importance of the mother in the home and equality between the sexes. It is also the area with the highest concentration of Roman Catholics, largely immigrants from Ireland or their descendants, and is the only area in England where Mariolatry is obvious to the visitor.

The Yorkshireman and the "Geordies" (men from Northumberland) consider themselves dour, hard-headed, and realistic. The occupations of the region, coal mining (*2*) and shipping and trawler fishing, depend on the traditional masculine virtues of strength, courage, endurance and self-reliance. The inhabitants of these regions tend to assume that these virtues have been transmitted to all inhabitants, whatever their sex or employment. In 1950 (*3*) this was the region which most stressed paternal authority in the home; in a metaphorical way, Yorkshiremen are liable to claim greater "masculinity" than other inhabitants of England.

The inhabitants of the two agricultural regions, the Southwest and East Anglia, tend to consider themselves more down-to-earth than the rest of the population, and more truly English. The most urban nation in the contemporary world dreams of itself as really rural ("There'll always be an England while there's a country lane . . .") and so the agricultural minority is "really" representative. John Bull was (or might have been) an East Anglian, Sir Walter Raleigh (and many others) a Devon man. The inhabitants of these regions tend to be blond and tall, (perhaps Saxon or Viking in ancestry) whereas most Englishmen are dark and short. But the "typical Englishman" is, I think, still envisioned as physically tall and fair-haired.

Although these rural areas tend to have high proportions of illegitimate births and of violent quarrels, I do not think either of these statistics play much role in the regional self-image. Perhaps the high percentage of unmarried mothers is an aspect of the down-to-earth quality on which they tend to pride themselves.

It seems possible that the relative unimportance of regional identity for the mass of the English population is connected with the relative lack of geographical mobility among the English; for I presume that regional identity becomes noticeable when one is constantly in contact with people from other regions. In a survey last year of a random sample of 2,000 people in England between the ages of 16 and 45 (*6*), 52% of the sample (59% of the men and 46% of the women) had grown up in the area where they worked and were questioned. Another 16% (13% of the men and 18% of the women) had grown up in the same region. Only 28% of the population (24% of the men and 31% of the women) who were English-born were working and living in a region to which they were not native. The higher proportion of women in this mobile group were presumably wives who had moved to their husbands' region at marriage. Nine percent of the sample interviewed were not English born, though most of them came from other parts of Britain and Eire.

Like regionalism, formal adherence to a religious creed or sect provides a frame of reference for self-identity only for a minority of the English. As I have mentioned, the concentration of practicing Roman Catholics is in the Northwest, while Methodists are mainly found in the Northeast and East. But in the country as a whole, only 12% of the population are regular in their church observances (*6*), and 37% of those who claim a religious denomination never enter a place of worship at all, or only for weddings and funerals. Twenty-three percent of the total of the young population interviewed disclaimed an adherence to any creed, amounting to 35% of those aged 16–20, 28% of those aged 21–24, 25% of those aged 25–34, and 18% of those aged 35–45. I do not think that this age-change in the rejection of religion reflects a change in baptismal experience. Rather, the young are rejecting the formal "C. of E." form-filling convention which their elders still maintain (possibly a carry-over from national service days, when "no religion" was not acceptable on military forms). Outside the regions, active adherence to a religious sect would seem to place the observant in a minority coterie, rather than providing a frame of reference for self-identity among the majority of unbelieving or unpracticing English.

In contrast to the minimal employment of region or religious belief as a frame of reference for self-identity, social class is an almost universal frame of reference for the English. A seven-category social class system—upper class, upper middle class, middle class, lower middle class, upper (or skilled) working class, working class, lower working class—is still valid today as a nationwide frame of reference. In the most recent survey, from which I have been quoting, fewer than fifty individuals (about 2%) refused to place themselves in a seven-class system. The proportion is slightly higher in two surveys dating from 1950 (*3*), but in that and in the intermediate surveys well over 90% of the English-born population had no hesitation in placing themselves in this seven-class system. And the refusal to place oneself in such a system is not based predominantly on uncertainty, but on conflicting ideological commitments. A small number of men (as far as I have observed this is an almost exclusively masculine response) who wish to reject the contemporary organization of English society state, in various formulations, that social class is "inappropriate" in contemporary society, that it is a feature of "the traditional society" which is a dead weight round the neck of progress, and so on; but these are purely ideological statements, and neither the people using them nor their fellow-English would have any doubt in the vast majority of cases of the social class these people belong to.

Another small group of middle and upper class men put themselves in the working class as a form of political statement. For them the working class has a positive connotation, while the bourgeoisie has a negative one. For a well-born, highly educated man to describe himself as working class is an apotropaic device.

A few orphaned and unmarried or widowed women are genuinely uncertain about their class position. Traditionally, and to a considerable extent today, a woman acquired her class position from her father and changed to that of her husband at marriage. The term *declassée* is a literal description of a woman who has married into a lower social class than that into which she was born. But if a woman has neither father nor husband, what is she? Her occupation, if she has one, may provide a secondary frame of reference; but although many correlations exist between social class and occupation, it is only one of the determinants.

(It may be remarked that the Registrar General's sex-partite system of social classification, which is used in nearly all English surveys, both official and unofficial, is based entirely on occupation for men, or occupation of the head of the household for women who are not living alone. This makes for many anomalies: any farmer, no matter how small his acreage or how little his education, is classified "professional and managerial;" any agricultural manager (bailiff), no matter how great his qualifications, nor how high his salary, is classified either C1 or C2 "skilled non-manual" or "skilled manual;" and so on. It is worth noting that both by the Registrar General's classification and by self-classification, there are considerably more women than men in the "middle class" categories.)

As portrayed in the turn of the century comedies of Ben Jonson, Beaumont and Fletcher and others, English society was then divided into three basic classes: the land-owning aristocracy, who may or may not have been titled; a middle class of merchants and tradesmen who owned their own property and their "means of production;" and a working class which in the towns was completely without property or in the country owned too little land to provide a family living without also hiring out their labour. Informal contact between the classes was relatively slight.

The aristocracy and landed gentry were and have remained well under one percent of the population. Their overt power has declined considerably in the last century, as has their wealth, with some individual exceptions, as other sources of wealth have in part replaced landownership. Large landowners have been a predominantly, but never entirely, endogamous group.

During the eighteenth century, the middle class was apparently subdivided into upper middle, middle and lower middle, partly on the grounds of education and occupation, partly on kinship. The differing manners, vocabulary and attitudes of the subdivisions of the middle class are one of the major sources of comedy in the novels of Jane Austen, Frances Burney and many other authors (predominantly women) of the end of the eighteenth and beginning of the nineteenth centuries. It is perhaps worth noting that these authors never, to the best of my knowledge, use the terms "upper middle" or "lower middle" class; characters are either "ladies and gentlemen" (upper middle), "in trade" (middle) or "clerical" (lower middle); the authors write as ladies, and their heroines belong to this class.

During the nineteenth century the working class was similarly subdivided into "upper working" or "skilled working," working class without modification, and "lower working," which class-position is never so described by members of this class. A considerable number of periphrases—such as "very modest," "very ordinary"—take its place. The claim to "upper working" or "skilled working" status is based either on prolonged apprenticeship or on representational activities; "lower working class" is accepted in the absence of technical skills, other than agricultural, or permanent employment.

For the vast majority of English men and women their membership in a social class is the most important component of their sense of social identity; it determines with which other English people they feel at ease or uncomfortable, as well as their vocabulary and (to a lesser extent) phonemes, their preferences in food, drink and meals, many of their values and political attitudes and their choices of entertainment. The only major aspect of their social personality which class membership no longer determines is dress. Until 1914, without exception, and until 1939, with some exceptions, an English citizen could place another English person at first glance by his clothes. This aspect of class discrimination has practically disappeared. Today one has to wait for a person to speak before class-identification is certain.

I should like to stress that self-identification by class depends on the real or fantasied presence of members of the other English classes; one is placing oneself in a nationwide schema. But English self-identity does not demand *more* than the real or fantasied presence of the other English social classes; people outside this framework are either irrelevant or a menace.

In contemporary England the proportions of the different classes are approximately as follows: upper and upper middle class, 2%; middle class, 25%; lower middle class, 8%; upper and skilled working class, 13%; working class, 50%; lower working class, 2%. In different surveys the percentages of the smaller classes vary somewhat, but there is fairly general agreement that a quarter of the population consider themselves middle class without modification, and half the population working class without modification. The proportions of the two intermediate classes (lower middle and upper or skilled working) are less certain. This is to some extent an artefact of changing technology: a bank clerk or shorthand typist will probably consider him or herself lower middle class, a keypunch operator skilled working class.

Traditionally, there was a very close correlation between occupations and positions, within the middle class. The only occupations that members of the upper middle class, the gentlemen, could engage in without destroying their class position were the professions: the armed services and government above all, and also medicine and the law. A gentleman (gentleman farmers apart) could have nothing to do with buying and selling—to be "in trade" was to be inexorably middle class and, at least up to 1914, to be unacceptable at court. The lower middle class were predominantly clerical, "white collar workers," and could not manufacture anything with their hands nor gain their living from their physical strength or skills.

The division within the working class between the skilled and the unskilled, between those who gained their qualifications through an apprenticeship and membership in a guild (more recently a crafts trade union) and those without such qualifications is also long-standing and can be discovered in literature from the seventeenth century on. Since the technical qualifications are predominantly acquired by men, it is understandable that the claim for upper working or skilled working status is advanced much more by men than by women. The small and typically feckless lower working class corresponds to the Marxist *Lumpenproletariat.*

As far as the middle classes are concerned, the rigid demarcation lines of appropriate occupations have been considerably eroded in the last half century and particularly in the last twenty years. Today a gentleman can be "in business" and a doctor be middle class; but the boundaries between the classes, which are maintained more by women than men, would not seem to have been weakened to any appreciable extent. Women are the chief initiators of invitations for hospitality; one invites people with whom one will feel "at home" or "at ease;" and, social climbers apart, this means people of one's own class, as far as the English middle classes are concerned. Typically, the English working classes do not entertain formally in their homes, with the exception of parties after christenings, weddings and funerals, but companions for entertainment and amusements outside the home are chosen on the same basis of congeniality as among the middle classes.

With very few exceptions (chiefly in the entertainment world and "cafe society") the English choose their companions in informal situations within their own social class. But since a person's notion of his social class is only valid in relation to the other social classes, I argue that the English sense of ethnic identity depends on some mental construct of the whole class-system of English society, and further, that this mental construct of the class-system is all that is essential for English ethnic identity. Foreigners (and these include the Scots, Welsh and Irish) don't matter unless or until they threaten to undermine or destroy this system.

Politically, both internally and overseas, it is the ethos and values of the relatively small classes, the upper middle, lower middle and upper working, which are the most influential. The core classes—the middle class and the working class without qualifications—tend to follow the lead of these smaller and more highly motivated groups.

The middle class proper, without qualification, corresponds in many ways with the bourgeoisie of classical nineteenth century economists, both Marxist and non-Marxist. This group includes small and medium-sized traders and manufacturers, and until thirty years ago included even large stores and factories. In the last generation, however, the rewards of top management have become so great that the upper middle and upper classes no longer disdain such positions. In fact, the demands of innovative technology have occasionally opened such positions to outstandingly gifted men of working class origin. Certain professions, which demand not very extensive specialized training, are held to confer middle class status on those who were in a lower social class before their training started. These professions include accountants, solicitors (the consultative and negotiation lawyers, but not the advocates nor the interpreters of abstruse legal questions), and teachers in the state educational system. When employed by others, members of the middle class tend to be paid a monthly salary rather than a weekly wage.

Although those who achieve middle class status by training are obvious exceptions to the generalization, members of the middle class are expected to be property-owners, typically of their shop or factory and their dwelling, and to accumulate enough to pay fees for their children's education and to provide for their own retirement.

Until the last decade the schooling the middle class paid for was generally for a grammar school or a denominational school. Working class children, unless exceptionally gifted, went to secondary modern schools and upper middle class children, unless exceptionally stupid, to the very expensive boarding preparatory and "public" schools (rich middle class parents might send their sons to "public" schools in order to enable them to achieve upper middle class status). In the last decade there has been a major effort to merge grammar and secondary modern schools into a comprehensive system, and some ineffectual rhetorical attempts to change the class composition of the fee-paying "public" schools, in the interests of fairness and egalitarianism.

Many of the middle class feel their status threatened by these changes and quite a lot of resistance has been generated on a local level.

As in nearly all other countries at a similar level of technological development, the middle class tend to live in well-defined areas of the towns and, even more markedly, suburbs. The middle class is far more numerous in the two southern regions than in the rest of the country, although some seaside towns on the south coast (where the climate is believed to be more clement) have retired middle class people as the major component of their population.

The middle class are distinguished by vocabulary rather than by phonemes. Nancy Mitford and Professor Ross's (*8*) "U and non-U" lists are basically devices for distinguishing between upper middle class and middle class speakers, although one or two words or attitudes may apply only to the upper class (such as the rejection of fish-knives, on the hypothesis that the family had acquired all its plate before these useful articles were invented in the early nineteenth century). Most euphemisms and the names given to the evening meal and to the room in which people sit are very general indicators of middle class status.

The working class, without qualification, represents more than half the English population. They typically left school (secondary modern or comprehensive) at the earliest possible date, according to the changing laws, and are paid a weekly wage for semi-skilled or unskilled work. Nearly all live in rented accommodations which tend to be massed into working class districts. The working class are usually more easily distinguished by their accent (phonemes) than by their vocabulary, other than technical working terms. Traditionally, working class speech was more direct and less euphemistic than middle class speech, but today, especially in the southern regions, it is likely to be riddled with genteelisms. In parts of the North, especially in one-industry towns such as mining villages, one can still occasionally hear the second person singular, thee and thou.

Most members of the working class start their heterosexual lives shortly after puberty, much earlier than the members of other social classes. Since they tend to reject the use of birth-control techniques, marriages precipitated by unwanted pregnancies are still not uncommon.

Ideologically, the working class tends to emphasize "fairness," which is primarily invoked as the guiding principle for parents in their treatment of siblings, and the antonym of which is "favoritism." In a social setting fairness and justice are treated as nearly synonymous, though where there is a conflict, the law should be fair rather than legalistic. For some of the working class other people's greater wealth or higher social status is the result of unfair "favoritism" on the part of fate or society. For others, the rich and the socially superior stand, not in the place of rival siblings, but in the place of parents, who should assure that fairness is observed. It is these two attitudes of the working class which make alternative party governments in England possible, for numerically the working class have an absolute majority over all other classes. If they all saw English society in terms of sibling rivalry, as do many of the more vocal spokesmen of the Labour party, the English would be a one-party state.

The "white dominions," Australia, New Zealand and English-speaking Canada were largely populated by members of the working class. The social and political life of New Zealand and Australia especially seems to continue to reflect this obsession with fairness and resentment of favoritism, even though the "favorites" are not physically present in significant numbers. Somewhat paradoxically one could describe these societies as having carried within them the attitudes appropriate to a multi-class society, although composed almost entirely of the members of one class and their descendants.

Although these two core classes, the middle and working classes without qualification, represent at least three-fourths of the English population, they are not nearly as influential, either in domestic politics or in the pattern given to the former Empire, as are the three smaller classes. Although the upper middle class represents at most 2 percent of the English population, its influence and its wealth is quite out of proportion to its size. Its difference from the even smaller upper class, or aristocracy, is almost entirely a matter of pedigree, with which the ownership of inherited land was traditionally associated. With the English system of primogeniture among the aristocracy, the children, other than the firstborn, of the higher ranks of the nobility receive a "courtesy title" (Lord or Lady for the younger children of marquises and earls). But these courtesy titles are purely personal and are not transmitted to the third generation, who become plain "Mr." and "Miss." They are then indistinguishable from the rest of the upper middle class who validate their status by their education, by their occupations, by their accent and vocabulary, by their manners, and by their anxious pre-occupation with the company they keep.

They appropriate for their exclusive use the labels of ladies and gentlemen, but this status can apparently be safely maintained only by excluding others who are *not* ladies and gentlemen. Good examples of this attitude could be found prior to 1939 in the tropical colonies, where perhaps five or six officials would be divided into two social groups, with the district officer or resident magistrate and especially their wives having no unofficial contact with the man from the public works department and his wife, and so on. These tiny groups of temporary exiles illustrate in starkly simple terms the theme of this paper, that English identity depends on the presence of other

Englishmen (sometimes only fantasied) from whom one is distinguished. This situation reached its most abstract form in the legendary figure of the English lady or gentleman changing for dinner in the jungle or desert, where none of the "natives" could be expected to recognize this affirmation of status, but any bounder or *box-wallah* ("trader") who might improbably turn up would immediately understand the superiority of the man in the dinner jacket.

Upper middle class education for males was presumed to impart automatically the qualities of "leadership," to produce "officer material," to equip those who had survived it with the ability and right to direct and protect the lives of others. The professions (7), which, with the armed services and public administration, were the only acceptable careers for gentlemen, all depend on the personal relationship between the professional and his client or patient or parishioner.

From the institution of the modern civil service in the middle of the nineteenth century, the administrative ranks have been an almost exclusively upper middle class reserve. In fact, during the century that Britain had a centrally administered tropical empire, the administrative ranks of the colonial and Indian civil services were almost entirely recruited from the same restricted group. Except when voluntarily exiled to escape disgrace or (occasionally) unseemly poverty, members of the upper middle class did not migrate to the "white dominions" or the "colonies of settlement" with temperate climates in Eastern or Southern Africa (members of the aristocracy might serve in them for limited periods in ceremonial or judicial positions). They were, however, completely dominant in the tropical empire, imposing their values and setting the tone. It is almost exclusively this class which still mourns the abandonment of this empire (in this context the word "freeing" is inappropriate) and its honorable career structure. Even though the inhabitants of Rhodesia or the Cape are clearly not "p.l.u." ("people like us") in the vast majority, most of the upper middle class voice a certain sympathy with those who are resisting the deprivation which has left them so bereft.

The upper middle class administrators were notably uncorrupt, just and considerate for all under their administration, provided the administered did not claim social equality. When equality was claimed it was callously resisted—"Dogs and Chinamen not admitted." The private clubs, centers of all social life in the tropical empire, for example, excluded not only "the natives," but all other Englishmen in lower social classes, such as those engaged in commerce or engineering. The clubs were places where one could "be at ease" when work was over, and one could only be at ease when surrounded by people "of one's own sort"—servants, of course, did not count. No analogies to these exclusive clubs existed in the former French or Dutch Empires.

Although sources of great bitterness, the clubs were not primarily racist.

"Natives" were excluded, but this was probably less wounding to all but a tiny minority than it was to the middle and lower middle class English who were also excluded. For example, probably a majority of white Rhodesians were lower middle class when they left England to settle in the colonies. For the lower middle class, whose position was and is precarious both at home and abroad, this exclusion was particularly poignant. It is my firm impression that it is this class which has initiated the fiscal and legal measures aimed at undermining the economic and social claims of the upper middle class to privilege. And it is certainly this class which is most vocally gleeful about such measures. One of the things which was most wounding to many of the excluded lower middle class is that this exclusion treated them and "the natives" alike, and with their precarious position within the English society, this was much more of a threat than it would have been to people secure in their social status. The more ethical among them may disapprove of or feel justifiably angry at those of their compatriots who use their authority to treat "the natives" unfairly. But this is more a rejection of oppression than it is a repudiation of racism.

The lower middle class wish to be considered "genteel" and completely distinguishable from the working classes, even though today their salaries are frequently lower than working class wages. In large part the lower middle class and white collar workers coincide—the literary archetypes of the lower middle class, Uriah Heep of *David Copperfield,* Mr. Guppy of *Bleak House* and Mr. Pooter of the *Diary of a Nobody,* were employed by solicitors and a bank. More than any other group in English society, the lower middle class feel themselves threatened from both sides. Their treatment was and is very similar in England in any of the associations in which the upper middle class plays a dominating role, such as groups connected with the Church of England or the Conservative Party. The lower middle class is more assiduous in its church attendance than any of the other social classes and has much the lowest percentage of those rejecting any sectarian label (17% against a national average of 23%). Not surprisingly, it has the highest proportion of any social class of members claiming adherence to one of the nonconformist Protestant sects. Among the English the lower middle class is the most representative of the "Nonconformist conscience:" their sexual lives, for example, tend to be restrained and regular, while they are loudly censorious about the real or supposed licentiousness of other groups.

In the earlier decades of this century the lower middle class and the Nonconformist conscience played major roles in the Liberal party, and when it was replaced by the Labour party, many sought and found influence there, too. In its earlier days the Labour party had political geniuses of undiluted working class origin, such as Bevin, Morrison, and Bevan, among others, but we are not likely to see their like again. With today's more egalitarian educational system, it is highly improbable that such gifted children will leave school at the minimum legal age and go down the mines or onto the shop floor. Rather they are likely to receive the best education the country can offer and end up as particularly brilliant and successful members of the administrative upper middle class.

When age and death had removed most of the authentic working class politicians, members of the lower middle class sought and found positions in the structure of the Labour party, perhaps even more markedly on the local than on the national level—but their tenure may be short. They may soon be replaced by members of the most influential social class in England today—the upper (or skilled) working class, a position claimed by 17% of the population between 16 and 45 (*6*). Nearly twice as many men as women claim these positions, and it will be remembered that 50% more women than men claimed to be middle class. The term "upper working" was preferred by respondents under 24; above that age the preference was for "skilled working" class. I think this difference in the way in which these respondents prefer to describe themselves may be more than terminological. The older respondents may well base their claim for superiority over the mass of the working class purely on the technical skills they have acquired through apprenticeship or other training, which justifies their higher earnings through the responsibilities they assume. The younger respondents who wish to be considered "upper working class" are likely to base their claims on their activities outside work, particularly their representational activities in local or factory politics and in the entertainment industries.

To my mind, the greatest social change which has occurred in English society since the end of World War II is the rise of the younger upper working class to national and even international significance. Today they are without question the trend-setters. Such international figures as the Beatles or Twiggy, and many more, would almost certainly have described themselves as upper working class at the beginning of their careers. The change which many observers see in contemporary English society is the replacement of the upper middle class by the upper working class as conspicuous models for emulation.

All the English working classes born since 1940 differ from their parents in not having known hunger or the threat of hunger in childhood, nor have they grown up under the burden of anxiety about the risks of poverty, unemployment or sickness. With the diminution of realistic anxiety there seems to have been a parallel diminution in free-floating anxiety. The gifted youngsters in this group could develop their talents without denying their working class origins, as their equivalents thirty years ago almost certainly did (outside Labour party politics). For a working class youngster to make a career, three or more decades ago, he or she would almost certainly have made the greatest efforts to cultivate a correct, BBC, upper middle class vocabulary and accent, the equivalent of passing in a multi-racial society. Today the reverse quite frequently takes place and one finds youngsters of impeccable upper middle class origin trying to pass as upper working class by adopting their vocabulary and attempting the slurred phonemes of their accent. Mick Jagger, the leader of the Rolling Stones, is one of the most conspicuous examples of this. The upper working class also tend to be hedonistic, leading a varied sexual life before marriage, with few puritans in their group, and they have the highest percentage of all groups rejecting a sectarian label.

Although the upper and skilled working classes lead a varied sexual life, they tend to start it later than their coevals who call themselves working class without qualification, and markedly later than that small group (under 2 percent) who can be described as "lower working class." This group represents the remnants of the vanished peasantry consisting of unskilled agricultural laborers and the descendants of those who have moved from country to city slum without making an adequate adaptation. They are of psychological importance for the respectable working class who live near them and who fear their children will be corrupted by associating with lower working class children by picking up their "bad" language and their disregard for sexual propriety and for property rights. The lower working class is also important in a different way to the rural aristocracy, for whom they often provided the most cherished childhood companions and, in the past, foster mothers, nurses and nursemaids. There are some similarities in the looseness or casualness in the highest and lowest social classes in England which are in conflict with the carefulness and constraint of the five intermediate classes.

I have thought it worthwhile to devote so much space to discussing the characteristics of the English seven-class social system because it is within this system that nearly all the English can place themselves without ambiguity. It is by the contrast between their own social position and the positions of other Englishmen that their sense of identity is maintained, although I do not suppose that many people who are not social scientists can be articulate about the differences between their own social class and those immediately above and below them; more distant classes are less sharply differentiated. It is my argument that the English sense of identity depends on the presence of other Englishmen of one's own class (with whom one feels "at ease") and of other classes to confirm one's place in the whole social structure, and that it depends on nothing more.

The presence in small numbers of foreigners is irrelevant—they can be treated either courteously or no, and they will go away soon. But what happens when the foreigners are numerous, or threaten to become so, and show no signs of going away? I have described, very cursorily it is true, the devices used by the English in the former tropical empire to preserve some corners of purely English society uncontaminated by "natives." If this were not done, the English feared they would be swamped, lose their identity and in a very telling phrase "go native." This self-preservation entailed both callousness and injustice, qualities to be repudiated in nearly all other settings. But if the English were to lose their identity, who would be left to be responsive and just to "the lesser breeds without the law?"

It is, I think, on this fear of English identity being swamped and destroyed by the presence of too many foreigners that the politician Enoch Powell and his associates play in their agitation to get the recent migrants from the West Indies, Africa, India and Pakistan "repatriated" before it is too late. They also play on this fear in their emphasis on the number of babies with colored skins being born in National Health hospitals, and on the number of darker pupils in elementary schools. There is, of course, some genetic nonsense mixed up in these and similar arguments, but I doubt very much whether an appeal on simplistic racial arguments would have gained the response it has in England if some more general fear were not touched upon. The fear that English identity would be annihilated by a wave of non-English who would not go away seems to me the most plausible explanation. Mr. Powell's actual followers are few, and he and his ideas have been forcibly repudiated in the rhetoric of the spokesmen of both political parties, but both political parties act, or plan to act, on his underlying ideas by ever greater severity towards further would-be immigrants. The current treatment of Indians from East Africa with British passports is one of the most shameful episodes in recent British history.

To my mind, the almost hysterical opposition from a vocal minority to Britain's "entry into Europe" (joining the European Economic Community) and the distaste for such a course shown by large majorities in most public opinion polls taken in early 1970 are rooted in the same fear that English identity would disappear if the barriers holding back those millions of foreigners are lowered.

As far as my limited observations go, this fear of losing one's identity if too many non-English are treated as English is shared by the majority of the members of all English social classes, except for the young upper working class. Their diminished anxiety, on which I commented earlier, seems to hold good in this inarticulate field too. They appear to be easily multi-national and multi-racial, without self-consciousness. Understandably, they choose companions with the same or similar interests and skills.

Although I believe that the upper working class has taken over from the upper middle class the role of models for many of their compatriots and tend to be treated as representative by non-English, they have not yet played any significant part in either domestic or international politics. This may be due to their relative youthfulness and also, perhaps, to lack of interest. If they do acquire an interest in conventional political activity, I believe English society will be transformed fairly rapidly.

REFERENCES

1. Allen, D. Elliston. *British Tastes.* London: Hutchinson, 1968.
2. Dennis, Henriquez, and Slaughter. *Coal is Our Life.* London: Eyre and Spottiswood, 1956.
3. Gorer, Geoffrey. *Exploring English Character.* London: Cresset Press, 1955.
4. Gorer, Geoffrey. "T.V. in Our Lives." *Sunday Times,* London, 1958.
5. Gorer, Geoffrey. *Death, Grief and Mourning in Contemporary Britain.* London: Cresset Press, 1965.
6. Gorer, Geoffrey. *Sex and Marriage in Contemporary England.* 1970.
7. Lewis, Roy, and Maude, Angus. *Professional People.* London: Phoenix House, 1952.
8. Mitford, Nancy, ed. *Noblesse Oblige.* London: Hamilton, 1956.

Ethnicity and Anthropology in America

MARGARET MEAD

7

Anthropology has depended—whenever it was a field science and not an armchair version of social philosophy—on human beings, as members of their own cultures, to serve as instruments for assessing and understanding other cultures. Inevitably, therefore, the forms of cultural or social anthropology developed in different countries each carry the stamp of cultural particularity. Since comparison is the basic method of anthropological work, I shall discuss here some of the parallels between American cultural attitudes towards ethnicity and American cultural anthropological practice.

Our early attitudes towards the American Indian, the African brought here as a slave and the European immigrant who spoke different languages or adhered to different religions have all been reflected in anthropological practice and theory. Whether he was Morgan meditating on the kinship behavior of his neighbors the Iroquois, or Franz Boas fresh from the university world of nineteenth century Germany, the anthropologist brought to his work the emotional and intellectual marks of his own place in the American ethnic mosaic and the perceptions shaped by that place.

Robert Lowie, born an Austrian, whose parents were products of the scholarly and humane traditions of Vienna, called on me the last time he was in New York. There was a formal air of farewell to that visit. I spoke of my intention to try to persuade him to go to Israel, where his combination of talents and experience would make him a strong advocate of field work and a formidable opponent of scholasticism. But the Sinai war had set in, and he said he had too little time left. As we parted he referred to Israel as "a last outpost of European civilization;" then he paused and added, "not that the Arabs aren't a very fine people!" Again a pause, and a confidential smile of recognition of the profession to which we had both given our lives, saying, "But you know that Sinai campaign did remind me of a Crow War party."

So in outlining the growth of American attitudes toward ethnicity, we can develop in parallel the expression of American perceptions of the people who were found here, the people who were brought here against their will, the people who chose to come—and the part of the science of anthropology that American anthropologists forged. I shall treat American consciousness and American anthropology together, without distinguishing in detail one from the other. For while the discipline of anthropology is international, this stamp of our own character forged out of our own experiences remains to further shape the cognitive emphases of Durkheim, Levy-Bruhl and Lévi-Strauss, the narrowly defined emphasis on social behavior of contemporary British anthropology, Malinowski's search for cultural integration (as dreamt of by Poles), and universality of a Ratzel and a Graebner.

Stocking has documented the necessity for anthropology to accept the psychic unity of mankind. He shows how Tyler, for example, had not yet arrived at the comprehensive idea of "cultures" rather than "culture," a concept vital to modern anthropology. Cultural pluralism and expressions of the validity of different cultures have flourished, been repudiated, reaccepted and redefined in the American scene. When the early settlers from Europe reached American shores, they had two urgent problems to deal with: the definition of themselves, branded at home as foolhardy adventurers, renegade family members or treasonable subjects of majesties, poorly equipped and unlikely to succeed in their new venture; and the early demand that they succeed despite every hardship and setback, and show the doubters at home that they had done so. Thus they laid the groundwork for those persistent characteristics of Americans, the exhibitionistic display of victories by the young, the weak, and the small before the eyes of their elders and betters. The need to succeed at any cost, the need to elevate not only each act but each person above the actuality, is well portrayed in the descriptions of the land speculators described in Martin Chuzzlewit, and in Dickens' contemptuous description of the Americans who spoke of "that lady across the way that takes in washing."

The vicissitudes of the early colonists in the north and south of the United

States also paved the way for the various styles of treatment of the Indians. The early explorers in the south painted the portraits of the Southeast Indians as royalty and nobles, placing upon their impressive physiognomy the mark of European aristocracy and dressing them in the clothing of the courts. Faced with a need to come to terms with those who possessed the land and knew how to live on it, the settlers elevated them to petty princes before whom it was no shame to ask for help or to admit failure, in the disease-ridden, inexpertly managed colonies of the Southeast.

The colonies of the Northeast faced the problems of cold and hunger rather than malaria, but they too admitted dependence upon the Indian to supplement their slender supplies and lack of the necessary skills. The Dutch in New Amsterdam, on the other hand, found it easy to wrest huge tracts of lands from Indians in return for small payments, because the Indians lacked an understanding of how land could be alienated. It was not long before Indian camps were burned and housewives kicked the heads of hapless Indians down the streets of New Amsterdam.

Slowly there emerged that curious image, which has lasted throughout our history, of the Indian as the noble savage with barbaric customs, speaking languages so strange that they became appropriate religious jargon for spiritualists; a people brave, proud, treacherous and cruel; impressive figures on their own lands and in their birchbark canoes—magnificent to contemplate but very inconvenient neighbors. From the Indian who took offense at the white man's ways, to the Indian who drives a broken-down Ford on the highway, dangerously drunk and disorderly on the white man's liquor, or who becomes a charge of public welfare, the double image has held and been periodically incorporated in our relationships to Europe and in European understandings of America.

Jefferson, angrily defending himself and all his kin against the denigrations of Buffon, had to include the American Indian among all those living creatures who grew taller and better on American soil. The Karl May stories for German readers, the young Czechs' symbolism after World War II, the Russian communist image of the American Indian as the victim of capitalism, the heroic Indians of children's stories, the Indian as a fit symbol on a coin and as a proper distant ancestor for a vice-president of the United States, the symbol of the match between equals which distinguishes American conflicts, whether cowboys and Indians or cops and robbers—in all of these the Indian has remained a symbol of our ambivalence toward technologically inferior people. No longer possessed of the true and exclusivist faith that guided the early settlers, we find the Indian emerging repeatedly as the symbol of the man of the land, the man who had held these boundless forests and rivers and plains as a trust—and it is in this sense that he has become a symbol of the new attitudes toward the earth's resources demanded by the present ecological crisis.

The early settlers (like all colonizing people who bring in a more developed technology and a religion with more universalistic claims) had to struggle with the contrast between the cultural style they found here and the subsequent breakdown and deterioration of that style. They watched as a proud tribal people, sure in their own traditions, were subjected to peonage, serfdom, proletarianization, exile into more and more remote reservations, or simple extinction.

Anthropologists, alert to the beauty and style of Indian culture, recognizing the intricate grammar of their unwritten languages, attentive to the precision of their technology, became the students of the Indian and the defenders of his right to remain an Indian, living as his forefathers had lived, and if possible on the same or similar territory. They developed a strong sense of the particularity of each of the Indian tribes, of their Indian informants as persons, as colleagues, in an atmosphere of collegiality which set the style of modern field work. Traits which the anthropologists found distasteful for moral or aesthetic reasons were systematically treated as the result of European conquest, and the Indians were fed back the mixture of ethnographic and folk images to which they themselves had contributed.

Thus, in the 1930s the Indians of Oklahoma who were oil rich used to go to New York and buy theatrical Indian costumes for the poorer members of other tribes to wear in local rodeos. In Florida the remnants of different tribes gathered into an artificial synthesis, costumed in European materials, and set themselves up in tourist-oriented Seminole villages. Throughout our history we have vacillated between treating the Indian as people to be eliminated or to be assimilated. Those who espoused the Indians' cause, romanticists and ethnographers alike, have concentrated on them more as carriers of a unique native culture, rather than as human beings. The Indians responded by insisting that boarding schools for Indians were bad because they did not prepare them for life on the reservation, and sending Indians to the local schools was bad because they could not learn English on a par with children of European origin!

So we, Americans and ethnographers, have come to half-terms with the men originally in possession of the soil, just as the United Kingdom settlers of New Zealand romanticized the Maori on the one hand and scorned him on the other. Away on their reservations Maori were considered bearers of a poetic cosmology equalled only by the Greeks. But once in town they sank to the position of a colored proletariat, carrying all the stigmata that Europeans accord people who have lost their relationship to their previous tribal status and differ in physique from the European colonizers.

Thus the ethnologists of New Zealand played the role of glorifiers of the Maori myth as did the American ethnologists of the ancient Hawaiian Polynesian and, to a lesser extent, the American Indian. But on the other side of the coin bearing the visage of the proud, aristocratic savage was the view, shared by Australians, of natives as "varmints." The British settlers of Australia, however, often made no such distinction in their treatment of the Australian aborigine, who was considered a deteriorated kind of man, a wooly marauder to be hunted like a rabbit.

Our experience with the Indian has had many repercussions on our treatment of the whole question of ethnicity in the United States. Those who wish to attack our notion of citizenship—which was originally a matter of choice, and a privilege that could be withdrawn—made copious use of the suggestion, "If you don't like this country, go back where you came from." This was said to an Indian Christian pacifist in World War I, and repeated in the demand that the Iroquois Indians, who had elected not to become American citizens, register as *aliens* in World War II. When, in the early 1940s, Arthur Raper was assigned the difficult task of treating Georgia sharecroppers, white and black, within the same economic framework, he found that by also including the Indians, the earliest inhabitants of Georgia, he could maintain a balance and even publish his discussions of all these groups in the local newspaper.

Whenever the political climate of the world or of this country becomes infused with a question of "rights to land," Indian claims to great built-up cities come up to parallel the demands of European minorities (Basques, Scots, Irish, Welsh, etc.) for autonomy. The recent theatrical gesture by American Indians taking the island of Alcatraz parallels the actions of Caribbean revolutionaries in either revolting against foreign rule and freeing their land [*sic*] or, in small bands, freeing other countries.

In the United States the demands of the increasingly self-conscious and powerful black minority are countered by requests that they think about other people also, and the Indians are sporadically included. Meanwhile, the lives of Indians on reservations, existing on miserably insufficient welfare payments, cut off from the larger world, cold, hungry, without adequate medical care, are perhaps equalled only by the misery of those Indians who have been, in their phrase, "turned loose too soon," who migrate to cities already overcrowded by other poorly educated and unskilled peoples.

Yet it is the conception of their differences, their uniqueness—the white settlers' insistence on a racial difference and the insistence of the Indians themselves, aided by anthropology, on each tribe's cultural distinctiveness—that has resulted in the Indians' present situation. On and off reservations they form a generally unhappy and unorganized minority. The right to a distinctive culture and language, to a distinctive adaptation to the environment, and the obligation of those in power somehow to preserve these rights has conflicted and conflicts today with the egalitarian, individualistic doctrines of the Protestant founders of the United States, who stemmed from a tradition where "every he in England is as good as every other he." It is illuminating to inquire what effect it might have had on the American attitude toward other peoples and other races as they arrived here, if the approach of the early missionaries to the Indians, like the enterprises set up at Carlisle and Hampton Institute, had prevailed. Individual American Indians were welcomed in the homes of English-speaking farmers and taught the style of life, of speech and of farming of the dominant culture in their day. The confusion between the rights of individuals to share fully in the duties, responsibilities, privileges and rewards of the dominant culture, and the demand that former suzerainty and traditional and archaic cultures be respected is now bedeviling not only the United States, but almost the entire world.

In the early days, when the first colonists, driven to succeed or at least appear to be succeeding in their first encounters with the wilderness, were shaping our attitudes towards ethnicity, the African slave presented as sharp a contrast to the American Indian as one could find. Where the Indian was on his own ground, secure in a superior knowledge of the natural environment, the African slave was far from home, separated from his fellow tribesman, and without communication except through his slowly developing grasp of the language of his white owner. His social organization totally disrupted, he was left to build a new culture, under the most adverse conditions, from the scattered remnants of many different groups.

Early anthropological interest in the Negro centered primarily around discussions about which of his customs, his way of singing, scraps of magic, his oratorical style, were or were not of African origin. The anthropologist and the folklorist reached back through the current generation of Negroes to reinvoke a primitive past, as the Indian buffalo-hunting ancestors had been reinvoked through the words of their reservation descendants. But where the Indians were independent equals vis-a-vis the early settlers and the anthropologist, the American Negro was simply abandoned, treated partly as any other ethnic group, partly as a group set aside not exactly by race or color, but definitely by origin.

Anthropologists shared the liberal traditions of the North and only very slowly, in the work of Powdermaker, and the group in Lloyd Warner's studies, came to understand something of the caste tradition of the old Southeast. Here were two peoples, deeply inter-related biologically, tied together by every kind of intimacy, yet preserving rigid caste distinctions, the violation of which upset the educated white man and robbed the uneducated, poverty-stricken sharecropper and mountain dweller of his single claim to distinction—his whiteness. The extent to which the color bar was a bar particularly against Negro Americans, those who shared part of the same white ancestry as their white neighbors, and not a bar against the darker or different peoples of the rest of the world was shown in the preoccupation in some Southern white circles with the fate of the Japanese in World War II, and in the fairly cordial treatment accorded old Jewish families. The desperate attempt to keep the black cousins in their place, and at the same time to emphasize kinship ties as all important, preoccupied the old South, blended as it was with the bitterness of conquest and Northern attempts to alter the caste system. Frank Tannenbaum has suggested that if there had been more immigration to the South from Europe and Asia, this obsessive preoccupation might have been broken, but recent experiences in introducing Negro Americans into parts of America where there are many different ethnic groups does not bear this out.

Mexican Americans shared a fate about halfway between that of Negro Americans and American Indians. Their general proletarian status, the fact that they were thought of as indigenous rather than as immigrants—a fact strengthened by our annexations of the Southwest and our conquest of the country where Spanish speakers had lived so long—contributed to their treatment as natives. At the same time, their European language, associations with Latin America and the Catholic religion distinguished them from North American Indians. Refusals of service in restaurants, signs forbidding Mexicans to remain overnight in a town, smack of the kind of restrictions that were applied on sight to people identified by dress, language, physique and lower class status. Efforts to improve the condition of Mexicans have been inextricably interwoven with questions of migrant farm labor, the farm workers' strikes of the 1960s and 1970s, the administration of welfare in the Southwest, and demands for the teaching of Spanish in the schools. Mexican-Americans may be contrasted to Puerto Ricans, who are often associated with Negroes, but who claim the status of American citizens, while Mexicans, even the Spanish speakers of the Southwest, are thought of as semi-indigenous foreigners.

In anthropological studies of the Southwest characteristic clusters appear, including Navajo, Mormons and Spanish-Americans, each distinct from the dominant culture of the United States. In contrast to attitudes towards Negro-Americans, Mexican-Americans outside the Southwest are typically looked upon as temporary residents whose homes are in Mexico, the country to which they periodically or eventually will return. Similar status has been extended to West Indian Negroes, people who come to the United States to work for money, who are accorded the restricted privileges of other low status colored peoples, and who will be expected to return to their own islands after a period of money-making in the United States. Members of each West Indian island community maintain active contact among themselves and with their home islands. If they become citizens, by birth or naturalization, they become indistinguishable in status from American Negroes.

The core definition of American identity, as white, Caucasian and blonder rather than darker, pervaded the American response to the appearance of Chinese coolies, and to Japanese immigrant families. They were treated as people apart, against which the country needed protection. The notion of the Yellow Peril as an Asian population of overwhelming proportions quickly blended with fear of their obtaining control of the land and with tales of tong warfare within their own communities. The success with which the Chinese maintained a closed community added to the sense of separation. The Chinese showed little interest in education and birth control, whereas the Japanese not only competed vigorously and successfully in school, but their birthrate in the second generation fell below that of native-born Americans.

Until World War II, the Japanese were seldom considered objects for study. Anthropology in Japan had hardly begun, and in the usual American studies of growth or intelligence the Japanese were treated as an Asian population with a different environmental history than Caucasians, and their ancient culture, complex and exotic, was taken for granted. As a class they fitted into the later pattern of European immigration, industrious and enterprising members of the peasantry who came to the United States to earn money, rather than to live here permanently. Those who did not want to settle permanently, or were believed not to want to, although not necessarily treated better, presented less of a problem to Americans, except in instances like World War II when, typically, the Japanese whom Federal security agents could trust as informants were Japanese Communists whose style was familiar; all other Japanese were felt to share Oriental inscrutability. Both Japanese and Chinese were temporary problems, felt to be "other," members of other societies.

For Americans the problem consisted of those who wanted to stay here, of those who had no other home—Indians who were here when the Europeans arrived, Africans who had no other home to return to and no language except English, and the children of non-American parents but who became citizens by birth. While the focal point of black-white contact was sex relations and marriage, the focal point of Japanese, Chinese, and at one time Armenian relationships was the ownership of land, particularly in California. There was a fear that such groups would remain a people, and would, as a people, become troublesome, as had some of the religious colonies like the Amish and the Mennonites. World War II, with the straight choice presented to American-born Japanese, sharpened the issue, as most of the Japanese, sure that man must have some absolute loyalty, transferred their allegiance to the United States.

Immigrants from Europe were subjected to the extreme racial ethnocentrism characteristic of the English-speaking settlers, who held Eastern and Southern European immigrants in low esteem. Such attitudes were primarily determined by the degree to which the foreigners stuck together, formed communities which ultimately exerted considerable political pressure, and became sufficiently assimilated to enter the economic structure at higher levels than the characteristic early positions of unskilled laborer, miner, and local boss and manipulator within their own ethnic group. When these groups also had a religious and communelike character, when they stood out against the ongoing culture by refusing schooling or military service, they strained the tolerance and hospitality of the core-culture Americans. To enter the mainstream of American culture it was on the whole necessary to change one's name, move away from an ethnic neighborhood and slowly adopt "protective coloration."

There were tremendous contrasts between the attitudes of the more established groups in any American community, and each group of newcomers, varying with the previous economic status of the immigrants, the sequence in which they arrived, their occupations, their religious allegiances, and the extent to which they contrasted in physique with the older groups. Frontier societies threw into prominence differential abilities to survive in the new environment, branding the newcomer a greenhorn, or a tenderfoot, but according considerable respect to the individual who adapted quickly. Thus the settler on the frontier was judged as an individual, on whether he established economic self-sufficiency and kept his fences mended. Small self-contained New England colonies maintained their early distinctions in which the most desirable locations in the new town went to those with the most economic resources, while the poor lived on the periphery of society and, later, in the deteriorating homes of former owners of high status. This became a persistent pattern in American towns and cities, a pattern which, in combination with the echoes of European residential restriction of various subordinated groups (Jews, gypsies, peasants), produced the pervasive American pattern that has culminated today in the ghetto-like concentrations of the poor. Most recent rural immigrants, the black and Puerto Rican populations, live in the deteriorated centers where the prosperous once lived, while prosperity and high status is accompanied by flight to the countryside and the higher prestige of the more distant suburbs.

Even in suburbs, however, the former patterns are repeated. In the suburbs there is an effort to exclude others of different ethnic identity, which often masks attempts to exclude those of a lower class position. Zoning to assure house lots and exclusive country club membership discourages those who differ in religion or style of living. Thus, today we have clusters of suburban communities that are predominantly Jewish, or Irish Catholic, or Italian-American in origin, comparable to the traditional ethnic quarters of cities.

The response of any particular American-born or American-acculturated person to each of the other ethnicities of Americans he knows or hears about is also very much determined by his experience in his own locality. Germans may have been experienced as the high-principled and prosperous burghers who fled Germany in 1848 to establish the orchestras and beer gardens of middle western cities; as the members of small, peculiar, specially garbed Protestant religious sects (Amish, Mennonites, Hutterites), as German Jews, patrons of music; or as isolated German immigrants who learned English quickly and resembled their English neighbors, in contrast to Southern Europeans who were darker in complexion, poorer and less skilled.

Italians may have been experienced as Southern Italians, Sicilians or Northern Italians, with their contrasting styles of behavior and complexion; as groups of peasants tilling the land in Southern New Jersey; as unskilled workers on roads and tunnels, as highly skilled craftsmen who came to shape their imported marble; as individuals of high culture; as our allies in World War I; as our prisoners of war in World War II.

Black Americans may have been experienced as a single colored family descended from runaway slaves in some Pennsylvania or New York State community; as the members of another caste in the plantation South; as the other half of the life of the aristocratic white man, a life from which poor white men, whose ancestors owned no slaves, were excluded; as urban dwellers pouring into Northern cities to become factory workers in World War I; as rural migrants fleeing into cities for work or for welfare, after World War II; as a group whose arrival broke the fragile fiction that there was no race prejudice in Hawaii and sent each ethnic group, precariously proclaiming their solidarity in different styles and racial origin, back into their enclaves. Today's small children in Northern urban communities are experiencing blacks as magnificently and exotically attired, with flaring Afro-headdresses. Their parents had learned to think of bright colors as distinctive, and therefore degrading, signs of the inalienable and genetic inferiority of American Negroes or of all colored peoples.

All of these contrasting local experiences are compounded into various negative stereotypes, widely but never completely shared, within larger categories of persons: "immigrants," "foreigners," "refugees," "colored people," "Orientals," "Indians," "Catholics," "hillbillies," "damn Yankees," "kikes," "shouters," "the poor," "people on welfare," "grape pickers," "factory hands," "the Mafia," "goyim." Each of these categories of persons, regarded invidiously, has been shaped by particular and differing circumstances, and the membership of each changed in different historical periods and in different parts of the country. Political partisanship—the activities of the Ku Klux Klan and the selection of political candidates because of their ethnically identifiable names—reflects the spectrum of differential valuation and rejection which in the United States is loosely known as "prejudice," an attitude that places some other group in a lower position than one's own. Thus, an American who takes for granted his own old American stock may excoriate any prejudice against Jewish Americans, but take it for granted that "Irish Catholics" have certain well-known undesirable characteristics.

Where different ethnic groups with contrasting styles of life or physique live close to each other, it is almost routine for children to be socialized by such perjorative comments on undesired behavior as "behaving like those *x*'s," whom the children have also seen denigrated in other ways. Jewish children are accused of having a *"goyisher kop,"* Irish children told not to behave like "dagoes," English-speaking children not to act like "dumb Swedes," or the ethnic element may be masked in admonitions not to be "common" or "behave like people in the slums."

The frequent use of such terms in the privacy of the middle class home, or in the open street fights of the new slum, form a basis for embarrassment when it is necessary to refer to the groups who have been denigrated in public or in their presence. Then transformations into the "great Polish people" from "Polacks," become the stock in trade of politicians, while individuals struggle for the contemporary acceptable phrase and may end up saying "colored," "Negro," "black," or "Afro-American," with the same kind of fumbling hope of being understood as the English speaker who, in travelling around the world, says, "turn on the spigot, faucet . . . er . . . tap." The contrast between public deference become expedient, either morally or politically, and private denigration, is a pervasive element in the experience of children who find their elders hypocritical. Significantly, during World War II, when members of every kind of group were packed together in trains, ethnic jokes disappeared and re-appeared as "moron" jokes, while in the 1960s a type of joke originally called "Polish jokes" spread from locality to locality with different ethnic negative heroes, even appearing as "Arab jokes" in New York City.

In wartime these differences are sharply accentuated, as the country of origin of a particular ethnic group becomes either ally or enemy, often necessitating a sharp reversal of previously expressed attitudes. Thus, before World War I, gramaphone records were made with the *Marseillaise* on one side, and *Die Wacht am Rhein* on the other, and children learned during the war that the record couldn't be broken because France was our ally, whose aid to us in the American Revolutionary War we were now reciprocating. After the war, when Germany was again becoming a valued friend and the French were being returned to the lesser popularity engendered among our troops abroad, the record again could not be broken because it contained *Die Wacht am Rhein.* Such shifting attitudes, compounded of distant political allegiance and foreign experience, curiously reinforced attitudes toward German neighbors ("German measles" were called "Liberty measles" in World War I), contributing to the sense of superficiality and shifting prejudices which are as much a part of American inter-ethnic attitudes as are the much deeper, extra-American prejudices of whites, black and Asians against each other.

The dilemma of most Americans has been that they experience, especially as children, a great number of these shifts. The dilemma of the black American is that he does not—in spite of the extreme contrasts between the caste attitudes of the South, which approve physical and emotional closeness as long as social distance is maintained, and those of the North which will concede some political and economic equality as long as spatial distance is maintained. His experience remains the same, independent of his economic class, personal success, or the behavior of his "country" of origin. True, the rise of the new African states has begun to necessitate a certain amount of diplomatic courtesy, just as the rise of Negro voting power has necessitated some degree of political courtesy to Negro political leaders. However, the Negro-American of yesterday and the black American of today is seldom treated as if his skin color or, if the skin color is non-definitive, his alleged possession of African ancestry were not of indelible significance. When we encounter a university professor who is Japanese in racial origin but completely "Americanized," this is a matter of mere curiosity. It carries with it, in most parts of the United States, no further stigma. It is the lack of alternative roots for the American of African, Indian, Hawaiian, Mexican, and often Puerto Rican descent, that carries a different degree of desperation and forms a basis for the periodic search for a separate identity with its own claims for racial exclusiveness, a glorious past, and the right to be underwritten economically by those who have, by conquest, exploitation and imperialism, robbed one's ancestors of their rights.

In considering deep-seated American attitudes towards social relationships, including marriage, residence and admission to an occupation, it is clear it is never possible to assert equality in one field without asserting it in the others. True, Myrdal found that equality of economic opportunity was placed highest by Negroes in desirability and by whites lowest in undesirability, but the three "rights" are really inextricably joined: the right to choose one's own spouse as an individual independent of parental, legal or social interference; the right to build one's house wherever one likes in total disregard of one's neighbors and without any recognition that one's house is part of one's neighbor's "view;" and the right to be employed at any job for which one is potentially qualified.

Counterpointed to these rights is the reflection of the way in which the country was founded—partly in fact, and wholly in myth—by those who, in choosing to risk exile and hardship and a trip across the dangerous seas for lofty religious and political reasons, earned the right to form a self-selected community and keep others out. Thus, the long history of religious, ethnic and racial discrimination in the United States has been a series of battles against one-sidedness in the exercise of these rights—either each group must have the right to form segregated communities of equally high value in pride, desirability and economic level, or the right must be denied to all.

So we have the uniquely American dilemma: the ethic of cultural pluralism, of ethnic separatism, pitted against the ethic of ethnic assimilation, the doctrine of the melting pot which states that the kind of product desired from the melting process may change through time, but the goal is always production of a standard product. Changes in the standard may be seen in the fact that Americans are no longer conspicuous in Italy. American children no longer reject pictures of fathers as brunettes, as they did 25 years ago, and the image of the fashion model or the airplane hostess as a beautiful black girl is gaining ground.

Changes in stance, in clothes, in kinetics, in speech have always been the criteria of the success of the melting pot—external, most easily acquired, waiting perhaps for two or three generations for corresponding "Americanization" in attitude. Skin color and hair have been the most intractable features to blend in, but slowly permanent waves, hair straighteners, bleaching creams and ultra-violet ray machines, cosmetic surgery and hairdos borrowed from another ethnic group are making it possible to simulate physical similarities also. Nevertheless, those for whom any of these simulations are difficult, those who are conspicuously non-European in looks, those who have difficulty in speaking or writing English, those who are both poor and ethnically identified, will continue to feel that the American view of Americanization is one-sided, that it demands higher prices from some than from others.

Rejection of this kind of unilateral Americanization—which demands change of name, if the name is foreign or hard to pronounce, change of hair and features if they are too far removed from American style, change of speech if one speaks a dialect instead of standard English, and set standards of hygiene, clothing and manners—has been called "cultural pluralism" in the past, and today is called "cultural separatism." In contemporary America separatism is symbolized by hippies, who resist Americanization by violating all of its canons. The hippies make an effort to look and act like the poor, the downtrodden, the outcast, the blacks, and the American Indian, combining dirt, bare feet, exaggerated hairdos, and Indian headbands with clothing made of dissected and disassociated bits of old uniforms and older styles, very much as newly exposed primitive people use the cast-off clothes of the civilized peoples with whom they come in contact.

Analogously, black Americans went through a long period of working very hard at acquiring the externals of membership in the American community: the men cut their hair short and the women straightened theirs, accents were modified, stance and gesture disciplined to white standards, and personal hygiene excessively insisted upon. The new move toward flamboyant difference in dress, speech and manners illustrates the other possibility. Both types of behavior point up the continuing importance of the issue: if the melting pot style is to win, the central product must be available equally to everyone, or there will be continuing inequality, resentment, and loss of dignity on the one hand, and guilt, unease and compensatory hostility on the other. If cultural pluralism is to win out, then there will be continuing demands to equalize the position of those in each segment of the mosaic, so that their part may be comparable to that of the others.

The progression from integration as a principle to black power has marked a shift from the demand, on the part of both black and white, that individual black people be admitted as pupils, physicians, lawyers, etc., into the larger society, to the demand that black people *as a group* and black people as residents of particular contiguous sections of large cities or rural counties be accorded recognition as a separate people which can itself confer dignity on each of its members. Integration expressed the melting pot idea: if you will make an effort to look, act, dress, speak as much like the standard white, then though not blond like the ideal American, we will act as if you were really entirely one of us. Black power expresses the rejection of this unilateral invitation, and the demand instead for equal recognition and value based on difference.

Class plays a complex role in the American sense of identity. There is no national society and no national class structure such as exists in England. High status in one city or one part of the country does not carry the same status elsewhere and although there are general nationwide criteria of class membership, there are no absolutes of income or education that can be invoked. But there is a tremendous amount of ranking within communities, and individuals whose education, wealth or achievement makes a radical amount of mobility possible usually have to leave the town or city where they have grown up and establish new ties appropriate to their newly attained status. There are also class hierarchies within each ethnic group, although the occupations followed by the different classes may vary widely from one ethnic group to another. Within many ethnic groups there are sharp breaks, as among preWorld War II Hungarian immigrants who divided themselves into gentry and peasantry; or as among Mexicans, who exhibit a high degree of cohesiveness when they are poor, but break sharply from other members of their ethnic group when they reach a certain level of affluence; or Italians who maintain family ties despite often tremendous difference in education and class level. Within the Jewish community the hierarchy that is partly derivative of Europe is complicated by the presence of "Spanish Jews" and "Syrian Jews," so that class and national origin interweave in the expression of social inclusiveness or exclusiveness.

The core class position in the United States may be said to be the lower middle class. This group is undistinguished in any way by dress or accent from the completely assimilated foreigner, whose clothes and behavior carry the suggestion that they perform no sort of manual labor and who will be treated respectfully by the police, hotel clerks, railway conductors, airline personnel and school authorities. This cherishing of a treasured inconspicuous respectability makes group members very sensitive to loss of status; they spend differentially on symbols of status, they are intensely conforming, and they are openly hostile to the invasion of their neighborhood by any of those who are conspicuously different—racially, religiously, or in dress or deportment. In many ways they resemble the lower middle class as described by Gorer for England, or by Fromm for Germany—extraordinarily clean, neat, careful, postponing satisfactions, fearful of loss of status by invasion. These similarities may be attributed to their common origins in the working class. At the same time this picture is complicated in the United States because their origins are not only working class but also very often distinctively foreign, and the attempt to mask the signs of past immigration is included in their behavior. They also include, in the United States, a large component of those who have newly-made money and are attempting to buy a way for their children if not for themselves into upper middle class society.

The lower middle class may be said to represent the general American values to which members of the lower class may aspire and by which the upper middle class are repelled: pride based on present position, occupation, residence and respectability; absence or even repudiation of ancestral ties; and fear of loss rather than hope for mobility. They represent a kind of immobile block in the middle of the ladder of American aspirations and American beliefs in upward mobility. They are people who are too busy keeping what they have to have much energy for impractical aspirations; if high school is necessary for their children, they send them to high school, and when college becomes necessary they send them to college. They also represent the traditional ideals of hard work, jealous egalitarianism, and puritanical self denial of the inappropriate pleasures of the dissolute and spendthrift poor and the dissolute and spendthrift rich.

The upper classes in the United States present the anomaly of lack of any secure position, and while the upper uppers—Lloyd Warner's categories—are preoccupied with a lack of definite role, the lower uppers are preoccupied with a fear of falling, somewhat analagous to the fears of the lower middle class.

The upper middle class, college educated, engaged in professional and managerial activities characterized by style of life, is perhaps the freest from class competition but is the most acutely involved in narrow rivalries within occupational and residential settings.

In most parts of the United States we have a distinctive six class system; there are no middle lowers, middle middles or middle uppers. The classes alternate in their fears; the lower lowers have no place further to fall, the upper lowers may become lower middles, the lower middles are afraid of falling; the upper middles are relatively secure, the lower uppers, mainly the descendants of wealthier people, are afraid of falling, and the upper uppers have no place to go. But all of these more general classifications are so overlaid by regional, ethnic and racial classifications that it is primarily within the narrow arena of a particular town or an industrial establishment that they come into play. As there are very few ways in which Americans of different local class orientation can associate socially, contacts tend to be very narrow.

Like members of other societies, Americans' sense of themselves as Americans is enhanced by any international context, war, travel or the presence of foreigners. But this sense of solidarity may also be fractured by internal dissension over a war, or some widespread social issue like the integration of the schools, and then the sense of being American becomes instead a sense of being Italian-American or Irish-American, and the sense of class and race and national origin all become highly confused, as in a recently described housing development inherited by working class Jews and Negro professionals, where each found the position of the other unexpected and inexplicable.

Within the context of American history, it may be said that the sense of being an American is seldom invoked positively. It almost always accompanies confrontation with foreigners or repudiation of some other group whose behavior is regarded as un-American. Reversion to European-derived values, upper class accents, "culture," socialism and the display of "taste" may all be regarded as un-American. In a sense this may be seen as the attempt on the part of the assimilated American to prevent any further differentiation from his recently attained status. This is perhaps why there is such a close correspondence between the idea of Americanization, core culture, and lower middle class status. They are all states only recently attained; the difference in the paths by which individuals reach them are so vastly different that conformity and similarity of present orientation are the only ways in which such a group can be held together. Freedom to criticize the domestic and foreign policies of the nation is, for example, almost completely an upper middle and upper class privilege. Whatever their status differences in national origin, social background or race, assimilated Americans all have in common this sense of precarious attainment.

American identity stands in strong contrast to that which Geoffrey Gorer has outlined for the English, where the presence of other English of their own and other classes, real or fantasied, is essential. Without the presence of those who are thought of as *non-American*—immigrants, foreigners, other races, the poor and disreputable, the radical and the bohemian—Americans define themselves much more narrowly as Jones or Livingstones, as people who attended a given college, belong to a particular local church, as men who served in the Marines or belong to the Oddfellows, as Democrats or Republicans. Scots and Poles are notable examples of peoples who invest many activities and character traits with positive national identity, and learn to study, or bear pain, or face adversity, as Poles or as Scots. But young Americans hear only negatively valued behavior invoked when they are told not to behave like those foreigners down the street. In the end, being American is a matter of abstention from foreign ways, foreign food, foreign ideas, foreign accents, foreign vices. So whiskey drinking becomes identified with the Irish and, by coincidence, with Catholics, beer drinking with Germans, and marijuana with black musicians and zoot suits with minority group adolescents.

Ethnicity has been a factor in the older battles against economic and political exploitation and in the newer battles against patronizing and unilateral benevolence. The slave, the mine worker, the agricultural migrant laborer has usually been characterized by ethnic difference from the master, the mine owner, the big fruit farmer. The perhaps unavoidable American emphasis on ethnicity has made possible the exploitation of disadvantaged groups by their own members who have obtained wealth and power. In such battles ethnic prejudice and unfairness have played an important role, intensifying the fight for justice and softening the hearts of those who cannot in good conscience defend their behavior.

Today there is a different kind of revolt, the revolt of those to whom "good" has been done by those who were their superiors, in age, knowledge, wealth, or expertise. So children, students, prisoners, patients and welfare clients are all rebelling against the unilaterality of institutions hitherto regarded as benevolent and dedicated by both practitioners and supporters. Similarly, ethnic groups who have been considered weaker or inferior and have experienced the same kind of benevolent, protective treatment are rebelling. It is black students, black patients, black parishioners and black welfare mothers who are most vociferous in their demands that this unilateral patronage cease and that they be given a voice in how they are to be taught, cured, rehabilitated, saved or given welfare.

The parallel in the behavior of professional anthropologists is fascinating. We have, it is true, treated our informants as colleagues, and we have refused to let them be demeaned in any way by white bureaucracy or by methods that would turn them into guinea pigs. We have clothed them in our professional identity within an atmosphere of collegiality of the highest order. (This in effect is what Talcott Parsons, in a paper on the use of human subjects in experimentation, has suggested. In a paper for the same conference, I suggested that medical experimenters might well use the anthropological field model of the trusted and respected informant.) We have, in fact, benevolently and quite sincerely offered to share our highly valued status as scientists, just as the majority members of a society—in working for integration—have offered minority individuals a share in their status.

This has been an admittedly unilateral, although benevolent, activity. And today's American Indians who are in search of a separate, economically viable ethnic identity, or today's African nationals intent on constructing workable historical views of their own pasts do not want a share in the anthropological enterprise, which values all cultures equally regardless of where they are placed in the ongoing socio-economic political marketplace of the wider world. So Vine Deloria complains about the very kind of behavior which accorded Ella Deloria, a Dakota Indian and professional anthropologist, such high status. He does not want a share in the particular kinds of culture-respecting activities that have been the hallmark of the traditional anthropologist. This was one of the points of extreme difference in the early arguments about action anthropology as compared to applied anthropology: the applied anthropologist maintained respect for a system, while the action anthropologist became an active partisan, even to the point of ignoring the historical records in favor of present socioeconomic needs. So, within these narrower battles, parochial and limited and essentially irrelevant to the importance of the concept of culture itself, one sees the reflection of national culture and contemporary social issues.

It seems important to recognize here the work of Erik Erikson, who has contributed so much to our understanding of identity. From his early work, notably his study of the Sioux Indians' loss of historical identity as hunters and warriors, he has continuously enriched the whole concept of the way in which the growing child, the young adult and the mature person may incorporate within his psychic structure the historical and contemporary elements of the wider culture as well as his specific place within the ethnic pattern. In his study of Gandhi, Gandhi's own caste position, the position of his friend and adversary Sarabhai, the experience of Indians in South Africa, Gandhi's own ambivalence towards the British culture in which he had once sought to participate, and the position of the untouchables within India are all given weight, and Gandhi emerges as a man shaped and informed by the ethnic complexities of his time.

In his earlier study of the Yurok Indians of California, Erikson recognized the significance of a cultural character which incorporates in detail the features of the landscape and the specifics of the major economic way of life. His own cross-cultural experience included a childhood in Germany, son of a Scandinavian father he had never known; migration to the United States as a young man; adaptation first to Massachusetts and then to California, working closely with Kroeber and Mekeel among the American Indians; a return to the study of German character in his research on the young Luther and finally, in response to time spent in India, a study of Gandhi's search for truth. His life as a whole illustrates the incorporation into illuminating theory of his own cultural experience.

In comparison, Kurt Lewin, after service in the German army (an atypical experience for a German Jew), and later participation in the Weimar Republic, was exposed to the particular style of the American WMCA, designed to induce some comradeship into the isolated lives of young white men of the lower middle class. At the same time, Lewin developed great respect for American democratic styles of behavior as opposed to the laissez-faire and authoritarian styles. His study of German social behavior as manifested in America by German and Austrian exiles also emphasized this. Brunswik, Adorno and Fromm discovered strains in American character which they identified with similar reprehensible traits in German character, and their work in America became the basis for restatements about Germans. Fromm also developed in interaction with American social scientists, and emphasized those elements in American culture which, with his respect for Jewish culture, for Marx, and for socialist aspiration, seemed to him most similar to the German lower middle class he hated and which were therefore most in need of repudiation. Lewin, on the other hand, utilized the contrasts between German and American democratic styles as the basis for his innovative experiments in group dynamics. These psychologists, all reacting within the American scene on the basis of their cross-cultural and ideological backgrounds, present a counterpoint to the earlier contributions of German and Jewish scholarship and the earlier and later contributions of English anthropologists to American anthropological theory, and to American multidisciplinary studies.

Interaction between anthropologists and the American scene also produced new insights. Levi-Strauss was in New York in the mid-1940s as a cultural attache to the French Mission, and had an opportunity for extended discussions with American anthropologists. And British anthropologists Geoffrey Gorer and Gregory Bateson both responded to their initial contact with American culture with provocative analyses.

In the 1970s furor broke out over the community studies that American anthropologists were carrying out in Thailand. It was argued that they might be endangering the mountain people whom they were studying. This issue intensified contemporary concern over the relationship between anthropologists and the people whom they study, necessitating attention to new ethical problems. Meanwhile, the politicizing of American Indian protests, combined with the symbolic resort to American Indian cultures by radical ecologists, has raised public consciousness of the relationship between American Indians and ethnologists. Finally, the television and magazine presentations of the Tasaday have given the general public a new sense of the dangers inherent in abrupt and unmodulated culture contact. At present, the invocation of primitive peoples as symbolic of deep ethical conflicts in the world is perhaps the most conspicuous development, a development that is often distorted by today's students into a belief that ethnologists are the ones who destroyed the old cultures, when in fact they attempted to chronicle them and cushion the contact.

REFERENCES

1. Adorno, T. W., et al. *Authoritarian Personality.* New York: Harper, 1950.
2. Antin, Mary. *The Promised Land.* Boston: Houghton Mifflin, 1912; reprinted 1963.
3. Ausubel, David P. *The Fern and the Tiki.* New York: Holt, Rinehart and Winston, 1965.
4. Bennett, John W. *Hutterian Brethren.* Stanford: Stanford University Press, 1967.
5. Berndt, Ronald M., and Berndt, Catherine. *The First Australians.* Sydney: Smith, 1952.

6. Bridges, Roy. *The League of the Lord.* Sydney-London: Australasian Publishing, 1950.

7. Brown, Dee. *Bury My Heart At Wounded Knee.* New York: Holt, Rinehart & Winston, 1971.

8. Cartwright, Dorwin, ed. *Field Theory in Social Science.* New York: Harper and Row, 1964.

9. Dark, Eleanor. *The Timeless Land.* London: Collins, 1950.

10. Davis, Allison, and Dollard, John. *Children of Bondage.* New York: Harper and Row, 1964.

11. Davis, Allison; Gardner, Burleigh B.; and Gardner, Mary R. *Deep South.* Chicago: University of Chicago Press, 1941; reprinted 1963.

12. Day, Beth. *Sexual Life Between Blacks & Whites.* New York: World Publishing, 1972.

13. Deloria, Vine, Jr. *Custer Died for Your Sins.* New York: Macmillan, 1969.

14. Dickens, Charles. *American Notes.* New York: Wilson, 1842; New York: Peter Smith, 1961.

15. Dickens, Charles. *Martin Chuzzlewit.* Leipzig: Tauchnitz, 1884; New York: Dutton, 1923.

16. Dollard, John. *Caste and Class in a Southern Town.* New Haven: Yale University Press, 1937; Garden City, NY: Doubleday, 1957.

17. Durkheim, Emile. *The Elementary Forms of the Religious Life: A Study in Religious Sociology.* London: Allen and Unwin, 1915; New York: Macmillan, 1926.

18. Durkheim, Emile. *The Division of Labour in Society.* London and New York: Macmillan, 1933; New York: Free Press, 1964.

19. Ella, S. "Samoa." *Report of the Fourth Meeting of the Australasian Association for the Advancement of Science*, 4, pp 620-645, 1893

20. Elkin, A. P. *Aborigines and Citizenship.* Sydney: Association for the Protection of Native Races, 1958.

21. Erikson, Erik H. *Childhood and Society.* New York: Norton, 1950; rev. ed. 1963.

22. Erikson, Erik H. *Young Man Luther.* New York: Norton, 1958; reprinted 1962.

23. Erikson, Erik H. *Identity: Youth and Crisis.* New York: Norton, 1968.

24. Erikson, Erik H. *Gandhi's Truth.* New York: Norton, 1969.

25. Franklin, John H., ed. *Color and Race.* Boston: Houghton Mifflin, 1968.

26. Frobenius, Leo. *Erlebte Erdteile.* 7 vols. Frankfurt/M.: Frankfurter Societats Druckerei, 1925-1929.

27. Fromm, Erich. *Escape from Freedom.* New York: Farrar and Rinehardt, 1941; New York: Avon, 1966.

28. Gorer, Geoffrey. *The American People.* New York: Norton, 1948; rev. ed. 1964.

29. Gorer, Geoffrey. *Exploring English Character.* New York: Criterion Books, 1955.

30. Gorer, Geoffrey. *The Danger of Equality: Selected Essays.* London: Cresset, 1966.

31. Graebner, F. *Methode der Ethnologie.* Heidelberg: Winter, 1911.

32. Graham, Edward K. *History Of Hampton Institute.* (In press.)

33. Green, Gerald (producer), and Reynolds, Jack (reporter). "The Cave People Of The Philippines." *NBC/TV*, October 10, 1972.

34. Handlin, Oscar. *The Uprooted.* Boston: Little, Brown, 1951; New York: Grosset and Dunlap, 1961.

35. Handlin, Oscar. *Immigration as a Factor in American History.* Englewood Cliffs, N.J.: Prentice-Hall, 1959.

36. Handlin, Oscar. *The American People in the 20th Century.* Cambridge: Harvard University Press, 1966, rev. ed.

37. Hicks, Granville. *Small Town.* Toronto: Macmillan, 1946.

38. Hostetler, John A. *Amish Society.* Baltimore: Johns Hopkins, 1968, rev. ed.

39. Jefferson, Thomas. "On the Character and Capacities of the North American Indians." In *The Golden Age of American Anthropology*, edited by M. Mead and R. Bunzel, pp. 75-81. New York: Braziller, 1960.

40. Kallen, Horace M. *Cultural Pluralism and the American Idea.* Philadelphia: University of Pennsylvania Press, 1956.

41. Kardiner, Abram and Ovsey, L. *The Mark of Oppression.* New York: Norton, 1951; New York: Peter Smith, 1963.

42. Kimball, Solon T., and Pearsall, Marion. *Talladega Story.* Drawer: University of Alabama Press, 1954.

43. Kluckhohn, Clyde. "Universal Values and Anthropological Relativism," Arthur T. Vanderbilt et al., eds. *Modern Education and Human Values*, vol. 4. Pittsburgh: University of Pittsburgh Press, 1952.

44. Kluckhohn, Florence R., et al. *Variations in Value Orientations.* Evanston: Row, Peterson, 1961.

45. Lantz, H. *Coaltown.* New York: Columbia University Press, 1958.

46. Leighton, Alexander H. *The Governing of Men.* Princeton: Princeton University Press, 1945; New York: Octagon Books, 1964.

47. Lévi-Strauss, Claude. *Structural Anthropology.* New York: Basic Books, 1963.

48. Levy-Bruhl, Lucien. *Primitive Mentality.* New York: Macmillan, 1923.

49. Lewis, Oscar. *Five Families: Mexican Case Studies in the Culture of Poverty.* New York: Basic Books, 1959; New York: American Library, 1965.

50. Lewis, Oscar. *The Children of Sanchez.* New York: Random House, 1961.

51. Lewis, Oscar. "The Culture of Poverty." *Scientific American.* 215:19-25, 1966.

52. Lewis, Oscar. *La Vida.* New York: Random House, 1966.

53. Lewis, Oscar. *Study in Slum Culture.* New York: Random House, 1968.

54. Lowie, Robert H. *Indians of the Plains.* New York: McGraw-Hill, 1954.

55. MacLeish, Kenneth, and Aunois, John L. "Stone Age Men Of The Philippines." *National Geographic.* 142:219-250, 1972.

56. McLuhan, T. C. *Touch The Earth: A Self-Portrait Of Indian Existence.* New York: Outerbridge & Lazard (Dutton), 1971.

57. McWilliams, Carey. *Prejudice: Japanese Americans, Symbol of Racial Intolerance.* Boston: Little, Brown, 1945.

58. Malcolm X and Haley, A. *Autobiography of Malcolm X.* New York: Grove Press, 1967.

59. May, Karl. *Winnetou,* 3 vols. Freiburg: Fehsenfeld, 1893; Englewood Cliffs, N.J.: Prentice-Hall, 1969.

60. Mead, Margaret. "Group Intelligence Tests and Linguistic Disability among Italian Children." *School and Society.* 25:465-468, 1927.

61. Mead, Margaret. *The Changing Culture of an Indian Tribe.* New York: Columbia University Press, 1932; reprinted with new introduction, Capricorn Books, New York, 1966.

62. Mead, Margaret. *And Keep Your Powder Dry.* New York: Morrow, 1942; reprinted 1965.

63. Mead, Margaret. "Trends in Personal Life." *New Republic.* 115:346-348, 1946.

64. Mead, Margaret. *Male and Female.* New York: Morrow, 1949; reprinted 1967.

65. Mead, Margaret. *The School in American Culture.* Cambridge: Harvard University Press, 1951.

66. Mead, Margaret. "Implications of Insight - II." In *Childhood in Contemporary Cultures,* edited by Margaret Mead & Martha Wolfenstein, pp. 449-461. Chicago: University of Chicago Press, 1955.

67. Mead, Margaret. Introduction to *The Golden Age of American Anthropology,* edited by M. Mead and R. Bunzel. New York: Braziller, 1960.

68. Mead, Margaret. "Research with Human Beings: A Model Derived from Anthropological Field Practice." *Daedalus.* Spring 1969, pp. 361-386.

69. Mead, Margaret. "Bio-Social Components of Political Processes." *Journal of International Affairs* 24 (1):18-28, 1970.

70. Mead, Margaret. "Field Work In High Cultures." In *Crossing Cultural Boundaries,* edited by Solon T. Kimball and James B. Watson, pp. 120-132. San Francisco: Chandler, 1972.

71. Mead, Margaret, and Baldwin, James. *A Rap On Race.* Philadelphia & New York: Lippincott, 1971.

72. Mead, Margaret, and Brown, Muriel. *The Wagon and the Star.* St. Paul: Curriculum Resources, 1966; Chicago, Rand McNally, 1967.

73. Mead, Margaret, and Metraux, Rhoda. "Town & Gown: A General Statement." In *The Universities in Regional Affairs.* Urban Research and Education in the New York Region: A Report to the Regional Plan Association, edited by Harvey S. Perloff and Henry Cohen, vol. 3, pp. 1-42. New York: Regional Plan Association, 1965.

74. Morgan, Lewis H. *Ho-De-No-Sau-Nee, or Iroquois,* 2 vols. New York: Franklin, 1901.

75. Muir, Margaret Rosten. *Indian Education at Hampton Institute and Federal Indian Policy: Solutions to the Indian Problem.* Master's Thesis, Brown University, 1970.

76. Myrdal, Gunnar. *An American Dilemma.* New York: Harper, 1944; reprinted 1962.

77. Parkinson, Richard H. *Dreissig Jahre in der Sudsee.* Stuttgart: Strecker and Schroder, 1907.

78. Parsons, Talcott. "Research with Human Subjects and the 'Professional Complex'." *Daedalus,* Spring 1969, pp. 325-360.

79. Pettigrew, Thomas F. *A Profile of the Negro American.* New York: Van Nostrand, 1964.

80. "Philippine Tribe Said To Live in Caves." *New York Times,* 27 March 1972.

81. Powdermaker, Hortense. *After Freedom.* New York: Viking Press, 1939; New York: Atheneum, 1968.

82. Raper, Arthur F. *Tenants of the Almighty.* New York: Macmillan, 1943.

83. Ratzel, Friedrich. *The History of Mankind,* 8 vols. London-New York: Macmillan, 1896-1898.

84. Reichard, Gladys. *Navajo Religion: A Study of Symbolism,* 2 vols. New York: Pantheon, 1950.

85. Ruesch, Jurgen, and Bateson, Gregory. *Communication: The Social Matrix of Psychiatry.* New York: Norton, 1951.

86. Smith, S. Percy. *Hawaiki,* 2d ed. London: Whitcombe and Tombs, 1904.

87. Soddy, Kenneth, ed. *Identity – Mental Health and Value Systems.* Philadelphia: Lippincott, 1961.

88. Spier, Leslie. *The Sun Dance of the Plains Indians: Its Development and Diffusion.* Anthropological Papers of The American Museum of Natural History, vol. 16, Part 7. New York: 1921.

89. Spier, Leslie. *An Analysis of Plains Indians Parfleche Decorations.* Washington University Publications in Anthropology, vol. 1, no. 3. Seattle: 1925.

90. Spier, Robert F. G. "Work Habits, Postures, and Fixtures." In *American Historical Anthropology: Essays in Honor of Leslie Spier,* edited by C. L. Riley and W. W. Taylor, pp. 197-220. Carbondale: Southern Illinois University Press, 1967.

91. Spitz, R. A. "Fruhkindliches Erleben und Erwachsenenkultur bei den Primitiven." *Imago.* 21:367-387, 1935.

92. Steward, Julian H. *The People of Puerto Rico.* Urbana: University of Illinois Press, 1956.

93. Stocking, George W. *Race, Culture and Evolution.* New York: Free Press, 1968.

94. Tannenbaum, Frank. *Slave and Citizen: The Negro in the Americas.* Toronto: Random House, 1963.

95. Tax, Sol. "Action Anthropology." *America indigena* (Mexico) 12:103-109, 1952.

96. Thomas, Dorothy S., and Nishimoto, Richard S. *The Spoilage: Japanese American Evacuation and Resettlement.* Berkeley: University of California Press, 1946.

97. Valentine, Charles A. *Culture and Poverty.* Chicago: University of Chicago Press, 1968.

98. Vidich, Arthur J., and Bensman, Joseph. *Small Town in Mass Society.* Princeton, N.J.: Princeton University Press, 1958.

99. Warner, W. Lloyd. *Yankee City,* abridged ed. New Haven, N.J.: Yale University Press, 1963.

100. Warner, W. Lloyd, and Lunt, Paul S. *The Social Life of a Modern Community.* Yankee City Series, vol. 1. New Haven, N.J.: Yale University Press, 1941.

101. Warner, W. Lloyd, and Low, J. O. *The Social System of the Modern Factory.* Yankee City Series, vol. 4. New Haven, N.J.: Yale University Press, 1947.

102. Warner, W. Lloyd; Junker, B. H.; and Adams, Walter A. *Color and Human Nature.* Washington: American Council on Education, 1941.

103. Warner, W. Lloyd; Havighurst, R. J.; and Loeb, M. B. *Who Shall Be Educated?* New York: Harper, 1944.

104. Warner, W. Lloyd, and Srole, Leo. *The Social Systems of American Ethnic Groups.* Yankee City Series, vol. 3. New Haven, N.J.: Yale University Press, 1945.

105. West, James. *Plainville, U.S.A.* New York: Columbia University Press, 1945; reprinted 1961.

106. Worth, Sol, and Adair, John. *Through Navajo Eyes.* Bloomington, IN: Indiana University Press, 1972.

107. Zborowski, Mark. *People in Pain.* San Francisco: Jossey-Bass, 1969.

Italian Ethnic Identity and Its Transformations

LOLA ROMANUCCI-ROSS

8

The "informed informant," that is, the ethnically enculturated investigator, can make valuable contributions to anthropological research in his role of informant-participant-observer. Investigating my native Italian culture, I found that this approach can be less verbal, less dependent on formal instruments, and still elicit full response. I applied this approach to the study of Ascoli Piceno, 130 miles northeast of Rome.[1]

Ascoli Piceno, the city, is in the province of Ascoli Piceno and in the region of Le Marche, which is surrounded by La Toscana, Umbria, Lazio, Abruzzi and the Adriatic Sea. The province has 228 *comuni rurali* ("rural communes") and five *comuni urbani* ("urban communes"). Of the working population, 25.6 percent are engaged in agriculture, 35 percent in industry, and 39.4 percent in other occupations. The industries include electric power plants, metallurgy, mechanics, textiles, and chemical products. About 39 percent of the population live in the hills, where the climate is Mediterranean, but frosts do at times destroy the fruit blossoms, and briny air causes crop

[1] I should like to express my appreciation for the assistance of Giudice Istruttore Dott. Alfonso Palumbo and Dott. Guido Marcolini, who were generous with their time and efforts in giving me access to materials.

damage on the coast. Much of the agriculture consists of cereals, grapes, and animal husbandry. Of the rural population, 46.1 percent farm their own land, 48 percent participate in a kind of sharecropping system called "*mezzadria,* 4.5 percent are hired laborers (*salariati*), and 1.4 percent do not fall in any of these categories.

Under the *mezzadria* system *il concedente* is the landowner whose land is worked by the *mezzadro,* also called *colono* or *contadino.* Theoretically the *mezzadro*'s entire family must work for *il concedente,* but this is no longer true in practice. Daughters and sons old enough to be hired by factories obtain fulltime jobs, much to the chagrin of the *concedente,* who can do nothing about it. The owner is under strict regulations to provide a domicile that meets hygienic standards and is of sensible construction. This is done. If he decides to leave, the *colono* must give notice and must remain until the following August. This is not done. The *mezzadro* gets 58 percent of the produce, along with all that he can appropriate, which can be considerable, for the opportunities are almost limitless. The owner never gets the best produce, nor does he know how much the *contadino* has sold and pocketed. Of the 42 percent that remains, the owners must pay 25 percent in taxes, 5 percent in contributions for social security for the *contadino* and his family, and must put 10 percent back into improving the land. With the migration to urban centers, and the desire to work in factories (or just *not* to be a *contadino*), agricultural produce brings a high price, but not high enough to encourage a return to the country.

This flow of rural people into the cities is unsettling to urban dwellers, who hold the view that all evil comes in from the country. The women, it is said, come into the city to be prostitutes, the men to set up small business, all *per fregare* (in polite terms, "to take others for all one can get"). Country children, it is said, use horrid language, and defile ordinary language in any case. And country people just generally are uncouth. Thus the incoming peasants are viewed by a people who have had millenia of the *civitas.* Those who leave the countryside for the city, however, do not regret it and do not go back to the country, preferring the unemployment pension. (Getting signatures on documents for pension eligibility is a common activity.)

The city of Ascoli is divided into *borghi,* or *sestieri,* or *porte (porta).* Each of these refers to a section of the city that is aware of its own history and its own characteristics. They also compete during the *quintana,* a yearly jousting bout and carnival which celebrates the returning of the keys of the city from the *comune* to the bishop, who represents the papacy. Sections referred to formally are Porta Romana, Porta Capuccina, and Porta Maggiore; Porta Tufilla is Borgo Solesta. These were the gates to the ancient and medieval city.

There is also an informal sectioning of the city, including "Korea" where the riffraff (*la marmaglia*) live, and "Shanghai," the black market, easy virtue section of town. There is another section "where all the communists live," and one where "all the vulgar new people live," like immigrants from Abbruzzi—in short, all those who do not reflect the core of the virtues of the ancient city-state. According to Ascoli's old guard, all that is bad (including prostitution and thievery) has been brought in by the uncivilized rurals and immigrants, for what can one expect of rustics who have not practiced the civic virtues for millenia, or at least centuries?

HISTORY OF ASCOLI PICENO

Italy is a conglomerate of many tribes and peoples that settled there over a 30,000 year period. Still there is an ancient, continuous cultural tradition by which the Italian defines himself and in which he lives, although regional differences remain extremely important. The Italian regional ethnography, which is not challenged by those whose regional origins differ, reckons Italianate ethnic perfection according to distance of origin from Tuscany (*la Toscana*). More prestige accrues to those born in or close to Tuscany, while there is deterioration southward and attenuation of authenticity northward. Ethno-ethnographies (group-appraisal of self and other groups) in Italy are a cultural tradition of long standing. Romans used to characterize people according to their barbaric habits or fine Romanic customs. They applauded other groups for their "liberation fronts," even if they wanted to liberate themselves from the Romans. It is no accident that the notion of group identity, a group's consciousness of its own history, comes to us from an Italian, Giambattista Vico (*54*).

Ascoli Piceno lies along the ancient Via Salaria, the Roman "salt road" to the east coast. Five hundred feet above sea level, it is found among wooded hills of oak and chestnut at the confluence of the Tronto and Castellano Rivers. It emerged historically during the Pelasgian invasions, and its earliest inhabitants spoke some version of the ghostly asterisked proto-languages that interlock with equally uncertain shades of pottery and sword people, who were quite probably Italics along with the Sabini, Volsci, Umbri, and Osci. At any rate there is archaeological evidence that Sabines from the north and Illyrians from the opposite coast came in and settled with the early neolithic inhabitants. The indigenes had inhumation burial rites, woolen clothing, bronze fibulae, torques, bracelets, girdles, amber, ornamental pendants, and inscriptions that utilized the Etruscan alphabet (*43*).

Some believe that the first attempts at Italian national unity occurred in the 90 B.C. war of the Socii against Rome, led by the Piceni. This enterprise included the Sabini, Tusci, Volsci, Brusci, Picentini, and Ascolani. Dating it then or later, as some do, it is agreed that eventually Italy conquered its conquerors, for the invaders stayed, abandoned their traditions, and became what they found. "Historical events" did not much interest the inhabitants. Even by the twelfth century, a national consciousness had not yet developed. With the formation of the *comuni,* local centers were handling their own problems without the help of outside authorities, but by the end of the thirteenth century, communal life was extinguished and factionalism took over once more. As far as we can tell, Italians became Italians simply through the institutions that they freely accepted: traditions, common language, art, music, heroic figures, poetry.

The Romans knew the ancient city as Asculum Picenum and captured it in 268 B.C. during the construction of the Via Salaria. Praeter C. Servilius provoked a massacre of the Romans in 90 B.C. in Asculum Picenum while leading the social war against Rome, but Rome won it back a year later. Caesar occupied the city after crossing the Rubicon. Christianity penetrated Ascoli in the fourth century. In 578 the city was occupied and sacked by the Longobards. In 781 Charlemagne gave it to Pope Adrian the First, who made it a papal state. In 1183 it became a republic with free judicial administration, but was then taken by Frederick II in 1242. In 1266 it became once more a papal possession. Under French domination from 1798 to 1815 (Carolingian Frankish Italy), it returned to papal jurisdiction after the fall of Napoleon. It became part of the Italian kingdom in 1860, and was captured by the Allies in World War II in July, 1944.

I chose these punctuation points because they have been memorialized in the city plan, the streets, buildings, monuments, the festivals and the daily lives of the inhabitants. Two of the main streets in Ascoli today correspond to the old Roman thoroughfares, and there are remains of the Roman city wall (fourth to second century B.C.), as well as much of the medieval wall. There are two Roman bridges (one partly destroyed by the Germans in 1944), the remains of a Roman theatre, amphitheatre, and a temple of Vesta. With the introduction of Christianity, circa 300, pagan temples became churches, and Benedictine cloisters were built. In 1006, civil power passed to the bishops and feudal lords. Because of internal quarrels, fortifications were built, including numerous towers, a few of which still stand, some truncated or incorporated into houses. The fortress of Malatesta (1349) is now a prison. By 1226 St. Francis had constituted his order in Ascoli, and the great Gothic church dedicated to him was built in 1265. The cloisters are now in the marketplace. The Palazzo del Arringo, earliest commune center, and the Palazzo del Popolo, now a museum, date from the thirteenth century. After 1300 the town declined because of internal strife and lack of trade.

BEHAVIORAL MODELS

In the "conscious model" of the family of the past the most conspicuous role in the good old days was that of the dominant male. He might be a grandfather or a mother's brother, this being determined by simple assumption of the role, accompanied of course by status, prestige and *carattere*, "strength of character." Others had to recognize the paterfamilias as such. He sat at the head of the table, kept order and discipline, decided what all the others could or could not do, and prescribed behavior. Discipline meant that one's language had to be circumspect at gatherings and that children were expected to eat everything at a meal. Meals often included peasant fare such as *polenta* (corn meal mush) and beans, because one had to learn to like to eat the food of the poor, since one never knew what one's circumstances in life might become.

This was the family of 65 or 50 years ago that is remembered with nostalgia. The dominant male was in command (*sapeva commandare*) and kept everyone in place. The patriarchal family is still considered ideal, and the woman who "marries in" constitutes a threat to family solidarity. She is seen as a vile and greedy woman who pits brother against brother, father against son, and husband against sister. She has strong allies—the Church, and the deep belief of her victims that a marriage must be saved at all costs, especially if there are children. She is considered to be assimilated when she has become loyal and subservient to her husband and his family. But even then it is rarely said that she was a good woman initially; rather, it is said that her husband had the *coglioni* ("testicles," i.e., manhood) to domesticate her. Her submission earns her the good offices of the paternal family. Against this family solidarity the Italian woman can expect no help from her brother; she must use all her ingenuity and cunning to get everything she can out of her husband.

Evidence abounds controverting the Banfield notion of "amoral familism," that is, the emphasizing of family loyalty above all other considerations. The courts have many records of brothers fighting, in some cases to the death, over a small inheritance, and every family has a story of the sister being done out of her small inheritance by the brother and his wife. But the woman who "marries in" creates a solidarity against her, where it did not exist before. Seduction of the woman is feared not from the stranger, but from the *compare, cugino,* and *cognato* ("godfather," "cousin," and "brother-in-law"). They have your trust, they have an entree into your house, and they will get at your wife. Very often one hears, *La vita e una fregature. Chi non sa fregare rimane fregato* ("Life is a rape scene. He who is not the aggressor in the act will be the victim"). Indeed the language does not lack idiomatic phrases alluding to phallic intrusion, most of it anal.

But despite the many tensions within family life, there are remarkably few problems between generations. The aged, the very young and all ages in between spend many hours together in the evening, in conversations and exchanges in which the observer notes no generational differences in style, speech, gesture or general attitudes—the very young have already assimilated all of these. On the other hand, at ten o'clock sharp everyone runs to look at the television commercials which are called *Carousel,* an arty twenty minutes of hard and soft sell of consumer items. The actors serve as new Americanized models for role-playing. These programs are not forbidden to the youngsters, but are enough removed from the acceptable for a mother to frown at the little nine-year-old who imitates the dress and body movements of a blues singer. Here, as elsewhere, body gestures are used to define relationships and to adjust to the idiosyncratic timing, the "personal clocks" of others.

Although a systematic collection of data on the patterns in the communication process is still needed, I feel I can safely say that the child is taught to trust the analogic message, and told overtly that information received when the sender is totally off guard is much more reliable. Explicit messages are well understood as "ceremonial," designed to fill in silences, to put up fences, or to build bridges between persons. I participated in the process myself and found I was correctly interpreted and most often correctly interpreted others.

A very important person just beyond the family unit is the *mediatore.* Licensed *mediatori* can arrange sales of land or articles, or settle disputes. Unlicensed *mediatori* arrange marriages. Rarely does anyone want to admit that he or she needs a *mediatore* to find a spouse, but specifications are drawn up and sought, and if found by the *mediatore,* a price is paid. The *mediatore* is a valued personality type because he has a facility with words and is not only a good but an easy-going bargainer. He knows that, as with most things in life, compromise is the real solution. He urges both sides to *ragionare*, to reason together.

A behavioral model outside the family is provided by the saints, who represent the externalization of sentiment and responsibility. Saints not only do not overeat, they literally starve and waste away. The cemeteries are full of those who died from heart attacks and other illnesses related to overeating while on long pilgrimages to pay homage to these self-denying saints. Also, they do not succumb to carnal desires, as others do. Saints, it is thought, are not different in nature from others, but they are more courageous and have more strength.

Saints often begin in role antithesis but then shift to role-reversal. Mussolini did so, going from an anti-authoritarian stance to its opposite. One woman said to me, "Don't let Italians lie to you about Mussolini. We loved him, he became strong and daring for awhile, as we knew we were not. It is doubtful whether it is he who led us or we who led him to destruction. But then we had to hate him because in the end he was really like us, pusillanimous." Another said, "Wasn't it so Italian of this man, who said, 'If I lead you, follow, and if I retreat, kill me,' to run off? and in a German sergeant's uniform yet! Only his mistress can be said to have had principles. Once in a while women surprise one."

On a lesser scale, priests and nuns give up family life and sex. For this they are respected, since they act out the purer desires. They are constantly fed and given gifts, and estates of the wealthy are willed to their various orders. If it is known that the private life of a bishop is not completely chaste, it is said that this does not impair his spiritual leadership. Temporary lapses are expected, but beyond a reasonable time, a lapse is not accepted. Then he must be transferred. But for a time the public attitude is that as long as a man of the cloth respects the codes of his status and the beliefs of his followers to the point of not confronting them with an ugly truth, then all should bear with him until it passes.

The *furbo* ("shrewd person") is the antithesis of the saint; he is the psychological survivor. He has others play all the roles, taking no risks, but also feeling none of the joys and traumas of achievement. He puts the risk-taking in the hands of the *ingenuo,* or the naive one. (Mothers always warn children not to become a *furbo,* but more importantly, not to become an *ingenuo.*) The active role of the *furbo* is that of psychological incitement. He creates the climate, sets the stage and directs the *ingenuo* who will plunge into the maelstrom, the love affair, the sexual misadventure, the economic disaster, or the revolt against authority that will demolish him.

POLITICAL ATTITUDES

The 1970 election results in Ascoli reported Christian Democrats receiving 37.29 percent of the vote. The *Movimento Sociale Italiano* (neo-Fascist party) received 8.95 percent, Monarchists, 1.41 percent, and the *Partito Communista Italiano,* 20.37 percent. The rest of the votes were all sub-varieties of Socialist or Communist or Maoist party votes. Although the Church proudly points out that it had the majority vote, over fifty percent of the voters expressed a desire for a drastic restructuring of the society, from left to extreme left. And this was not in industrial Northern Italy, where it would be most expected. Still, individualism keeps the smaller parties from ever coalescing. Although a great deal of social legislation is being passed, the country remains too poor to implement it properly.

In a survey of political attitudes, I found that regardless of party affiliation or professed voting preference, basic political attitudes prevailed. According to the *Ascolani,* Italy needs *il bastone,* "the club," so that Italians learn respect for the law. But it is felt that although Fascists had the right idea about this, one simply cannot allow others to tell one *how* and *what* to think (religious doctrine is not taken seriously). Anyway, no matter what the political structure of the region or the country, political activity, say the Ascolani, will be determined by Italian character, which is hopeless. And even if the Communists took over, it could never be Soviet-style, because everyone would still try to get through life by chicanery and little or no work. They would continue to worry about what others think, and they would keep going to mass because there is nothing else to do. Therefore, there is no real objection to a Communist coup, but only to the type of Italian who is attracted to the Communist party and especially its leadership, for he is likely to be the pigheaded one, unable to recognize that social life is made possible by compromise. That type of person would not give up power easily, and it is above all necessary to have a government that can be toppled easily over any issue.

ATTITUDES TOWARD SOCIAL INSTITUTIONS (FEUDAL REMAINS)

Italian institutions as seen in Ascoli are characterized by patterns of interpersonal relationships that Erich Fromm called feudal, for they depend on giving and receiving favors and on formal rules of dependency and responsibility in crises or everyday life. Inadequate salaries are regarded as justification for everyone to be entitled to a little bribe, a bit of *prosciutto* ("ham"), to get papers moving from desk to desk, to get one's rightful pension, to collect one's insurance, to be sure that the teacher promotes a child, to get one's case on the court calendar. One informant said to me, "This is the place where a man will say he is wrong when he is right because he has no faith in his rights, only in the kindly disposition of a superior." On several occasions, I asked people if they wanted my intervention on higher levels to get into a hospital or a school. The reply was always, "No, please, I will be punished in some terrible way in the future after you are gone, for my presumption."

Barzini wrote, "in all of Italy there is 'lower-case *mafia*' " (5). I would say *mafia,* "writ small." The code cannot be violated without disastrous effects, for it is a guide on how to get things done. It is not difficult to see how this might have come about. With frequent changes in the ruling class, justice came to mean an unwritten moral code. "Sardinian justice" intrigues those interested in the effectiveness of legal sanctions in Italy. I was told by justices, and I have also read, that few cases ever get to Italian courts in Sardinia, although there are murders over kidnappings and infringements of land rights. Infrastructural codes exist, however, as is seen in the case of some kidnappers who were not protected by villagers because they broke the rule on never kidnapping a woman. Sardinian justice is concerned with what you must not do, while Sicilian justice tells you both what you must and must not do. The *mafia* was a pre-political, or para-political organization, an institutionalized system of justice outside the law. Its first code of *omerta* ("manliness") was that one did not give information to the state. The social structure became one of patronage, retainers, dependents and networks of influence, which later also became a perfect organization for criminal activity.

Italians are convinced of the corruptibility of men and women. And they are certain that the tyranny of the weak is not to be less feared than that of the strong. I asked the more sophisticated why psychoanalysis had not become popular in Italy. The reply was always, "the Church." I think this answer reflects the attitude that of course evil is repressed, and ought to be, because *repression is good.* It forces people to be non-egoistic, and protects families and children. Repression is the *fundamenta* of civility and polity and even self-respect.

I noted that crime patterns change from south to north, and in various regions. "Carnal crimes" abound in the South, with the purpose of undermining the position of an antagonist by desecrating the "honor" of his woman. In Sardinia, kidnapping in order to obtain large ransoms is common. It is easy for the kidnappers to hide in the hills and then escape to the north of Italy, to try and set up a business. In Naples, petty pilfering and large-scale theft are rampant. As one goes north, "declared bankruptcy with full pockets" becomes common. This crime has come as far south as Ascoli, where one important case involved a shoe factory from which forty million lira were sent off to Belgium. And there was the notorious wine case, *Vini Piceni,* involving wine made of banana peels, ox-blood and Tronto River water. Ascolani say of these lawbreakers, "they are not from here," and actually they were not.

Both homicides and suicides are generally from the *contadino* ("peasant") or working classes. There were forty-seven homicides in the province of Ascoli between 1930 and 1968. Victim and aggressor were usually in the same occupation and had the same social rank. Only three cases were related to jealousy. Seventeen homicides were the result of arguments, of which the majority were about money matters. Twelve murders were the result of political hatreds (almost all of these in post-war years). There were nine passion killings (two for revenge, three as a result of robberies, four unknown), five cases called *futile* by the court—the result of insults, drunkenness, or a fight over a card game, and one undescribed homicide. From 1930 to 1965 there were twenty-nine *reported* cases of infanticide. Infanticide is defined by article 578 of the penal code as "bringing about the death of a newborn immediately after parturition, or of a foetus during labor, to safeguard one's honor or the honor of a conjoined person." Honor is defined as the sexual honor of a woman who became pregnant without being married.

In Ascoli, the prison had only eleven inmates. They were allowed to walk about freely and talk with each other, were sent on errands within the prison and kept busy. Two had been imprisoned for exploiting prostitutes, one for murder. He explained to me that although he heard all the others telling me they were not guilty and were there by mistake, he wanted me to know that he was guilty and it was only fair that he got 21 years. Everyone shook his hand respectfully as we left, attorneys, physician, the justice and myself. There was a remarkable civility about it. One young boy of sixteen was there for having raped a 62-year-old woman. The speculations on whether or not it was true were interesting. The physician's interpretation was that the old woman used to pay the young man, but this night she knew they had been seen so she screamed "rape," and he hit her. The very young judge expressed anxiety about his sentence because, he confided to me, his best affair was with a 51-year-old German tourist when he was twenty—and did that mean he was utterly depraved? My only conclusion about the boy in prison is that he was thoroughly Sicilian and would not cooperate with the judge (i.e., authority), even when it became clear to him that the judge was trying to help, for he must have been sure that the "help" was a trick. He explained his refusal to admit his guilt by asking, "What would my mother think if she knew I slept with an older woman?"

The judge said, "I like much older women."

"Each to his peculiar tastes, sir," he answered, at which point everyone laughed.

In Ascoli, through an unusually heightened consciousness of culture, even all those people beyond the prison walls know they are not free. Their past slaveries are commemorated in bronze and in stone, and in their paintings. The churches and priests are reminders, like punctuation marks, through the day and year and life crises that they are not in control of their destiny.

I spoke earlier of the notion of life being a *fregatura,* a rape. I was often told, "You do not know, even after you have been given a discount or have been done a favor, whether you have been *fregato* or not." Such feelings add further to the sense of loss of control. The belief that there exists an ethic of *me ne freghismo* is total; children are taught this very early. All agree that Fascism curbed this attitude for a while. In fact, the only thing wrong with Fascists was that they got Italians involved in wars and mixed up with barbarians like the Germans and the Russians. Work is in the long run counterproductive, for in addition to working long years to make a big ceremonial splash, or to appear important in an affinal exchange, one also has to contend with the marketplace and its endless bickering and game strategies as to how much one is going to overcharge before discounting, with the fear and avoidance of long-term business commitments, and with a general distrust of government. The individual knows he is alone, and in his solitude he does not really hope for help even from his family. People in government are all thieves, he thinks, be they local or federal. And they have to be bribed in order for him to receive what is rightfully his. The *prosciutto* is the symbolic allusion for the transaction.

CLASS DISTINCTIONS

Consciousness of class is so keenly honed that if someone demonstrates even slight pretensions in *comparaggio* ("godparentage") or marriage choice, much will be made of the fact that his antecedents were *contadini* or *garzoni* (peasant "work boys"). Barzini writes that "Italians are not class conscious" (5), and it is true that caste and class among Italians is sometimes subtle, so that a person may not know he was "out" until he is "in." I would say that Italians are extremely conscious of class and caste when they marry, merge, ritualize and socialize. But there are situations in which class differences break down, and these situations, interestingly enough, I was always able to classify as those events where *ragionando* ("reasoning," "problem-solving") was of paramount importance. In the courts of law, for instance, attorneys, minor judges, prisoners and the prisoner's relatives speak to each other familiarly and frankly, and respect each other's opinions. This is also the case where a crime or its motivations are being discussed, even between magistrate and prisoner, or on the street, between a traffic policeman and a violator. The gestures, the tones, even at times the grammar are "familiar," because one must *ragionare*, reason together, try to understand something. But one never finds the breakdown of class barrier symbols in a hospital or clinic, or in a church or a school. Here interclass relations follow traditional and rigidly defined styles.

In ordinary situations, class distinctions are respected as far back as the memory allows. Much was made to me of the fact that my mother's family (the Celani) were landowning aristocrats, though untitled. Although some are still successful in modern terms, others live in shabby gentility. Everyone seemed to know that my maternal grandmother's mother, Caterina Lalli-Cafini, was a noblewoman, and they never tired of letting me know that the hyphenated name alone gave that information, and of telling me that when she came to marry her intended, she had one hundred of everything in her *corredo* ("dowry"), including an elegant coach, horses, and a retinue. I was never spared the fact that her husband had nothing to recommend him but his wit and his *prepotenza* ("exaggerated self-confidence"). His parents had an estate on which they trained and bred dogs for nobility, but after all, what is a dog breeder and trainer? To those who described these things, it is as though it were in the present, not events that happened over a century ago. I enjoyed status-contamination from my great-grandmother; attenuation does not seem to occur. The high sensitivity to status difference in addressing another person is evident, but not constantly expressed. It varies with the information one wants to convey. My uncle, for example, in speaking to the judge who had been helpful to me, would sometimes say "Signor Guidice" and sometimes "Alfonso." It depended, of course, on what he wanted to say. "Alfonso" meant, "I know that you are much too attentive to my niece." "Signor Guidice" meant, "I have some very fine wines if you will remember I am Lola's uncle and do me a favor when I need it." Such intimations are often ignored; the response is also cryptic in form of address.

The use of titles also varies in a situation, particularly if one wishes to inject humor. A lawyer, who has the title *dottore di legge,* is called by his first name by people who know him, by his last name by people who do not. This is because he is purchased and can be replaced, and he cheats anyway. I am called, depending on the situation and the information one wishes to convey, Lola, our Lola, Loletta, *l'Americana,* or *la dottoressa.* When I am not in Italy, I have been told, I am referred to as *la divorziata* ("the divorced one") or *la sorella del chirurgo, i divorziati* ("the sister of the surgeon—the divorced ones"). I asked about the titles *suor* and *don.* It was explained this way: *suor* implies "you are like us but better than we are within the similarity"—e.g. in ownership of property. *Don* implies "you are different from us, and better and more worthy in the difference"—e.g. the parish priest and his spiritual ascendancy *regardless of class origin*.

Achievement is often equated with abominable morals, an attitude always elaborated upon by the clergy whenever an opportunity presents itself. Evidence that not only successful, but also lower class people have "pig morality" is totally ignored when this point needs to be made. But when the courts want to demonstrate that immoral behavior is punished, it is the lower class person, never the upper class one, who pays the price. Two cases of a murdered lover have occurred in Ascoli in recent years, one involving a noblewoman and the other a man of no particular social standing. The *contessa* was sentenced to a year in a private mental hospital, with maid service, classical music and visitation rights by family and friends. Her affair was described as a "sentimental attachment." In the other case, the man killed his mistress after she had persuaded him to leave his wife, because she took all his money, planning to join her husband who had emigrated to Belgium. This murderer was sentenced to 21 years in prison.

Class distinctions are handled quite consciously, as in the celebration of the mass, where seats are reserved or available according to status, and masses are tailored for class participation, that is, different masses are designed for and attended by people of a particular class. These avoidance rules are observed by everyone. Many upper middle class persons no longer go to the cinema now that working class people go.

The status differences are marked in the choosing of the *compare* or *commare* ("godfather" and "godmother"). The optimal strategy is to get someone who is just slightly above you, but not too far above you (because you then are a rude, uncivilized person who is asking another to lower himself for your gain—in terms of favors possibly receivable. One should emerge from the contract as a person of honor, discretion and understanding, who is also unpretentious. Optimizing is a prized skill, carefully cultivated in the young.

The uses of dialect, other than in the multi-level discourse to which I allude below, is tribal, by which I mean that it strengthens in-group ties, the feeling that "We are like ourselves and others are not like us;" standard Italian has this function, and so does the dialect. Individuals do not, however, want their voices taped in dialect. For the most part I could only obtain tapes in dialect from children, although I did get one tape in dialect from a poet.

REGIONAL PERCEPTIONS

In their own eyes, the *Ascolani* are better than Italians of other regions. All bad influences are from the South. Neopolitans, for example, are sentimental, do not reason, are thieves and sycophants, and non-authentic—for example, they say "Good day, captain" to a sergeant. The North is pure and honest, the South is base and evil. One writer compared the people of the North "male people" (*popolo uomo*) with people of the South "female people" (*popolo donna*), describing the latter as irrational, capricious, untrustworthy, imprudent, impulsive, servile, "cannibals." Another writer considered

Southerners inferior because they commit fewer suicides and manifest less mental disease. Dialects often are distinguished as "dirty" or "clean." In the presence of blacks and Jews, Italians usually demonstrate their tolerance with pride, thus refusing a nod to the sophisticated racist attitudes of the *nordici* toward the *sudici.* This externalization of the base *id* to another group has a "vast storehouse of history" to fortify the nursery memories of the *nordici.* The greatest paranoid fears are elicited by the South, where they rape, they kill, they take juice out of oranges with a syringe before sending them North for the gentle *Ascolani* to be *fregati* out of their *lira* when purchasing oranges.

Romans are *fettendi* ("stinking") and use terrible language such as *i mortacci tuoi* ("your evil dead"). They give you wrong directions and then laugh as you add 40 kilometers to your odometer, only to end up one block from where you started. Everyone has a collection of Roman stories. *Ascolani* do not, however, consider themselves to be as industrious or precise as the people of Ancona, which is 123 kilometers north of Ascoli. Ancona is where one has a car fixed or an operation performed, because Italians generally are, as one physician of Ascoli said, *approssimativi* (not precise, not scientific). Many *Ascolani* often say, *me ne freghisti* (in French, *je m'enfoutiste;* in English, "I don't give a hang"). And one does not trust people who do not care about others. In 1798, the *Anconitani* said through their mayor, "If we get together with Rome, their natural laziness will destroy us and we will lose all the advantage of our commerce. Let us get all our Jews together with us in a new enterprise to get commerce going with France and the Orient." The *Anconitani* consider the *Ascolani* mild-mannered and rather pusillanimous (Ancona was a revolutionary center against the papacy, Ascoli a papal state). *Veneti* are *i piu educati* ("the more cultivated"). Florentines and Tuscans are vicious, mean, cold (as Curzio Malaparte has them describing themselves) and distant (*31*). With horror, many recite the epitaph:

Io sono Aretino Fosco Giachetti
Che di tutti dissi mal fuor di Dio
Dicendolo—io non lo conosco.

(I am Aretino Fosco Giachetti
Who spoke ill of all except God,
Saying, "I don't know him.")

Those from Abruzzi are thick-skulled and stupid, and can only go into business, which is a lowly activity. They are called *regnicoli* ("those who favor the kingdom"), a term which reveals the tenacious influence of history on Italian attitudes. Since the wars between the papacy and the kingdom of Italy took place before our American Civil War, it is as if we still derisively called all Southerners the "grays" or the "rebs."

The characterization of some places leads to satiric doggerel. Thus the tourist resort of San Remo is described as having *mare senza pesce, donne senza onore, uomini senza parola* ("sea without fish, women without honor, men without words"). And Campobasso is the place where *se non piove, tira vento, se non tira vento, suonan le campane funebre* ("If it does not rain, the wind blows, if the wind does not blow, the funeral bells ring").

The *Ascolani* see Italians in general as thieves, lower than Africans, who after all are good people whom Mussolini freed from slavery and civilized, building schools, roads, and hospitals for them. The Africans understood that what Mussolini gave them were good things. Italians are not only inferior to Africans, but they are even worse than Arabs, who are seen as lying, cheating, undependable, moral idiots, and a total disaster as a culture.

At the community level *Ascolani* see themselves as kind to the stranger but mean, invidious, nasty and carping with each other. When immigrants point out to them those acts which are not kindness to the stranger, it is said that these are *vizii* (acquired bad habits). I noticed in talking with *Ascolani,* that if, in three-party conversation, one person should depart, the others gave me a quick moral accounting of the person who had left. Asked what Italians are like, *Ascolani* say without exception, "We are *schifosi, disgraziati, vergognosi, ladri*" ("shameless, disgusting thieves, fallen from grace"). In Mexico, villagers generally say something of this sort, but not in such negative terms and adding *asi somos,* which means "This is what we are like and what can anyone do about it? Nothing." (*45*). But the Ascolano's *siamo cosi* means, "But we don't have to be, if only the system would change, if only the Americans, or the government, or the Fascists or the Communists or someone would set up a system in which our expectations would permit us to be honest and hard-working and trustworthy, it would be such a relief." More than a few suggested to me that we Americans should simply bomb the whole countryside, themselves included, since their lives were without hope. Then a new race and culture of decent people could begin. My father's sister said, "Italy will never change unless you have a strong ruler, born of a foreign woman who comes here when she is pregnant and keeps the child totally out of touch with anything Italian until he begins to rule over us. Then we may find honor again." Which foreign country hardly matters—"Who is worse than we are? Anything is an improvement."

SOCIAL BEHAVIOR

The two major concerns in living are food and the division of property. Should the matriline or the patriline inherit? This is a highly charged subject.

If the conversation concerns affairs of illicit sex, everyone yawns and says, "What else is new? We all know that men are basically *porci* ("pigs") and women are *puttane* ("whores")." But mention a property division and all eyes light up, all bodies move forward in their chairs.

As for food, almost everyone is fifteen to twenty pounds overweight by American standards. Only then it is said, "You look good." The concern is that a person might waste away, based on a lump-sum theory of the body with no notion of function. An Italian *signora* in Sydney, Australia, once said to me as I hesitated over lamb chops and spaghetti for breakfast, "Eat, eat! As my mother used to say, the fat ones get thin, the thin ones die." One eats defiantly in the presence of one's enemies, conspicuously exhibiting one's prosperity. If doctors advise them against eating, they do not believe the doctors. Doctors, like everyone else, are out to get first your money and then to do away with *you,* delighted at the prospect of one less person hanging on in a crowded society to diminish the goods available. (Overpopulation has *this* kind of effect, also.) Someone will probably pay the doctor off when you are dead and the insurance is collected—but never let the doctor know that you do not trust him, or he will give you noxious medications.

Sometimes people are characterized in terms of food. There are, for example, people who are *mangioni* and those who are *complimentosi.* The first come to eat you out of house and home and are insatiable. (You of course compulsively cannot stop feeding them.) *Mangione* also, by extension, means corruptible. The *complimentosi* must be begged to eat. They really *want* to eat what you have set before them, but the energy you must expend to get them to do it is excessive in American terms. For when you beg them to eat, you are showing that you love them, and when they finally do eat they are demonstrating their belief in your protestations and reciprocating your love and care. Conversations on how long another must be begged to eat are long and intricate, and just as long are the descriptions of how much was devoured after the acceptance. The function of these descriptions of *complimentosi* seems to be to expose someone's facade of elegance and courtliness, and to reveal the underlying corruption.

If it is generally true that "most of you is outside of you," then in Ascoli "all of you is outside of you." The feeding behavior and the division of property, which I have suggested are central foci of energy expenditure, are the major indicators of self-perception within the group. But all other areas of activity also point up the externalization of sentiment and responsibility, and the renunciation of free will. The children's games show this dramatically, for these games are great shaming techniques. For example, the child who loses in several games is put into a circle, shamed in rhyme and then playfully beaten over the head by the children who surround him. The games all say, "You are nothing without our approval." My son was thus shamed and shaken out of his jealousy of my playing with the other children. Even in games the child learns of the renunciation of free will, and that outside of the opinions of honor and shame that others give him, he does not exist.

So too are the serious games on the adult level. The *passatella* is now illegal, although it is still sometimes played. The game consisted of a group of men playing *morra,* which consists of guessing the total of the aggregate of fingers exposed on cue by the players. The winner is the *padrone* ("patron"). He who comes in second is the *sotto-padrone* ("sub-owner"). The *padrone* then offers the others drinks (feudal giving of favors or land), but the *sotto-padrone* can veto his offers, with the result that someone is in the end the *ulmo,* who gets nothing at all. But the real message is on another level and is known to all, for the game is always played for vengeance, and is a means of local justice, even if it does not end in explicit accusations. Out of such challenges and passions and anger came knife fights, woundings and killings. The *ulmo* could choose not to get angry, but his manhood, his credibility, his very existence (the esteem of others), was threatened and was known to be threatened.

The esteem of others plays a large part in the psycho-cultural life of Italy, and takes on another dimension in the concept of *rispetto,* which is granted to a person who can do one a favor. (This kind of information may not, however, show up on a questionnaire, since such a definition is inadmissible, perhaps even to oneself.) It regularly happens that the respected person is more powerful than the one who bears him the respect. I have seen and heard of situations in which families have hated and not "respected" each other for decades, yet who become sudden allies over a common hatred. One informant said, "You may not believe this, since you know I have said nasty things about so and so for many, many years, but really I have always had *rispetto* for him." In this situation he had quarreled bitterly with a man who had now taken sides against his own nephew in a quarrel between the nephew and the informant. Conversations are filled with echoes of the concept of *rispetto,* but it loses its force as one goes from southern Italy to northern Italy.

Rispetto also seems to be related to suicide in Italy. If we look at the statistics, we find that the suicide rate for the province of Ascoli Piceno is about 6 per 100,000, based on the figures for 1950 to 1968. Compared to Austria or Sweden, where rates are about 23 per 100,000, this rate is not very high. (In the United States regional rates vary from 10 to 24 per 100,000.) But there are between 26 and 30 suicides per year to one or no homicides, a striking comparison. Who are the suicides? They include the aged and the woman alone, who has more responsibility than she can bear raising her children, and who is perhaps ill in the bargain. It is difficult to ascribe suicides to a sense of shame, for I learned of many situations in which their notion of shame *could* have been a powerful motive and was not, such as incest (mother-son, father-daughter, brother-sister) or infanticide. There are many indications that the suicide is the person who has dropped out of the exchange system. It might be said that a person comes to suicide when he can no longer do anyone a favor and cannot ask for help because it cannot be returned.

There is much to prevent suicide, since it is first of all a mortal sin in a country where all are Catholics. Many people attribute suicide simply to *squilibrio mentale* ("mental disequilibrium"). Poverty alone is not sufficient motive, but if it reaches a state in which a person no longer has *rispetto*, then one's outlook becomes grim. Suicide is generally by means of firearms, or by hanging or poisoning, the latter method preferred by women when they know they are no longer needed or "respected." Then the rules have obviated the individual's existence, and this is disastrous in a culture where one's self-esteem depends on the opinions of others.

Like the early Greeks, these are a public people coerced by public opinion; they are thus shame-sanctioned not guilt-sanctioned. Like the early Greeks they feel manipulated by external forces and seek glimpses of themselves in the eyes of others. One is closed in by vertical and horizontal restraints, as sociologists are fond of saying. Thus in Ascoli, all of a person's internal drama is externalized. He strives to eat well, live off rents or pensions, and keep others from gossiping about him, because he has to manage this good life without loss of *onore* and *rispetto*. Again, it is much more important to be virtuous if one is poor than if one is rich.

Gossip is another powerful sanctioning technique. But although everything is known about another individual, he must never be confronted with it. For the ordinary folk, the center for the dissemination of gossip is the washing fountain (which also gives rise to fights for the clearest water). For the upper or upper middle class it is the cafe in the piazza, and the cemetery, for even the expression of grief must follow prescribed codes. For example, while assisting a physician with an autopsy in a cemetery, I was told that I had missed "a most Italian phenomenon," the wailing widow of yesterday's corpse. The widow threw herself on the coffin, but friends and relatives pulled her off it. She protested she wanted to go with him. "Ah, no, you will see him in heaven." She fainted, but a few minutes later she pulled herself together and walked to the car. The doctor explained to me, "You see, she cannot win. If she doesn't go through this they will say she had no feelings for her husband. But since she has, if she dares smile or look at a man in a year or two, it will be said of her, 'Ah, ha, and how she cried and wanted to be thrown into the grave with her husband.' At any rate, for the moment, the focus of attention will be on how much insurance she will collect and what she is going to do with it."

The "death cult" is an important economic and social activity. A person must observe proper etiquette about visiting the dead, with the number of visits depending on the relation of the deceased to the bereaved. There are also rules as to who goes to visit the dead together—a widow and widower would cause a stir, even though friends of thirty years standing find studious avoidance difficult. Proper deference to the dead also requires meticulous attention to how one dresses, how much is spent on flowers, whether they are fresh or artificial, whether one pays to have poetic prayers recited to the dead and how often. The living must have black-edged posters put on the walls in the city at least once a year to commemorate their dead, and it is a source of gossip if they do not. The survivors must also pay to have masses celebrated. If they do not, they are unloving and disloyal, and not to be trusted by the living.

It would be irrelevant to criticize such practices as wasteful of psychic energy—if they led to healthy and happy people. But they are not healthy people (as the doctors assert), nor happy (as the priests and psychologists can attest). Most importantly, they do not nourish the illusion that they are. The greater part of almost all lives is spent in frustrating attempts to conform to the opinions of others. "We never tell each other the truth under any circumstances, not even the most trivial," said the director of the library of the *comune*, curiously echoing one of my uncle's *contadinos*. One physician said of this constant fabrication that if one were scoring these people on an index for fantasizing, they would score very high indeed. The general opinion is that such fabrication is not good, that it is a self-inflicted slavery. Several physicians talked with me at great length on what they consider a very high incidence of hysterical illnesses, and how these illnesses are attempts to control others. I would add that certain organs are the loci for specific situational controls. The liver is to get away from a spouse for a certain length of time each year; the stomach is for short-term, interpersonal altercations.

Illness, if frankly and openly acknowledged, is taken as a plea for help. A thorough study by a medical-psychiatric-anthropological team demonstrated that not all *tarantati* (persons reporting symptoms of the tarantula bite) were bitten by tarantulas (*12*). *Tarantati* fell into certain age groups and were involved in extremely stressful situations, of the sort that the culture does not recognize and certainly does not allow to be openly expressed. The tarantulas that "caused" the attacks were of various colors, "totemic" of attributes such as jealousy, hate, and love. The sick person becomes the center of attention, the senses of the afflicted are flooded with music and color, and the sick person then dances herself or himself into exhaustion in a dancing mania that sometimes lasts for days.

In extreme circumstances, the individual relies heavily on the church, and believes that when everyone has abandoned you, *il ricovero* ("the poorhouse") will take you (though it is a disgrace to be old and in a *ricovero*). The Church, too, is "reasonable." It was common for very wealthy men of exaggerated sexual appetites to buy their salvation by willing all their possessions to the *ricoveri* in their death. Ascoli has three *ricoveri* instituted in such a manner. One aristocrat, for instance, insisted that he have the young daughters of his *contadini* as soon as they were ready to please him. All of this was bearable only because he had drawn up a will leaving much land and money to a *ricovero*. He met an untimely death when one of his *contadini* slit his throat as he asked for the second daughter.

Attitudes toward sex can be briefly disposed of: persons of the opposite sex cannot be left alone, regardless of age or status difference, or their sexual drives will overwhelm them. And dishonor reigns. (Even repression is not trustworthy!)

With respect to the modern world, television has had remarkably little effect on the general pattern of behavior and attitudes described above. It has influenced styles of clothing and consumer goods, but not much else. Children and adults alike tend to watch only the musical specials and old movies. The news is not considered worthy of attention, which fits in with their wariness of politics and their notion that no matter who says what about the state of the nation, nothing will be done, even though prices and taxes will soon be higher.

THE IMMIGRANT

When *Ascolani* can escape their society, they do, going to America, Australia, or Canada. There was even a period when Africa and Oceania were popular. Many have come back, though, all giving as a reason, "The wife had to come back here, she couldn't take it." Investigating the immigration statistics, I found that those who gave in to their wives were now disillusioned and angry with themselves. They had been tailors, mechanics, or workers of all sorts abroad. One had had a pineapple farm in Brisbane and had been doing very well indeed. But his wife missed the home country, the climate, and especially the relatives. The wives are *not* sorry, for they have regained their sense of worth. Said one repatriated male, "I knew I was coming back to unemployment, hopelessness, and the *prosciutto* scene. I could make money here too if I worked as hard as I did in Australia, but here I have already slipped back into their—I mean *our* sense of time and work." The wife retorted, "I told you that you yourself should have stayed in Australia, and the children and I would have come back to Italy." Then she turned to me and asked, "What's wrong with him anyway?" The Italian immigrant in a foreign country is maximally stressed to learn how the generated self "works" in a foreign setting. The immigrant adapts because adapting is taught to be a virtue: You do not make enemies, you try to be like others, and then you can succeed. Immigrants succeed abroad and then fail again at home, because to come home is to know once more that they must step back in the old, frustrating ways. Such comments as those of the returned immigrant above fill others with shame, but they already had that sense of shame. Nothing has changed and the immigrant's wife is happy to be once more on familiar landscape.

Immigrants abroad view each other as they did in Italy, as I learned when I designed and carried out a psycholinguistic project to study the correlation between variations in linguistic structure and the group-sanctioning of these variations. Holding American socio-economic status constant, I selected first- and second-generation Italian immigrants to take part in a "word-creating" exercise. The task involved creating words for job and social situations for which there were no Italian equivalents. The first-generation participants made the stem conform to their original phonetic system: Italian prefixes and suffixes were added and Italian syllabicity retained. No violation of the consonant-vowel-consonant pattern was permitted. Any deviation from these rules made one the object of invidious gossip and suspicion. De-culturation was a function of necessity, not choice. Second-generation individuals created words arbitrarily, for humor or for the exclusion of non-Italians in certain situations, usually where it was felt that someone might be excluding them. Particularly interesting were the results indicating that second-generation participants from more respected regional groups of Tuscan and the North *retained* the mother tongue almost completely, in contrast to others who retained it only in occasional joking behavior, when they might use Italian phonemicization of American utterances.

Accommodative behavior among immigrants is also an index to notions of identity as defined in a person's native region. There has always been, in the United States at least, a decided trend for Italians from one region to settle in defined areas and to exclude groups from other regions of Italy by mutual consent. This is so that cultural expectations will be fulfilled and not violated. The most frequently cited studies of Italian immigrants in cities draw erroneous ad hoc conclusions about their "propensity to huddle in cities" (*23*). The few studies (*44, 36*) on immigrants in rural areas, in the South and west of the Mississippi, reveal a remarkable capacity on the part of the Italian immigrant to succeed in these vast marginal areas that have been abandoned by several previous waves of settlers. The huddling thesis can be refuted with more than ample data. My view is that both the huddling and anti-huddling theses fallaciously assume the absence of a dominant high-status ethnic group defining the permissible in myriad ways. Activities of Italians in the West were so consonant with the ethos of the dominant white population there that Italian immigrants emerge as positively Puritan-ethic Anglo, even giving significant aid for the liberation of the West for our joint manifest Christian destiny. They have played this role extremely well in California, even managing to beat Max Weber to the West Coast (*55*). This Protestant ethic-spirit of capitalism dignity was short-lived, however, for Americans now explain Italian success stories by present or past Mafia connections—only early white Americans could amass a great fortune without committing at least one small crime.

Rolle laments the lack of literary effort among Italian immigrants, although he mentions some novels in which authors depict Italian immigrants in a manner not totally untrue, which gave maximum comfort to the average American reader. Since the publication of *Soul on Ice* and *Custer Died for Your Sins,* I might point out that significant contributions were made by Italians to the literature of protest, including works by Giovanitti, Tresca, Gori, Salvemini, Borghi, Malatesta, Vacirca, Serrati, all men of considerable talent, even though they generally were not read by Italian immigrants. Immigrants had high hopes for their children, but accommodation to the anti-intellectual stream of American life (*24*) had more positive assimilation value. Although groups that had been assumed to be assimilated are now displaying eloquent anger, it is doubtful that the Italian will raise much protest against the excesses of the American "power elite" of one or two generations ago. Their low expectations were easily fulfilled, and short of being lynched, as they were in Louisiana and other Southern states, all else was sheer windfall.

For a vivid contrast in non-Italian behavior, we may look to Giacomo Matteotti, an aristocrat and socialist deputy in the early Fascist era. He was assassinated because of his intransigent resistance to the Fascist corporate state. Italians do not know what to do with such behavior. My father's decision to leave Italy to escape incarceration or assassination by the Fascists made sense to Italians. Mussolini's tactic of changing himself a bit to get the job done—or even to escape as a German non-commissioned officer—made sense. His mistress' behavior made sense, for a woman can rise to great heights through a man she loves. But to die for an idea! To choose non-survival! Others do this, of course, but Italians are not so courageous, not so competent, not so foolish.

To the greeting, "How does it go?" Italians reply with various metaphors that signify "I've gotten through another day, haven't I? It's not like winning but it's not like losing either." Winning and losing are irrelevant categories to specialists in survival.

SOME COMMENTS ON METHOD

Explanation has many facets: the historical (how an event came about); the reasons given for events (the conscious models); the structural-functional (how events are placed and how the system works); the nomothetic (search for general laws); and the idiographic (determining how to treat a case that does not fit in with the general laws). Some anthropological studies that begin with description, run through analysis and end with explanation seem to lose sight of the need to integrate all of the above. Admittedly it is difficult, and in some cases, impossible. Partial explanations, however, result in, for example, the documentations of empire-collapse that are based on well-selected anecdotes of moral lapses. (A snowy silence covers the tranquil ignorance of the easy virtues that have accompanied the vigorous beginnings of some Puritan cultures.) In gathering and analyzing the material just presented, I was interested not only in describing a cultural system, but in ascertaining how it works and eventually arriving at an explanation.

Ethno-studies have made exclusive use of conscious models. But social relations and structure are not always evident; they must be distilled and abstracted from many events. The selection of these events is often a product of the collusion or collision of the experience, cultural background and biases of both the investigator and the informants.

Because of these considerations I was interested in learning not only the conscious models of my informants, but also the interplay between their models, and the relation between conscious models and the underlying structures of Italian culture. By underlying structures I mean the assumptions or organizational principles which are often paraconscious. These include expectations, sense of chronology, event boundaries (acts that are continuous as contrasted with discontinuous), the paradigmatics of memory association, the use of the body in health and in illness, and the control of events or the control of others. Often the organizational principles are explicit, as in legal codes or highly intellectualized versions of an event, or in social fantasies and the recognized roles of fantasy producers. Underlying structures also include the notion of behavioral complementarity, by which I mean that *an agent plays not only a role, but the whole scene,* and that he can reverse the role in the same scene in a subsequent state.

Identity can be defined as *self-conscious self percepts.* These percepts are produced through strategy usages over time, and I wanted to learn about them in my examination of Italian identity and its transformations. Identity, in this context cannot be limited to the self-concept most reconcilable with the social reality that signals back its correctness and acceptability. This self-concept is the easiest for the individual to generate from the parts and combinatorial rules for each event and situation, but it is also modified by a series of transformations in slightly or greatly varying social contexts that can eventually lead, in the extreme case for the immigrant, to the wall of unintelligibility. This is the foreign situation in which the generated self does not work, or may work to one's detriment. For example, those qualities of propriety, courtesy, and silent participation that one learned as appropriate to a particular status and role may cause one to lose the race, or the prize, or the game to the *sfacciati* (those without "face," i.e., pride, or grace or dignity). That acquired finesse which enables one to hide the training and toil behind a finished product is often interpreted by another culture as non-dedication, a Harlequinade. Identity Italian-style requires one to wear his learning lightly, to conform to the emotional tone of the occasion, to become other than himself for contingencies, even if only to give others pleasure. But in a foreign setting, this may be misunderstood, just as Niccolo Macchiavelli was misunderstood in the English-speaking world for centuries.

Actually, all my informants were quite adept at describing what happens in the system if certain states are assumed. Given an initial situation, they delighted in predicting the distribution of elements over states and the set of transition probabilities. They also described the roles they would play, and their moral despair over their doing it, and how they would not do it if they were in a different system. All the immigrant experience of which I am aware through reading, personal experience, and long interviews with returned immigrants validated what they believed would happen.

The concept of "areal integration" (*50*), which served as a useful model for subsequent research in the Admiralties, is highly appropriate for transformal studies in Italy. There are important differences, of course, for in Manus, or in some of the newly created developing nations, space is vast (in Manus this is so because the scale of distance is predicated on the difficulty of getting there), but the time dimension is short. In Italy, however, it is historical time that holds the greatest meaning with respect to diversity, while space furnishes images not only of the limited, but of the diminishing good. Still, I consider these two dimensions of inquiry important for Italy, and I pursued them in the linguistic, economic, political, legal, moral and religious spheres. I should like to emphasize legal and moral, since these are the areas most difficult to appraise for a person who is only an outsider or only an insider. For me understanding is reached when I can predict with accuracy which legal, moral or other information-abstracting code will take precedence in a given situation. Being a participant-observer did not absolve me from gathering all the statistics on voting patterns, past and present. But mainly I wanted to understand the walls of symbols between classes and how these are handled in various situations. How is it, for example, that the peasantry is looked down upon by the upper classes, but nevertheless remains an endless repository of ancient tradition (poetic, romantic images for food, dress or moral codes).

For the linguistic study I tried to assemble data not only on the phonetic shifts between dialects but on the libidinal investment in that original language of Pier delle Vigne, which originated at the court of Frederick Hohenstaufen at Palermo—Dante later froze it into classicism in his *Divine Comedy.* This is the language that seemed to writers to evoke the ancient boundaries of Italy since the times of Augustus. Highly prized, Italian is still the lingua franca of the nation, although dialects have enormous tribalization value in certain circumstances. Use of dialect also provides a mechanism for exteriorization of that which is "base" in behavior (e.g., certain dialects are "clean" and others "dirty"). Dialect usage can also be more complex. If one is secure in status, one lapses into dialect to spice the multi-level discourse, either in playful exclusion of a guest, or among professionals to indicate peasant affinities which, of course, are belied by status. (Many events are used to say "observe how we are also peasants" in a sort of incorporation of the whole culture, including the use of peasant foods in a twelve-course meal.)

Central to data-management in my ongoing field study is the development of a model for describing Italian identity and its transformations. It is a three-dimensional widening spiral, with the added dimension of time. It allows for change in the notion of a personal identity and the necessary component of group identity. With ego at the base point, the spiral model provides a convenient structure to represent the intensity of experience, transition to other-level ego base points, and possibilities of information flow which give the self-concept, as experienced, its viability. How the self goes about processing informational inputs shapes the identity, as George Herbert Mead pointed out long ago in his own idiom (*37*). But the presence or absence of restricting or amplifying mechanisms of information flow, or the change in the process of processing in the individual, are also important. For example, one observes, throughout the city and province, what I call tight-linked cultural transmission (in the groupings that ignore age, for example, as I have indicated).

The widening spiral is the hierarchical notion as experienced by the person whose identity is defined and manageable through this model. The more attenuated the experience of membership, the further it lies from the base point, not only vertically but in the widening arch. Throughout his lifetime the individual expands his awareness of his identity at some rate or other, either through concerted effort or serendipity. The spiral may become more compressed for him (e.g. experiencing many facets of his identity with equal intensity—such as feeling American-Italian, Italo-American or Italian). This is unlikely in a rigid society. A good example is the Italian male who has lived in the U.S. for the years 1919–22 and who feels that he has a vocabulary and a point of view which make him not exclusively Italian.

The widening spiral model for my data is preferable to a network representation, because it can accommodate points along a continuum of identity or a continuum of intensity of awareness and/or participation in the knowledge systems, codes, and symbols of one or more societies. The top of the spiral represents the weakest experience of identity, both in time and space. It represents roots of identity barely visible in proto-history, the barely acknowledged myths that shape social images. Compressed into a compact identity, the top of the spiral springs out in analysis, revealing the levels, the distances from the central point of reference, the differences of intensity between levels and the relations that obtain between them, and the information flow both to and from the self. In addition to information flow possibilities, relations that obtain between levels contain rules as, for example, for marriage, godparenthood, fictive relationships, the educational levels aspired and actual, preferred relationships with other individuals, markets, and religious excursions or festivals.

My approach presupposes that a subculture of a complex society *cannot* be examined with the same methods employed in the study of primitive societies. (It is annoying to ask a question in New Guinea and get the reply, "We don't know, the only old person who knew *that* died last year.") We have no recourse in primitive societies, since they do not and cannot overwhelm us with their complex recorded past, their interpretations of it, and their interpretations of interpretations. Mannheim's appraisal holds—that "there are modes of thought which cannot be adequately understood as long as their social origins are obscured," and that "men participate in thinking further what other men have thought before them. . . . [Man] has inherited a situation with patterns of thought" (*32*). Of this, the investigator must be aware, not only in the subjects he studies, but in himself. Patterns in history are often put forth as hypotheses by their captives after an appropriate ritual of scientism, to "explain" other cultures. Witness Banfield's hypothesis of amoral familism and his seventeen logical implications in his search for the morals of a backward society (*2*). He arrived at an explanation when his mind "came to rest." "Mind" can find instant repose when unencumbered by knowledge of the languages, the dialect, the history and the aesthetic structures of an Italian community.

REFERENCES

1. Alessandrini, Mario. *Cecco d'Ascoli.* Fermo: La Rapida, 1969.
2. Banfield, Edward C. *The Moral Basis of a Backward Society.* Glencoe, Ill.: Free Press, 1958.
3. Baroja, Julio Caro. *The World of the Witches.* Chicago: University of Chicago Press, 1964.
4. Baron, Hans. *The Crisis of the Early Italian Renaissance; Civic Humanism and Republican Liberty in an Age of Classicism and Tyranny.* New Jersey: Princeton, 1955.
5. Barzini, Luigi. *The Italians; a Full-Length Portrait Featuring Their Manners and Morals.* New York: Atheneum, 1965.
6. Bloch, Marc. *Feudal Society.* Chicago: University of Chicago Press, 1961.
7. Burckhardt, Jacob. *The Civilization of the Renaissance in Italy.* New York: Mentor, 1960.
8. Cagnucci, Emidio. *Agre e dogge; poesie e canzoni in dialetto Ascolano.* Ascoli Piceno, S. D'Auria: Gennaio, 1969.
9. Castelli, Giuseppe. *Curiositá storiche nella Provincia.* V. Gazzetta d'Ascoli. a II 1871, no. 3.
10. Daraul, Arkon. *Witches and Sorcerers.* New York: Citadel, 1969.
11. de Coulanges, Fustel. *The Ancient City; a Study on the Religion, Laws and Institutions of Greece and Rome.* New York: Doubleday.
12. De Martino, Ernesto. *La Terra del Rimorso; Contributo a Una Storia Religiosa del Sud* Milano: 11 Saggiatore, 1961.
13. Dolci, Danilo. *Outlaws.* New York: Orio Press, 1960.
14. Dolci, Danilo. *Spreco.* Torino: Einaudi, 1960.
15. Erikson, Erik H. *Identity; Youth and Crisis.* New York: Norton, 1968.
16. Fabiani, Giuseppe. "Collana di Pubblicazioni Storiche Ascolane." *Ascoli nel Quattrocento,* vol. I and vol. II. Ascoli Piceno: Societa Tipolitografica Editrice, 1958.
17. Fabiani, Giuseppe. "Collana di Pubblicazioni Storiche Ascolane." *Ascoli nel Ottocento.* Ascoli Piceno: Societa Tipolitografica Editrice, 1967.
18. Fouillée, Alhedo. *Bosquejo Psicologico de los Pueblos Europeos.* Buenos Aires, 1943.
19. Fromm, Erich. *Escape from Freedom.* New York: Reinhardt, 1971.
20. Fromm, Erich. *Man for Himself.* New York: Reinhardt, 1946.
21. Gabrielli, Giulio. *Saggio di Bibliografia Storica Ascolana.* Estratto dal Vol. II. *Atti e Memorie della Deputazione Marchigiana di Storia Patria.* Ancona: A Gustavo Morelli tipografo editore, 1896.
22. Gans, Herbert J. *The Urban Villagers: Group and Class in the Life of Italian Americans.* New York: Free Press, 1962.
23. Glazer, Nathan, and Moynihan, Daniel Patrick. *Beyond the Melting Pot.* Cambridge, Mass: Massachusetts Institute of Technology Press, 1963.
24. Hofstadter, Richard. *Anti-Intellectualism in American Life.* New York: Vintage Books, 1962.

25. Hostetter, Richard. "Anarchism versus the Italian State." In *The Anarchist.* New York: Bell, 1964.

26. Homo, Leon. *Primitive Italy and the Beginnings of Roman Imperialism.* London: Kegan Paul, 1926.

27. Lévi-Strauss, Claude. *The Raw and the Cooked: Introduction to a Science of Mythology,* vol. I. New York: Harper and Row, 1969.

28. Lévi-Strauss, Claude. *Structural Anthropology.* New York: Basic Books, 1961.

29. Lévi-Strauss, Claude. *La Pensée Sauvage.* Paris: Plon, 1962.

30. MacGregor, Hastie. *The Day of the Lion: The Rise and Fall of Fascist Italy (1922-1945).* New York, 1963.

31. Malaparte, Curzio. *Maledetti Toscani.* Vallecchi Editore, 1959.

32. Mannheim, Karl. *Ideology and Utopia; an Introduction to the Sociology of Knowledge,* translated by Luis Wirth and Edward Shils, 1963.

33. Malinowski, Bronislaw. "Culture." In *Encyclopedia of the Social Sciences.* New York, 1935.

34. Marselli, G. A. "American Sociologists and Italian Peasant Society: with Reference to the Book of Banfield." In *Sociologia Ruralis,* vol. 4, 1963.

35. Mariotti, Cesare. *Il palazzo del Comune di Ascoli Piceno,* 2d ed. Ascoli Piceno: Casa Editrice di Giuseppe Cesari, 1941.

36. Mead, Emily Fogg. "Italian Immigration into the South." *South Atlantic Quarterly,* July 1905.

37. Mead, George Herbert. *Mind, Self and Society.* Edited by Charles W. Morris. Chicago: University of Chicago Press, 1934.

38. Murray, Margaret Alice. *The Witch Cult in Western Europe.* Clarendon: Oxford, 1967.

39. Musa, Mark. *Machiavelli's "The Prince."* St. Martin's Press, 1964.

40. Nietzche, Frederick. *The Genealogy of Morals.* New York: Modern Library, 1937.

41. Pais, Ettore. *Tradizioni Antiche e Toponomastica Moderna, a Proposito di Liguri, di Umbri, di Etruschi e di Picene.*

42. Pizzorno, Alessandro. "Familismo Amorale e Marginalita Storca Ovvero Perche non c'e Niente da Fare a Montegrano." *International Review of Community Development* 15(6), 1966.

43. Pulgram, Ernst. *The Tongues of Italy; Pre-History and History.* Cambridge, Mass.: Harvard University Press, 1958.

44. Rolle, Andrew F. *The Immigrant Upraised; Italian Adventures and Colonists in an Expanding America.* Berkeley: University of California Press, 1968.

45. Romanucci-Ross, Lola. *Conflict, Violence and Morality in a Mexican Village.* Palo Alto, CA.: National Press Books, 1973.

46. Romanucci-Ross, Lola. "The Hierarchy of Resort in Curative Practices: The Admiralty Islands, Melanesia." *Journal of Health & Social Behavior* 10(3), 1969.

47. Romanucci-Ross, Lola. "Conflits fonciers a Mokerang, village Matankor des Iles de l'Amiraute." *L'Homme* 6(2):32-35.

48. Saitta, Armando. *Dal Fascismo alla Resistenza; Profilo Storico e Documenti.* Firenze, 1961.

49. Schwartz, Theodore. *The Paliau Movement in the Admiralty Islands, 1946-1954.* Anthropological Papers of the American Museum of Natural History, no. 49, pt. 2. New York, 1962.

50. Schwartz, Theodore. "Systems of Areal Integration: Some Considerations Based on the Admiralty Islands of Northern Melanesia." *Anthropological Forum* 1(1), 1963.

51. Silverman, Sydel F. "An Ethnographic Approach to Social Stratification: Prestige in a Central Italian Community." *American Anthropologist* 68(4):899-921, 1966.

52. Speranza, Giuseppe. *Il Piceno Dalle Origini alle Fine d'ogni sua Autonomia* (1 I 20). Roma e il Piceno, n.d.

53. Spiro, Melford E. "Causes, Functions and Cross-cousin Marriage: an Essay in Anthropological Explanation." *Theory in Anthropology: A Sourcebook,* edited by Robert A. Manners and David Kaplan. Chicago: Aldine, 1968.

54. Vico, Giambattista. *Scienza Nuova. De Antiguissima Italorium Sapientia.* 1719.

55. Weber, Max. *The Sociology of Religion.* Beacon Press, 1963.

56. Whyte, William Foote. *Street Corner Society.* Chicago, 1966.

57. Yates, Frances A. *Giordano Bruno and the Hermetic Tradition.* London: Routledge and Kegan Paul, 1964.

Political Conflict, Religion and Ethnic Identity

PART THREE

PART THREE

POLITICAL CONFLICT, RELIGION AND ETHNIC IDENTITY

Religion is the crucial element for many groups in defining their ethnic identity. In some instances it is the only distinguishing feature separating groups which share all the other attributes of a common cultural tradition. Separations arising from religious differences occur both between and within given political units. Religious difference within a culture seldom exists without tension. "Incompatible" religious loyalty tends to be considered a threat to political allegiance. Those who know the cultural history of Western civilization are aware with what frequency religious difference results in war or civil disorder. Although much less pressing than in the past, religious conflict related to ethnic loyalty has not yet disappeared, as the situation in the mideast or in Ireland between Catholic and Protestant well illustrates. Similar relationships between religion, ethnic identity, and political conflict are less known outside of Europe. Gananath Obeyesekere acquaints us with an example from Ceylon.

Obeyesekere forcefully brings out three major points that will receive further attention in our conclusions. The first point is that past events have meaning for the individual only in so far as they are turned into easily communicated legends symbolizing continuity between past and present. Present identity thus is influenced more by myths of the past than by actual historical occur-

ences. In Ceylon, Sinhalese identity is inextricably interwoven with Buddhist mythology.

A second major issue raised by Obeyesekere is that crises in identity tend to occur at certain characteristic times of life for certain individuals or groups; therefore, ethnic identity must be assessed in the context of a total life trajectory. This perspective takes on added significance when viewed in the light of Erik Erikson's psychoanalytically oriented frame of analysis for the life history of the individual.* Erikson's analysis relates crises in identity to the ways in which resolved and unresolved past vicissitudes continue to influence new experiences. Here again, in a sense, it is the mythic meaning of past events, not their behavioral details, that determines how new situations will precipitate crises in the individual's concept of self.

Finally, Obeyesekere aptly illustrates how "identity affirmation" can bolster self-esteem. In crises involving a perceived threat to the unity of an ethnic group, identity affirmation acts to resolve internal stresses resulting from political and social degradation of the group. What takes place, in other words, is a collective "revivalist" response to a political defeat or dissolution. Ethnic revivalist movements commonly are manifestations of defense against threatened extinction when a ruling polity seeks by its policies to secure the ultimate loyalty of all those it governs. Some form of identity affirmation can counter the effects of a period of dispersion and degradation by evoking old images and emblems around which members can rally to shed shame, renew ethnic pride, and gain a sense of self-acceptance.

In highlighting the life of Amagarika Dharmapala, Obeyesekere succinctly yet sensitively illustrates the difficulties of individual identity management in Ceylon in the latter period of colonial rule as the country moved toward political independence. Amagarika Dharmapala experienced a fierce intrapsychic struggle in growing up as Sinhalese in that society—i.e., as a member of a politically and economically submerged people. He conceptualized his own struggle as an irreconcilable conflict between two bodies of religious teaching. In his case, a sustaining identification with Christian mentors failed to take hold and ultimately, through an enduring and ascendant attachment to maternal models, he reaffirmed his familial allegiance to Buddhism and successfully transmitted his conviction to thousands of his countrymen.

Today in Ceylon, to be Sinhalese is to be Buddhist; pluralism is denied as a possibility. The Sinhalese majority has attempted to resolve its problems of ethnic identity by forming a religious state. Like modern Israel, however, Ceylon may have created problems for itself in its religious definition of nationhood. It is still unclear how the Christian, Muslim, and Hindu minorities that together comprise a goodly percentage of Ceylon's population are to be included in the concept of citizenship.

*See Erik Erikson, *Identity, Youth and Crisis* (New York: W. W. Norton, 1968).

Sinhalese-Buddhist Identity in Ceylon

GANANATH OBEYESEKERE

9

The thesis of this paper is that, as far as Ceylon is concerned, being Buddhist is inseparable from being Sinhalese, which is Ceylon's major ethnic group. Up to the sixteenth century being a Sinhalese implied being a Buddhist. After that time, with the advent of the European powers, a split in the Sinhalese identity occurred as a result of the existence of Catholic and Protestant Sinhalese who were clearly not Buddhist. Sinhalese ceased to be an ethnic identity. Buddhism also lost its prominence as the national religion; its position was usurped by Protestantism. Though Sinhalese Christians were economically and politically dominant, the majority of Sinhalese were Buddhists living in peasant villages. We can then document a revival of Buddhism in the nineteenth century with the emergence of a leader who, in solving his own personal identity conflicts, helped to refashion the identity of Sinhalese Buddhists. If the Buddhist aspect of the Sinhalese identity was traditionally taken for granted, it had to be affirmed and vindicated in the nineteenth and twentieth centuries. I describe this process of identity affirmation and its culmination in the mid-twentieth century, when Buddhists, having obtained political power, are affirming through symbolic acts their claim to a Sinhalese Buddhist nation.

In the contemporary Sinhala language the term for Buddhism is *Buddha-*

gāma, the *agama* ("religion") of the Buddha. In general when a Sinhalese wants to refer to his religion he says, *mama Buddāgamē,* "I belong to the religion of the Buddha." The term *Baudhayek* or "Buddhist" is also used, but it is not in general vogue, it sounds almost neologistic, and perhaps is a translation of the English term, "Buddhist." I suggest that these self-reference terms are cultural labels of recent development in the history of Ceylon, that they came into use after 1505, the date of the arrival of the first Portuguese colonizers. The widespread use and diffusion of these terms, however, is a phenomenon of British rule in Ceylon, which lasted from 1795 to 1948.

The situation is in some sense analogous to what happened in India, where an overall religious label, "Hindu," was used to include various types of indigenous religious systems, such as Vaishnavite, Shaivite, and Lingayat, although in India, Hindu pantheism also fostered to a great extent the coalescence of diverse sectarian identities into the overall religious identity of "Hindu." In India, as well as in Ceylon, these newly introduced cultural labels have been accepted by many people in a manner that has a great deal of significance for their collective identity. It is the aim of this paper to examine the newly emergent identity of "Buddhist," and relate it to its historical and social background, and the immediate socio-political and economic factors that led to its development. The reader is requested to bear in mind two distinctive uses of the words "Buddhist" and "Buddhism" in this paper—one as the anthropologist's own reference to the practitioners of the religion, and secondly as a self-reference and self-identification term used by the people themselves.

The traditional Sinhalese word for Buddhism was the Pali term, *Buddha sāsana,* "the universal Buddhist church." Though the meaning of the term *Buddha sāsana* was universalistic in Pāli form, its significance for the Sinhalese was almost entirely particularistic. The *sāsana* was inextricably linked with the country's dominant ethnic group, the Sinhalese. The great historical chronicles of the Sinhalese, the *Mahāvamsa* and *Cūlavamsa,* written in Pāli, as well as literary and historical works written in Sinhala from about the thirteenth century onwards, constantly emphasize the identification of the destiny of the *sasana* with that of the Sinhala people. This identification is also legitimized in a particular genre of myth, which for want of a better term may be referred to as "legend" or "historical myth." These myths are found in the chronicles and in Sinhala literary works and are sung in rituals. They have been and still remain part of the current beliefs of the Sinhala people. As such, these myths are vitally important for understanding the equivalence of the terms "Sinhalese" with "Buddhism," and the whole problem of Buddhist identity.

According to myth, Ceylon was originally inhabited by non-humans—

yakkhas ("demons") and *nāgas* ("snakes"). The first chapter of the *Mahāvamsa* records three visits of the Buddha to Ceylon (Lanka). The first visit was when "at the ninth month of his Buddhahood, at the full moon of Phussa, himself set forth to the isle of Lanka, to win Lanka for the faith. For Lanka was known to the Conqueror as a place where his doctrine should [thereafter] shine in glory; and [he knew that] from Lanka, filled with the *yakkhas*, the *yakkhas* must [first] be drawn forth"(*3*, p. 3). In this first trip he quelled the *yakkhas* at Mahiyangana, in Eastern Ceylon, which today is a leading pilgrimage center where people go to worship the collar bone relic of the Buddha and propitiate the guardian deity of the area, the god Saman. During his second visit he quelled and converted the *nāgas*, "snake beings," who dwelt in the northern tip of Ceylon, known as *nāgadipa*, which is also a center of Buddhist pilgrimage. "When the Master, having alighted on the earth, had taken his place on a seat there, and had been refreshed with celestial food and drink by the nāga-kings, he, the Lord, established in the [three] refuges and in the moral precepts eighty kotis of snake-spirits, dwellers in the ocean and on the mainland." His third visit was to Kelaniya, near Colombo. During this visit he also "left traces of his footprints plain to see on Sumanakuta"(*3*, p. 8). From there he went to Digavapi on the East Coast, and to various places in Anuradhapura, which later became the first capital of the Sinhalese kings. All these places consecrated by the Buddha have been, and still are, great centers of Buddhist pilgrimage in Ceylon. The significance of the myth is clear: The island has been consecrated by the Buddha himself, and evil forces have been banished or subjugated preparatory to the arrival of the founder of the Sinhala race, Prince Wijaya.

The *Mahāvamsa* states, "The prince named Wijaya, the valiant, landed in Lanka, in the region called Tambapanni on the day the Tathagata [i.e., Buddha] lay down between the two twin-like sala trees to pass into nibbana" (*3*, p. 54). But before the Buddha died he summoned Sakka, the king of the gods and the divine protector of the Universal Buddhist Church (*sāsana*) and instructed him thus: "Wijaya, son of King Sinhabahu, is come to Lanka from the country of Lala, together with seven hundred followers. In Lanka, O Lord of gods, will my religion be established, therefore carefully protect him with his followers and Lanka"(*3*, p. 55). Sakka in turn handed the guardianship of Ceylon to a god named Uppalavannassa ("the colour like the lotus"), later identified with Vishnu. Vishnu, in the guise of an ascetic, met Wijaya as he landed in Ceylon with his followers and "sprinkled water on them from his water-vessel and . . . wound a thread about their hands,"(*3*, p. 54) in order to protect them from evil demons, much as contemporary monks do for the lay followers in Buddhist *pāritta* ceremonies.

Wijaya's men are lured into a cave and captured by a demoness, Kuveni.

Wijaya rescues them, and afterwards marries the demoness who begets him a son and a daughter. Later Wijaya discards the demoness and banishes her with the two children. He himself marries a princess from the royal family of South Madura; his followers also marry women from the same region and from these unions spring the Sinhalese race. The son and daughter of Wijaya and Kuveni, banished into the forest, also marry incestuously and from them spring the Veddhas of Ceylon (ethnologically the aboriginal people of the island). Thus the myth records the development of one contrastive set of Sinhalese versus Veddha.

These myths which are repeated time and again in the course of history in various contexts—literary, ritual and historical—crystalize the situation of Sinhalese identity until about the sixteenth century. This identity simply equates Sinhalese=Buddhist —the two cultural labels are the constituent elements of a single identity. The myths are also an expression of the self-perceived historical role of the Sinhalese as a nation. They are the guardians and protectors of the *sāsana,* a historic role decreed by the Buddha himself. This self-perceived role is not lacking in objective validity, so that one could further argue that the myths are a summary of the actual relationship between the Sinhalese state and Buddhism, between laity and monk, between the imported Hindu gods and the Buddha. Myths, in a sense, are more powerful than actual historical events, for Sinhalese history in the true sense of that term is a series of events which have little bearing on or meaning in the life of the people. Myths, by contrast, are always present in the minds of the people at any given point in history, and sum up for them the "meaning" of their country's history. Historical events, which we know from verifiable sources to have occurred, may also be "mythicized," that is, repatterned in accordance with the pre-existent dominant myths of a nation. They then become part of the larger corpus of myth that gives meaning to the self-perceived historical role of any nation.

The historical events as depicted in Ceylon's chronicles had until the sixteenth century one unvarying pattern: with a few exceptions Ceylon was consistently invaded by South Indian peoples who were generally Tamil speakers. Very soon the major contrastive set was not "Sinhalese versus Veddha" but "Sinhalese (Buddhist) versus Tamil (Shaivite unbelievers)." Thus there were historically two major opposed ethnic identities, Sinhalese and Tamil. The historical conflicts between Sinhalese and South Indian invaders reinforced and stabilized the Sinhalese-Buddhist identity. However, while Sinhalese was equated with Buddhist, Buddhist did not always imply Sinhalese, for Ceylon as an ancient center of Theravada Buddhism attracted Buddhist monks and perhaps laymen of other nationalities—Tamil and Indian generally, but also Chinese, Burmese and others. However, since their numbers were small, it is likely that as far as the masses were concerned, the label "Buddhist" also implied "Sinhalese."

The historical experience of conflict with South Indian invaders produced a new pattern of myth and mythicized history, which incorporated another theme: "Sinhalese as defenders of the *sāsana* versus Tamil as opposers of the *sāsana*." This theme is not always in accordance with the facts of history. Tamil kings who ruled Sinhalese kingdoms, either through conquest or through complicated rules of succession, often took upon themselves the traditional role of Sinhalese kings and protected the official religion of the state; and Sinhalese kings sometimes pillaged temples and robbed monasteries of their wealth. Yet the myths were not fictions, for insofar as this was the Sinhalese "definition of the situation," their self-perceived historic role was real to them. In fact, Sinhalese people could be mobilized by their rulers to fight foreign invaders by appealing to the sentiments underlying the myths, so that these myths became, on occasion, rallying points for Sinhalese nationalism. Finally, actual historical events began in turn to be interpreted as validating the themes of these myths.

Ceylonese history mentions a king, Vattagamini Ahaya (29–17 B.C.) who, defeated by the Tamils, left Anuradhapura, the capital, and sought refuge in the principality of Ruhuna in South Ceylon. There he mobilized an army, but soon an incident occurred which nearly ruined his cause. "One day the King, when climbing the narrow and steep path . . . met one of his generals, named Kapisisa, coming down. Kapisisa sat down and gave way to the king, but the latter was enraged that the general did not prostrate himself as one should have done before royalty, and struck the warrior down with his sword. When this incident became known to the other leaders of the army, they left Vattagamini in a body. At this critical juncture in Vattagamini's career, a *thēra* ["monk"] named Tissa of Hambugalla and the king's former benefactor, Mahatissa [also a monk] intervened to reconcile the captains to the king, using the powerful argument that it was by serving him that they could further the interests of the Buddhist religion"(*4*, p. 71). The argument was in fact successful, and Vattagamini defeated the Tamils and recaptured the capital.

Let us now turn to the myth of Dutugemunu, for while there is no doubt regarding the historical authenticity of this king and the main events of his career, I am largely interested in his mythicization, for he is preeminently the Sinhalese-Buddhist hero who saved his country from the Tamils. In the second century B.C. the capital of the Sinhalese kingdom fell into the hands of the Colas of South India, and the Tamil King, Elara, reigned there (145–101 B.C.). Resistance to Elara was to come from Dutugemunu, the son of the ruler of the southern principality of Ceylon. The *Mahāvamsa* and other chronicles describe how Kavantissa asked his two sons, Dutugemunu and Sadhatissa, to promise that they would not fight the Tamils. They both refused, and Dutugemunu crawled into bed. "The queen came, and caressing Gāmini spoke thus: 'Why dost thou not lie easily upon thy bed with limbs stretched out, my son?' 'Over there beyond the Gange (the river Mahaveli) are the Damilas (Tamils), here on this side is the Gotha-ocean, how can I lie with outstretched limbs?' " Subsequently Dutugemunu defeated the Tamils and after having killed Elara, assumed the kingship of the whole country. Since I am not interested here in the historical account of Dutugemunu, I shall list certain items in the *Mahāvamsa* account which had mythic significance:

(1) In the war with the Tamils, Dutugemunu used a spear within which was embedded a Buddha relic. Having mobilized his army he said, "I will go on to the land on the further side of the river [where the Tamils were entrenched] to bring glory to the doctrine"(*3,* p. 171).

(2) He marched into battle with five hundred ascetic monks; never before or after have monks taken such an active part in a military campaign. In fact, one of Dutugemunu's warriors was an ex-monk, Theraputtabhaya, who, after the conquest of the Tamils, reverted to the order.

(3) Dutugemunu felt guilty about the lives lost in the war. Like Arjuna of the *Mahabharata* he tells the eight *arhats* who came to console him: "How shall there be any comfort for me, O venerable sirs, since by me was caused the slaughter of a great host numbering millions?" But the *arhats,* like Krishna of the Hindu epic, reply: "From this deed arises no hindrance in thy way to heaven. Only one and a half human beings were slain here by thee, O lord of men. The one had come unto the [three] refuges, the other had taken on himself the five precepts. Unbelievers and men of evil life were the rest, not more to be esteemed than beasts. But as for thee, thou wilt bring glory to the doctrine of the Buddha in manifold ways; therefore cast away care from thy heart, O ruler of men"(*3,* p. 178).

(4) After his death Dutugemunu went to the heaven of Tusita where the next Buddha-to-be, Maitreye, also lived. The *Mahāvamsa* goes on to say: "The great king Dutthagamini (Dutugemunu), he who is worthy of the name of the king, will be the first disciple of the sublime Metteyya [Maitreye Buddha], the king's father [will be] his father and the mother his mother. The younger brother Saddhatissa will be his second disciple, but Salirajakumara, the king's son, will be the son of the sublime Metteyya"(*3,* p. 227).

This is the only instance in the Ceylon chronicles where there is an explicit justification for war and killing in terms which perhaps better fit the *Bhagavata Gita* than the Buddhist *suttas.* I have heard historians of Ceylon argue that this was simply a lone exception in the history of Ceylon. Although this may be the case statistically, the mythic significance of the episode totally outweighs its statistical import. While the details of the wars fought by Dutugemunu, and recorded faithfully in the *Mahāvamsa,* may easily have been forgotten, the mythic significance of Dutugemunu as the savior of the Sinhala race and of Buddhism grew through the years and developed into one of the most important myths of the Sinhalese, ready to be used as a powerful instrument of Sinhalese nationalism in modern times. Although the justification for killing is unusual, the general message that emerges is everywhere the same: "The Sinhalese kings are defenders of the secular realm and the *sāsana*; their opponents are the Tamils."

Certain institutional arrangements in Ceylon, from very early times, gave further expression to the idea of a Sinhalese Buddhist nation. The first Buddhist missions were sent by the Indian Emperor Asoka, and during this time occurred an event of great symbolical importance. A branch of the *bōdhi* tree under which the Buddha received enlightenment was placed in Anuradhapura, and survives to this day. Also enshrined were relics of the Buddha, including the right collar bone and the almsbowl. The collar bone was enshrined in the Thuparama Dagaba in Anuradhapura. Rahula sums up well the significance of these events: "The planting of the *bōdhi* tree was symbolic of the establishment of Buddhism and Buddhist culture in the island. The relics of the Buddha were regarded as representing the Buddha himself and their enshrinement was as good as Buddha's residence in Lanka. The *pātra-dhātu,* or the almsbowl, of the Buddha was kept within the king's house, and it became a national 'palladium' of the Sinhalese, just as happened later in the case of the 'tooth-relic' "(*8,* p. 58).

Thus very early in Ceylon's history two ideas developed: (1) Not only was Ceylon consecrated by the Buddha himself, but he was immanent in his relics enshrined in the great centers of Buddhist pilgrimage in Ceylon. (2) Two of these relics became associated with Sinhalese sovereignty and the legitimacy of kingship. Earlier it was the bowl relic, and subsequently the tooth relic, which is now housed in Kandy, the last capital of the Sinhalese kings. These relics were preciously guarded, housed in a special building and paraded ceremonially every year. No foreign invader or claimant to the throne felt himself secure or rightfully sovereign unless he had with him the possession of the relic. Thus the relic not only symbolized the living presence of the Buddha, it also symbolized the idea of the Sinhalese Buddhist state and the legitimacy of its rulers. Soon a third idea developed—that the king was a future Buddha or bodhisatva. This idea was the Sinhalese version of the divine right of kings. Thus the king was the "defender of the faith;" the order of monks were its visible representatives; the laity represented the Buddhist congregation. The major guardian deities of the Sinhalese religious pantheon were also supernatural defenders of the faith and future aspirants to Buddhahood.

I have argued that up to the sixteenth century, the term "Sinhalese" meant also Buddhist and that were was no self-reference term for the latter. The self-reference and identification term was Sinhalese, and Sinhalese was the "ethnic identity." As Barth says, the critical feature in ethnic identity is the characteristic of self-ascription and ascription by others: "A categorical ascription is an ethnic ascription when it classifies a person in terms of his basic, most general identity, presumptively determined by his origin and background"(*1,* p. 13). He goes on to say: "regarded as a status, ethnic identity is superordinate to most other statuses, and defines the permissible constellation of statuses, or social personalities, which an individual with that identity may assume. It constrains the incumbent on all his activities, not only in some defined social situations. One might also say that it is imperative, in that it cannot be disregarded and temporarily set aside by other definitions of the situation. The constraints on a person's behavior which spring from his ethnic identity thus tends to be absolute"(*1,* p. 17).

The ethnic identity "Sinhalese" is the superordinate identity within which are contained several other subordinate identities, such as the primary group identities of family, kinship identity, larger group identities like caste, or even a still larger regional identity. As far as the Sinhalese, or any ethnic group, is concerned, the subordinate identities may reveal a great deal of areal variation and cultural differences, yet these differences can be subsumed by the larger, all-inclusive ethnic identity. Thus for example two Sinhalese persons may have radically different caste affiliations and concomitant cultural differences, yet they both share the ethnic identity "Sinhalese" (and, as also implied, "Buddhist"). Yet we must ask what characteristics distinguish the Sinhalese from the Tamil.

Culturally there are two distinct markers of the Sinhalese identity. First, there is the common language, Sinhala, which in spite of minor dialect variations is intelligible to all who consider themselves ethnically Sinhalese. Second, there is Buddhism, which involves belief in the three "refuges"—the Buddha, the *dhamma* ("doctrine, moral order") and the *sangha* ("the monkhood"). All Sinhalese (note that we are dealing with the pre-sixteenth century situation, though I am using present tense) worship the Buddha, who is a super-deity, heading the pantheon. This universal worship of the Buddha is important, for many Sinhalese groups may worship other deities in the pantheon, and these lower deities (particularly regional gods and demons) may vary from one region to another. Yet while variations in belief occur on the lower levels of the pantheon, all Sinhalese beliefs merge at the apex of the pantheon in the worship of the Buddha (*5, 6*). Furthermore, Tamils and Veddha may worship some of the gods that the Sinhalese also worship (Vishnu, Skanda, etc.), but the Sinhalese alone worship the Buddha. Moreover, while ethnic Tamils view gods like Vishnu and Skanda as primary deities, these gods occupy only a secondary place in the Sinhalese-Buddhist pantheon and are clearly subordinate to the Buddha.

The *dhamma* is also considered by all as the true teaching of the Buddha, yet the belief in the truth of the doctrine must be distinguished from the knowledge of the doctrine. Sinhalese believe that the true doctrine is enshrined in Pali texts, the *suttas,* and the true knowledge of the doctrine is the prerogative of the order of monks, the *sangha.* As far as the laity is concerned, their knowledge of the doctrine is highly variable, yet I think it is true that all Sinhalese share a common set of concepts or ideas derived from the doctrine. These concepts are of crucial importance in giving meaning to their everyday lives and shaping their worldview. Concepts like *karma, dāna* ("giving"), *sīla* ("virtue"), *bhāvanā* ("meditation"), *pav-pin* ("sin and merit"), *karunā* ("compassion") and many others in common use are all derived from Buddhist doctrinal sources. In addition, all Sinhalese share a common knowledge of *Pāli* prayers, particularly the knowledge of the "recital of the five precepts." Thus all Sinhalese share a common idiom—I call it a salvation idiom—which constitutes their shared knowledge of the *dhamma.*

The *sangha* ("monk order") is crucial to maintaining the Sinhalese knowledge of the *dhamma,* for the *sangha* is the repository of the *dhamma.* The *sangha,* through their sermons, propagate and diffuse among the Sinhalese laity the knowledge of the *dhamma.* The laity in turn support and pay homage to the *sangha.* The *sangha* by virtue of their vestments are a clearly identifiable body of men worshipped by the ethnic Sinhalese, and by no other group in the island.

The cultural markers we have described set off the ethnic group as a moral community, that is, as a body of men sharing common norms. But what is the sociological significance of belonging to an all-inclusive moral community of Sinhalese? It is obvious that an ethnic group as a moral community is not a group in the strict sociological sense of the term, yet the ethnic moral community has a sense of ethnic self-consciousness, a sense of belongingness, which is characteristic also of primary group identities. Yet the latter constitute groups while the former does not. I suggest that the model for the we-feeling is earlier primary group identities, largely because the markers of ethnic identity discussed above are inculcated in the process of socialization in the family. But this is not sufficient to create a sense of identification. We have to consider an added factor, the presence of other ethnic groups which, insofar as they are viewed as threatening or alien, create within the ethnic group a sense of community. I further suggest that ethnic groups are latent groups, that the possibility exists for members of an ethnic group, with divergent other-identities and values, to interact as groups, and that sociological mechanisms may exist which help translate the possibility of interaction into a reality.

In other words we are interested not only in the cultural aspect of the idea of an ethnic moral community (shared norms), but also its sociological aspects (interaction). The idea of a moral community is, in our view, crucial to maintaining the ethnic identity of a group as a superordinate identity within which are contained the individuals' other-identities.

The most important sociological mechanism which creates a sense of group consciousness, the sense of belonging to a moral community, is what I call the "obligatory pilgrimage." Each village is a moral community, and there are various rituals to deities that define the limits (*sīma*) of the moral community and bring blessings on its members. For example, in Rambadeniya, an isolated village in the central province of Ceylon, where I engaged in field research in 1958, annual rituals to the chief deity of the region brought the village together as a moral community participating in common worship. The deity worshipped here was a regional deity who might be unknown outside one particular region in the Central Province. However, once a year people from Rambadeniya go on pilgrimage to Mahiyangana, 35 miles away, where the Buddha relics are enshrined. As soon as the pilgrim group (*nadē*) leaves the village, it joins other pilgrim groups in other villages, and after a few hours of travel, there is a literal expansion of the moral community—people of different villages and regions, different castes, now merge into one large mass as they approach Mahiyangana. At Mahiyangana they temporarily renounce the worship of their local parochial deities. Instead they worship the guardian god of the shrine, Saman, and the Buddha present in his relics. If the rituals of the village define the limits of the moral community of the village and validate the status differences in the village social structure, the rituals of Mahiyangana are open to all irrespective of caste, sex and other status factors. The once discrete and separate moral communities of the several villages now lose their identity in the larger moral community of Sinhalese Buddhists. Interaction is made possible in these centers because of the common language spoken and the common subscription to Buddhism. The rituals and prayers uttered are part of the common "salvation idiom" of all Sinhalese and thus communal participation in rituals are realized. People from various parts of the country listen collectively to sermons preached by the monks of the temple and participate in other acts of communal worship. Lay *virtuosi* from different areas who have observed the higher precepts may congregate in one area and meditate, while others may read from sacred texts to a motley congregation, while others preach lay sermons. Thus the notion of belonging receives concrete sociological expression in the mechanism of the obligatory pilgrimage. The sacred pilgrimage centers are scattered through the island, and the ideal pilgrimage takes a person throughout the length and breadth of the island. While it is doubtful whether in the past many individuals had the time or opportunity to undertake such a tour, some of these places were obligatory for most villagers, so that the individual perceived and developed a sense of community and common identity outside of the limited universe of his village or region (*6*).

DECLINE OF SINHALESE HEGEMONY IN CEYLON

I have just discussed the traditional Sinhalese identity in the early period of Sinhalese civilization. Let me now discuss it in relation to the decline of Sinhalese civilization, which roughly consists of two periods, one of systematic South Indian invasions which resulted in the abandonment of the old centers of civilization and the later period of colonial rule which brought about a radical change in the Sinhalese ethnic identity.

The wars between the Sinhalese and the Tamils continued until the sixteenth century. In the tenth century the old capital of Anuradhapura had to be abandoned because of the Tamil invasions, and the capital was moved eastward to Pollonnaruva. Sinhalese fortunes reached a low point in the late tenth century, with systematic invasions from South India which were unlike the sporadic incursions of the earlier periods. Ceylon was a principality of the Tamil Cola kings until 1070, when the Sinhalese chieftain Kirti raised the standard of revolt successfully and assumed the crown as Vijayabahu I (1059–1114 A.D.). Later under Prakramabahu, Sinhalese civilization reached new heights, and Pollonnaruva, the new capital, became a great city. But the respite was temporary. In 1214 Magha of Kalinga landed in Ceylon with a large army of South Indian mercenaries. The Pāli and Sinhalese chronicles mention the devastation of the kingdom by Magha and the sorry plight of the Sinhalese. The *Rājāvaliyā,* a seventeenth century Sinhalese chronicle, writes of the event: "As moral duties were not practiced by the people of Lanka, and the guardian deities of Lanka regarded them not, their sins were visited upon them and unjust deeds became prevalent. The king of Kalinga landed on the island of Lanka with an army of 20,000 men, fortified himself, took the city of Pollonnaruva, seized King Parakrama Pandi, plucked out his eyes, destroyed the religion and the people, and broke into Ruwanvali and other *dagabas.* He caused the Tamils to take and destroy the shrines which represented the embodied fame of many faithful kings, the pinnacles that were like their crowns, and the precious stones which were as their hearts, and the relics which were like their lives. He wrought confusion in castes by reducing to servitude people of high birth in Lanka, raising people of low birth and holding them in high esteem. He reduced to poverty people of rank; caused the people of Lanka to embrace a false faith . . . turned Lanka into a house on fire, settled Tamils in every village, and reigned nineteen years in the commission of deeds of violence"(*9*, pp. 61-62).

As a result of these invasions, centers of the old civilization in the northern dry zone of Ceylon were abandoned, and the Sinhalese kings gradually moved to the southwest. The new capital was Dambadeniya to the south of the old kingdom. In the middle of the fourteenth century it was moved to Gampola near Kandy in central Ceylon. In the beginning of the sixteenth century there were three virtually independent kingdoms in the country—Kandy, Kottē near Colombo, and the independent Tamil kingdom in the northern Jaffna peninsula. The existence of a Tamil kingdom in the north implied the existence of an ethnically homogenous Tamil community which persists to this day. By the beginning of the sixteenth century there were also groups of Tamil-speaking Moslems scattered in various parts of the island and having an identity distinct from and opposed to both Sinhalese and Tamil.

This period of the decline in Sinhalese civilization may have resulted in the demoralization of the Sinhalese, but did not affect their identity in any other way. Sinhalese still implied Buddhist, and they were opposed to Tamils (and a minority of Moslems). The division of the country into autonomous Sinhalese kingdoms no doubt produced conflicts between Sinhalese, but similar divisions also existed in previous periods in the country's history. The Sinhalese ethnic identity transcended political boundaries, and is perhaps one reason for the instability of these boundaries, for massive numbers of people crossed from one kingdom to another. The really radical change in ethnic identity came with the advent of European powers, beginning with the arrival of the Portuguese in 1505.

By the end of the sixteenth century the Portuguese were in virtual control of the whole coastal region known today as the "low-country." The kingdom of Kandy alone remained independent. In 1655 the Dutch successfully defeated the Portuguese, and retained control of the seaboard until they were defeated by the British in 1795. In 1815 the British marched into Kandy, defeated the last king, and brought the whole country under their rule.

The advent of the European powers had serious implications for Sinhalese identity, for the historic equation of Sinhalese=Buddhist ceased to have the kind of universal validity it had once had. As a result of European proselytization, Sinhala people were converted to Catholicism and later Protestantism. In the areas that came under Portuguese rule, Catholicism was the politically dominant religion. Later, with the Dutch and the British, Protestantism became politically dominant, and Sinhalese Protestants became economically dominant also. Thus the old Sinhalese ethnic identity split into several contrastive sets: Sinhalese Buddhist versus Sinhalese Catholic; Sinhalese Buddhist versus Sinhalese Protestant; Sinhalese Catholic versus Sinhalese Protestant. There developed, then, three separate Sinhalese identities, each distinguished by religion. Furthermore, these identities were characterized by regional, occupational and class differentiation. The bulk of Sinhalese peasants living in villages were Buddhists, while Catholics were largely confined to the fishing communities on the coast, and Protestants became a bureaucratic elite under the Dutch and British. To compound matters further, the Tamil ethnic identity was also split in the same fashion; and then there were the Moslems, who could also be characterized as an ethnic group. Thus the present major groupings are Sinhalese-Buddhist, Sinhalese-Catholic, Sinhalese-Protestant, Tamil-Hindu, Tamil-Christian, Moslem, and whites.

It is likely that from the Sinhalese-Buddhist point of view the major contrastive sets were: Sinhalese Buddhist versus Sinhalese Christian, Sinhalese Buddhist versus Tamil (both Christian and Hindu), Sinhalese Buddhist versus Moslem, and Sinhalese Buddhist versus whites (*suddho*). Thus the complexities of the objective situation were reduced by an ethnic reclassification into a limited number of contrastive sets. The first set, with which we are now concerned, resulted in the development of new cultural labels. The Christians were all classified into one group, *āgama* ("religion," literally, "tradition"). Perhaps this term developed as a result of the missions' claim that their religion was the only religion, or *āgama.* In opposition to *āgama,* or Christianity, the term *Buddhāgama* was used to refer to Buddhists. This term, now also a self-reference term, is a new one, but one that has come to stay as a result of the split in the Sinhalese identity into Christian and Buddhist.

THE NEW SINHALESE BUDDHIST IDENTITY

I shall now describe the process whereby a new Sinhalese-Buddhist identity emerged as a result of Western colonial rule. Let me briefly sum up the effects of colonial rule on Sinhalese identity. First, there was the split in the Sinhalese identity, as I have described above. Second, Buddhism ceased to be the official and dominant religion. It lost its position of prestige, and simultaneously Sinhalese-Buddhists lost political and economic power. Under British rule Protestantism was the dominant religion, and Protestant churches were built in the proximity of old Buddhist temples, acts which symbolized the supercession of the old religion by the dominant one. The demoralization of the Sinhalese is clearly manifest in the millenial type myth which became popular under the British among Sinhalese peasants—the Diyasena myth. According to this myth a new Sinhalese culture hero, Diyasena, will arise, kill all Christians and non-believers, and reestablish the glory of the Buddha *sāsana*. This millenial fantasy is the product of the hopeless plight of Sinhalese-Buddhists, unable to take positive action to reestablish their lost prestige, for the majority of them were still living in peasant villages, while power was in the hands of colonial rulers and a few elite educated and westernized Sinhalese Protestants in the cities.

The middle and late nineteenth century saw a revival in Buddhism led by a non-peasant intelligentsia under the leadership of educated Sinhalese Buddhists and of monks from the Sinhalese low country. The educated Sinhalese Buddhists were mostly schoolteachers trained in Sinhalese vernacular schools, and the influential village intelligentsia consisting of Ayurvedic physicians and village government officials such as headmen, coroners, and registrars of marriages, all created by the British bureaucracy. Some members of the intelligentsia came from city elites educated in English in Christian mission schools, but they were not numerically significant, since the mission schools were largely the preserve of Christians. This period also saw the establishment by the Venerable Sumangala of a Buddhist college, the Vidyodaya Pirivena in Colombo, which was devoted to the study of Pāli and Buddhism. This was followed by the establishment of another college, Vidyalankara Pirivena. In the 1880s there was a series of public debates between Buddhist monks and Christian priests. One of the most popular of the Buddhist debaters was Mohotiwatte Gunananda, whose fame spread all over Ceylon as a champion of the Buddhist cause. Shortly afterwards, an American Colonel, H. S. Olcott, and Madame Blavatsky who had organized the Theosophical Society of New York in 1875, arrived in Ceylon to organize the Buddhist Theosophical Society of Ceylon. These theosophists took under their tutelage a young brilliant Buddhist, born in Colombo as Don David Hewavitarana, who in resolving his own identity conflict also helped refashion the identity of the Sinhalese Buddhists. Since he is best known as the Anagarika Dharmapala, I refer to him by that name.

Anagarika Dharmapala was a prolific writer in both English and Sinhalese and, like Luther and Gandhi, provided us with information about his childhood. Let us examine his identity crisis, as stated in his own words when over sixty years old, and see how this crisis was symptomatic of the identity crisis facing the Sinhalese in general.

Dharmapala was born in 1864 in Colombo. His father was an indigent carpenter when he arrived in Colombo from the South of Ceylon, but later made a fortune. His family background, I think, would have been of some significance to Dharmapala, for it is likely that his family would have been treated as wealthy *parvenu* by the Sinhalese elite of his day. He was given the name Don David because "children of Buddhist parents born in Colombo had to be taken to a church where the minister would record the names of the parents and the birth date of the child, [and] would give a Biblical name to the infant" (*2*, p. 697). But be that as it may, this was a period when many Sinhalese were in fact adopting English names, and Dharmapala's father merely followed this practice.

As a very young child, Dharmapala was sent to a girls' school in the Pettah in Colombo, "where Dutch burgher girls were taught English." At six he went to the Pettah Catholic School, and at eleven to a "boarding school of the Church of England, seven miles from my home"(*2*, p. 684). Between eight and ten he attended a Sinhalese vernacular school. He attended the mission schools because, in his words, "the Buddhist temple schools in Ceylon had been forcibly closed, because, in view of a commission appointed by the government to investigate them, the children attending them were too loyal to the traditions of old Ceylon." Again it is also very likely that Dharmapala's father, who had high aspirations for his son, simply wanted to give him an English education, which then was available in the mission schools.

The upshot of Dharmapala's early life and education had serious implications for the identity problems of an intelligent and sensitive child. In the first place, his father, who belonged to the *goyigama* (farmer) caste had given up his primary group identities (his kinship and caste obligations) and emigrated to Colombo, where, in all probability, he was not accepted into Colombo's elite society, which was Protestant. Dharmapala then was born into a family which had no established place in the community. It is likely that Dharmapala was conscious of this fact, and that his later activities were attempts to find roots, not in any specific locality or grouping, but in the whole historical tradition of Sinhalese Buddhism.

Secondly, the religious education he received in the schools contrasted strongly to the religious education in his home, posing a moral dilemma of the first magnitude to the child, in addition to creating identity problems. In school he was nurtured in Catholicism, and later Protestantism: "in the years six to ten I was associated daily with Catholic teachers. I was a favorite with my padre teachers because I brought flowers from my father's garden to decorate their altars on feast days." In all likelihood he was a good, obedient pupil, as he was a good son, and he probably reflects on his own attitudes when he says: "As boys, the Sinhalese are good and obedient and love their teachers"(*2*, p. 683).

At twelve he was reading the Bible "four times a day" in the Protestant boarding school. "During the two and a half years I stayed there I was taught very little history or arithmetic, but pored over Bible lessons from morning till evening"(*2,* p. 684). Though later on he developed a great hatred of the missions, he had respect for the Bible, particularly the New Testament, and the personality of Jesus himself. In fact, wherever he went he carried copies of Buddhist texts as well as the Bible "heavily underlined with references and cross references and falling apart from constant use"(*2,* p. 682).

In contrast to his enculturation in Christianity at school, Dharmapala was socialized in Buddhism at home. The village Buddhism of his father's ancestral home in the South, with its heavy orientation towards magic and exorcism, had little relevance in the urban society in which Dharmapala was raised. The Buddhism practiced by his parents had a more fundamentalist character. "My family, which is Sinhalese, has been Buddhist without a break for twenty-two hundred years" (*2,* p. 682). This sentence shows that Dharmapala is not identifying his family with any other identity, outside of an idealized Buddhist identity. "All the members of my family were devout. I had to recite passages from the *sutras* and holy poems to my mother; and always she had ready, as a reward for good work, special sweets which she knew I liked"(*2,* p. 282). His mother's charity toward beggars and the poor, and his mother's sister's qualities as a "ministering angel" created in him, he says, a sensitivity to "human suffering from bodily privation, and I always want to help those who are poor"(*2,* p. 682). The whole family observed the precepts, meditated and fasted "once a month on full-moon day" (*2,* p. 682). The contrast between this socialization into Buddhism at home and into Christianity at school comes out dramatically in the following sentence which refers to his early childhood: "Every half an hour the class had to repeat a short prayer in praise of the Virgin Mary, and I got accustomed to Catholic ways, *though I was daily worshipping my Lord Buddha*"(*2,* p. 698, italics mine).

The conflict between the home and the school environment was manifest in the child's sensitive conscience at a very early age. He speaks of the humiliation that Buddhism and he as a Buddhist bore through the taunts of the missionaries. He says of his early education in the Catholic mission school: "The *padres* gave us bonbons and stroked our hair to show us that they loved us. But they also would say to us constantly: 'Look at your mud image. You are worshipping clay.' *Then the small Buddhist boy would turn in shame from his native religion*"(*2,* p. 683, italics mine). The loss of self-esteem suffered during these onslaughts must have been great. The young boy, not yet ten, reacts to these insults by abusing the *padres* in fantasy. "But my teachers could not win me away from the Buddhist training I had received at home. The *padres* were great pork eaters. I thought: 'The dirt pigs eat is disgusting. These fellows must be very dirty.' That thought was enough to breed an early contempt for my missionary teachers"(*2,* p. 683). At twelve, while studying in the Protestant mission school, an incident occurred which profoundly affected him, for he repeats it several times in his writings. "One day when I was at this school—I was twelve years old—I saw one of my teachers go out into the field with his gun and shoot down a bird. I was horrified. I said to myself—and at that time I was reading the Bible four times a day—'This is no religion for me. He is a preacher of Christianity and he goes out cold bloodedly and kills innocent birds.' The teachers in that school also drank liquor, a practice that was against my earliest teachings. Not long after this time one of my classmates died. As we looked at him, lying so still on his bed, our teacher told us to pray. Suddenly I realized that we were praying because of fear. From that moment freedom of thought was born in me. I ceased to pray. And I soon became very critical of the Bible"(*2,* p. 684). Later "I became a Biblical critic in the boarding school, and I was threatened with expulsion if I continued to attack Jesus Christ"(*2,* p. 699).

Thus it seemed that the home environment prevailed, due largely no doubt to the influence of his devout mother and the monks with whom he came into contact, particularly the great orator Mohotiwatte Gunananda, who was a friend of the family. At ten Dharmapala listened to Gunananda's famous debate with the Christians. At the age of thirteen he joined St. Thomas' College (a famous mission school) and on his way to school he passed Gunananda's temple daily. From Gunananda he came to hear of the Theosophical Society and of Col. Olcott and Madame Blavatsky. From the age of fourteen he took a great deal of interest in theosophy and was a voracious reader of the occult sciences.

We have mentioned two types of conflicts, the social and the religious, that posed identity problems to the growing child, and now we must mention the third, the familial. There was no doubt that Dharmapala's father was a hardworking, wealthy and upwardly mobile man who had probably not too much time for his son, though he showed remarkable tolerance of the boy's needs. (Another son became a doctor, a highly prestigious profession.) It was his mother, however, to whom Dharmapala was devoted. "I adored my mother. Often, in the midst of my play, I would say to myself, 'May my mother enter *nirvana* when the next Buddha comes' " (*2*, p. 682). Toward the end of his life he wrote about other "mother figures:" "I owe everything to my parents, to the late Madame Blavatsky and to the late Mrs. Foster of Honolulu." (The latter was his patroness and helped him financially and morally; he referred to her as "my foster-mother!") (*2,* p. 769). His identification with his mother comes out in a reference to the loss of his baby sister at the age of two, when he was seventeen: "I saw her quietly weeping over the loss of *our* precious baby" (*2,* p. 686, italics mine).

The little evidence we have suggests that the boy adored his mother and probably identified strongly with her. In this regard an incident that occurred at age nine is interesting: "In my ninth year I was initiated into the Brahmachariya vow by my father at the Temple, and on that day he advised me that a Brahmachari should be contented with what he is given to eat, and that he is expected to sleep little. The vow was taken only for 24 hours; but in my case it had made a permanent impression in my mind"(*2,* p. 698). The reference is to the custom of observing meditation on holy (*pōya*) days; one of the ascetic vows that one observes on such days is *brahmachariya,* that is, total sexual abstinence. Perhaps we are not reading too much into this incident if we infer that the strong impression that the *brahmachariya* vow had on the child was due to his identification with his mother, and the association of sex with incest. Much later the British noted in their confidential files that Dharmapala was a homosexual. While there is no independent evidence for this, it is likely that he was at least latently homosexual. Like Leonardo da Vinci he was fond of keeping young boys around him as his disciples or acolytes, and in his own adolescence he was closely associated with the English theosophist, Leadbeater who, it turned out later, was a homosexual. In any case, homosexuality, latent or otherwise, fits in with the child's early and close identification with his mother.

Though lesser in stature to either Luther or Gandhi, the case of Anagarika Dharmapala reveals with even greater clarity the situation that arises when the identity crisis of an individual has significance for the identity problems of a larger ethnic group. The impact of the man on his culture was highly dramatic. By the age of sixteen he had come under the influence of the monks engaged in the famous religious debate; thus when Col. Olcott and Madame Blavatsky visited Ceylon, he had conversations with them and became an ardent disciple. He left school at eighteen and spent his time reading "ethics, philosophy, psychology, art, and especially biography and history." His father did not approve of his interests and wanted him to pursue a career "and see if you can't be practical." In deference to his father, he joined the government department of education as a clerk.

In 1884, when he was twenty, Olcott and Blavatsky again visited Colombo on their way to Madras, and this visit was of crucial importance to the young Dharmapala. Olcott and Blavatsky were drawn towards the young man and invited him to come with them to Madras, but his father, and even the monks, objected. "Though I did not know what to do, my heart was determined on this journey, which I felt could lead to a new life for me. Madame

Blavatsky faced the priests and my united family. She was a wonderful woman, with energy and will power that pushed aside all obstacles. She said: 'That boy will die if you do not let him go. I will take him with me anyway.' So the family were won over. My mother blessed me and sent me off with the parting words, 'Go and work for humanity.' My father said, 'Go, then, and aspire to be a *bodhisatva*' and he gave me money to help me in my work"(*2*, p. 687).

The passage to Madras was also a rite of passage for the young man from confused adolescence to a mature adulthood. He also cut his connections with his family and sought a new identity under the guidance of another mother figure. Dharmapala was so enamoured of Blavatsky that he wanted to study occultism, but, to Blavatsky's credit, she encouraged him to devote his life to the "service of humanity" and to Buddhism. Back in Ceylon in 1886 he took over the management of the Buddhist section of the Theosophical Society. In the same year two Buddhist theosophists—Olcott and Leadbeater—visited Ceylon, and Dharmapala obtained three months' leave from his government job to go with them on a tour of Ceylon. The impact of this tour was profound, for he was convinced of the real decay of Buddhism, and the necessity to regenerate it. He resigned from the government job, in spite of his father's objections. "With delight I left." From this point onward he devoted his full time and energy to Buddhism. He renounced sex, took the *brahmachariya* vow, and became Anagarika, "the homeless one." He shed his Western name, Don David, and his family name, Hewavitarana, and adopted a new name, Dharmapala, "guardian of the doctrine."

ANAGARIKA DHARMAPALA AND THE SINHALESE-BUDDHIST IDENTITY

Let us examine how the resolution of Anagarika's identity problems affected the identity of Sinhalese Buddhists. It will be noted that his family problem of attachment to and identification with his mother could be resolved in the new role of *anagārika*. He broke away from his mother and home largely with the help of another mother figure, Madame Blavatsky, and took up the homeless life dedicated to a cause. Guilt feelings regarding sex are also resolved through the *anagārika* role with its ideal of chastity. The ascetic denial of sex, originally a personal psychological problem, became a higher, impersonal way of life. Latent homosexuality is expressed in sublimated form in the sentimental attachment to the acolytes he collected.

His lack of roots in the traditional social structure—the absence of village, caste or regional identities—impelled him to seek his identity in Buddhism. Moreover, insofar as he lacked local identities like caste, he could appeal to all sectors of the educated Sinhalese. His religious conflicts led him to be an inveterate and implacable foe of the Christian missions, and he brought into Buddhism the zeal, enthusiasm and bigotry that characterized the missionary dialectic. In 1902 he writes (in English): "The sweet gentle Aryan children of an ancient historic race are sacrificed at the altar of the whiskey-drinking, beef-eating belly god of heathenism. How long, O how long will unrighteousness last in Lanka?"(*2*, p. 484). And: "Practices that were an abomination to the ancient noble Sinhalese have today become tolerated"(*2* p. 494). And again: "Arise, awake, unite and join the army of Holiness and Peace and defeat the hosts of evil"(*2* p. 660).

He became a Protestant-Buddhist, a reformer of the Buddhist church, infusing that institution with the puritan values of Protestantism. All these had tremendous influence on a group of people who were in a sense like Dharmapala himself, alienated from the traditional culture of the village, and from the politico-economic system controlled by the British and the English-educated elite of Colombo. Though his initial impact was on members of the alienated Sinhalese intelligentsia living in the villages, he later had an impact on all Sinhalese Buddhists.

AFFIRMATION OF THE SINHALESE-BUDDHIST IDENTITY

Anagarika Dharmapala started a process in Ceylon which I call "identity affirmation." His affirmation of his Buddhist (Sinhalese) identity was the result of his personal identity conflicts. On the personal level, identity affirmation helps to enhance an individual's self esteem, when it has been lowered by shame or humiliation. Dharmapala insisted that others affirm their identity also. Here is an instance where the needs of the individual matched the needs of the group, so that today Sinhalese Buddhists are constantly affirming their collective identity as an ethnic group. As a collective phenomenon, identity affirmation is a partly conscious process whereby an ethnic group is impelled to display its unity through visible symbols, and overt symbolic actions, or through the reiteration of grandiose ethnic myths. The psychological function of identity affirmation is to enhance a group's low self esteem. Viewed sociologically, the process is complicated and probably always occurs as a part of ethnic identity consciousness, but is accelerated (a) when there is an actual or perceived threat to the unity of the group, so that the ethnic group must affirm its collective solidarity and maintain its self-image; (b) when the ethnic identity is disintegrating and new attempts are made to reconstruct or resurrect the ethnic identity, as happened to the Sinhalese under European rule; and (c) when an ethnic group attempts to define or redefine itself for political, economic or other purposes where the self-image is not well defined, e.g., American blacks.

I shall now examine the manner in which Anagarika Dharmapala initiated the process of identity affirmation, and shall describe the people he influenced. These people, I said earlier, could be characterized as a village *intelligentsia*: schoolteachers, monks, *ayurvedic* physicians, various types of government officials, representatives of local bodies ("village committees"). They lived in the village, but did not belong to the peasant class. They were educated in Sinhalese schools, had high aspirations for themselves and for their children, but were cut off from the sources of political and economic power. It was for these people, who constituted the leadership of Ceylon's villages, that Anagarika Dharmapala provided a new and regenerated Buddhist ideology. If the old identity, before the advent of Europeans, was Sinhalese, but implied Buddhist, the new identity had to affirm both Sinhalese and Buddhist, in opposition to Sinhalese who were non-Buddhists, and non-Sinhalese who were non-Buddhists.

How did he set about the process of identity affirmation? The technique was powerful, though simple. He *shamed* people into realizing their folly, and ridiculed their aping of Western ways, and religious beliefs. His psychological intuition, as far as Sinhalese personality was concerned, was incisive and effective. Having reduced their self-esteem, he then provided a means for enhancing it—the glorious Sinhalese past. In his speeches and in the newspaper he founded, the *Sinhala Baudhaya* ("the Sinhalese-Buddhist"), he castigated the Westernized upper classes and idealized the glories of the past. The following passage is typical:

> My message to the young men of Ceylon is . . . Believe not the alien who is giving you arrack whisky, toddy, sausages, who makes you buy his goods at clearance sales . . . Enter into the realms of our King Dutugemunu in spirit and *try to identify yourself with the thoughts of that great king who rescued Buddhism and our nationalism from oblivion*(*2* p. 510, italics mine).

He held up the glories of the Sinhalese past as an ideal worth resurrecting: "No nation in the world has had a more brilliant history than ourselves"(*2*, p. 735). "There exists no race on earth today that has had a more triumphant record of victory than the Sinhalese." The present degradation is due to evil Western influence on the part of missionaries and colonialists. The country, as he perceives it, is a Sinhalese-Buddhist one, and there is hardly a place in it for Tamils and Muslims, who are viewed as exploiters. The Christians are condemned as meat eaters of "low caste." "The country of the Sinhalese should be governed by the Sinhalese" (*2*). While on occasion he addresses himself to Sinhalese *qua* Sinhalese, rather than Buddhists, the general bias in his polemics is for a Sinhalese Buddhist nation.

The immediate effect of Dharmapala's teaching was quite dramatic—it took the form of massive name changing. Names are identity badges, and name changing implies self-consciousness about one's identity. European-type personal and surnames were changed into Sinhalese or Buddhist personal and surnames. Again, this name changing was not a peasant phenomenon; it was confined largely to the alienated *intelligentsia.* But it soon became the general pattern, so that by the 1930s practically all parents, including Sinhalese Christians, gave Sinhalese or Buddhist personal names to their children, even if they did not change their own names. A similar dramatic effect was almost immediately felt in the area of female fashions. Well-to-do Sinhalese females in the low country—that area that had been subject to three centuries of Western contact—generally wore Western dresses. Dharmapala mercilessly ridiculed these clothes in his speeches and in cartoons in his newspaper. Again, the technique was the same—shaming, lowering of self-esteem and the provision of an alternative. In this case he exhorted the women to wear the Indian *saree.* Anagarika's own mother was the first to wear this new dress, but soon it became the standard "national" dress for women in the low country. The most important innovation was the Buddhist flag, an invention of Col. Olcott, but popularized by Dharmapala. Hitherto Buddhists had no flag. Since the identity Sinhalese implied Buddhist, the *Sinhalese* national flag was all that was in existence, and all that was necessary. With the *identity affirmation* initiated by Dharmapala, the Buddhist flag became popular very soon, so that on all ceremonial and ritual occasions, this flag was hoisted also. The flag has been so effectively assimilated into the national life that few are aware of its comparatively recent American origin.

As Erikson says, identity makes no sense except in relation to the "core of the communal culture."[5] Traditionally the core of the Buddhist culture was adapted to a peasant way of life. In the twentieth century, social changes had produced the growth of cities and massive economic change. Dharmapala provided a new orientation in Buddhism, consonant with the new identity. This orientation was an active involvement in the world. The model for this involvement was a Protestant model: the *anagārika* is the modern Sinhalese Buddhist analogue of an early Calvinist type of reformism with its increasing this-worldly asceticism. Though Anagarika Dharmapala is more a symbol than a person for most contemporary Buddhists, the *anagārika* role is a function of a specific socio-political context. In the Buddhist Pāli texts, the term *anagārika* ("homeless") was exclusively applied to *monks. Anagārika* and "monk" were equivalent; the resurrection of the term *anagārika* by Dharmapala to designate a specific status between monk and layman was an innovation. Its popular acceptance was the result of the necessity for a "homeless life" (*anagārika*) while living in the world.

The life and work of Anagarika Dharmapala anticipated much of contemporary Buddhism. In his Sinhalese writings his audience was never the peasant, it was the educated Sinhalese-speaking or bilingual *intelligentsia.* He not only enhanced their sense of self-worth, but also in the political changes of the mid-century, provided a "charter" for modern Buddhism, which included two basic aspects. The first was a this-worldly asceticism, in which he castigated the laziness of the Sinhalese, emphasized thrift, saving, hard work. He exhorted people to reject the propitiation of *dēvas* and to worship the Buddha daily at home and every week in the temple. He exhorted parents to get their children interested in meditational (*sil*) activity (generally accepted in contemporary Buddhism, but an innovation at that time, for traditionally such activity was confined to old persons). He condemned again and again the consumption of meat and alcohol, though he remained singularly silent about fish.

The second aspect of his charter for modern Buddhism involved a code of lay ethics. Buddhist doctrine has no systematic code of lay ethics, though the rules of conduct for the order (*sangha*) are minutely regulated, great emphasis being placed on personal decorum and good manners. As far as the layman was concerned, only broad generalizations were available in texts like the *Sigālōvada Sutta.* This absence of specificity regarding lay ethics facilitated the spread of Buddhism among peasant societies with diverse and even contradictory moral codes. However, in 1898 Anagarika Dharmapala laid down a systematic code for the laity in a pamphlet published in Sinhalese, entitled *The Daily Code for the Laity.* When the nineteenth edition appeared in 1958, nearly fifty thousand copies of this work were sold. Rules were given in detail on the following subjects:

The manner of eating food (25 rules)
Chewing betel (6)
Wearing clean clothes (5)
How to use the lavatory (4)
How to behave while walking on the road (10)
How to behave in public gatherings (19)
How females should conduct themselves (30)
How children should conduct themselves (18)
How the laity should conduct themselves before the *Sangha* (5)
How to behave in buses and trains (8)
What village protection societies should do (8)
On going to see sick persons (2)

Funerals (3)
The carter's code (6)
Sinhalese clothes (6)
Sinhalese names (2)
What teachers should do (11)
How servants should behave (9)
How festivities should be conducted (5)
How lay devotees (male and female) should conduct themselves in the temple
How children should treat their parents (14)
Domestic ceremonies (1)

Anagarika thus devised a total of 200 rules guiding lay conduct under 22 headings. In examining these rules we may conclude that the pamphlet is addressed to a literate Sinhalese intelligentsia. The rules proscribe behavior that peasants are generally given to, for example, "bad" eating, dress, and lavatory habits, indiscriminate betel chewing, use of impolite forms of address (though Anagarika uses those same terms in a letter to one of his servants). This is a code of conduct for an "emerging Sinhalese elite."

But alongside traditional norms of conduct are many Western norms. Even the condemnation of peasant manners is based on a Western yardstick. That is, Anagarika attempted to formulate a code based on traditional norms, as well as on the norms prevalent in the wealthy society in which he was reared. Here is an aspect of the process we have mentioned earlier, in which Protestant and Western norms have been assimilated as pure or ideal Sinhalese norms. The case of Anagarika was especially interesting, for his avowed intention was to reject Western ways. Yet regulations about the correct manner of using the fork and spoon are also given! Elsewhere, his admiration for the West breaks through the polemic and comes out into the open. "Europe is progressive, Her religion is kept in the background for one day in the week and for six days her people follow the dictates of modern science. Sanitation, aesthetic arts, electricity, etc., are what made European and American people great. Asia is full of opium eaters, *ganja* smokers, degenerating sensualists, superstitious and religious fanatics. Gods and priests keep the people in ignorance"(*2,* p. 717).

Anagarika Dharmapala provided a role model for a this-worldly asceticism for Buddhism. In his own day his influence on constitutional reform was negligible. His influence was with the "not yet emerged" Sinhalese elite (the village monk, the school teacher, the notary, the *ayurvedic* physician and the government clerk) who, according to Wriggins, spearheaded the 1956 election which brought about a radical shift of power in Ceylon's politics. For them he provided a model for emulation— a national consciousness, a nativistic sense of past glory and present degeneration, and very importantly, an ascetic involvement in this-worldly activity, not primarily of an economic, but of a socio-political nature. Few people since his day have actually adopted the *anagārika* status with its associated vestment. But the *anagārika* role has come to stay. A this-worldly asceticism comprised of a puritan code of morality is part of the higher code of urban elite Buddhism—a greater commitment to the doctrine, an emphasis on a "rigid" moral code, meditational activity for young and old, an intolerance towards other faiths, an identification of Ceylon with Buddhism and the Sinhalese language, and an involvement in social and political (though not economic) activity. However, there is one important difference between the *anagārika* role symbolized by Anagarika Dharmapala and the contemporary adoption of that role. The *anagārika* status is celibate, while the contemporary puritanism is for all, including married persons. Anagarika Dharmapala emphasized the doctrinal aspects of Buddhism. In accordance with the doctrine, he scorned the intercessionary powers of *dēvas* and demons. For elite Buddhists of today involved in the family and the larger society, this is not easy, for the Buddha is not a conventional deity that grants favours. Thus among the elite there is a dependence on *dēvas* that contradicts the doctrinal position, which devaluates the power of these beings.

SOCIO-POLITICAL CHANGE AND THE SINHALESE-BUDDHIST IDENTITY

I think it is clear from the preceding account that the Buddhist (Sinhalese) identity is an important one for those who profess it. But is it an ethnic identity in Barth's sense of an all-inclusive identity? In other words, is the ethnic identity *Sinhalese* or is it *Sinhalese-Buddhist*? My own view is that it is the latter. The Sinhalese Buddhists today perceive the Sinhalese Christians as not only non-Buddhists, but also in a sense as non-Sinhalese, for their Christian cultural markers are viewed as alien. To affirm their Sinhalese identity, the Christians have adopted national dress for their rituals, have taken up Sinhalese (but not strictly Buddhist) calendrical rituals like New Year, and in many ways have implicitly recognized Buddhism as the dominant religion. It may be that eventually the cultural markers that distinguish Sinhalese Buddhists from Sinhalese Catholics and Protestants may be evened out and an overall Sinhalese ethnic identity may develop. But right now it seems to me that Sinhalese-Buddhist is an all-inclusive ethnic identity. Whether ethnic or not, the identity is a crucial one, separable from other collective identities. In this section I discuss how contemporary Sinhalese-Buddhists collectively affirm their identity and claim Ceylon as a Sinhalese-Buddhist nation.

Anagarika Dharmapala died in 1933; in 1948 the Ceylonese achieved independence, and in 1956 effective political power was in the hands of the Sinhalese Buddhist population. It was an inevitable consequence of universal suffrage, mass education, and the identity consciousness that Anagarika Dharmapala instilled into the Sinhalese Buddhists. The details of this transfer of political power are available in Wriggins' *Ceylon: Dilemmas of a New Nation.* In addition to these political changes there was an acceleration of the pace of socio-economic change: universal education and mass literacy, massive population increase, migration into cities, and the development of a large middle class and industrial proletariat. These changes led to a loosening, if not disintegration, of local identities of family, kinship, caste and region and of the ideologies of values that centered on these identities. It is my view that *when an individual's commitments to his other identities have weakened, his commitment to his ethnic identity will be enhanced.* The reason for this is fairly straightforward. A man's other identities, including those of his primary group, provide him with a sense of inner security and outer (group) support. With the dissolution of these other identities the ethnic identity, often revitalized and refashioned to suit the changed social conditions, helps to give a sense of meaning and coherence to the individual's existence. It is possible that the same needs may be met by an entirely new identity and its associated ideology, as in Communism, but even political ideologies like Communism can become a revitalized, all-inclusive ethnic identity (Chinese Communism, Russian Communism). In Ceylon, with increasing urbanization the new Buddhist identity forged by the Anagarika became the normative one for the urbanized and educated segments among the Sinhalese Buddhists. Then in 1956 political power effectively passed into the hands of the Sinhalese Buddhists, so that it became possible for them to claim for Ceylon the status of Sinhalese Buddhist (not simply Sinhalese) nation. All this resulted in a new and fascinating form of identity affirmation that has occurred in urban areas in Ceylon: symbols of the Buddhist identity are found everywhere in public places in the urbanized areas of the country. In another paper I have emphasized the somewhat complex socio-economic factors that have produced this change (the omnipresence of "identity labels" all over urban Ceylon), but here I focus on one aspect of this phenomenon, that of *identity affirmation,* which claims that Ceylon is a *Buddhist* nation, which by definition means a *Sinhalese* Buddhist nation. Although all Sinhalese today are not Buddhists, all Buddhists in Ceylon are Sinhalese. If before the sixteenth century the term Sinhalese implied Buddhist, today the term Buddhist implies Sinhalese. Thus the affirmation of Buddhism implies the affirmation of the old Sinhalese ethnic identity. Let us see how this identity affirmation occurs.

Imagine a drive down a major highway in Colombo, formerly known as Turret Road, but recently renamed Anagarika Dharmapala Road. If we turn right, we come to a traffic roundabout at a point where three roads meet. Behind the roundabout is a large *bo* tree (*ficus religiosa,* the tree under which the Buddha received enlightenment). On the roundabout are four huge concrete maps of Ceylon, about five feet high, facing the four directions in a square. In the middle of each map is engraved a precept of Buddhism: *mudita* ("sympathetic joy"), *upekka* ("equanimity"), *karuna* ("compassion"), *metta* ("universal love"). At the top of each map is printed the traditional national emblem of the Sinhalese, a highly stylized lion with a sword held aloft in one paw. The lion relates to the origin myth of the Sinhalese, the themes of which deal with bestiality, incest, and parricide (7). Thus the abstract universal ethical concepts of Buddhism are juxtaposed to a symbol representing the very opposite. This concrete edifice expresses a simple, but telling fact: Sinhalese Buddhists are claiming Ceylon as their nation.

This juxtaposition of Buddhism and Sinhalese myth is no isolated instance. In Colombo and in Ceylon's densely populated towns of the western and southern provinces, similar changes have occurred in the urban landscape. Statues of Buddha, often aesthetically crude, have been placed in traffic roundabouts, at city junctions, in front of government buildings, in the polluted atmosphere of the Ceylon Transport Board's bus garages, in practically every government school, in the former premises of the Ceylon Turf Club. Some of these statues are of huge proportions, suggesting an attempt to regain the self-esteem of the Buddhists, which sank very low during colonial rule. For example, a statue of Buddha which is claimed to be the largest (and also probably the ugliest) in the world has been erected in Matara, South Ceylon. In Kurunegala (Northwestern Province) the Protestant Bishop had an impressive church built; a Buddhist organization has now decided to erect a statue of Buddha on an adjacent hill so as to completely dwarf the latter, exactly in the manner of Christian missionaries who planted churches in centers of Buddhist worship all over Ceylon. The Ceylon Harbour Workers Buddhist Association is now constructing a huge statue mounted on a massive concrete pedestal, so that all ships entering the harbour will be confronted with this spectacle. The Buddhist images and edifices located in central places in urban Ceylon express the active involvement of urban Buddhists in the affairs of the world. They are visible public symbols of the new Buddhist (Sinhalese) ethnic identity, like a flag or the totem animal in Durkheim's analysis of Australian aboriginal religion, and they are an affirmation of that identity.

NOTE: I am grateful to Mike Lieber for critical comments on this paper.

REFERENCES

1. Barth, Fredrik. *Ethnic Groups and Boundaries.* Boston: Little, Brown, 1969.
2. Dharmapala, Anagarika. *Return to Righteousness.* Colombo: Government Press, 1965.
3. *Mahāvamsa.* Translated by W. Geiger, Pali Text Society, 1912.
4. Nicholas, C. W., and Paranavitana, S. *A Concise History of Ceylon.* Colombo: Ceylon University Press, 1961.
5. Obeyesekere, Gananath. "The Great Tradition and the Little in the Perspective of Sinhalese Buddhism." *Journal of Asian Studies* 22:2, 1963.
6. Obeyesekere, Gananath. "The Buddhist Pantheon in Ceylon and its Extensions." In *Anthropological Studies of Theravada Buddhism,* edited by M. Nash. New Haven, N.J.: Yale University Press, 1966.
7. Obeyesekere, Gananath. "Religious Symbolism and Political Change in Ceylon." In *Modern Ceylon Studies,* vol. 1, no. 1, pp. 43-63.
8. Rahula, Walpola. *The History of Buddhism in Ceylon.* Colombo: Gunasena, 1956
9. *Rajavaliya.* Translated by G. Gunasekera. Colombo: Government Press, 1900.

Problems of Ethnic Ascendency and Alienation

PART FOUR

PART FOUR

PROBLEMS OF ETHNIC ASCENDENCY AND ALIENATION

The papers included in this section differ from those comprising Part I in that they deal with ethnic identity in the context of ethnic groups seeking to achieve psychological as well as political independence from other cultures which have been more advanced technologically, if not politically and socially. In Part II we discussed societies (China, England, the United States and Italy) in which the sustaining self concepts held by their members have been influenced by forces arising from within the society. In the following discussions of black Africa, Senegal, Egypt, and Japan, we see instances of social identity influenced by psycho-cultural reactions to external cultural forces that have compelled and continue to compel emulation.

Uchendu touches upon the complexity of ethnic problems in a rapidly changing Africa where post-colonial political changes, urbanization and other forces are influencing social and personal consciousness. Uchendu sees the search for identity in black Africa as comprised of four sometimes conflicting alternatives. First, there is an identity with the entire continent, based on newly achieved post-colonial political independence. Second, one finds a uniting "black" racial identity. Third, there are new, somewhat synthetically achieved African national identities, and fourth, the continuing force of separate local ethnic identities.

Uchendu finds that identity shifts with the frame of reference of social interchange. He cites Gluckman to support the contention that many Africans are situation-oriented and can easily be "tribal" or "urban," for example, depending on context. Uchendu views ethnic groups as social categories providing a basis for status ascription, a basis which can fluctuate with rapid political and economic change. He deals less with the presence of more internalized dilemmas about identity than the other contributors, Hamamsy and Wagatsuma.

The two articles by Hamamsy and Wagatsuma on national cultures with highly different histories illustrate similar problems related to the sense of alienation that can selectively attack the elite segments of a society heavily influenced by an outside culture. During certain periods of a people's history a particular segment of the society (usually the elite) finds psychological and social as well as technological, economic, or political advantages in taking as a model the behavior of the elite segment of another culture. But they may then alienate themselves from other segments of their own society, and may well suffer from a subjective sense of inner alienation that affects individuals who are caught up in the vertigo of normlessness discussed so well by Durkheim.

Stress from attempts to adapt to the cultural ascendency of a dominant but ethnically different group is not limited to those situations in which members of an ethnic minority find themselves in a politically or socially subordinate position within a larger dominant society. They also usually occur when a politically dominant conquering elite minority is superimposed on a subjected majority. Ethnic ascendency as a social force, however, is not limited to situations of political dominance by either a majority or by a minority elite. It is also found in situations where there is no direct political occupation. Emulation of another culture may be first inspired by a superior technology, which permits the consequent introduction of other culture traits that arouse a need for affirmative choice. A superior technology from another culture often carries with it an alternative world view and implicit moral system which may alienate an individual or even a whole group from its cultural origins. The group most easily alienated tends to be not only the one in greatest direct contact, but the one most able economically to afford the emulation of an alien pattern. Hence the elite of a society are most susceptible to outside influences.

Egypt and Japan, highly dissimilar in culture content, are both instances of this process at work in response to what has been a politically aggressive as well as technologically advanced Western culture. In both cases, members in the elite segment of the culture have had to face serious dilemmas with respect to their own ethnic identity.

Egypt is one of the oldest of the world's cultures, yet the history of Egypt since the time of Alexander the Great has been that of a people under continuous domination by foreign rulers until the expulsion of the British in 1952. Hamamsy documents briefly the re-creation of a modern ethnic identity as a consequence of political independence. Like the situation of black

Africans, there is also a trend toward the development of a supra-national Arab identity. Hamamsy, however, limits herself to discussing Egyptian identity and its long history. One historically derived tension relates to the question of how such minority religious groups as Christian Copts and Jews, both of whom have distinct subcultural features, are to be considered Egyptian, within the context of a Moslem majority. There are also the unresolved tensions related to borrowing and integrating a modern European technology without becoming alienated from a prior loyalty to an Egyptian national identity. With its long history of foreign domination, this tension is not new for Egypt, which has long suffered a split in its life style and world view between a small outward-oriented elite and a large inwardly preoccupied peasant population. The need to direct social energies inward is a pressing problem for a state having no alternative but modern technology to relieve the plight of a burgeoning population.

Internal problems of identity in modern Japanese are less immediately visible to outsiders. Japan was fortunate in escaping direct political colonization by aggressive Western powers in the nineteenth century. The internal social resources and diplomatic sagacity of its social elite were sufficient to resist their being overwhelmed. In effect, the intellectual elite of Japan, although intrigued by Western cultural blandishments, did not in general become alienated. Rather they were able to overcome the internal barriers of a severely restrictive class structure to unite the nation in common effort. In broad terms, the Japanese have been able to modernize without any radical social dislocation. Nevertheless, individual Japanese have manifested alienation. Some intellectuals have communicated in their writings the internal tensions experienced as a result of sustained contact with an ascendent Western alien culture. Wagatsuma, in his chapter, documents some of the more subtle aspects of problems in cultural identity to be found in modern, economically successful Japan.

The Dilemma of Ethnicity and Polity Primacy in Black Africa

VICTOR C. UCHENDU

10

Of the many factors determining human action, two stand out in discussion of ethnic identity. The first factor consists of cultural values, which partly determine ethnic identity, its persistence, its change over time, and the "dilemma" of ethnic identity, especially in a plural social system. The second factor consists of the historical processes which tend to redefine a people's self-identity, to reinforce it, or to compel a search for a new identity. Among these historical processes two elements, imperial control and the demand for political independence cannot be ignored, because of their pervasive influence on the identity of the black man in Africa. The background of ethnic identity, then, lies in contrasting value systems, contrasting social categories, and the dynamics of history.

We assume that ethnic identity is an imposed value over which its bearer has absolutely no control in his formative years, because of his protracted dependence. Koestler (*1*) argues that the "overwhelming capacity and need for identification" with a social group and/or a system of beliefs, which can even be "indifferent to reason, to self interest and even to the claims of self-preservation," is a central feature of the human predicament.

This paper explores the predicament of ethnic identity in black Africa, especially in its political context, and puts the problems of ethnic identity in a wider sociocultural context. Among man's unique qualities is the power to transcend the narrow bounds of an imposed social identity and thus compensate for the shortcomings of his utterly helpless dependence on his early cultural environment. Man also has the capacity to contract rather than to expand his social frame of reference. When is it psychologically rewarding to maintain, expand, or contract the social frame of reference which confers a person his group identity?

Shils argues that the values or belief system of a society can be lived up to only "partially, fragmentarily, intermittently and only in an approximate way" (*16,* p. 130). He asserts that ideals and beliefs can only influence conduct "alongside of personal ties, primordial attachments, and responsibilities in corporate bodies." With respect to ethnic identification, Shils' arguments can be framed as three propositions, all depending on the "principle of choice," or cultural alternatives. First, ethnicity is impermanent in that individuals, communities, and territories change their identification over time. Second, members and nonmembers may use ethnic terms or labels differently, depending on whether the criterion of identity is self-identification or identification by others. Third, members of an ethnic group may not always use the same term for themselves. This introduces a segmentary or situational principle in ethnic identity.

Empirical studies of factors contributing to ethnic identity in black Africa are rare. Studies suggesting the problems which ethnic identity poses to political integration, while more frequent, are neither abundant nor definitive (*18, 4, 11*). Although the question of ethnicity is academic in a stable, homogeneous social system, the recent social, economic and political developments in Africa have so fundamentally shaken traditional African society that competing ethnic interests not only are asserting themselves but are violently striving for accommodation, sometimes domination.

Although recent works in psychiatry, social psychology and sociology have tended to ignore African ethnographic background, they are stimulating and contain many theoretical insights. We shall ignore much of the work by those psychologists and psychiatrists who have studied the acquisition, loss or severe disturbance of identity solely from the individual point of view. These limits are consistent with our limited goal of examining problems of ethnic identity in black Africa in their political context.

Psychologists have tended to regard the self as an independent structure, comparable to the ego but developed in adolescence. Eissler (*2*), who subscribes to this view, believes that experiences of identity also occur during adolescence. This might well be true at the personality level, but at the group level, one's ethnic affiliation and identity might well be taken for granted long before adolescence (*15*, p. 184).

Erikson (*3*), Wheelis (*19*), and Lynd (*10*) have tended to emphasize a sociological orientation to identity, an approach which Jacobson (*6*, p. 24-32) has criticized as unbalanced. Erikson's thesis is that identity formation is a "lifelong development." He uses the term "ego identity" to "denote certain comprehensive gains which the individual, at the end of adolescence, must have derived from all his pre-adult experiences in order to be ready for the task of adulthood" (*3,* p. 101).

Both Wheelis and Lynd view identity in terms of generalized group phenomena, pointing out that the search for identity is a general problem of structural change, especially rapid social change. This view is consistent with African data if we interpret structural change to be an increase in political scale which has created a polyethnic society. Whereas Wheelis (*19*) tended to emphasize the disturbances in the feeling of identity caused by the "generation gap," especially the breakdown of the value systems of the past, Lynd (*10,* p. 215) attributes identity disturbance to social change processes which prevent a person from finding "aspects of his social situation with which he can clearly identify."

Emphasizing a psychiatric orientation, Jacobson stresses the continuity as well as the personality integration of identity formation. In her view, identity formation is "a process that builds up the ability to preserve the whole psychic organization—despite its growing structuralization, differentiation, and eomplexity—as highly individualized but coherent entity which has direction and continuity at any stage of human development"(*6,* p. 27).

Lichtenstein (*9*) points out that in a dynamic world, man as a culture-bearing and culture-creating animal cannot take his identity for granted. He attributes the origin of identity formation to the earliest mother-child relationship and emphasizes the experience of continuity in the normal feeling of identity. In his view, man's quest for identity is unique. Unlike animals, man lacks the preformed, adaptive identity which is guaranteed to animals by their genetic inheritance. On the other hand, because of his ability to profit by learning, man inherits an existence with self-defined, self-created identity which he must struggle to maintain.

This brief survey indicates that ethnic identity lends itself readily to a psychosociological study in which individual identity and group identity can be related. A person's identity as it develops cannot be easily divorced from his cultural background or from his subjective experience. Positive group identification or group belongingness is not a problem for any social group that has status and power and enjoys prestige in a society. The problems of group identification arise for those who are deprived of these advantages and those in competition for them (*15,* p. 213).

Approaches to Ethnicity

The tribe, as an anthropological concept, derives from the premise that there are aggregates of people who essentially share a common culture (tribe), and that there are interconnected differences which distinguish one tribal culture from all other tribal cultures. Barth (*1*) takes issue with this type of reasoning. He makes two observations which I consider relevant to ethnic processes in modern Africa. First, he asserts that ethnic boundaries persist despite the interpenetration of cultures and that ethnic distinctions do not depend on an absence of physical contact. Rather, they entail social processes of exclusion and incorporation, whereby discrete categories are maintained *despite* changing participation and membership. The persistence of ethnic enclaves in urban environments in modern Africa lends support to this proposition. Second, he asserts that ethnic distinctions do not depend on absence of social interaction and acceptance; quite to the contrary they are often the basis on which embracing social systems are built. This indicates that cultural differences can persist despite inter-ethnic contact and interdependence (*1,* pp. 9-10).

Ethnic group boundaries are maintained by a limited set of cultural features. What are these features and how definitive are they? Naroll (*14*) lists six criteria: trait distribution, territorial contiguity, political organization, language, ecological adjustment, and local community structure. In a critique of these criteria, especially of their diagnostic value, Moerman (*13,* p. 1215) argues that language, culture, political organization, etc., do not correlate completely, so that units delimited by one criterion do not coincide with the units delimited by another.

Barth (*1,* pp. 10-38), who has grappled with the "defining characteristics" of ethnicity, suggests that when an ethnic group is viewed as a social organization, the critical feature becomes "the characteristic of self-ascription and ascription by others" (*1,* p. 13), a point also stressed by Moerman (*13,* p. 1219). When "self ascription" is used as the critical mark of ethnicity, it becomes obvious that this definition imposes a series of constraints on the kinds of roles an individual is allowed to play, and the partners he may choose for different kinds of transactions. It is this self-definition, reinforced positively or negatively by the actions of other relevant social groups, that tends to perpetuate ethnic boundaries.

The Search For Cultural Roots

Membership in a traditional African ethnic group is a matter of social definition, the result of the interplay of members' self-definitions and the categorization and stereotyping by other groups.

In rural Africa, tribal identity persists because the colonial government gave it an institutional and political support and because the tie to the tribal, communal, or lineage land, often phrased in the idiom of filial loyalty to ancestors, is still an important social and economic asset. In the urban area, factors contributing ethnic loyalty include the competition for jobs, the uneven distribution of government patronage, and the insecurity of urban employment. There is also an element of "ethnic patriotism"—an important value which conflicts with a wider national loyalty.

If tribal Africa took its identity for granted, the developments of the last seven decades—especially the fact of colonialism and the presence of white minority governments in Africa—have dictated a search for identity. Whether the frame of reference is at the continental, regional, national, or ethnic level, political considerations overshadow the recent search for identity in black Africa. This factor also illustrates a critical principle in the problem of African identity: its segmentary or situational orientation.

The search for identity in black Africa can be considered from four perspectives. First, there was the demand for a "political kingdom," which compelled a search for continental identity. Continental identity became an instrument for decolonization and a weapon for post-independence international diplomacy. Second, there is the search for black identity which is motivated by racial pride—a search which makes it meaningful to speak of three Africas: Arab Africa, black Africa, and white minority Africa. Third, there is the search for national identity. And finally there is the demand for ethnic identity within the polyethnic state system. Whatever its immediate concerns, the search for identity in black Africa has always faced a dilemma in its choice of symbols. Which symbols should project continental, racial, national, or tribal identity?

Lacking a written culture, black Africa was not heir to any great traditions. Since what could be considered "great traditions" in black Africa enjoyed no higher status than the "little traditions," ethnic patriotism compelled African scholars and social thinkers to adopt continental identity. Nkrumah's "African personality" and Senghor's "negritude" are identity labels which are pan-African, trans-national, and trans-territorial. Similarly, the demand for political independence had a pan-African ideology. Nkrumah set the tone by declaring that he would not consider Ghana as truly independent until all Africa was liberated. This new emphasis in continental identification is a radical departure from an early outlook which regarded Egypt as the fountainhead of all African civilization. As Kopytoff (*8*, p. 55) points out, "this scientifically untenable interpretation of Egypt's role in world history" was first used to deprive black Africa of all credit for indigenous achievement, and is at present used "by some Africans to bolster the historical importance of Africa as a whole."

Mazrui (*11,* p. 88) has called attention to the dilemma of continental identification in Africa. He asserts that Africa has "a negative common element . . . [that Africans] are like one another to the extent that they are collectively different from anything in the outside world." Arguing that the continental feeling built up by colonialism was more emphatic in black Africa than it ever was in Arab Africa or in Asia, Mazrui (*11,* p. 90) observes that "Nasser is an Egyptian in a deeper sense historically than Nkrumah is a Ghanaian, but he is an African in a shallower sense emotionally than Nkrumah is an African."

The dilemma of selecting an appropriate symbol of cultural identity is not restricted to the continental level; it also persists at the national level. Throughout black Africa, the policy of decolonization is accepted as a political imperative, although the speed at which this policy is implemented varies widely. On a fundamental question of decolonization, such as language policy, the challenge of choice is rarely faced. Tanzania seems to be the only exception, thanks to a colonial policy which encouraged Swahili as a lingua franca and to the political courage of the leadership in adopting this language. It is difficult to see any aggressive language policy emerging in many black African countries. Although the idea of an African language to act as the vehicle for the new political cultures which African political leaders envision for their countries is attractive, there is no "politically neutral" language in a polyethnic state. The dilemma is compounded when it is realized that in a polyethnic system, where the competing languages are almost equally "politically visible," the foreign language becomes the only "politically neutral" language that can command consensus.

Shifts in Ethnic Identity

What are the factors which tend to shift ethnic loyalties, and to what extent are they operative in black Africa? Obviously many factors are involved but two will serve to illustrate the role they play in ethnic processes—political integration and urbanization.

The expansion and contraction of political scale are important factors in ethnic processes. Until the independence movement, the peoples of black Africa were not "African" by self-identification; they were Igbo, Zulu, Akan, Yoruba, Hausa, Kikuyu, Ganda, Lunda, and so forth. In this time perspective, one's self-definition and ascription by others rarely coincided. Independence and national consciousness are gradually bringing about the convergence of the two criteria, especially among the elites of African society.

Ethnic identification, even in the political frame of reference, can be segmentary in articulation. A Nigerian student in London or New York is more likely to identify himself as an African than as a Nigerian unless the situation clearly indicates that identification of his country is expected or required. To a fellow Nigerian, he is most likely to identify himself with his state or region; if he is speaking to his co-ethnic, he is likely to name the provincial or administrative headquarters to which he belongs. Thus identity is likely to change as the frame of reference changes.

Economic development leads to increasing specialization of functions, one of the most dramatic being an ecological rearrangement. Students of the emergent urban cultures in Africa have noted the widespread shifts of loyalty among Africans. This "shifting loyalty" has been termed "detribalization." To me, the concept of detribalized man is the product of bad sociology and of Western ethnocentrism (*17,* p. 54). The concept implies the existence of a tribal order of society which was the desirable state. Its logical implication is that detachment from this tribal order results in normlessness. It appears to me that the image of the detribalized African—the counterpart of the marginal man—who stands in the corridors of two cultures but belongs to neither is an ethnographic myth. Tribal loyalty has a number of aspects: loyalty to the family or lineage, loyalty to the tribal community, and loyalty to the tribal chief or government, where one exists, may be isolated. As Wallerstein (*18,* p. 130) points out, "it does not necessarily follow that an individual who is no longer loyal to his chief has rejected as well the tribe as a community to which he owes certain duties and from which he expects a certain security."

Gluckman argues that the ethnic identity of the urban African is situation-oriented. He asserts that "the African in rural area and in town is two different men: he tends to be 'detribalized' outside the tribal area, and 'tribalized' or 'de-urbanized' when he leaves the town" (*4,* p. 55). The view that persisting loyalty to a tribe operates for a man in two quite distinct situations and that different "spheres of identity" can be segregated is an interesting hypothesis which seems to receive wide ethnographic support in black Africa.

It is in the urban environment that the expansion and contraction of ethnic identity is manifested. The fact that ethnic groups must have a minimum size to function in an urban environment forces individuals to expand the social frame of reference which confers to them an ethnic identity. The dynamics of Igbo Unions illustrate the operation of this principle. It is common knowledge that the Igbo of Nigeria have a strong in-group feeling which is manifested in their tradition of founding urban associations wherever they happen to be immigrants. The structure of the Igbo Union, like the traditional Igbo polity, tends to be segmentary. The Igbo from one village group are more likely to have an independent "family meeting" to which other co-ethnics are excluded if the number of this particular village group in the town justifies a viable, independent union. However, if the number of people is limited, the village group in question is likely to be absorbed by a larger social unit. In this context, ethnic identification is constantly redefined according to new criteria which might not be considered socially relevant in the rural areas. The tendency, especially in West Africa, to define ethnic groups in terms that are not necessarily traditional but rather reflect the urban social situation indicates that ethnic identity is not a fixed phenomenon.

In the African urban environment, two major trends reinforce ethnic identity and loyalty. The first is the persistence of ethnic enclaves and the second is the dramatization of joking relationships in a pan-ethnic framework.

Especially in West Africa, "strangers' quarters" are an important feature of the urban ecology. Whether in the forest areas or in the savannah lands, towns are zoned into indigenous and strangers' areas. In the copper belts of Central Africa as well as the eastern region of Africa, residential segregation tended to follow racial lines, with Europeans in their own reservation, the Asian population in the commercial center, and the African populations at the periphery. This pattern of development has tended to promote greater ethnic interpenetration in Central and East Africa than in West Africa.

Ethnic enclaves in urban Africa have two basic characteristics: they are "poverty pockets" which resemble many parts of the rural environment, and they are relatively homogeneous ethnically. On the question of poverty, the Hannas (*5,* p. 5) argue that "the deprivational conditions found in large sections of most African towns are not created by urban-specific factors, but are imported to the town and clustered in . . . ethnic enclaves." Because Africans in towns tend to reside, associate, and work with their co-ethnics, ethnic enclaves are marked by "ethnic clustering." In this environment, rural occupational training, ascriptive hiring practices, and the desire to work side by side with co-ethnics lead to occupational clustering.

Tensions arising from ethnic group rivalry may be transformed into joking relationships. Mitchell (*12*) provides a dramatic example of such tension management in his discussion of the Kalela dance in the copper belt of Central Africa. Performed by teams of Africans who come from single tribes, the Kalela dance is probably the most popular entertainment in the copper belt. During the dance, a team of tribal dancers deride other tribes, alleging that the target tribes have, among many unpleasant habits, loose and even perverted sexual lives. The team praises the virtues of its own tribe. There is no ill-feeling provoked and everybody enjoys the performance. Gluckman (*4,* pp. 63-64) suggests that the Kalela dance reflects the persisting significance in towns of tribal allegiance. In this particular context, ethnic identification in town operates as a primary mode of classifying into manageable categories the heterogeneous masses of people a man meets. Ethnic identity in urban

Africa is in this frame of reference a social category by which people group one another.

CONCLUSION

Ethnic groups are social categories which provide a basis for status ascription. Because the factors which lead to status ascription are not static, the social frame of reference which categorizes ethnicity is subject to expansion and contraction. We cannot understand the dynamics of contemporary ethnicity in black Africa unless we take the political environment into consideration. Political competition, especially in the urban areas, tends to upset the criteria of ethnic definition which might be socially relevant in the rural areas. Ethnic identity is least segmentary in a homogeneous society and most segmentary in a heterogeneous society. In a small, homogeneous society, the criteria of "self-definition" and the "definition by others" tend to coincide. This is not so in an urban environment. Although ethnic groups tend to shed some of their cultural peculiarities in town, their ethnic identity—which is often expanded to make political competition effective—is perpetuated through common residence and common political interests.

The boundary-maintaining mechanisms which perpetuate ethnic identity in urban areas are embarrassing to political elites, who find themselves in role conflicts as national leaders and cultural brokers for their ethnic groups. This is the dilemma of ethnic identity: how to "keep faith" with competing loyalties.

Politics and tribe play an important role in the identity of black Africa. At the macro-level, it was colonization, based on power politics and superior technology, that imposed on Africa a negative self-identity. The expansion in political scale, which followed imperial expansion, created modern states such as Kenya, Uganda, and Nigeria. Reaction against imposed national labels also created modern Ghana, Zambia, Malawi, and Tanzania. The struggle for independence in parts of southern Africa finds expression in new national identities, of which Namibia and Zimbabwe are notable examples. The ambivalence toward anthropology as a scientific discipline in Africa is not unrelated to the early association between colonial administration and anthropology, and the wholesale imposition of pejorative terms such as "noble savage," "primitive," and "preliterate" on non-Western peoples.

At the national level, politics and tribe are still important in self-definition. In pre-colonial Africa, the national society tended to coincide with the tribal society. Because of the ramifying role of kinship and the absence of a written language, clear-cut class stratification did not emerge. In areas where immigrants were in political control (as in parts of the interlacustrine Bantu), a polyethnic social system became the pattern of the social structure. Here the polity was the integrating factor under a power system dominated by immigrant rulers but large areas of cultural diversity were left in religious and domestic spheres. In such a polyethnic system, ethnic identity was not coterminous with the political society. The traditional Rwanda society composed of three hereditary groups—the Batwa, Bahutu, and Bututsi—is a classic example.

The inclusiveness of the kinship system and the extended family obligations created an estate rather than a class system. It is not surprising that African leaders, who emphasize the continuity of traditional African past, resent the idea of a class society, which they view as highly divisive. Their ideology is one that seeks to create a nation of one extended family with which all must feel an equal identification.

This concept of a trans-class society, in which hierarchy and rank do not create social distance and in which the extended family-feeling is the center of identity, is the challenge of modern African society, and the contemporary dilemma of African identity.

REFERENCES

1. Barth, F., ed. *Ethnic Groups and Boundaries.* Boston: Little, Brown, 1969.
2. Eissler, K. R. "Problems in Identity." *Journal of American Psycho-analytical Association* 1958, pp. 131-142.
3. Erikson, E. H. "The Problem of Ego Identity." *Psychological Issues* Monograph I, 1956.
4. Gluckman, M. "Tribalism in Modern British Central Africa." *Cahiers d'Etudes Africaienes,* 1:55-70, 1960.
5. Hanna, William, and William, Judith. "The Integrative Role of Urban Africa's Middleplaces and Middlemen." *Civilization* 17:1-16, 1967.
6. Jacobson, E. *The Self and the Object World.* New York: International Universities Press, 1964.
7. Koestler, A. "The Urge to Self-destruction." *The Observer.* London: 28 September 1969, p. 11.
8. Kopytoff, I. "Socialism in Traditional African Societies." *African Socialism,* edited by W. H. Friedland and C. G. Rosberg, Jr., pp. 53-62. Palo Alto, Calif.: Stanford University Press, 1967.
9. Lichtenstein, H. "Identity and Sexuality: A Study of their Inter-relationships in Man." *Journal of American Psycho-analytical Association.* 9:179-260, 1961.
10. Lynd, H. M. *On Shame and the Search for Identity.* New York: Harcourt Brace, 1958.
11. Mazrui, A. A. "On the Concept of 'We are all Africans'." *The American Political Science Review,* 57(1):88-97, 1963.

12. Mitchell, J. C. *The Kalela Dance: Aspects of Social Relationships Among Urban Africans in N. Rhodesia.* Rhodes-Livingstone Paper no. 27, 1956.

13. Moerman, M. "Ethnic Identification in a Complex Civilization." *American Anthropologist* 67(5):1215-1230, 1965.

14. Naroll, R. "On Ethnic Unit Classification." *Current Anthropology* 5(4):283-312, 1964.

15. Proshansky, H., and Newton, P. "The Nature and Meaning of Negro Self-Identity." *Social Class, Race and Psychological Development,* edited by M. Deutsch and I. Katz, pp. 178-218. New York: Holt, Rinehart and Winston, 1968.

16. Shils, E. "Primordial, Personal, Sacred and Civil Ties." *British Journal of Sociology.* 8:130-145, 1957.

17. Uchendu, V. C. "The Passing of Tribal Man: A West African Experience." *Journal of Asian and African Studies,* 1969, pp. 51-65.

18. Wallerstein, I. "Ethnicity and National Integration in West Africa." *Cahiers d'Etudes Africaienes.* 3:129-139, 1960.

19. Wheelis, A. B. *The Quest for Identity.* New York: Norton, 1958.

The Assertion of Egyptian Identity

LAILA SHUKRY EL-HAMAMSY

11

This paper examines Egyptian identity from a historical perspective and in its current manifestations—what Egyptians consider to be their own attributes and how far and in what way they identify themselves as Arabs. In the process, it may also be possible to achieve a better understanding of the connotation of the term "Arab" and, more importantly, to appreciate the complexities involved in trying to define Arab identity.

In writing this paper, I have tried to exercise as much detachment and objectivity as is possible for a student examining his own culture. I would like to add that my observations are not based solely on personal experience; I have drawn upon historical and literary materials and, at certain points in my presentation, on field research.

In discussing the identity of the Egyptians, I am likely to present concepts which reflect the views of the urban Egyptian population. A people's identity is affected by their experience of the world, especially by the extent and intensity of contact with other cultures. In Egypt, a somewhat geographically isolated country, the points of contact with other peoples are the urban areas. Therefore, a broader view of the world and a greater awareness of identity vis-a-vis other ethnic groups should exist among the urban population rather than among the non-literate, more isolated peasants. It is also evident that the urban educated class, because of their greater articulateness and wider use of mass media of communication, will influence considerably the concepts of the rest of the population. Hence, confining the presentation to the urban group may not be as serious a limitation as one might at first assume.

EGYPTIAN IDENTITY FROM A HISTORICAL PERSPECTIVE

From the beginning of recorded history, Egypt constituted a national entity. It has been a nation in the dictionary sense of "a community united under a single independent government" since 3400 B.C., when Menes united its northern and southern regions to form a single state. The country has been overrun time and again by foreign conquerors—the Hyksos, Persians, Greeks, Romans, Turks, French and British. For long periods, it was simply a province of a larger empire. Yet it always remained a distinct geographic and cultural entity. Indeed, it has always succeeded in reverting to its independent state and in so doing has frequently shown a resilient capacity to absorb its foreign rulers. Cleopatra was of Greek origin, yet fought the Romans in the name of Egypt. Muḥammad 'Alī, of Albanian extraction, came to Egypt in 1801 as an officer in the Turkish army; his descendants remained to rule over an independent Egypt. It is not surprising, then, in the light of their history, that the Egyptians, unlike the inhabitants of many emerging nations, should be conscious of their national identity and consider themselves above all Egyptians, with an awareness of the continuity and uniqueness of their own past and of their own contribution to civilization.

The Ottoman Period

Egyptian identity can best be understood from a historical perspective. In the Ottoman period, prior to the Napoleonic invasion of Egypt, we find the country under the titular rule of the Ottoman Turks, but under the virtual rule of the Mamlūks. Mamlūks were white slaves, originally Qipchak Turks from the Black Sea area, but later of Circassian, Georgian, Kurdish, or even Greek origin. They were first introduced into Egypt in the thirteenth century by the 'Ayyūbids (Saladin's successors). At first they constituted a militia, then a military elite. Finally, on the death of the last 'Ayyūbid ruler in 1260, they revolted and became a ruling class, making one of their number, Baibars, the sultan. In 1517 they were conquered by the Ottoman Turks. The establishment of Ottoman suzerainty, however, did not mean the end of the Mamlūk system, even though it brought an end to Mamlūk rule. In order to be able to exploit Egypt to the full financially, the Ottoman sultanate in Constantinople imposed upon the country a politico-administrative superstructure. This consisted of the governor (*wālī*) and various military and non-military corps whose officers held the title of *bey.* The political and administrative posts in the government and the upper level of judiciary were filled from these corps, all of whose officers were Turks appointed directly by Constantinople. For example, in the case of the judiciary, not only the chief judge (*qāḍī 'askar*) but also the district *qāḍīs* were appointed by the High Porte (*61*, p. 59).

Shaw makes a distinction between this "hierarchy of function" and the parallel "hierarchy of power," which still consisted of the Mamlūk princes (*61,* p. 2). As he points out, "the history of Ottoman Egypt is a story of repeated conflicts among the members of the Mamlūk hierarchy and between them and the representatives of the Porte in Egypt, conflicts whose object was the control of the Ottoman hierarchy of government" (*61,* p. 3). As the power of the Ottoman Empire declined, its control over Egypt became less effective. By 1798, when the French invaded the country, the de facto power rested with the Mamlūk princes, even though the Turkish "hierarchy of function" still existed. The Mamlūks constituted a feudal aristocracy whose system was an adaptation of Turkish Seljuk feudalism. In lieu of pay, a Mamlūk officer received a grant of land and was obliged to supply a stipulated number of Mamlūk soldiers. These grants were not hereditary and involved the eviction of the Arabised descendants of the Mamlūk officers. The Mamlūks perpetuated themselves by bringing in new slaves who were educated and trained in Egypt and eventually freed as vassal knights (*50,* p. 155; *73,* p. 23).

The majority of the Egyptian population over whom the Mamlūk princes ruled were peasants reduced to the position of serfs on the land. They were not free to leave the land without facing severe punishment. The workers in the towns were not much better off than the peasantry. The only privileged groups among the Egyptians were some of the wealthier merchants and the religious leaders, or *'ulamā',* who were below the Mamlūks in the societal pyramid. The *'ulamā'* were the only class of native Egyptians to enjoy civil and economic rights. They possessed feudal estates like the Mamlūk princes and their property was protected from usurpation or confiscation. Few other people could accumulate wealth without the risk of confiscation by the predatory Mamlūks. When persons outside the privileged classes of the Mamlūks and *'ulamā'* acquired wealth, they took pains not to advertise the fact. This class of clandestine rich included merchants and tax collectors and sometimes those in the employ of the wealthy—often Christian Copts acting as secretaries or stewards.

The *'ulamā'* were the real leaders of the people; they had power over the masses, in whose lives religion played a major part. They could appease them and keep them in a state of resigned acceptance, or rouse them to open revolt. The Mamlūk rulers recognized their power and treated them with deference. They acted as intermediaries between the rulers and the people, for they were the only means of intercession with the ruler available to the masses.

Like the Turkish officials, the Mamlūk princes kept themselves culturally separate from the rest of the population and avoided any cultural assimilation. They remained foreign in dress, traditions and speech. They spoke mainly Turkish or Circassian, and some of them hardly spoke Arabic (*50,* p. 156). According to al-Maqrīzī, they even followed some of their own laws and did not adhere to the Islamic *sharī'a* law in their relations to one another (*70,* p. 90). However, they were Muslims and as such shared with the population certain cultural values. For example, they were patrons of Islamic art and architecture and left for posterity an impressive legacy of mosques, schools and mausolea. Furthermore, unlike the Turks, they had a local identity, for Egypt was their only home.

The Egyptian population also maintained an identity separate from their rulers—in fact, they considered themselves the real sons of the country. We can get an idea of how they regarded themselves vis-à-vis other ethnic groups from the chronicles of the famous Egyptian historian, al-Jabartī. Al-Jabartī had a sharp eye for the social scene and left a rich record of day-to-day events in the life of urban Egypt from the end of Mamlūk rule through the Napoleonic invasion and into the period of Muḥammad 'Alī. In his history, he mentions the variety of ethnic groups existing among the urban population of Cairo (*54*). He refers to the urban Egyptian as *awlād al-balad*, which means "the sons of the country or town," a term still used today to differentiate the Egyptian from all other ethnic groups. A synonymous term used by al-Jabartī is *ahl al-balad,* "the people of the country or town." A study of the various contexts in which the term is used by al-Jabartī shows that *awlād* or *ahl al-balad* clearly did not refer to the Turks—the Turkish *wālī,* the Turkish *qāḍī,* or chief judge, and other government and army officials—nor did it include the Mamlūk princes. The *'ulamā'* on the other hand, were from the people and were identified by al-Jabartī as *awlād al-balad.*

The relationship between the people and their rulers was a tense one, for the people suffered much oppression and injustice (*44,* p. 238). The Egyptians were not only conscious of their own distinctive identity vis-à-vis the governing elite, but also in relation to other ethnic groups in the country, including the few hundred Europeans and such Arabic-speaking groups as the Syrians, Tunisians, Moroccans, Sudanese, and Yemenites. Al-Jabartī makes several references to other *ajnās,* or "races." For example, one passage describes how "a crowd of *ajnās* and *awlād al-balad* gathered under the arcades and barrages . . . where boats and ships carrying people from these groups were moored" (*44*, p. 518).

Members of these ethnic groups, even if they had lived for generations in Egypt, tended to emphasize their separateness by preserving their own distinctive dress and some of their traditions and customs. In fact, Middle Eastern society as a whole has been characterized, not as a melting pot, but as a mosaic pattern in which various ethnic groups have their special roles within the total structure, while maintaining their own identity and cultural distinctiveness (*18*). In the large cities of Egypt, especially Cairo and Alexandria, these ethnic groups, as well as non-Muslim Egyptians, tended to live within special quarters, which were named after them, such as the Turkish quarter, the Moroccan quarter, the Jewish quarter, the Christian quarter, and the European quarter.

Among the Egyptians themselves, groups were distinguished on religious lines, such as Muslims, Jews and Coptic Christians. By "Jews," I mean native Egyptian Jews. I assume that al-Jabartī would have referred to them by his customary epithet for Europeans, *al-lfrang,* had they been, for example, of Italian or French origin. In the eyes of the Muslim majority, the Jews and the Copts seem to have been associated with the foreigner. In regard to the Copts this may seem odd, since the Copts are of true Egyptian origin and have always considered themselves, as they still do today, racially purer and more truly Egyptian than the rest of the population, on the grounds that Coptic Egypt antedated Muslim Egypt. However, the Muslim Egyptians, while recognizing the Egyptian origins of the Copts, have always associated them with aliens, because of their long history of service to the foreigners. During the Mamlūk period they were the tax collectors, administrators of the land registry and managers of the feudal Mamlūk estates (*28*, p. 259).

Later when Napoleon invaded the country, some of them served the French during their brief stay in Egypt. Even the ruling aliens, the Mamlūks, identified the Copts with the Europeans. This was most likely due to the affinity between the two latter groups which existed, or was assumed to exist, as a result of a common religion. We see the association of the Copts with the foreigners in a passage from al-Jabartī (*44*, p. 295), in which he describes the reaction of the Mamlūk princes and of the local population to Napoleon's unexpected entry into Alexandria—they searched the houses of Copts, along with those of the European foreigners, Syrian, Christians, and Greeks. He also describes the effect that French favour had upon the behavior of minority groups, including the Copts and the Jews: "The lowest among the Christians from the Copts and Syrians, the Greeks and the Jews, because they served the French, rose to the point of riding horses and carrying swords. They swaggered around and humiliated the Muslims." (al-Jabartī, *4*, p. 295.)

The First Impact of Europe

Mamlūk rule and feudal society was brought to an end by Napoleon's conquest of Egypt. Though of short duration (from 1798 to 1801), the French occupation was a deeply significant event in the history of the country, for it paved the way for modern Egypt. The reaction of the Egyptians to the French invaders is worth noting, not only because the latter were the vanguard of European civilization, but also because they were the first of a variety of European groups to attempt to control Egypt politically and economically. The reaction of the Egyptians to the French was ambivalent, a combination of admiration and rebellion—an attitude that persists toward Western influence.

Napoleon took the stance of a liberator. Before coming to Egypt, in his speech to his army, he emphasized the need for tact and understanding: "The people of Egypt are Moslems. Do not contradict them: respect their *muftīs* and *imāms,* as we have respected rabbis and bishops. They treat their women differently from us and he who dishonours a woman is a monster of depravity" (*22,* p. 74). He had studied the manners and customs of the country and even adopted oriental dress. His proclamations began with traditional Islamic phrases and were larded with complimentary references to the Prophet and Islām: "I worship God more than the Mamlūks do and respect the Prophet and the glorious *Qur'ān*" (*44,* p. 246). One of his generals, Menou, even embraced Islam. Yet, as explained below, Napoleon failed to achieve a rapprochement with the Egyptians.

A more successful venture, incidental to his military designs, was the introduction of French culture. Napoleon had brought French savants along with the army: the Egyptologists and other scientists began to study various aspects of Egypt. After the *Institute d'Egypte* was founded, its libraries and laboratories were open to interested visitors. A printing press was set up and the administrative and fiscal systems were reorganized. The immediate results of these innovations were perhaps not very impressive, but they represented the beginning of Egypt's cultural contact with Europe. The response of Egyptians to French science and technology was one of awe. Shaykh Ḥasan al-'Aṭṭar, who later became rector of al-Azhar, is representative of the small group of liberally minded religious leaders who were stimulated and challenged by contact with the French savants. "He welcomed contact with the French and taught them Arabic and attempted to learn their sciences. 'Our country,' he urged, 'should change its way of life and introduce modern sciences which it lacks' " (*56,* p. 15). The fruits of his contact with the French are to be seen not only in his cry for change, but more practically in his attitude toward the pattern of teaching at al-Azhar. At the turn of the eighteenth century, the standards of teaching at al-Azhar had declined, with both subject range and educational outlook extremely narrow. (Shayyal, in Holt, 1968:118, 119) He himself introduced into his lectures references to the natural sciences, mathematics, philosophy and logic—no easy matter when one considers that the atmosphere prevailing at the time was no different from that existing in the seventeenth century, when Shaykh 'Alā' al-Dīn al-Hasafkī admonished: "Know that learning is a personal duty insofar as it is necessary for one's religious needs and voluntary if it is for others . . . and forbidden when it deals with philosophy, sorcery, astronomy, the natural sciences, magic and fortune-telling" (*1*, p. 30).

In spite of Napoleon's efforts to strike a chord of sympathy in the local population by emphasizing his solicitude for the cause of Islam, and in spite of the admiration that some Egyptians, such as al-'Aṭṭar, began to feel for the achievements of French culture, Napoleon was not successful in eliciting the support of either the *'ulamā'* or the people. The reaction of the religious leaders to Napoleon was negative from the start. We can see this clearly in al-Jabartī's account of how they responded to Napoleon's special bid for their support a few months after his landing in Alexandria:

> On September 1, 1798, Bonaparte summoned the *shaykhs*. When they had settled themselves down in his company, Bonaparte left the *majlis* and returned holding in his hand shawls of three colors, consisting of sections in white, red and dark blue. He placed one of them upon the shoulder of al-Shaykh al-Sharqāwī, but he threw it onto the ground . . . The interpreter said: 'O shaykh, you are beloved of the Commander-in-Chief; he wishes to show respect to you and honor you by [presenting you] with his own garb and insignia, so that you will be distinguished thereby and respected by the army and the people and find a place in their hearts' They said to him: 'But we will lose standing in the eyes of God and our brother Muslims' " (*44*, p. 262).

The people were clearly not convinced by Napoleon's expression of affinity to and sympathy with their customs and religion. The Egyptians regarded him as a foreigner—even more foreign than their Turkish and Mamlūk rulers, who at least shared with them a common religion. Reaction against the French gained group with great rapidity during the Autumn of 1798, exacerbated by such actions on the part of the French as the imposition of a special tax, the confiscation of goods and the tearing down of the gates of the quarters. It culminated in the active insurrection of the population. The revolt was firmly suppressed by the French troops and ended with their capture of the mosque of al-Azhar on October 21, 1798 (*44*, p. 275).

Napoleon's stay in Egypt ended as suddenly as it had begun. A British force of 16,000 men under Abercrombie landed at Alexandria in March 1801, and three months later the French capitulated and withdrew. Egypt itself was restored to the Ottoman Empire. The French, however, had made an important impact. By the ease of their military victory and by the display of their science and technology, they had undermined the complacency of Egypt's traditional society. By exposing the Egyptians to new administrative methods, as well as political beliefs and educational concepts, they had generated the first signs of a mood of self-questioning and self-doubt which acted as an important stimulus for change.

The Beginning of Modernization

In the century and a half following Napoleon, the genesis of modern Egypt took place. New social forces were at work with two seemingly contradictory processes finally dominating the scene—the gradual modernization of society along Western lines and the Egyptianization of the life of the nation. The latter trend did not start and continue along a straight line. The nation had to suffer the influx of numerous privileged foreigners before the trend towards Egyptianization finally asserted itself. A survey of these trends is given below.

The withdrawal of the French was followed by a period of anarchy, with groups of Mamlūks and Turks struggling for supremacy. The Mamlūks had lost their military power, but they still retained a large measure of political power. The Turks on the other hand were anxious to eliminate them and reassert Turkish rule, while the Egyptians hated them both. Although they seemed not to be involved directly in the conflict, it was the Egyptian people and their religious leaders who helped decide the outcome of the struggle by giving popular support to still a third party, the leader of the Albanian garrison, Muḥammad ʻAlī. A Turkish-speaking Ottoman officer of Albanian stock, Muḥammad ʻAlī had jockeyed for power by playing one side against the other.

In 1805, the *shaykhs,* notables, merchants and artisans of the various guilds demonstrated at the High Court of Justice against the Turkish governor. When they received no response to their complaints, they deposed the Turkish governor in the name of the people and proclaimed Muḥammad ʻAlī governor without permission from Constantinople. This was a significant step for the Egyptian people, as Rifaat has pointed out, for in so doing "they asserted their full right of self-determination in choosing their own head of state and in investing him with the insignia of office without even waiting for the approval of the Sultan" (*60,* p. 20). After sending an unsuccessful expedition to Egypt to depose him, Constantinople had no recourse, finally, but to accept Muḥammad ʻAlī as governor in 1806.

Muḥammad ʻAlī's first move was to make his power absolute by eliminating the Mamlūks and all other powerful groups in the country. In 1811, he massacred 400 of the Mamlūk leaders, whom he had invited as his guests, and had thousands more killed in the provinces. He then turned against his own Albanian forces and replaced them with Egyptian and Sudanese troops. He also set about undermining the positions of the Egyptian religious leaders who had brought him to power. He confiscated the religious *waqf* estates and ousted the *'ulamā'* who had been administering them. Henceforth, he ruled with total autocratic power. Thus, Egypt came once more under the suzerainty of a foreigner and was to remain under this foreign dynasty until the Nasser revolt of 1952.

Muḥammad 'Alī introduced far-reaching changes in all aspects of the country's development, including agriculture, industry and education. He had grandiose political designs and wanted to modernize the nation in order to make it powerful economically and militarily. These efforts, some successful and some less so, set in motion the two processes of Westernization and Egyptianization.

After confiscating all lands, Muhammad 'Alī redistributed them in a discriminatory fashion. To some he gave fallow land to reclaim, to others he gave good land. To the Egyptian peasants he gave three- to five-acre plots against payment of taxes. Al-Jabartī records that the tax levied on the peasants was heavy, at times twenty times more than they used to pay the Mamlūks. Many neglected the land and fled to the towns, or even emigrated to other countries, which called for repressive measures restricting their movements (*53,* p. 9). Other lands were distributed, free of taxation, to notables and officials—these were mostly "Turks"—and to members of his own family. He thus created "a class of new landowners . . . who supported his rule and had an interest in maintaining it" (*53,* p. 11). In effect, Muḥammad 'Alī's agricultural policies left Egyptians in a worse state than before vis-à-vis the dominant 'foreign' aristocracy.

Muhammad 'Alī developed modern industries and owned the large-scale enterprises he established. He set up wool and cotton textile factories, as well as factories for the production of sugar, glass, paper, oil, ropes, etc. He also established the iron and copper foundries which were to form the basis of an armament industry. He brought in Europeans to manage the factories; the engineers were French, Italian or English, while the workers were Egyptian (*60,* p. 45). He also used foreigners as technical advisers. But innovations in agricultural and industrial development failed to give the Egyptian any important new place in society. It is apparent, also, that the relationship between the ruling group and the people was little better than it had been in the earlier period. There are numerous accounts of arbitrariness and oppression by the authorities. The oppressive taxation of peasants has already been referred to. Al-Jabarti describes similar extortionary taxes levied on the artisans and merchants, based on false assessments of property ownership. No matter what the evidence presented, shopkeepers, merchants, silk craftsmen and others would be beaten and imprisoned (*44*, p. 757). There were also strained relationships between the local population and the military in their role as representatives of the punitive power of the state.

Although Muḥammad 'Alī's policies for agriculture and industry did not seem to change the status of the Egyptians significantly, the educational measures did. The traditional educational system of the mosque college was not equipped to meet Muḥammad 'Alī's needs. He wanted the system to produce employees for his industrial and military enterprises: he needed engineers and doctors, technical officers for the army and translators to make available European knowledge. Instead of reforming the old educational system, he chose to set up a parallel secular system along European lines (*56*, p. 84). The new system, strangely enough, started at the topmost level, with schools of medicine, pharmacy, veterinary science, engineering, minerology, applied chemistry, arts and crafts, and military sciences. Later, primary and secondary schools were established to underpin the system.

Since the first teachers were from Italy, Italian was the first European language to be taught (*36*, p. 53). This was soon replaced by French, as Muḥammad 'Alī turned to France for the model for his education system (*56*, p. 87). Most of the students at the first schools were Turks or Christians, but later the Egyptian Muslims, recruited from the students of al-Azhar, were introduced and gradually became more numerous. It was this element which became the first intelligentsia of modern Egypt, thus changing the earlier fossilized class structure.

Groups of students were also sent on study missions to France. In 1826, an Egyptian school was set up in Paris and 44 students were sent there for training. Their areas of specialization constitute an impressively catholic list: civil administration, military administration, naval administration, hydraulics, mechanics, military engineering, artillery, metallurgy and armaments production, printing and lithography, engraving, chemistry, medicine, surgery, agriculture, biology, mining and translation. Other students were sent to specialize in the manufacture of surgical instruments, textile, gunpowder, and in shipbuilding (*56*, p. 87).

In the career of al-Ṭahṭāwī (1801-1873), one of the first Egyptians to be sent on educational missions abroad, we have an example of the leavening effect of the ideas inherent in the new education to which the Egyptians were now being exposed. He not only developed new concepts on the function of education but also ideas on the state and society. He became an early apostle of the Egyptian national movement and gave articulate expression to Egyptian national self-consciousness. Al-Ṭahṭāwī, like succeeding generations of the intelligentsia, developed a questioning attitude toward the traditionals of his society, which he felt should look to its own rehabilitation and reform. The reform of the educational system was one of his main concerns, for he believed that the traditional religious education must allow for modern concepts. He held that the way to the regeneration of the society was through the education of both boys and girls (*36,* p. 77).

By laying the foundations of a modern educational system modeled on the methods and curricula of European schools, Muḥammad 'Alī brought to Egypt the influence of Western thought and technology. By recruiting Egyptian students, he set the stage for the emergence of a new class of Egyptians, imbued with a new national consciousness which expressed itself in a desire to improve society and to secure for themselves a greater share in its control and development. However, apart from this nascent and as yet insignificant growth of a class of educated Egyptians, the rule of Muḥammad 'Alī did nothing to loosen the grip of the foreigner upon the state. The governing elite, as is clear from Lane, remained Turkish, even down to the lower levels of the army and the administration (*48,* pp. 116, 129). All officials above village headmen were Turks and all commissioned and non-commissioned army officers of all ranks were Turks.

Modernization Versus Egyptianization

Under Muḥammad 'Alī's successors, Egypt became prey to a new group of foreigners, the Europeans. His immediate successor, 'Abbās, was in fact hostile to the Europeans, especially the French, and closed some of the schools established by Muḥammad 'Alī. Sa'īd, who followed 'Abbās, was more friendly to them—it was he who in 1854 granted de Lesseps the concession to build the Suez Canal. Paradoxically, Sa'īd was at the same time responsible for increasing the Egyptianization of the army and promoting many Egyptians to the rank of colonel, among them 'Urābī, who was to lead the 1882 revolt. Sa'īd was also instrumental in creating an Egyptian landowning class through the decree promulgated in 1858 which gave the Egyptians the right to own land (*75,* p. 334). Sa'īd, himself a Turk, was obviously bowing to already existing popular pressures when he delivered the following speech to a party of religious leaders and members of the government and the army:

> Brothers, I have examined the circumstances of this Egyptian people in relation to history and have found it oppressed and in enslavement to other nations, such as the Hyksos, Assyrians, Persians, even the people of Libya and the Sudan, the Greeks and the Romans, before Islam and after it. Many conquering nations have overrun this land—the Umayyads, 'Abbāsids and Fātimids from among the Arabs, the Turks, Kurds and Cir-

> cassians. France has frequently raided it, prior to occupying it at the beginning of this century under Bonaparte. Because I consider myself Egyptian, it is incumbent upon me to educate and train each son of the people, so that he is fit to serve his country properly and get rid of the foreigners. I have dedicated myself to changing this idea from thought to action (*68,* p. 16).

Ismā'īl, under whom the Suez Canal was completed, was a European-educated Egyptian who sought to modernize Egypt in order to bring it to a level of parity with Europe. Under Ismā'īl, an increasing number of foreigners flocked into Egypt and were protected by the immunity granted them under the "capitulations"—a system established in the sixteenth century to protect European traders within the Ottoman Empire. Under the capitulations, the foreign litigant was given the right to appeal to his own consular courts. Apart from the basic inequity of this process, the system was open to exploitation (*46,* p. 66).

In 1875, the "mixed courts" were established to replace the consular courts in deciding commercial and civil cases involving Egyptians and foreigners. Although an improvement, the mixed courts, which consisted largely of foreign judges appointed by foreign governments, was inevitably "offensive to Egyptian national sentiment" (*53,* p. 15).

The foreigners took advantage of Ismā'īl's extravagance and gullibility at every turn. Their looting of Egypt was described by Lord Milner as follows: "It is hard to imagine the complete unscrupulousness with which diplomatic agents used their influence to make a weak Egypt yield to their most extravagant demands. At the time, the purpose behind obtaining a concession was not to carry out some project, but to invent some complaint which would allow the contract to be broken and then turn to the government for compensation" (*46,* p. 67). Lacouture, using even stronger words, refers to the behavior of the Europeans during Ismā'īl's period as "this whirl of intrigues, this solemn ballet of tricksters, this auctioning of Egypt by a Europe whose thieves were disguised as diplomats, and the diplomats as thieves" (*46,* p. 67).

In the 1870s, Ismā'īl's wild speculations brought tighter controls over Egypt by the creditor nations, France and England. At the beginning of the decade, a *Caisse de la Dette* was set up, with French and British controllers to supervise the Egyptian budget. In the face of Ismā'īl's attempt to modernize Egypt "even at the price of ceasing to be Egypt," a counter-reaction was inevitable. The same period also witnessed the rapid growth of a nationalist sentiment, which was demanding the protection of Egypt and the Egyptians from the depredations of the Europeans and from discrimination in favour of the local but alien Turkish aristocracy.

Three groups of the more enlightened Egyptians took part in the nationalist movement—the civil servants, 50 percent of whom had become Egyptian under Ismā'īl, the Egyptian landowners, and the higher-ranking Egyptian officers in the army (*75,* p. 334). In 1879, Ismā'īl was deposed by the Porte as a result of British and French pressure, and Tawfīq succeeded him. In the same year, Egyptian nationalist sentiments were given more active expression in the organization of the first political party, the National Party, which had previously been just a secret society. It was composed of both army officers and landowners—the former especially concerned with discrimination against them in favor of the Turks in the army, the latter concerned with the establishment of a constitutional government to do away with the Khedive's aristocratic rule and to give the Egyptians a share in the running of their own country (*75,* pp. 334, 335).

Under Tawfīq, Egyptian feeling against discrimination culminated in the 1882 revolt led by 'Urābī and other Egyptian officers. This is considered the first genuine expression of modern Egyptian nationalism. 'Urābī was an Egyptian army colonel, the son of a village *shaykh* and a former student at al-Azhar. Young describes the situation in the army under the successors of Muḥammad 'Alī as follows:

> Under Sa'īd the colonelcies had been open to Egyptians, but Ismā'īl had promoted only Circassians, Syrians, and Arabs as being more showy. The general officers had always been Turks. Thus, the Egyptian regimental officers found themselves relegated with their rank and file to serve as navvies on canals and roads. Or if they had to fight, found their lives thrown away, as in Abyssinia, by the bad strategy and staff work of the palace proteges. And the accession of Tawfīq brought no redress but only reduction of pay and promotion, to pay the foreign control and the foreign creditors (*74,* p. 105).

Egyptians in the army had also been dismissed in large numbers on the recommendation of the British and French debt controllers (*46,* p. 69).

At first, 'Urābī and his supporters won many concessions from the Khedive. The prime minister, an Armenian, was dismissed, while the war minister, a Turk, was exiled, and a nationalist government was formed under Muḥammad Sāmī al-Bārūdī, who appointd 'Urābī as minister of war. A liberal constitution calling for a national assembly was proclaimed. The Khedive, however, appealed to the British, and on July 13th, 1882, they landed in Alexandria and crushed the 'Urābī revolt. In September 1882 the British occupied Cairo, and they remained in occupation of Egypt for nearly three-quarters of a century. From then on, Egyptians had to struggle against the domination of three types of foreigners—the British, who controlled the country politically and economically; the resident foreigners, mostly Europeans, who dominated its economic life; and the local aristocracy of foreign origin.

The Egyptian nationalist movement, which picked up momentum again after a period of quiescence following the 'Urābī defeat, expressed the reaction of the Egyptians against all three types of foreigners, with a change of emphasis at different periods. Following the British occupation, reaction against their control became the most vocal. But the struggle to imprint an Egyptian character on the nation was going on beneath the surface, even though such a goal may have seemed at times utopian in the face of an increasingly powerful European presence.

Achievement of Independence

In 1883, Lord Cromer was appointed British consul general in Egypt and remained the de facto ruler for over twenty years, although Egypt continued under the nominal suzerainty of the Ottoman government. Under the British, the Egyptian nationalist movement steadily gained strength and was focused on the fight for independence from Britain. In 1907, with the coming to power of the Liberal Party in England, British controls were relaxed and two Egyptian political parties were formed, the Umma and the National Parties. In the following three years, five other new political parties were established.

The program of the Umma Party represented the political thinking of the nationalist Egyptians. Their platform was that "Egypt could not be liberated except by the Egyptians themselves and through reform. The Khedive's power . . . should be assumed by the representatives of the people. Turkey was regarded as helpless, and actual Turkish rule was out of the question. Foreigners in the service of the government should be gradually replaced by native Egyptians" (75, p. 338).

On December 19th, 1914, the British Government deposed the Khedive, made Prince Husayn Kāmil sultan, and established a protectorate over Egypt. Britain thus replaced Turkey as suzerain and assumed responsibility for Egypt's defense and for its foreign relations. In spite of military occupation and censorship, however, the nationalist movement gained momentum. In 1918, Sa'd Zaghlūl, now spokesman for the movement, decided to form a delegation to present Egypt's case at the Peace Conference and secure the latter's recognition of its independence. The British rejected this move and deported him and three of his followers to Malta. As a result, a revolt broke out in 1919, with systematic sabotage of communication, followed by a general strike, then a political boycott. Zaghlūl and his followers were allowed to proceed to Paris only to face serious disappointment, for the Conference recognized the British protectorate over Egypt (75, p. 342).

As a result of continuing nationalist pressure, however, Egypt was eventually proclaimed independent in 1922 and Fu'ād, one of Muḥammad 'Alī's progeny, was made king. A constitution was promulgated in 1923 with the following provisions: "Legislative power was to be exercised in conjunction with the king by a parliament comprising an elected Chamber of Deputies and a Senate; executive power was to be exercised under the king by a Council of Ministers. Two-fifths of the members as well as the president of the Senate were to be appointed by the king; the latter also had the power to dissolve parliament and to appoint and dismiss cabinet ministers" (*45*, p. 354). The constitution also stipulated that public and military employment was to be restricted to Egyptians, with special exceptions to allow for the continuing employment of some British officials. Islam was to be the religion of the state and Arabic its language. In the elections which followed the promulgation of the constitution, the Wafd Party under Zaghlūl was swept into power.

These developments, however, did not mean the end of British control over Egypt, for the declaration of 1922 had affirmed Britain's responsibility for the defense of Egypt and the protection of foreign residents. A threefold nexus of power now existed, consisting of Britain, the Wafd Party, and the Monarchy. This combination determined the political development of Egypt over the next thirty years. Nationalist pressures against British control continued to gain ground, however, and culminated in the Anglo-Egyptian treaty of 1936. Under this treaty, Britain, while remaining responsible for Egypt's defense, was to withdraw her forces to the Suez Canal. Perhaps more important, the capitulations were to end, while the mixed courts were to assume the judicial responsibilities of the consular courts. The Montreux Conference of 1937 confirmed that the mixed courts should themselves hand over all their judiciary powers to Egyptian courts by 1949.

The Second World War delayed the withdrawal of British troops from Egypt. It was not until 1947 that the earlier British commitment to withdraw to the Canal Zone was complied with. Although it had also been agreed that complete evacuation was to take place by September 1949, it turned out that the British troops continued to occupy the Canal after that date. Demands for complete evacuation continued, and in October 1951 the 1936 Treaty was unilaterally abrogated by Egypt. It was not until after the Nasser revolution and the signing of the Anglo-Egyptian treaty in 1954, however, that the British finally left Egypt.

We need now to go back a little and review some of the other important developments during the latter part of the nineteenth and first half of the twentieth centuries, including the expansion of modern education and the growth of an Egyptian professional and business class, the domination of the economy by the foreigners, and the deteriorating position of the Turks. One consequence of the increased Egyptian participation in government was the expansion of educational opportunities for Egyptians. In order to modernize the nation, without at the same time perpetuating its status as a foreign exploited fief, educated Egyptians were needed to undertake all the tasks necessary for the functioning of a modern state. After the early efforts of Muḥammad 'Alī and of Ismā'īl to develop a modern educational system, the British had attempted to reverse these trends (*56,* p. 94). They had been influenced by their experience in India and had tried to avoid creating a difficult-to-control intelligentsia. They had reverted to the old-fashioned *kuttāb* system, where little more than the three R's were taught. The few modern schools left in operation could accommodate only a limited number of students (*66,* pp. 326 ff). Until the British occupation, the schools had been free at all levels, but the British abolished this system. The result was that only the well-to-do could afford to send their children to school.

The British tried to replace Arabic with English in the primary and secondary schools. They further encouraged the establishment of missionary schools "which were foreign in their language, curricula and traditions. They never tried to understand Egyptian society or mix with it or serve the local communities in which they existed" (*33,* p. 11). The foreign schools were mainly French and English; there were also special schools for foreign minorities—Italians, Greeks, etc. In some of the foreign schools, Arabic was hardly taught at all, and the history and geography courses were more concerned with Europe than with Egypt. The people these schools produced were naturally somewhat alienated from their own cultural traditions and sometimes showed little pride in its values. While they were limited in number, they did, unfortunately, form part of the upper class.

With the declaration of Egypt's independence in 1923, an ambitious educational program was launched which provided free and compulsory education for children between seven and twelve years of age. Primary and secondary schools, with Arabic as the language of instruction, multiplied. Cairo University was established in 1925, followed by Alexandria University in 1942, and Ain Shams University (Cairo) in 1950; numerous missions for higher studies abroad were also organized. In ever increasing numbers Egyptians took advantage of the wider educational opportunities now available to them. Total school population increased from 342,000 in 1913, to 942,000 in 1933, to 1,900,000 in 1951 (*42,* pp. 96, 97). The school and university graduates found ready employment in the rapidly expanding civil service.

As the Egyptians were gaining greater control over the political life of the nation and over public administration, however, the foreigners were increasingly coming to dominate important aspects of the economy. During the late nineteenth and early twentieth centuries the development of the economy, particularly the production and export of cotton, had encouraged a tremendous influx of foreign capital accompanied by large-scale immigration of foreigners, so that in 1836 there were 3,000 foreigners, over 68,000 in 1878, and as many as 221,000 by 1907 (*34,* p. 343).

The presence of foreigners and the influx of European goods had also undermined locally controlled commerce based on the guilds. During most of the nineteenth century, in the larger towns, a system of guilds existed, consisting of the gainfully employed segment of the population. During the second half of the century, guilds started to decline and by the end of the century, local crafts lost out to European imports. The importance of the traditional *suq* and the effectiveness of the Egyptian merchant guilds had likewise been affected. Foreign trade, which had dealt with Arabian and Sudanese goods and which had been handled by Egyptian, Syrian and Turkish merchants, gave way to trade with Europe which was controlled by Greeks and other Europeans (*12,* pp. 142, 144).

The predominance of foreigners had become most marked in the higher levels of finance, trade, and to a lesser extent industry—most likely because the British had discouraged industrialization (*42,* p. 29). The Egyptians had difficulty competing with foreign businessmen for a number of reasons. The latter had more links with the European markets and wider experience in modern business organization and management than the Egyptians, while the legal and fiscal protection of the capitulation system had given them undue advantage over the natives. Consequently, the Egyptians left the field to the foreigners and the educated among them gravitated to government employment, while the wealthy invested mainly in land.

After Egypt's independence, however, things began to change. In the 1920s, industrialization efforts by pioneering Egyptians, helped by government measures to protect local industry, encouraged Egyptian participation in industry and commerce. As a result, an Egyptian professional and business class emerged and continued to grow over the years. However, the foreigners still remained in control of much of the business world, even as late as the 1950s. An analysis of the ethnic background of 1406 company directors shows that in 1951, 31 percent were Egyptian Muslims, 4 percent Copts, 18 percent Jews, 11 percent Syrians or Lebanese, 8 percent Greeks or Armenians, and 39 percent Europeans (*42,* p. 89).

The foreigners of Egypt, while exploiting the country for their own benefit, made little effort to assimilate into the local culture. Many of them felt it advantageous to keep their foreign passports even when they had become permanent residents and had lived in Egypt for generations. They spoke their own language and lived their lives unmindful of Egyptian traditions. In fact, it was the Egyptians, mainly the wealthy and the educated, white-collar and professional classes, who came to accommodate themselves to Western ways. They had become exposed to Western influences through direct contact with the Europeans in Egypt and abroad, and indirectly through modern education and the mass media. For many, the change involved mainly material aspects of culture—clothing, housing, etc.—while for others the change touched deeper levels of thought and behavior. Some members of the upper classes, to the resentment of the rest of the Egyptians, went so far as to identify almost completely with the foreigners: they spoke English or French more frequently than Arabic, knew more about the roots of European culture than about their own, and adopted patterns of social behavior which were at times so discordant with the traditional norms as to be offensive to the local population.

With progressive Egyptianization, the Turks had gradually lost their special position. Early in the nineteenth century, Turkish immigration ceased and the Turks remaining in Egypt became more acculturated with each succeeding generation, especially as they began to intermarry with the Egyptians (*12,* p. 149).

Until the Nasser revolution, however, a small group of Turks, including the royal family, remained at the apex of society. They boasted of their Turkish blood and retained a sense of social superiority over the Egyptian, or the "fellah" as they often called him. Standards of personal beauty emphasizing Turkish standards, such as lighter shades of skin, eyes, and hair were still prevalent. Egyptian reaction against this residue of Turkish superiority could be seen in the lampooning that the Turks suffered in popular jokes and plays, and in the tribute that novels and folk songs repeatedly paid to the dark beauty of the Egyptian. The last vestiges of Turkish superiority only disappeared after the 1952 revolution.

MODERNIZATION WITH EGYPTIANIZATION

In spite of the many political, social and economic gains which the Egyptians had made in the first half of this century, political tensions kept building, culminating in the Nasser revolution. Several factors contributed to the restlessness: the irresponsibility of King Farouk, which exacerbated the hatred felt for the "alien" Muḥammad ʿAlī dynasty; the continuing presence of the British forces in the Canal Zone; the deep disillusionment which both the people and the army felt as a result of the Arab-Israeli war of 1948; and the conduct of the political parties and their leadership.

An additional important cause of disenchantment among many liberals and intellectuals was the socio-economic structure which had developed. Although Egyptians had managed to take over most of the important functions in the state and now had the opportunity to exploit its resources for their own benefit, it was mainly the numerically small upper classes who profited from these developments and who wielded the political power. Land, as has already been noted, was the major form of investment for well-to-do Egyptians. When the parliamentary system of representative government was introduced in Egypt, land became not only a source of wealth and a symbol of prestige but also an important means of gaining political power. Those who owned the land controlled the livelihood, hence the votes, of the peasants. With 80 percent of the population of Egypt living in the rural areas, the rural votes were very important. Consequently, there emerged a large group of absentee landlords, city dwellers who had little interest in agriculture except for the economic and political power that the land bestowed.

The number of Egyptians who benefited from the economic growth of the country can be surmised from the pattern of land distribution just before 1952. Whereas 80 percent of the people lived by farming, only 14 percent owned any land at all; over 70 percent of these owned less than one acre. The rest, who constituted less than 4 percent of the total population, owned over 85 percent of the land, while less than .04 percent owned about 64 percent of the land (*53,* p. 27). Members of the royal family were among those who owned vast estates.

The 1952 revolution came to rid Egypt of the foreigners—the British and the foreign aristocracy—and to spread the benefits of Egyptianization more widely. Rather than "Egypt for the Egyptians," the revolution aimed at an "Egypt for *all* the Egyptians." Perhaps the finest evaluation of the forces which brought about the revolution can be best looked for in the pronouncements of the men who made it. In the introduction to the National Charter, President Nasser states the conditions which instigated the revolution as follows:

> The foreign invaders occupied the land; close by were their military bases, fully armed to intimidate the Egyptian motherland and destroy its resistance. The alien royal family ruled according to its own interests and whims, and imposed humility and submission. The feudalists owned the estates which they monopolized, leaving nothing to the toiling farmers except the straw following the harvest. Capitalists exploited Egyptian wealth in several ways after they succeeded in dominating the Government and made it serve their own interests . . . Political leaderships . . . were lured by class privileges and were drained of all power or resistance [and] were even used to deceive the masses under the guise of a spurious democracy. The same thing happened with the army, which the dominating powers, operating against the interests of the people, tried to weaken, on the one hand, and divert from supporting the national struggle, on the other.

In its first decade, the revolution achieved a number of its important goals.

First of all, it brought an end to British occupation, and the last British troops left Egypt in 1956. Second, the revolution effected serious changes in the socio-economic structure, changes which have had implications for the foreigners of Egypt as well as for the Egyptians. It did away with the alien aristocracy by abolishing royalty and confiscating the property of the members of the royal house. It undermined the economic and political power of the landed upper classes by promulgating the Agrarian Reform Law in 1952. This law at first limited land ownership to 200 feddans (1 feddan = 1.038 acre), but was changed in 1962 to allow only 100 feddans per family. Finally, the revolution succeeded in almost completely Egyptianizing the economy through the nationalization of important industries and through large-scale enterprises, among other measures. The Suez Canal was nationalized in 1956; the British-French-Israeli attack which followed led to the sequestration of British and French assets and to the expulsion of British and French nationals. From 1957 on, further nationalizations led to an accelerated exodus from Egypt of foreigners and of Jews and other Egyptians, who had been in control of business and industry. As a consequence, the influence of the foreigner on the Egyptian economy today is practically non-existent.

Another important long-term goal of the revolution has been social and economic growth through the transformation of existing socio-economic structures in accord with the socialist philosophy of the revolution and through the modernization of technology. In order to escape the pitfalls of earlier ventures, modernization was to be attained not through the importation of foreigners, but through the importation of new ideas and new techniques to be implemented by the Egyptians themselves, with the help of the foreigners if need be, but without their control. In other words, the short-term foreign expert is now welcome, but not the long-term resident foreign businessman and industrialist.

Further expansion of modern education was deemed necessary to provide the additional technical and professional manpower to carry out the ambitious schemes of agricultural, industrial, and social development. The availability of free education, even on the university level, encouraged students from all classes of society to take advantage of the educational opportunities.

It is not within the scope of this paper to evaluate the successes or failures of the educational and modernization efforts. What is of interest here is the impact of these on Egyptian identity. It is interesting that, concomitant with the strong desire to modernize the nation, which involved the wider adoption of foreign ideas and foreign techniques, there developed a powerful counterbalancing mood demanding the reassertion of Egyptian cultural traditions and values. This reassertion has taken several forms.

First, we find current national educational policies consciously aim at creating in the students a sense of their cultural heritage. Arabic language and literature, Egyptian history, geography, politics and society are included as a basic part of all curricula in both government schools and private schools. Many of the foreign schools have been nationalized, while others have been compelled by law to Egyptianize the administration and to limit the number of foreign teachers. Greater homogeneity in educational programs has also been achieved by imposing a basic curriculum for all schools enrolling Egyptian students. The French or German schools still functioning are allowed to offer advanced foreign language, or other special courses, so long as they also follow the basic curriculum set by the Ministry of Education. All examinations for the primary, intermediate, and secondary certificates are set by the government. The result of all these measures is the development of a greater intellectual and cultural affinity among today's school graduates, and a greater awareness of their cultural heritage than was the case for earlier generations of graduates, who were products of a variety of school systems based on a variety of cultural traditions.

Other efforts to strengthen traditional Egyptian culture can also be seen in the development of the arts, which today seem to be undergoing a real renaissance. Many of Egypt's new painters and sculptors, although influenced by modern art techniques, try to incorporate into their works older Egyptian art forms—Islamic, Coptic or Pharaonic. Themes from Egyptian life inspire and give local color to much of today's art production, leading to a revival of folk art, folk music and folk dances—sometimes with modern adaptations to appeal to contemporary taste.

The current trend to glorify the Egyptian common man and to reject the Turkish aristocracy and the alienated, westernized Egyptian can be seen clearly in the themes of contemporary novels and plays. In fact, social pressures today are such that it would be difficult to find someone who would boast publicly of his Turkish origin. Similarly, there are few who would not feel ashamed if they did not master the Arabic language, or if they appeared uninformed about Egyptian society and its cultural traditions.

In my opinion, the effect of the recent simultaneous attempts to modernize the country and to affirm Egyptian culture has been the development of a more culturally integrated, less schizophrenic society. As compared with earlier modernization efforts, which produced deep cleavages between foreigner and Egyptian and between traditional and westernized Egyptians, the new type of modernization is spreading westernization more broadly and more homogeneously, but in a sense, less deeply and with less cultural uprooting. With wider educational opportunities for all, change is reaching people of all social levels. As a result, a kind of continuum has developed between the most traditional and the most modernized levels, instead of the earlier sharp distinctions. There still exists, of course, a cultural cleavage between the urban and peasant societies.

A comparison of Cairo's business center as it was a few decades ago with what it is today will serve to illustrate the difference between the old and the new type of modernization. With the advent of the European businessman, Cairo developed two different business centers, one modern and the other traditional, each center physically separated and catering to different clienteles. The modern center could not have been distinguished from that of any European Mediterranean city: the signs on the shops were in French or English, and the streets teemed with Europeans, long-term residents or tourists. The girls at the counters were mostly of foreign background and for the most part spoke French, while the goods exposed were mainly European, catering to the elegant taste of the wealthy and the upper classes. Less westernized Egyptians shopped in the *suqs* in the older quarters of town. Today, the local foreigners have practically disappeared from the streets and the shop counters, replaced by Arabic-speaking Egyptians, who are also capable of using French or English to communicate with the tourist. All shop signs are in Arabic and Roman letters, and the articles displayed are by and large locally manufactured by Egypt's modern industries. Some of the goods still represent the latest European styles, but products appealing to local Egyptian tastes and needs are also available. The shoppers are overwhelmingly Egyptian, representing all levels of society and varying degrees of westernization.

The "Sons of the Country" Today

Little empirical research has been done on the effect of westernization and Egyptianization on the Egyptian self-concept, but a small study undertaken recently in Cairo, by Sawsan El Messiry, on contemporary *awlād al-balad* offers some interesting insights. We have already met *awlād al-balad,* the "sons of the country," in al-Jabartī's chronicles of the nineteenth century. This was the expression the Egyptians used to differentiate themselves from foreign rulers and foreign visitors. Today the term still applies to "the real Egyptian who has no foreign blood," "those who are born from an Egyptian father and mother," "The Egyptian son of Egypt." (*54,* p. 58). *Awlād al-balad* do not include persons of Egyptian nationality who are known to be of foreign origin, such as an unassimilated Greek or Italian who has retained the speech, manners and customs of his foreign background.

The interesting thing, however, is that other more exclusive meanings are currently conferred on the term, meanings which I believe are a consequence of the gradual westernization of urban society. In its more exclusive meaning, it is used to designate one particular type of Egyptian: unless the speaker is obviously using the term to differentiate an Egyptian from a foreigner, *ibn al-balad* (singular form of *awlād al-balad*) is used to designate a traditional, less westernized Egyptian. According to Egyptian informants from all classes of society, an *ibn al-balad* is someone who lives according to behavior patterns that are truly Egyptian. From the El Messiri study, it is clear that what are considered "truly Egyptian" ways are those traditional patterns which were once common among Egyptians prior to the introduction of European manners and customs. This is clear from the following definitions provided by respondents: "Not all Egyptians are *Awlād al-balad.* They are a special kind of people of the old days. They are the 'baladī people'." [*baladī* is an adjective derived from *balad.*] "It refers to the person who follows our forefather's way of life." "It is said of the person whose way of life does not differ from that of the old days." "*Ibn al-balad* is one who represents our old Egyptian traditions" (*54,* p. 86).

There is an even narrower meaning attached to the phrase *Awlād al-balad,* and that is perhaps its most common usage today. It is used to designate the lower middle and lower classes among urban residents. From the context of the conversation one can usually tell which of its several meanings is intended. These are the groups that can be considered the repository of the older traditional Egyptian ways, those who have been least subjected to the influence of European or western ways. They live in the older, less Europeanized quarters of Cairo; many of them still wear traditional robes or *galabeyas*; they speak Arabic without intrusion of foreign words, and use the customary salutations and proverbial expressions with which their language is richly endowed; they still observe many of the older customs and ceremonial behavior which in earlier times were practiced by most Egyptians; they have preserved the male-dominant Muslim family pattern with its emphasis on strict codes for women and for sexual behavior; they eat traditional foods and listen to traditional Arabic music; the *baladi* coffeehouse is still an important source of entertainment.

As a whole, they are poorer and have less formal schooling than other urban groups. However, according to most of the Egyptians who were asked to list the criteria for distinguishing the *awlād al-balad* from all others, education and wealth were not alone sufficient. There may well be among them educated as well as wealthy individuals. The most important criterion is the extent to which a person follows the old ways and identified himself with *awlād al-balad.* Formal education, however, is seen as a danger to this kind of identity, because of the changes it tends to induce in a person's thinking and way of life (*54,* p. 82).

The narrowing of *awlād al-balad* to refer to the more traditional class of society seems to be a reflection of the changes which westernization has brought about. As Egyptians became westernized, they were excluded from *awlād al-balad,* just as the Copts had been excluded in the nineteenth century because of their association with the foreigners. Interestingly enough, today's Copts who live in the traditional quarters and exhibit traditional outlooks are now called *awlād al-balad.* It seems that as westernization touched all parts of Egyptian society, the Copts no longer remained prominent as "culturally foreign." In other words, they seem to have become more integrated within the total society once westernization ceased to be their exclusive characteristic.

The antithesis of *awlād al-balad* are *awlād al-zawwāt,* a term used to designate a person from the upper classes. The stereotype of *ibn al-zawwāt* in the popular Egyptian conception is a highly westernized person whose lifestyle is European, who is fluent in foreign languages, which he sometimes masters better than his own, who is sophisticated as in European manners but ignorant of his own, and who does not follow religious observances and is often a libertine. In between *ibn al-balad* and *ibn al-zawwāt* stand the middle classes, somewhat westernized but still adhering to many traditional cultural patterns. Persons from this group may identify themselves with *awlād al-balad* or *awlād al-zawwāt,* depending on whether they adhere to behavior norms typical of the one or of the other. Whereas in an earlier day, more of them aspired to be considered *awlād al-zawwāt,* recently the pendulum has swung the other way. People now find it awkward to be designated as *awlād al-zawwāt,* and many are anxious to prove their peasant or *ibn al-balad* background.

What are the special attributes or qualities considered characteristic of *ibn al-balad*? This is a question that was asked of urban Egyptians who represented different socio-economic and educational levels and varying degrees of westernization. Since most respondents considered *ibn al-balad* to be the "true Egyptian," the answers would seem to reflect an Egyptian concept of self. It does not appear, however, to represent a realistic concept of what a contemporary urban Egyptian actually is, that is, a mixture of westernized and traditional personality. Rather, it represents an idealized concept of what a "real" Egyptian is—someone rooted in his traditions and untouched by foreign ways and values. It is as if today's Egyptian considers the westernized part of him not truly himself.

According to the people interviewed, the *ibn al-balad* is gay, jovial of spirit and possesses an acute sense of humor. He lives for the moment and is heedless of the morrow; he lacks foresight and tends to be fatalistic in his attitude towards life's events. He is generous and hospitable; he is deeply loyal to his kin and neighbors and is always there to help when needed. He is ready to share with others both their joys and their sorrows. He is very quick, intelligent and *debrouillard,* but he lacks discipline and meticulousness, while his sense of time is hopeless. He is deeply empathic and can easily adjust to the demands of a social situation. As some have described it, "he speaks to everyone in his own language." He has respect for tradition and is ceremonious in his social behavior.

The *ibn al-balad* possesses two complex traits: *shahāma* and *fahlawa. Shahāma* is a combination of a number of the qualities just cited; it is a compound of gallantry, nobility, boldness, generosity and manliness. *Fahlawa* on the other hand implies sharpness, shrewdness and social adaptability. Hamid 'Ammār describes *fahlawa* as the capacity for quick adaptation that requires suppleness, alertness and readiness to adjust to novel situations and ideas, although it can also refer to a superficial acquiescence and a surface politeness used to cover up real feelings (*9,* p. 81). A *fahlawī* is also someone who can bluff his way to attain his own ends but who may overplay his hand to his own detriment.

The Egyptian as an Arab

How is the Egyptian, with his strong sense of Egyptian identity, able to look on himself as an Arab, too? Before answering this question, the term "Arab" must first be defined. In its earliest usage the word is applied either to the nomadic Bedouin or, more generally, to the inhabitants of the Arabian peninsula. Both usages relate to what was essentially the same "racial" group, for the inhabitants of the towns and villages of pre-Islamic and immediately post-Islamic Arabia consisted almost entirely of sedentarized Bedouin. When, in the seventh century, the Arab armies emerged from Arabia on their fantastic path of conquest, they were still largely organized and led as tribal units, but fighting under the unifying banner of Islam. As such, they were the bearers not only of a dynamic monotheistic faith, but also of an ancient culture and a mutually accepted system of values.

On their borders with Syria, Palestine and Iraq, the Arabs encountered peoples of Arab stock and Arabic language, who were the product of earlier population movements out of Arabia. In such cases, conqueror and conquered were readily merged. Elsewhere, they met people of non-Arab stock possessing ancient cultures, such as the Greco-Aramaic people in Syria, the Sassanian in Iraq and the Berber in North Africa. These held out a little longer against the tide of Arabism, but within the space of three generations they too had adopted the language, mores and, for the most part, the religion of their conquerors. The Arab world today, stretching from Morocco in the west, through North Africa and including the Arabian Peninsula and the Fertile Crescent, consists of countries whose inhabitants have remained dominated ever since by these same social and cultural influences.

As a result of the expansion and cultural assimilation by the Arab armies, the connotation of the word "Arab" changed: It is no longer used solely to denote a member of the nomad tribes who peopled the Arabian Peninsula. It gradually came to mean a citizen of that extensive Arab world—not any inhabitant of it, but the great majority whose racial descent, even when it was not of pure Arab lineage, had become submerged in the tide of arabisation; whose manners and traditions have been shaped in an Arab mould; and most decisive of all, whose mother tongue is Arabic (*10,* p. 18). Arabization, then, meant the diffusion of a set of cultural patterns and values which the people who have been Arabized are aware of sharing. I propose now to examine some of the elements which generate this sense of Arab cultural affinity, with particular reference to Egypt and the Egyptians. At the time of the Arab Conquest (639–641), Egypt was a province of Byzantium; it was Greco-Roman in culture, Christian in religion, Greek and Coptic in language. Within fifty years Arabic had replaced Greek as the official language, with Coptic confined to liturgical use. The spread of Islam was slower, but by the beginning of the ninth century, the Muslims were in the majority and the churches were being turned into mosques (*73,* IV, p. 24).

The fact that Egypt is an Islamic country—indeed, plays a leading role in the Islamic world—obviously produces a sense of cultural affinity with respect to the other Arab Islamic countries. But the bases for that affinity are more subtle and permeating than such a simple statement indicates. Islam tends to induce cultural similarities among its adherents that transcend the religious observances and beliefs. The broad cultural impact of Islam arises from the comprehensiveness of Islamic beliefs, statements and injunctions, which cover not only man's relationship to God, but also to his fellow men. This comprehensiveness has been given explicit expression through the medium of the *Qur'ān* and the *sharī'a* the corpus of Islamic law. Although it no longer applies in totality in any Islamic country, the *sharī'a* law, which was developed by jurists from the *Qur'ān* and the Prophetic traditions, has helped to impose a stamp of similitude upon Arab Islamic cultures. Islamic law, in its traditional formulation, covered every action of the individual, secular as well as religious; it regulated and conditioned all aspects of life. Thus the basis of Islamic law is not legal but ethical (*28,* p. 114). As such, it postulates certain norms of behavior governed by set moral values. Thus, whole areas of social behavior, including patterns of family relationships, the attitude to elders, social greetings, and social obligations such as mutual help, benevolence, and charity, stem from injunctional elements in the religion. These norms will be shared by other Muslims, so that the Egyptian, for example, finds in Iraq or Morocco behavioral patterns and beliefs which are familiar facets of his own culture.

As Antonius has emphasized, a further basis of affinity between Arabs, and an important vehicle for the diffusion of ideas, is the Arabic language. Dialect differences exist and are extreme among various Arab groups. Without the *Qur'ān* to keep alive a uniform base of purest Arabic to aspire to, there is no doubt that Arabic would have fragmented into regional forms, as the Romance languages did. By perpetuating a community of language the *Qur'ān* kept alive a community of culture—a process which was reinforced by the use of the *Qur'ān* as a basic teaching text throughout the Arab world. The net result has been the development of a lingua franca which enables all Arabs to communicate with one another. We also find among the Arabs an almost mystical regard for the Arabic language. The Egyptian, like other Arabs, responds readily to oratory and verbal felicity, to which Arabic lends itself, because of the richness of its vocabulary and because of its morphological structure, which encourages the euphonic use of words. This reverence for the Arabic language transcends sectarian considerations so that one finds an Egyptian Copt such as Makram Ebeid acknowledging that his powerful oratory owed much to the study of the *Qur'ān.* Similarly, we find that the Syrian and Lebanese Christians, who were involved in the infant Arab nationalist movement in the Levant towards the end of the nineteenth century, took great pride in the Arabic language which, in fact, made acceptable the Islamic coloring of Arabism.

As with the Arabic language, pride in Arab history is an important element in generating a sense of affinity among Arabs. Egyptians, like other Arabs, identify with the great figures of the Arab past. The clemency of Abū Bakr, the noble self-effacement of 'Umar, the intrepitude of Khālid Ibn al-Walīd, the glitter of Hārūn al-Rashīd, the chivalry of Saladin—these are not simply historical personalities, but ideal types. Gibb has rightly stressed the importance of pride in Arab history as a central point in feeling oneself to be an Arab. This identification with an Arab past also expresses itself powerfully in popular culture. Egyptian folk lore is studded with Arabian themes, such as the ill-starred lovers of antiquity—Qays and Lubnā and Majnūn Laylā—who died of unrequited love. Such Bedouin heroes of antiquity as 'Antar and Abū Zayd al-Hilālī, were among the most popular themes in the oral mass culture of Egypt until the advent of radio and television. They were the stock in trade of the professional storyteller in the coffee houses and were presented as a melange of poetry and prose, to the accompaniment of the single-stringed fiddle. The contemporary writer, Neguib Mahfouz, opens his novel Zuqāq al-Midaqq with a moving account of a blind ballad singer, specializing in these Arabian sagas, being forced to leave a coffee house when a radio was installed.

Many aspects noted in the last section of the idealized Egyptian concept of self seem to have been influenced by ancient Arabian values, transmitted and kept alive by tales of Arab chivalry. To the Egyptian, the image of the Arab is a glorified one, embodying the virtues of *muruwwa* (manliness), including courage, fierce loyalty to one's kind, clemency towards and consideration for others, and a generosity and hospitality which border on the flamboyant.

Egyptianization has meant the rehabilitation of the Arabic language, not simply as the official language of administration and government, but more importantly as the language of instruction in schools and universities. The result has been an increased tempo of Arabization, for facility in the Arabic language opened windows onto the rich legacy of Arabic culture. The new emphasis on the study of the historical roots of Egyptian society inevitably entailed classes in Arab-Islamic history, which in terms of present Arab-Egyptian culture, is more directly relevant than pre-Islamic and Pharaonic history. The study of literature, however, included the totality of Arab literature, reaching back to the literary legacy of pre-Islamic Arabia. As a result, within the last fifty years, Egyptian literature has reflected an increasing preoccupation with Arab themes. Even within the writings of a single author, such as Taha Hussein or Tewfik El Hakim, it is possible to trace the change from a preoccupation with Pharaonic or Classical themes to Arab ones. Thus, in seeking a cultural identity, Egypt has revived its Arab cultural heritage.

Relatively recent political and economic developments have caused the Egyptians to become increasingly conscious of their own identification as Arabs. In an earlier period the word "Arab" was often used in Egypt to designate the Bedouins living on the fringes of the Nile valley, as well as the Arabs of Arabia and the Levant. More recently, Egyptians have come to refer to themselves as Arabs. In recent decades, political leaders in Arab countries have made a conscious effort to build on the existing cultural affinities and common historical experience, to create a political and economic unity. As an expression of this effort, Egypt has changed its official name to the United Arab Republic, and the Egyptian constitution today speaks of "the Arab nation."

The creation of Israel and the subsequent Arab-Israeli conflict, while generating great tensions in the area, has given rise to a stronger sense of collective Arab identity. A common enemy cannot fail to create a common response and a sense of common purpose. Furthermore, the usual reference to the problem in the mass media as the "Arab-Israeli conflict," without differentiating between the various Arab states involved, may be partly responsible for the increasing readiness of Egyptians to regard themselves as Arabs.

Since World War II, Egyptians have come into much closer contact with the other Arab countries. This interaction is the result of the great degree of consciously generated interaction between the newly independent Arab nations, but it is also attributable to economic and social development in the last quarter of a century. The effort of these countries toward development has created an urgent need for technicians, teachers and specialists of all kinds. This is particularly so in the case of the oil-rich countries, which had so far remained relatively isolated and underdeveloped. Egypt, with its resources of manpower, has stepped in to meet the need. Thousands of Egyptian teachers, technicians and professional men have travelled and worked in other Arab countries. This is itself an interesting phenomenon, for the Egyptian has traditionally been closely tied to his own country and been reluctant to leave it. Such movement of trained personnel has brought about interaction between Egyptians and other Arabs, reversing the trend toward compartmentalization in the Arab world, a trend that has been strengthened by the ease and speed of modern travel and the effectiveness of the mass media. The latter are helping to diffuse ideas and to standardize taste in various parts of the Arab world. Books, magazines, films and radio programs are understood and have currency throughout the area. Egyptian films are shown everywhere, so that an artist like Umm Kulthum can acquire a stature which is not so much Egyptian as Arab, for the entire Arab world, from Morocco to Iraq, listens to her daily program. In fact, at many levels, from popular mass culture to the esoteric, a greater degree of "cultural consanguinity" is being created among the Arab nations.

REFERENCES

1. 'Abd al-Raziq, Mustafa. *al-Durr al-Mukhtār fī tanwīr al-aksār.* Cairo, 1944.
2. Abdel Nasser, G. "The Egyptian Revolution." *Foreign Affairs,* 33, 1955-56.
3. Abdel Nasser, G. *The Philosophy of the Revolution.* Cairo, n.d.
4. Abdel Nasser, G. *Speeches and Press Interviews, 1958.* Cairo, n.d.
5. Abdel Nasser, G. *Speeches and Press Interviews, 1959.* Cairo, n.d.
6. Ahmed, J. M. *The Intellectual Origins of Egyptian Nationalism.* London: 1960.
7. Amin, Aḥmad. *Qāmūs al-Ādāt wa'l-taqālīd wa'l-ta'ābīr al-Miṣrīya.* Cairo, 1953.
8. Ammar, Ḥamed. *Growing up in an Egyptian Village.* London, 1954.
9. Ammar, Hamed. *Fī binā'al-bashar* (in Arabic). Cairo, 1964.
10. Antonius, George. *The Arab Awakening.* London, 1945.
11. Arnold, Thomas, and Guillaume, Alfred, eds. *The Legacy of Islam.* Oxford, 1931.
12. Baer, Gabriel. "Social Change in Egypt 1800-1914." In *Political and Social Change in Modern Egypt,* edited by P. M. Holt. London, 1968.
13. Berger, M. *Bureaucracy and Society in Modern Egypt.* Princeton, 1957.
14. Boktor, Amir. *Development and Expansion of Education in the U.A.R.* Cairo, 1963.

15. Central Agency for Public Mobilization and Statistics. *Statistical Handbook, 1952-1966.* Cairo, 1967.

16. Charles-Roux, F. *Bonaparte: Governor of Egypt.* London, 1937.

17. Colombe, M. *L'Evolution de l'Egypte, 1924-50.* Paris, 1951.

18. Coon, Carleton S. *Caravan: The Story of the Middle East.* New York, 1951.

19. Crouchley, A. E. *The Economic Development of Modern Egypt.* New York, 1938.

20. Dickson, H. R. P. *The Arab of the Desert.* London, 1949.

21. Dodwell, H. *The Founder of Modern Egypt: A Study of Muhammad 'Ali Pasha of Cairo.* Cambridge, 1931.

22. Elgood, P. G. *Bonaparte's Adventure in Egypt.* London, 1931.

23. Enan, Moḥamed Abdulla. *Ta'rīkh al-Jāmi' al-Azhar* (in Arabic). Cairo, 1958.

24. Faḥmy, Moustapha. *La Révolution de l'Industrie en Égypte et ses Consequences Sociales au 19ème Siècle.* Leiden, 1954.

25. Faris, N. A. and Husayn, M. T. *Hadha 'l-'alam al-'Arabī* (in Arabic). Beirut, 1953.

26. Gadalla, Saad M. *Land Reform in Relation to Social Development Egypt.* Missouri, 1962.

27. Gibb, H. A. R. *The Arabs.* Oxford, 1944.

28. Gibb, H. A. R. and Bowen, Harold. *Islamic Society and the West.* Oxford University Press, 1957.

29. Goldschmidt, Arthur, Jr. "The Egyptian Nationalist Party: 1892-1919." In *Political and Social Change in Modern Egypt,* edited by P. M. Holt. London, 1968.

30. Goldziher, Ignaz. *Muslim Studies I.* London, 1967.

31. Grohmann, Adolf. *"al-'Arab." Encyclopaedia of Islam,* new ed.

32. Ḥamady, Sania. *Temperament and Character of the Arabs.* New York, 1960.

33. Harby, Moḥamed Khayri, and El Azzawi, El Sayed Moḥamed Moḥamed. *Education in Egypt (U.A.R.) in the 20th Century.* Cairo, 1960.

34. Heyworth-Dunne, J. *Introduction to the History of Education in Modern Egypt.* London, 1938.

35. Holt, P. M., ed. *Political and Social Change in Modern Egypt.* London, 1968.

36. Hourani, Albert. *Arabic Thought in the Liberal Age.* Oxford, 1962.

37. al-Husri, Sati'. *'Arā' wa aḥādīth fi'l qawmīya al-'arabīya* (in Arabic). Cairo, 1957.

38. al-Husri, Sati'. *al-'Urūba bayn du'ātihā wa mu 'aridīhā* (in Arabic). Beirut, 1957.

39. U.A.R. Information Department. *Eleven Years of Progress and Development, 1952-1963.* Cairo, 1963.

40. U.A.R. Information Department. *The Charter.* Cairo, n.d.

41. Issawi, Charles. *Egypt: An Economic and Social Analysis.* London, 1947.

42. Issawi, Charles. *Egypt in Revolution.* London, 1963.

43. Issawi, Charles. *Egypt at Mid-Century: An Economic Survey.* London, 1954.

44. al-Jabartī, 'Abd al-Rahman. *Ta'rīkh al-Jabartī.* Cairo, 1958.

45. Kedourie, Elie. "The Genesis of the Egyptian Constitution of 1923." In *Political and Social Change in Modern Egypt,* edited by P. M. Holt. London, 1968.

46. Lacouture, Jean and Simone. *Egypt in Transition.* London, 1956.

47. Landes, David. *Bankers and Pashas, International Finance and Economic Imperialism in Egypt.* Cambridge, Mass., 1958.

48. Lane, E. W. *Manners and Customs of the Modern Egyptians.* London, 1908.

49. Levy, R. *The Social Structure of Islam.* Cambridge, 1965.

50. Lewis, Bernard. *The Arabs in History.* London, 1954.

51. Little, Tom. *Egypt.* London, 1958.

52. Marçais, George. "al-'Arab." *Encyclopaedia of Islam,* new ed.

53. Marei, Sayed. *Agrarian Reform in Egypt.* Cairo, 1957.

54. el Messiri, Sawsan. "The Concept of Ibn al-balad." Unpublished thesis, 1970.

55. Nicholson, Reynold A. *A Literary History of the Arabs.* London, 1923.

56. Radwan, Abū Al-Fūtouh Aḥmad. *Old and New Forces in Egyptian Education.* Columbia University, 1951.

57. al-Rāfi'ī, 'Abd al-Raḥmān. *'Aṣr Ismā'īl* (in Arabic). Cairo, 1948.

58. al-Rāfi'ī, 'Abd al-Raḥmān. *Ta'rīkh al-harakat al-qawmīya.* Cairo, 1944.

59. al-Rāfi'ī, 'Abd al-Raḥmān. *'Aṣr Muḥammad 'Alī.* Cairo, 1951.

60. Rifaat, Moḥamed. *The Awakening of Modern Egypt.* London, 1947.

61. Safran, N. *Egypt in Search of Political Community.* Cambridge, Mass., 1961.

62. Shaw, Stanford J. *The Financial and Administrative Organization and Development of Ottoman Egypt, 1517-1798.* Princeton, 1962.

63. el-Shayyal, Gamal El Din. "Some Aspects of Intellectual and Social Life in Eighteenth Century Egypt." In *Political and Social Change in Modern Egypt,* edited by P. M. Holt. London, 1968.

64. al-Tahṭāwī, Rifā'a. *Manāhij al-albāb al-Misrīya* (in Arabic). Cairo, 1912.

65. al-Tahṭāwī, Rifā'a. *al-Murshid al-amīn li'l-banāt wa'l banīn* (in Arabic). Cairo, 1872.

66. Tignor, Robert L. *Modernization and British Colonial Rule in Egypt, 1882-1914.* Princeton, 1966.

67. Tomiche, Nada. "Notes sur la Hiérarchie sociale en Égypte à l'époque de Muḥammad 'Alī." In *Political and Social Change in Modern Egypt,* edited by P. M. Holt. London, 1958.

68. 'Urābi, Ahmad. *Kashf al-sitār 'an sirr al-asrār* (in Arabic). Cairo, n.d.

69. Vatikiotis, P. J. *History of Modern Egypt.* New York, 1969.

70. Von Grunebaum, G. E. *Islam.* Wisconsin, 1955.

71. Wahida, Subhi. *Fī usūl al-mas'alat al-Misrīya* (in Arabic). Cairo, 1950.

72. Warriner, Doreen. *Land Reform and Development in the Middle East.* London, 1962.

73. Wiet, Gaston. *Histoire de la Nation Égyptienne.* Paris, 1937.

74. Young, George. *Egypt.* London, 1927.

75. Zayid, Mahmud. "The Origins of the Liberal Constitutionalist Party in Egypt." In *Political and Social Change in Modern Egypt,* edited by P. M. Holt. London, 1968.

76. Zurayq, C. D. *al-Wa'ī al-qawmī* (in Arabic). Beirut, 1938.

Problems of Cultural Identity in Modern Japan

HIROSHI WAGATSUMA

12

Japan was the first non-Western country to become an industrialized nation. This was accomplished within a surprisingly short period of time, following 1868, in the wake of three hundred years of feudalism and isolation. Since the end of World War II in 1945, Japan has again accomplished a miraculous industrial recovery within a short time. Japan today is the only country in Asia that has a fully developed modern society, constituting the third largest industrial complex in the entire world. From this industrial accomplishment, however, arises an important question the Japanese must answer—the question of national purpose, or cultural identity, individual and collective.

One of the characteristics of Japan's modern history from 1868 to 1945, and one of the themes that runs through this period, is that Japan, first overwhelmed and threatened by the Western powers, attempted to become as powerful as, or even stronger than, the major Western nations and to act like one of them. In the years following 1868 Japan transformed herself from a tiny feudal country into an industrialized nation by learning from the West. A second wave of Westernization (or, more specifically, Americanization) occurred from the mid-1920s to the mid-1930s. At this time not only Western technology, but also liberal democratic ideas and even American music, movies and fashions left their impact on urban Japanese. Then came the war.

After her defeat Japan found herself once again learning "lessons of democracy" from her American teachers during the Occupation. As a result of the mass media, the impact of American culture was unprecedented. Things American flooded Japanese society. With the end of the Occupation the flood began to subside. Recent political, diplomatic and economic developments indicate an increase of nationalistic feelings. Intellectual and political leaders both appear to be grappling continuously with the problem of relating national purpose and cultural pride to present economic affluence.

This problem was first recognized by Japanese intellectuals soon after Japan had begun its vigorous efforts to "Westernize herself in order to resist the West" (*42*). Japanese intellectuals struggled to escape from their "historical predicament" (*43*), the conflict between national pride and the desire for cultural borrowing; in short, the need to be both modern and Japanese. The Japanese tried to settle by a series of wars the problems of their cultural identity by defining a unique Japanese political order and social morality superior to those of the West. It was an impossible task, and it ended with Japan's disastrous defeat. Then came the "cultural colonization" (*42*) during the post-war Occupation that shattered once and for all not only the militarism and ultra-nationalism, but everything that appeared to be associated with it, namely, Japanese tradition itself.

Amid economic affluence the hundred-year-old question seems to remain largely unanswered, and the dilemma unresolved. How can we become Westernized and yet remain Japanese? What is it that makes the Japanese uniquely Japanese, and that they can be proud of? Japanese intellectuals are still trying to find some meaningful way of relating the past to the present and future, but apparently without much success.

One finds no easy answer to the questions of how Westernized Japan is and to what degree the Japanese have become like Westerners in their mode of thought and world view. Japanese intellectuals disagree about a future course of action for Japan, and this disagreement seems to derive from differences among them concerning the degree of Westernization that they perceive in Japan. Some see their country and people as too Westernized and are indignant, while others feel confident that Japanese culture remains basically unaffected and unchanged. Regardless of degree, it is a fact that certain sectors of contemporary Japanese life *are* Westernized.

Although not limited to Japan, fads and fashions in dress, music and the arts come directly from American and European cities, arriving in Japanese cities perhaps more quickly than they reach corners of rural America and Europe. Well-known books by Western intellectuals, particularly Americans such as Herbert Marcuse or Peter Drucker, are quickly translated (or mistranslated) into Japanese and avidly read by white collar workers in overcrowded commuter trains. In television commercials two-thirds or more of the words used for brand names and descriptions of products are English or French, although such words are systematically mispronounced so that they fit into the Japanese phonological system, a process that renders them quite incomprehensible to speakers of English or French. Some linguists estimate that a Japanese needs to know about 2,200 foreign words for ordinary daily conversation, and about 3,000 additional words to engage in sophisticated discourse. This means that a Japanese intellectual is expected to know more than five thousand foreign words. This is a large number when one recalls that there is a total of 5,642 words in the Old Testament, and 4,800 in the New Testament.

The number of "words of foreign origin" (*gairai-go*) included in Japanese dictionaries published at different times in Japan's modern history indicates a definite increase in words which first came into Japanese as "foreign words" (*gaikoku-go*) and were eventually adopted. In a dictionary published in 1889, of the total of 39,104 words, 551 (1.4 percent) were words of foreign origin. In a 1956 dictionary, of the total of 40,393 words, 1,428 (3.5 percent) were of foreign origin. In a third dictionary, published in 1963, of the total of 57,000 words 2,918 (5.1 percent) are of foreign origin. It should be noted that the number of these words of foreign origin in the dictionaries gives no indication of their frequency in conversation and writing at the time, because only after a foreign word is used frequently and long enough (although there does not seem to be any standard for measuring such frequency and duration), is a word considered adopted into Japanese and included in a dictionary. This is particularly the case in recent times, when dictionaries can hardly keep up with the foreign words that are constantly flowing into the country, or are sometimes even being invented by the Japanese themselves. The mass media are much less conservative than dictionaries in using these lexical borrowings.

One can also point out the "conceptual Westernization" of Japanese academic theory. For example, in most of the recent writings by Japanese social psychologists a variable "Japan" is characteristically lacking. They do not pay enough attention to the social psychological reality that is uniquely Japanese, but tend to be satisfied with Western theories which are, after all, based upon Western psychological reality, not necessarily directly applicable to Japan (Wagatsuma:1969).

"Westernization" is also found in what one might call the sexual esthetics of the Japanese. As analyzed elsewhere in detail (*61, 63, 64*) prior to any sustained contact with the Caucasoid Europeans, the Japanese valued white skin as beautiful and depreciated "black" (actually, suntanned) skin as ugly. With the introduction of Western technology and values in 1868, the Japanese perception of feminine beauty also began to change. Although they noted with admiration the white skin of the Westerners, they found the hair color and the hairiness of the Caucasians distasteful. Wavy hair was not attractive to the Japanese until the mid-1920s, for curly hair was considered characteristic of animals. During the second peak of Westernization in the 1920s and 1930s the Japanese, especially those in cities, adopted Western customs and fashions, including singing American popular songs and dancing in dance halls. They watched motion pictures with delight, and made great favorites of Clara Bow, Gloria Swanson and Greta Garbo. Motion pictures seem to have had a strong effect in finally changing hair styles and notions of beauty. During this period, many Japanese women had their hair cut, and in spite of the exhortations of proud samurai, had it waved and curled. They took to wearing long skirts with large hats to emulate the clothes worn by Greta Garbo. Anything Western was considered modern, and therefore superior. This trend lasted until the mid-1930s when, under the pressure of the ultra-nationalist militarist regime, the ties with Western fads and fashions were systematically broken. On the other hand, the subtle, almost unconscious trend toward an idealization of Western physical features apparently became of increasing importance in the 1920s. It remained, it seems, a hidden undercurrent throughout the last war, when Japan, as the "champion" of the Asian nations, fought against the whites. The rapidity with which Western standards of beauty became idealized after the war attests to the continuous drift that was occurring in spite of ten years of antagonism and military hostilities.

In the post-war flood of things American the standard of beauty also went through a drastic change. The straight black hair of the past is all but gone. Even most *geisha,* the preservers of many feminine traditions, have permanents and wave their hair, resorting to wigs when they appear at parties that require the traditional hairdo and kimono. Among other women one periodically sees extreme examples of bleached hair, although this is no longer as frequent as it was during and just after the Occupation. Many more women have their hair dyed a purplish or reddish hue. Some young girls even buy blond and brunette wigs. Plastic surgery, especially to alter eye folds and to build up the bridge of the nose, has become standard practice among movie actors and actresses and also among many ordinary people. Japanese women also attempt to increase the actual or apparent size of their breasts by surgery or by wearing padded brassieres. These various attempts among younger Japanese, and among women in particular, to alter their physical appearance suggest that the Caucasian standard of beauty and sexual attractiveness became the standard for the Japanese.

Japanese attitudes toward the physical features of the Caucasians, however, are more complicated. Interviews with present-day Japanese men and women seem to indicate that their attitudes toward the skin of Caucasians fall into opposites of likes and dislikes. These two opposite attitudes may coexist within an individual, either appearing alternately or being expressed simultaneously. Caucasian skin may be considered inferior to that of the Japanese because it is rough in texture, with many wrinkles, blemishes and furrows, whereas Japanese skin is smooth, tight and resilient, with far fewer spots and speckles. Most of the Japanese, however, admit that the Caucasian facial and body structure is more attractive than the "flat face" and "less shapely body" of the Japanese. This attitude has been discussed by intellectuals. For instance, the ethnologist Ishida wondered "if it is not true that the idea, or the complex, that Westerners are superior to the Japanese in regard to physique and appearance always existed in the subconscious of the average Japanese *after 1868*" (*14*). Aida, a professor of French history, is of the same opinion: "too many discourses among us Japanese that discourage the attention to one's external appearance might be a reflection of our preoccupation with our appearance . . . and I think this proves that we have inferiority feelings about our ugly appearance and are hypersensitive to it" (*1*). This attitude—maintaining a Japanese "skin supremacy" while at the same time admitting the desirability of the Caucasian facial and body structures—is exemplified by a widely held notion that a Eurasian child will be very attractive if it takes the Japanese parent's skin and the Caucasian parent's bone structure, but that the result of the opposite combination could be disastrous.

It seems that Japanese men, especially those over forty years of age, tend to be concerned more with the skin texture of a Japanese woman than with the measurement of her bust and hips, while Western men will first think of the shape of a woman rather than her skin texture. One might say that the Japanese man's taste with respect to sexual esthetics has traditionally been "surface-oriented," whereas the Western man's is "structure-oriented." Among the younger generation, however, structure-orientation is quickly replacing surface-orientation, as the popularity of plastic surgery amply exemplifies. Here one notices the Westernization, or more specifically the "Caucasianization," of the sexual esthetics of the Japanese.

Positive attitudes toward Caucasian skin center on the idea that it is, in actuality, whiter than the so-called white skin of the Japanese, and therefore more attractive. Many Japanese men, especially those in the United States, admit the beauty of white skin in Caucasian women, but also point out the sense of the inaccessibility of Caucasian women. For most Japanese without much personal contact with Westerners skin is only one of several characteristics making up the image of a Caucasian. Other components of this image are the shape and color of the eyes, the hair color, and the height, size and weight and hairiness of the body. The image of a Caucasian with white skin, deep-set eyes, wavy hair of a color other than black, a tall, stout, hairy body, with large hands and feet, seems to evoke in many Japanese an association with vitality, superior energy, strong sexuality or even animality, and the feeling that Caucasians are basically discontinuous with Asians. This attitude of ambivalence toward Westerners is found in mixed feelings of admiration, envy, fear or disgust, and the sense of being overwhelmed or threatened that are evoked in the Japanese mind by the image of a hairy giant whose great vigor and strong sexuality can easily satisfy an equally energetic and glamorous Caucasian female.

Although most Japanese may not be aware of the "Caucasianization" of their sexual esthetics, when one looks through the pages of those women's magazines which show the newest fashions, one often sees Caucasian models posing on the first pages, followed by pictures of either Eurasian models (or models whose make-up makes them look like Eurasians), with clearly Japanese girls appearing only on the last pages.

Such trends have certainly invited criticism from intellectuals. Particularly among the older generation one observes dissatisfaction and irritation with "too much Westernization." For example, Takeo Kuwabara, a professor of French literature at the University of Kyoto and a prolific writer, used bitter words in criticizing the Japanese preoccupation with things Western:

> I want the Japanese to be more proud of themselves as modern people (*kindai-jin*) with human dignity and individual rights. The Japanese should have "guts" (*konjō*) as a nation. They should stop worshipping foreign countries and stop regretting that Japan never had the same history as the West. . . . I detest the indiscriminate use of too many English words. . . . I detest the tendency to translate into Japanese Western books of a third rate quality, or to quote from them in academic articles. . . . All Japanese keep facing toward Tokyo, and all the people in and around Tokyo keep looking toward New York, Paris, or Moscow. Somewhere in their minds the Japanese harbor a hidden wish to have the color of their skin changed into white, and would pray before a "skin whitening shrine" (*iro naoshi jinja*) if such a shrine existed. However, the only real way possible for Japanese to become respectable is to keep their yellow faces (*29*).

In October 1969 the PHP Institute, headed by Konosuke Matsushita who is chairman of the Matsushita Electric (Panasonic) Industrial Company and a most influential man in Japan's business world, published a special issue of its monthly journal with the subtitle, "Thinking about Japan" (*Nippon o kangaeru*). As of April 1970 it had sold 200,000 copies. All seven articles, including one by Matsushita, criticized contemporary Japan for being only a prosperous "economic animal" and urged a restoration of pride in the nation's traditional culture. Matsushita wrote:

> Since the end of the war we have been preoccupied with the recon-

> struction and development of the material aspects of our society, and have hardly reflected upon our state of mind. The autonomy of a nation is based on its traditions. In contemporary Japan our traditions have been all but ignored, and even replaced by the customs and thoughts of foreign lands. Those who grow up in present day Japan are no longer Japanese but a group of people without selves and without self-confidence . . . We must become clearly aware of our being Japanese, and, keeping this basic awareness, we must adopt and digest both Eastern and Western thought and by so doing make ourselves and our country better and richer

Where should the Japanese look to find self-confidence? Yoshishige Ashiwara, president of the Kwansai Electric Company, stresses that Japanese should be proud of their "loyalty to their company," "solidarity between labor and management," and "the traditional diligence"—the characteristics that form "the strength of Japanese industry which most Western industries cannot imitate" (5). A cynic may indeed wonder if he is not teaching pride to an "economic animal." Shun'ichi Kase, once a well-known diplomat and now the president of a publishing company[1], accused contemporary Japan of being in *gyōki mappō no yo* (a Buddhistic term meaning "last degenerate days") in which no "spiritual prosperity accompanies economic success," and emphasized, among other things, the importance of "the spirit of the tea ceremony" (*17*). Masataka Kosaka, a Kyoto professor of international relations and an active commentator on world politics, suggests that the Japanese emphasize again the importance of the old politeness and etiquette (*25*).

Such simplistic advice does not work (and one might even wonder if the writers themselves did not know it), because they do not address themselves to the complicated nature of modern Japanese culture. The masses in Japan could perhaps be advised to stop receiving plastic surgery, and one day they might actually stop doing it. But the mass of Japanese people also know that they are Japanese and nobody else. The problem of cultural identity, to which this paper is addressing itself, is *not* the problem of ethnic or group identity and does not concern most of the Japanese. In spite of plastic surgery Japanese know very well, perhaps too well, who they are and especially *who they are not.* For the Japanese, group identity is an assured given. They tend to believe that there is a greater degree of physical homogeneity among themselves than actually exists. They tend to believe that they look uniquely alike, and always look different from other Asians. In the Japanese mind only those born of Japanese parents are Japanese—nobody can *become* a Japanese.

[1] The PHP Institute was founded in November 1946, and began publishing its monthly magazine in April 1947. "PHP" stands for "Peace and Happiness through Prosperity." The magazine, with the same title, contains essays, articles and short stories. It sells approximately 1.5 million copies every month.

However, the problem of cultural identity, or the matter of pride in things Japanese, has deeper and more difficult historical problems behind it, and this is what the Japanese intellectuals have been concerned with.

Early in the nineteenth century Japan began feeling the threat around her shores of the expanding Western powers, and soon her nearly three hundred years of peaceful isolation came to an end. By the turn of the century, the Russians had begun exploring the Kurile Islands and Sakhalien. They came to Nagasaki in 1804 for trading, and when refused they began to enter the Kurile Islands and even Hokkaido freely. English ships came to Uraga in 1818 for trading. In 1837 an American ship, the *Morrison,* tried to enter the ports of Uraga and then Yamakawa (in Kyushu), but was driven away by Japanese cannons. French naval ships came to the Ryukyus in 1846.

Many Japanese of high status in the ruling warrior class were ignorant of the world situation and Western civilization, and, confident of their mythical superiority over the hairy barbarians, did not want the Westerners to bother them by coming to their "sacred land." However, many others, especially those later instrumental in the eventual overthrow of the Tokugawa feudal regime, understood such Western approaches as a grave threat to Japan's political security. Because they were aware of what was happening to the rest of Asia (for example, to China after the Opium War of 1842) these knowledgeable scholars, critical of the government's ineffectual and inadequate policies, warned against Western threats and proposed a nationwide campaign for the defense of the country.

This sense of crisis toward the end of the Tokugawa feudal era was expressed in two contrasting forms, the first one based on a recognition of the material superiority of Western civilization and of the necessity to learn from it in order to maintain Japan's political independence, and the second one was based upon the recognition of fundamental differences between Japanese and Western civilizations and of the necessity to reject the Western influences in order to maintain Japan's cultural autonomy. The followers of the first line of thought emphasized that Japan should open herself up to the West and were called *kaikoku-ha ("the open country wing").* Those who followed the second line of thought insisted that Japan drive the Westerners away, and were called *joi-ha* ("the expulsionist wing"). It might be that the *kaikoku-ha* was more realistic and practical, whereas the *joi-ha* was more proud and/or ignorant. In any case, however, both groups, in spite of the fierce and often bloody battling between them, shared the same goal—Japan's survival in the face of the Western threat.

After the visit of Commodore Perry's "black ships" to Uraga in 1853, the Tokugawa government changed its policy from "expulsion of the barbarians" to "opening up the country." After complicated changes of alliances among the lords and among the anti-government forces, and after battles and bloodshed, the Tokugawa regime was finally overthrown in 1867. The Meiji emperor was restored to the throne, and the building of a new modern nation was begun under those who were anti-Tokugawa, some of whom had been for the "expulsion of the barbarians" and others of whom had advocated "opening up the country." All these young leaders agreed on the clear goal of making their country as rich and powerful as the Western countries so that Japan would not become a foreign colony of the West. Most of the leaders were ex-samurai, and they were sensitive to the grave threats which the Western powers posed to Japan's independence and autonomy. They focused their efforts upon the building of "a rich nation and a strong army" (*fukoku kyohei*). The first major objective in their foreign policy was to remove the blemish of unequal treaties, thereby attaining complete independence and equity with the Western powers. Toward this end the Japanese leaders decided to learn and adopt from the West whatever was necessary for building a modern country and to "civilize and enlighten" (*bunmei kaika*) the nation, with the Western countries as the model.

Some intellectual leaders even advocated the "physical" Westernization of the nation. Arinori Mori, later to become the first Minister of Education, was in the United States in 1871 as Japan's first ambassador, at the age of 24. He expressed his opinion that the Japanese students in the United States should marry American women and bring them home so as to produce physically and mentally stronger children (*37*). In 1883 a book proposed that the Japanese should import women from the West and marry them, in order to produce "racially superior offsprings" (*51*, pp. 38-39). Incredible as it may sound today the Prime Minister, Prince Hirobumi Ito, took this proposition seriously enough to write a letter to Herbert Spencer asking for his opinion. Around the same time, a newspaper article advised that the Japanese eat more meat and drink more milk. "Japanese are intellectually smart by nature, but, unlike the Westerners, they lack persistence and tenacity," said an article. "Japanese lack persistence and tenacity because they do not eat beef and drink milk. . . . Cows are stupid animals but they are persistent and tenacious. Those who eat their meat and drink their milk become persistent and tenacious like cows" (*24*). As a matter of fact, Emperor Meiji, setting up a model for the nation, had begun drinking milk twice a day in 1871, and in 1872 the Imperial family had started eating meat regularly (*47*).

Generally speaking, however, it is hard to believe that most of the Meiji leaders were genuine admirers of Western civilization and particularly of Westerners. Rather, they decided to learn from the West out of sheer practical consideration. They believed that Japan had to become like a Western country because that was the only way to survive—a lesson they had learned from the experiences of India, China and Southeast Asia. Such basic attitudes among the Meiji leaders are clearly summarized in an essay, "Getting Out of Asia" (*Datsu-a Ron*), written in 1885 by Yukichi Fukuzawa, the most influential opinion leader of the time. Fukuzawa emphasized that, in order to survive among the Western powers, Japan had to "get out of Asia" and act like one of the Western powers, even to the extent of invading and colonizing her Asian neighbors (*11*, pp. 238-240). (This idea was a major tenet of Japanese foreign policy from 1871 to 1920.) Known for his belief in individual equality and people's rights (*min ken*), Fukuzawa was also an advocate of "a rich country and a strong army." The goal of Westernization, or "getting out of Asia" was for him, as for other leaders, none other than self-defense against Western threats. The implication was exactly the same when Kaoru Inoue, the Foreign Minister, submitted a recommendation to the government in 1887, and emphasized, "Let us make our empire like an empire in Europe, and our people like European people. Let us create a new European empire here in the Orient" (*12*).

However, to what extent and how selectively was this to be carried out? This question already confronted Tomomi Iwakura, an envoy extraordinary and minister plenipotentiary, who, with an entourage of eighty, traveled through the United States and Europe from 1871 to 1873. Looking for "secrets" in building a rich nation and strong army, Iwakura saw a close relationship between the wealth and power of a nation and its democratic system. He understood there was "character and temperament" of the people behind the Western democracy, cultural history behind the technological development, and religion behind the moral values. While in the United States, he wrote in his report:

> People of this country all grow up in a democratic way and have a fraternal spirit. Toward other people they are frank and friendly. Toward their tasks they are composed and impartial. They are true citizens. . . The Bible is the code of the West and the basis for people's conduct. To compare it with the Orient, the Bible penetrates people's mind like the Four Books of Confucianism. The Bible is valued by men and women like Buddhist Sutras. Nothing in the Orient, however, is as widely and greatly respected as the Bible is in the West. After all, the people's piety is the source of their diligence, and their moral conduct the basis of national security. The wealth and strength of a country derives from this source and basis (*15*).

Iwakura did not, however, ask if it was possible for his own people to build a modern nation without adopting the modern principles of democracy, freedom and equality. Instead, as his long journey approached its end, Iwakura resorted to racism and rejected the basic values and principles that he had so perceptively recognized in the Western societies. Perhaps otherwise he could never have returned to his Emperor. He wrote:

> The white race has strong passion and lust. They are enthusiastic about their religion, lack self-control, and are avaricious. The yellow race has less passion and lust, and possesses strong self-control. They are modest. Accordingly, the Westerners need a protective government, while we Easterners can have a moralistic government. . . . Because the white race is passionate and lustful, their government must be suited to their nature so as to maintain social peace. The white race is vicious, and greedily seek their individual happiness and welfare. They need their religion to train their nature. Their religion is incompatible with the Oriental moral teachings that regard human nature as basically good, instead of evil (*15*).

Iwakura and other leaders of the Meiji government knew that industrialization of the country was absolutely necessary for building up a modern army and navy, but at the same time they wanted to, and actually did, base national unity on the cult of Emperor, rather than introducing Western democracy. Iwakura's inner conflict—his understanding of Western values and then rejecting them on a racist basis—is of special interest to us, because it foreshadows the later efforts of many Japanese intellectuals who, sometimes under the slogan of "Japanese spirit and Western skills" (*wakon yosai*), tried to emphasize the mysterious superiority of Japanese cultural elements and to give them priority over Western liberal, democratic thought.

For the early leaders, who had grown up in the pre-Restoration tradition and whose identification with the warrior-Confucian values was firm, things were relatively easy. The initial Westernization was more or less limited to the adoption of technology, or at least the leaders could focus their attention mainly on the introduction of industry. The problem became a painful one, however, for those who were younger—those whose impressionable youth was spent in the period of drastic political, social and ideological change that quickly followed the introduction of Western technology. Characterizing this period of tremendous disruption of tradition, Takeo Kuwabara has written:

> In early Meiji, the leaders drove the top ranking artists of traditional painting out of their ateliers and forced them, without compunction, to work on blueprints in the national arsenal. . . . Children at school were never taught the traditional music and folksongs so dear to their parents' hearts. Such complete disruption of tradition has never been found in any Western country (*29*).

A foreign visitor of this period describes the social climate as follows:

> Whatever you do, do not expatiate, in the presence of Japanese of the new school, on those old, quaint and beautiful things Japanese which rouse our most genuine admiration . . . generally speaking, the educated Japanese

have done with their own past. They want to be somebody else and something else other than what they have been and still partly are (*8*).

The young people who had spent their formative stage in this period suffered from historical and cultural dislocation, or "spiritual breakdown" (*6*). The identity crisis among such young intellectuals is well analyzed by Kenneth Pyle's excellent work. With remarkable clarity and insight, his analysis (*43*) shows the prototypes of major dilemmas with which the Japanese intellectuals of later times have grappled and are apparently still struggling.

In 1885 a book entitled *Youth of the New Japan* was published. Urging youth to seek total Westernization of Japan, the book soon became widely popular among young people (*55*). Its author, Soho Tokutomi, organized young intellectuals into a group called the *Min'yusha* ("Friends of Nation"); by writing for the group's periodical, *Kokumin no Tomo* (subtitled in English "The Nation's Friends"), he became the leading spokesman of the new generation. Following Herbert Spencer, Tokutomi believed that a universal process of social evolution, impelled by historical forces, was molding all nations, including Japan, along similar lines. Accordingly, in Tokutomi's opinion Japan would inevitably become more like Western societies, and her progress should be measured by her acquired similarities to Western nations (*56*). This outright rejection of Japan's traditions was enthusiastically welcomed by the youth, who, in the period of both drastic social changes and of intense national consciousness, had been painfully sensitive to the self-degrading implications of the ongoing process of nation building, which involved replacement of much of the Japanese traditions with things Western. Pyle points out that Tokutomi's future oriented belief in a universal evolutionary process became popular partly because it offered a soothing justification for the prevailing cultural alienation of the new generation—that if Japan was to move entirely out of her past into a higher stage of civilization, there was no need to worry about or lament over the loss of the traditions (*43*).

When the Government made it an official policy (particularly with the promulgation of the Imperial Rescript on Education in 1890) to adopt the past oriented Confucian ethics as the moral backbone of national education, Tokutomi severely attacked this policy of proceeding with industrialization while maintaining identification with the East. He argued that Western science and Eastern morals were fundamentally incompatible, and that the civilizations of the Orient and of the West, with their contradictory characteristics, could never coexist or be successfully integrated. In his opinion, teaching Western utilitarian principles alongside traditional Confucian morality would only lead to confusion. In De Vos' terms there was no possibility that Japan could reconcile past oriented ethnic traditions with a future oriented belief in a universalistic social evolution.

There was, however, an inherent difficulty in the propositions of Tokutomi and his group. Like all other leaders of that time they urged national self-confidence at the same time that they repudiated the only possible basis for such self-confidence—that is, the worth of Japan's traditional culture. Furthermore, their belief in the universal process of social evolution could not long offer satisfaction, because the political reality of unequal treaties and foreign settlements was a constant reminder of Japan's weakness and the self-effacement implied in Westernization.

An alternative to the *Min'yusha*'s Westernism was proposed by a second group of intellectuals, the *Seikyosha* ("Society for Political Education"), founded in 1888. Their emphasis on the preservation of Japan's cultural autonomy gained increasing popularity. Although its members—Setsurei Miyake, Katsunan Kuga and Shigetaka Shiga being the most prominent—had been strongly influenced by Western values and were committed to the adoption of many Western institutions, they believed that only by maintaining a distinct identity could the Japanese feel equal to the Westerners, and recover their own national pride. As an alternative to the *Min'yusha*'s universal evolutionism the Seikyosha offered a view of the world as multi-cultural. In Kuga's opinion, for example, all nations had different characteristics due to their unique histories, and what was of value in one society might not be equally valuable when transplanted to a different society. Society did not progress according to fixed laws; rather, progress varied with individual cultures. "World civilization progresses through the competition of different cultures" (*28*). Miyake, too, in his widely read book on the cultural missions of the Japanese, asserted that the progress of civilization was the product of competition. Although the culture of the Western nations was the highest stage of civilization, concepts of value other than those of Western culture were necessary if world civilization was to progress to an even higher stage. According to Miyake, the Japanese had an obligation to preserve and develop their distinctive talents and values in order to supplement the contribution of Western culture.

Even further, Miyake proposed three major missions for the Japanese: first, the application of their Western-trained scholarship to the study of the history, society, and culture of the Far Eastern countries, so as to test the applicability of Western knowledge; second, becoming the protector of weak Asian nations against Western imperialists; and third, the preservation and development of their unique conception of beauty, with its emphasis on the delicate and the exquisite (*36*). It is noteworthy that such a "sense of mission" seems to have a strong appeal to many Japanese intellectuals, both past and present, when they are concerned with the national purpose of their country.

The *Seikyosha* members, however, did not reject Westernization. They knew it was necessary for Japan's survival. Kuga, for instance, believed that the Japanese with their unique character would successfully borrow from the West, just as they had done centuries ago from China. He stressed, however, that borrowing had to be kept in perspective, and care taken to strengthen Japan's national spirit. "To the degree that it does not damage the national character, we can adopt Western things," he said. He believed that traditional morals and customs would perform a binding integrative function, and would help to maintain a continuing ethnic cultural identity upon which Japanese nationalism could be built (*28*).

What was it, however, in Japan's traditions and history that the Japanese could value and be proud of? The *Seikyosha* members wanted to re-evaluate Japanese ethnic traditions to find something in their national past that they and the world could esteem, something by virtue of which they could define their uniqueness and thus feel themselves the equals of Westerners. They were not, however, very successful in their "search for a usable past" (*43*). In trying to make national progress and national pride compatible, they created no small amount of conflict and confusion among themselves over what constituted the essential traditions and preservable elements in the Japanese heritage. The difficulty was that "the very fact of building the nation-state had already involved disowning the past and adopting the techniques and institutions of an alien culture" (*43*).

Neither the *Min'yusha* nor the *Seikyosha* was able to offer any total solution to the dilemma of early modern Japan. Meanwhile, international tensions mounted in Asia. During the 1890s, a third way of extricating Japan from her "historical predicament" (*43*) became prominent. A far more conservative nationalism, it intended to end Japan's cultural subservience to the West by asserting the distinctiveness and superiority of the Japanese way of life. It erected "a myth of distinctive national virtues flourishing within a framework of a completely separate ethnic-national identity. It set forth the mystic idea of an entire people supernaturally bound together by the common heritage of a national soul" (*43*).

In 1894 and 1904 Japan won its wars with C'hing Dynasty China and Czarist Russia. One should note that Japan was able to make the Western nations agree to relinquish their extra-territorial privileges only after winning these two wars, and not after the Rokumeikan masquerade of 1887, when high Meiji government officials and their families dressed in Western clothes and invited foreign diplomats to balls in order to persuade the foreigners that the Japanese were civilized enough to deserve equal treatment. This improvement in their international status made the third answer to the problem of cultural identity increasingly convincing.

The Meiji government formulated and propagated a national ideology that justified its power and called for great loyalty on the part of the people to achieve the nation's industrial and military goals. In the newly established universal education and military training the government reasserted the old values of loyalty, filial piety, solidarity and duty to superiors, and promoted ethnic myths about the sacredness of the Emperor. It should be noted that the pressure to conform to this national orthodoxy came not so much from the government as from "forces within Japanese society" (*16*). This receptivity to a national ideology represented a natural reaction to the sense of uprootedness and the emotional stress and dislocation produced by the rapid changes during the first two decades of the Meiji period. This national ideology helped the Japanese to compensate for their lost sense of security.

It is relevant to note how the victory in the war with Russia gave a temporary basis of national pride to Soseki Natsume, one of the greatest authors of modern Japan. While in London, lonely and homesick, Natsume was critical of the inferiority of Japan to the Western nations. "I want to go back to Japan," he wrote in his diary on April 9, 1901. "But as I visualize Japan, I feel miserable.[2] I am annoyed by the lack of virtues, physical strength, and aesthetic appreciation of Japanese gentlemen. I feel annoyed by their being proud of something worthless, their superficiality, emptiness and vanity—their being content with the present situation of Japan and leading the nation into corruption." Compared with the West, Japan in Natsume's eyes was a miserably small and backward country. On January 25, 1902, he wrote in his diary, "The Europeans are surprised at the development of Japan. The reason for their surprise is obvious. People are surprised when someone whom they feel contemptuous toward suddenly talks or acts in a brash way. Most of the Europeans, however, are not surprised nor interested. I do not know how many years it will take Japan to be able to make the Europeans respect her." On March 15, 1902, still in London, he wrote, "Why do the Japanese feel annoyed when mistaken for the Chinese? The Chinese are a much more glorious nation than the Japanese, except that presently the Chinese are in an unfortunate stagnation. Thoughtful Japanese should feel honored when mistaken for Chinese." After Japan's victory over Russia, Natsume showed a different attitude. In an article he wrote:

> "Now we can have self-confidence. Admiral Nelson was a great man but Admiral Togo is even greater . . . People have been feeling that Japan was inferior to Europe in everything, and that Japan had to imitate Europe, that we should respect it and devote ourselves to the cult of Europe. Now we have our self-confidence. Japan is Japan. Japan has her own history.

[2] At this time, the editor of the widely read new magazine *Taiyo* ("The Sun"), and one of the leading spokesmen for the new nationalism, wrote, "By the end of the Sino-Japanese War the long entrenched Westernism had vanished" (*52*).

The Japanese have their own characteristics. We should not devote ourselves simply to imitation of the West. Europe is not the only model. We can be a model too" (*39*).

Unfortunately, however, his "self-confidence" did not last very long. Increasingly, he became disillusioned with "superficial modernization" (*40*), and he came to fight with the government from his individualism as the last stronghold of moral values. And yet, like so many other Japanese intellectuals, Natsume himself was caught in the painful state of anomie and alienation, finding the meaning of life neither in the West nor in the East. He, too, looked for ways to reconcile the conflicting needs of cultural borrowing and national pride, to be both modern and Japanese, and yet he could find none (*9*).

Opposition against the nationalistic policy of the government came from many other intellectuals. For example, Kanzo Uchimura, a great Christian leader, opposed the government and its engagement in wars from his stand of absolute pacifism. His was, however, impossible for a government preoccupied with survival. Nor did Uchimura ever offer any alternative to the government's policy. Another opponent was Sakuzo Yoshino, an eloquent advocate of democracy, who opposed Japan's "rich country and strong army" policies, by emphasizing the importance of morality in international relations after World War I. Inazo Nitobe, as the Secretary General of the League of Nations (1919–1926), criticized Japan's expansionist policy.

In 1910, Shusui Kotoku, a noted anarchist-socialist, was executed for an alleged plot to assassinate Emperor Meiji. This incident marked the beginning of an accelerated process through which, despite a period of short-lived liberalism, the government's militarist-expansionist policies became stronger. The intellectuals in turn became increasingly disillusioned and dissatisfied with the government. Some were to escape from reality into art: Kafu Nagai, a famed novelist, for instance, in total disillusionment with modern Japan, escaped from it into the world of esthetics, portraying love, pleasure and women in his art (*21, 49*). Another author, Ryunosuke Akutagawa, known to the West for his novel *Rashomon*, was then still a young student of the First National Higher School, idealistic and concerned with his country. In 1913 as a class assignment he wrote an essay on Japan–U.S. relations in which he pointed out as causes of anti-Japanese prejudice in the West "not only the racial prejudice of the white, but also the inferior status and situation of the yellow countries." He was of the opinion that "the low standard of moral and ethical consciousness throughout Japanese society invites the laughter and contempt of the Western powers." Therefore, he proposed, "we must train our minds and make progress not only to build our own character but also to enable our country to assert its own right in international relations" (*4*). As he grew older, however, Akutagawa became bitterly disillusioned with his country, and escaped into estheticism, seeking the meaning of life in art for art's sake, until he ended his own short life (*65*). Other intellectuals simply became quiet, and the majority even joined Japan's war efforts.

During the 1920s, following its industrial expansion and economic depression, Japan had its first government in which the majority party leader also served as prime minister. The government tolerated more or less liberal ideas, both in foreign and domestic policies. Liberalism was encouraged in the academic world and in journalism. Marxism also became popular among urban intellectuals, as did certain political and labor movements. As mentioned before, things Western (this time mainly American)—jazz, dress, dance and movies—also attracted the urban Japanese. This new tide of Westernization not only did not offer any solution to the problems of Japan's cultural identity, but further aggravated them. Reminiscing about the past the late professor Eiichiro Ishida, a Vienna-trained cultural historian and ethnologist, stated that his childhood in Japan prior to World War I was spent during "an age of vague feelings of inferiority toward the West" and that "all imported goods (*hakurai hin*) were considered superior to Japanese products." The countries of the West continued to be regarded as advanced nations (*senshin koku*), and Japan as backward (*kōshin koku*). Ishida describes the period after World War I as "an extension of the previous age of inferiority feelings among the Japanese toward the West."[3] According to Ishida, many young intellectuals, frustrated by the lack of democratic freedom, regretted "the unhappiness of having been born in Japan" (*13*).

Then came the war, first in Manchuria in 1931, then spreading to north China, then to the whole of China, and finally to the Pacific and Pearl Harbor. Ultra-nationalism, with its mythical glorification of the "descendants of the Sun Goddess," drowned all liberal thought. The problems of cultural identity were answered by a clear definition of the national goal of the "sacred war," in which Japan's role was to become the leader and protector of the Asian nations and to drive out the Western imperialists. During this disastrous war, the importance of "Japanese soul and spirit" was greatly stressed, and the chauvinistic emphasis on the superiority of the traditional warrior-Confucian-Shinto value system over the "corrupt Western civili-

[3] In 1918 Japan sent her army to Siberia, in 1921 the liberal Premier Hara was attacked by an assassin, in 1923 members of the Japan Communist Party were arrested in great numbers, in 1925 the notorious Law for Maintenance of the Public Peace (*chian iji ho*) was enacted, in 1928 the Special Secret Police (*tokubetsu koto keisatsu*—Japanese Gestapo) was instituted, in 1931 Japan sent her army to Manchuria, and in 1933 Japan seceded from the League of Nations.

zation" became almost hysterical, for the "corrupt" West proved to be much more powerful and there was no sign of the "divine wind" (*kamikaze*) blowing to protect the "land of gods."

Once the war ended, Japan found herself receiving a "democratic education" from her American teachers toward whom she felt rivalry mixed with admiration. It is totally inaccurate to say that Japan had not known about democracy and that the post-war political, social and ideological changes were all forced upon Japan by the American Occupation. However, the very fact that Japan went through drastic social changes under American "guidance," with the United States as the model, left a significant mark on Japan's history. The impact of the American culture was something almost unprecedented in Japan's past. Things American literally flooded Japan, ranging from the new constitution and the separation of administrative, legislative and judicial powers, through "Parent-Teacher-Associations" and the "National Institute of Mental Health," to chewing gum and Coca Cola.

Japanese society and traditions were all put on trial, not by the Americans, but by the Japanese intellectuals. Historians separated Japanese history from the myth of the origins of the Imperial line. The mechanisms of Japanese fascism were analyzed for the first time in scientific terms (*30*). Sociologists pointed out the predominance of small communities in Japan, and particularly the institution of the patriarchal family (*23*). Psychologists analyzed the "irrational," "Pre-modern," or "feudal" characteristics of the Japanese (*34, 35, 33, 50*), and emphasized the necessity to overcome such characteristics in order to accomplish the "democratization" of the Japanese people. All this demonstrated a "wide-spread realization of Japan's backwardness (*21*). Anything associated with defeated Japan—be it the Emperor cult, calligraphy, judo, a-father-who-tells-his-daughter-to-come-home-before-supper, or a-mother-who-wants-her-son-to-marry-her-best-friend's-nicest-daughter—was condemned as "feudal" (*hōken-teki*), and therefore to be rejected. Intellectuals, through lectures and writings, urged the Japanese to become "modern" (*kindai-teki*), "rationalistic" (*gōri-teki*) and "democratic" (*minshu-teki*), and not infrequently the implication was "like the Americans." In the minds of those intellectuals, as in the minds of the *Min'yusha* members of the 1880s, there seemed once again to be an assumption that Japan should move along the ladder of unilineal social evolution, from the "feudal" or "pre-modern" stage to the "modern" and "democratic" stage. Moreover, many of them, pointing out what the Japanese should no longer be, seemed too busy to think what the Japanese will eventually become when they are fully "democratized" and "modernized."

The Occupation ended and the flood of things American subsided. In terms of economy and in the sphere of material life the Japanese rebuilt everything they had lost and more, "except for a sense of values and national purpose to replace those shattered by the war" (*44*). Bad as the old system might have been, "it had given meaning and purpose to life, a way of viewing the world, and an opportunity for service and sacrifice to a larger cause" (*42*). Or, "the thought that the Japanese were not passively accepting Western civilization, but were holding themselves as the last fortress in Asia against the Western powers, gave the nation pride and a sense of mission" (*25*). This was all lost, and the rapid changes, the confusion, the "transvaluation of values" and the discrediting of the old authority without its replacement by a new one created what the Japanese themselves refer to as "a spiritual void."

The drive toward Westernization has slowed down somewhat since the middle of the 1950s, especially with the recent economic prosperity of the country. Japanese intellectuals now seem to be again increasingly concerned with the century-old question of cultural identity. Let us turn to some of the examples of such intellectual efforts.

The post-war quest for cultural identity is, however, much more difficult than it was in pre-war Japan, because the defeat shattered the traditional value system. Unable to turn to the search for the "usual past," many intellectuals tried to propose a new point of view that separates "modernization" from "Westernization." A proposal was made to reconsider the whole process of Japan's modernization in the context of the modernization of Asia as a whole (*53*). Others contended that, in contrast to all other Asian countries, there is no longer any significant difference between highly modernized Japan and Western societies. Thus the modernization of Japan has not been Westernization as such, but a process which happened to be parallel to that of the West (*59*). An extension of this argument is the proposition that Japan, already fully modernized, must strive to go beyond the modern stage, overcoming all its defects and evils—slum, smog, delinquency and many other things.

Saburo Ienaga, a noted historian, had perhaps a similar view of Japan when he wrote:

> . . . modern culture, which had its source in Europe and America, does not simply belong to the Westerners only . . . it is the world's culture and no one can overlook that . . . [but] it must not be forgotten that it [modern culture] has contained from birth not a few contradictions and deficiencies . . . Now the Japanese together with the other peoples of the world are facing the great task of overcoming [these contradictions and deficiencies] (*6*).

Simple replacement of the word "Westernization" with "modernization," however, does not seem to solve the problem. Japan *is* Westernized in one way or another, and there are discontinuities between contemporary Japan and her traditional past. The Japanese people need to find something uniquely *theirs* that they can be proud of, largely because of their century-old ambivalence toward Western civilization. Shuichi Kato, a physician and writer, in his efforts to solve the problem, proposed a new way of looking at Japanese culture. He suggests calling it a "hybrid culture" (*zasshu bunka*) in contrast with English or French culture which he terms "pure" (*junsui*). The Japanese culture is a hybrid of East and West, because Western culture has penetrated irrevocably into the roots of Japanese culture, and, Kato asserts, there is nothing wrong with a hybrid culture. "The mass of people accept our hybrid culture just as it is and enjoy a life rich with variety and conveniences. They never think of purifying this hybrid culture. . . . It is only the intellectuals who have that ambition. The history of complicated cultural movements since the Meiji Restoration is none other than the history of intellectual efforts to 'purify' hybrid culture" (*18*). His proposition is to give up the wish to purify Japanese culture, either into a purely Japanese or into a purely Western culture, because such a task is simply impossible. "The English or French culture is pure and it is acceptable as such. The Japanese culture is hybrid and it is also acceptable as such. Or, even if it is not acceptable at present, we must make it acceptable." But how? In another article Kato writes:

> Imported Western ideologies have long deprived many Japanese of the ability to think. New thoughts have been imported one after another, made popular, and then forgotten without leaving any trace of influence. Those who ran around in pursuit of the imported thoughts have had the illusion that running around is thinking (*19*).

He seems to suggest that, in order to make the hybrid Japanese culture acceptable, the Japanese should stop "running around" and look into their own cultural history, instead of trying to catch up with the West. He says that if the development of humanism outside the Christian world is the social task for all the Asian countries, it is the task of the Japanese to think and predict what form such humanism will take in the arts and literature. For instance, the Japanese should study the role played by Confucianism and *Kokugaku* (the Japanese classics) in Japanese history, in comparison with the role played by Catholicism and Protestantism in European history. Kato is no doubt looking for what makes the Japanese uniquely Japanese (in addition to its having a "hybrid" culture), when he says that no country in the world ever produced so many poems and songs about nature and the changing seasons, and that the Japanese are characterized by a kind of sensualism (*kankaku shugi*)—a world-view which sees the empirical world as the only reality and existence, and does not recognize any being that transcends such sensual reality. According to Kato, gods in the Japanese world have never been absolute, perfect and infinite, nor thought of as transcending human relativity, imperfection and finiteness. In the same way, no principles or values inherent in human nature have ever become absolute principles which transcend things sensual and empirical. Two years later, however, Kato no longer used the word "hybrid," but still denied the discontinuities between contemporary Japan and its traditions. The conscious efforts at Westernization, he contended, were limited to the urban intellectuals and were totally alien to the farmers. "The Japanese culture has never been disrupted. It has only been conceived as disrupted" (*30*). Kato names a few aspects of Japanese culture that remain valid among the general population: Shinto animism, a sensual conception of nature, estheticism, the tendency to beautify everyday life, and the lack of an absolute, transcendent god or principle. Granted that these characteristics make Japan uniquely Japanese, what are the implications of such recognition? In Kato's opinion the only logical basis of the values concerning human equality and individual dignity is the Christian notion that all human beings are equal in their relationship with the absolute God. This is precisely what is lacking in the uniquely Japanese traditions. Accordingly, Kato wonders, not without a tone of pessimism, how democracy is possible in the East without Christian traditions. "How can this social system, conceivable only on the basis of individual dignity and equality, develop in Japan which has its own historical background and unique mental structure?" (*20*).

More recently, Shunpei Ueyama, a professor of philosophy in Kyoto, made a proposition essentially in agreement with Kato. Instead of using the term "hybrid," Ueyama calls the Japanese culture "concave" because "practically every culture and civilization has flowed into Japan" and "no original civilization has ever flowed out" (*57*). He clearly believes that the Japanese should be proud of such a culture, because, "like a 'blast furnace' of many cultures, Japanese culture can provide the motive force for the establishment of a world community of mankind." Somewhat like the *Seikyosha* members, Ueyama tries to base Japanese pride on their ability to contribute to a world civilization by being a unique mixture of East and West. He never tells us, however, whether or not the Eastern and Western traditions, apparently so different from each other, can "melt" and produce something meaningfully new and valuable, nor how that might be accomplished.

In the special issue of *PHP* magazine, Michio Nagai, a former sociology professor at Tokyo Institute of Technology, offered a view that is essentially the same as Ueyama's, namely, the view of Japan as "the melting pot of many cultures:" "The Japanese, who embrace within their small insular state Western traditions, Buddhism, Confucianism, and Shinto traditions, are by accident in charge of a great experimentation of mankind to create something new out of the mixture of the Eastern and Western cultural traditions" (*38*).

Nagai thinks that Japan's success during the 1970s depends solely upon whether or not the Japanese can become "more than economic animals." "It is our task," he concludes, "to grow economically, and to build a society and culture that values humanity. We must contribute both to the Orient and to the Occident by adopting all that is excellent from both our own and other cultural heritages, and by creating a new modern non-Western culture" (*38*). However, Nagai, too, leaves us wondering just how the East and West can be mixed and synthesized.

Yuji Aida, a professor of French history at Kyoto University, almost exactly echoes the sentiments of the *Seikyosha* members, especially Shigetaka Shiga, when he deplores extreme Westernization, and urges Japanese to restore their pride and regain their "Japanese soul," without ever explaining just what the Japanese soul is.

> Miserable examples are abundant in post-war Japan. Probably as a reaction to the war-time ultra-nationalism and due to the shock of an unprecedented unconditional surrender, we seem to have thought that we could improve everything and solve every problem by condemning that which is Japanese and discarding all our past and even our present. The changes in political structure, the removal of factors detrimental to economic growth, and the elimination of a mistaken sense of national superiority all made sense. Our success in these changes brought about the present economic prosperity. However, the post-war changes did not stop there, but went further and destroyed all the beautiful and refined customs and consciousness uniquely Japanese. . . . The cultural traditions that our nation had built through its three thousand years of history have become almost extinct. The educational system and methods that once trained our unique Japanese mind and body are gone. What is left is technology and a state of nationlessness (*mukokuseki*—"citizenlessness") common to all the colonies. . . . Hidden beneath the contemporary economic affluence are spiritual emptiness, apathy and decadence. . . . We must return to our real selves, and restore the soul (*kokoro*) that we have lost in the imitation of the West. Only when we regain our Japanese soul will people of the world stop blaming us for being an economic animal (*3*).

Much more self-assured is Yoshio Masuda, professor of anthropology and comparative civilization at University of Tokyo, who believes that in spite of the imported fads and fashions of foreign cultures, Japanese culture has remained essentially unaffected and undisrupted throughout its history. Reversing the opinion of Kato, mentioned earlier, Masuda calls Japanese culture "pure" (*junsui*) and European cultures "hybrid." After reviewing the history of Japanese culture, Masuda concludes:

> It is true, indeed, that the elements of foreign cultures which flowed into Japan like torrents during the sixteenth and seventeenth centuries and

again in the nineteenth century, and which we have adopted without much worry, are overwhelmingly varied and miscellaneous. One might very well be tempted to call the Japanese culture "hybrid." However, judging from the historical examples we have seen so far, I would think that the Japanese attitude toward the various impacts of foreign cultures has remained the same throughout. What is important in considering Japanese culture is not the varied elements of foreign cultures themselves, but the skills or attitudes of the Japanese who have cooked, swallowed and digested the foreign elements, or at times have looked at them and thrown them into the garbage can with no qualms. We must not overlook the fact that every time these foreign elements were integrated into a culture complex through the uniquely Japanese "cooking method," the end result was curiously uniform and definite. Seen in this perspective, Japanese culture is far from being "hybrid;" it is essentially "pure," with its basic patterns unchanging and consistent (*3*).

In Masuda's view the Japanese nation has, on a number of occasions in its history, imported higher civilizations from outside. This has occurred "intermittently, on a large scale, but without any painful experience of invasion, conquest or violence, allowing Japan its own autonomy and freedom to be selective." At the initial stage of learning and adoption the imported foreign elements often looked overwhelming and varied. However, as the tide ebbed, the Japanese have been able to digest and "Japanize," in relative isolation and peace, what they had adopted and learned. The repetition of such avid and massive adoption of foreign cultures and their subsequent assimilation contributed to the formation of unique Japanese culture patterns, and, as the result, "the Japanese, as a homogeneous ethnic group, have maintained a homogeneous culture since the pre-historic age."

While they are greatly fond of foreign cultures and willing to accept almost anything new from abroad, the Japanese, in Masuda's opinion, are extremely suspicious of the people who created and who carry the foreign culture. "The Japanese do not like to see foreigners coming into their country in large numbers, getting settled, and marrying Japanese. . . . This suspicious attitude and resistance toward foreigners must have derived from the historical fact that the Japanese have rarely experienced military conquest by a foreign cultural group. . . . Japanese are shy and closed to outsiders, and deep in their mind they feel absolute mistrust toward them" (*31*). Making such comments as "Japan is a rare example of a nation which has had the 'happiness' of acquiring superior foreign civilizations without paying the price or experiencing the pain of foreign conquest," "the Japanese are naive toward foreign cultures, unsuspicious and unguarded like a virgin," Masuda, as an anthropologist, remains basically free from any value judgment as to the nature of the "pure" Japanese culture. Nor does he take the trouble to give a concrete description of what he calls "unique Japanese culture patterns." What is it that has persisted all through Japanese history in spite of the impacts of the foreign culture elements that flowed into it?

Another anthropologist, Mitsusada Fukasaku, in basic agreement with Masuda, offers an opinion in regard to the "sources of the persistent Japanese culture patterns." Discussing the history of Japanese culture as well as Japanese clothing and house structure (made for warm and humid summers) and diet (which consists of rice as the main source of calories with side dishes basically as appetizers), Fukasaku comes to the same conclusion as Masuda. "In spite of changes on the surface," he writes, "there is something deep in the Japanese culture that has remained unaltered since ancient times, something that has lasted undisturbed, despite the restless shifts and movements on the surface" (*10*). He points to the "agricultural nature of the Japanese people" as a basic characteristic of the Japanese culture. As derivatives of this basic agricultural nature of the Japanese, Fukasaku describes five major characteristics: (1) "a trust in and dependence on self-sufficient agricultural production among the farmers who believe that as long as they work like ants they can live" (this emphasis on diligence and hard work is still prevalent, even among the present-day urban Japanese); (2) a basically inner-directed conservatism based on rice cultivation by means of irrigation; (3) an assumption of "sameness" and homogeneity among Japanese people and preference for "similar people"—the psychology of the farmers who work and live in basically the same way; (4) an emphasis on adaptation to the course of nature and avoidance of artificial techniques; and (5) an emphasis on the priority of a cooperative working group over its individual members and the required loyalty to the group, as well as the inter-group competitiveness and antagonism. Fukasaku contends that with these basic unchanging characteristics the Japanese have adopted various foreign cultural elements "without ever really understanding their essential nature." He asserts that the Japanese adoption of foreign cultures has been no more than "monkey's imitation" (*saru-mane,* a superficial imitation), and the Japanese have remained essentially the same in the relative isolation afforded by a self-sufficient rice agriculture. Fukasaku further argues, however, that such traditional patterns of life and thought are no longer possible, because Japan is no longer geographically isolated from the international community, agriculture is no longer the basis for the Japanese economy, because Japan's once beautiful nature has been destroyed by pollution and urbanization, and because the traditional culture has been completely commercialized. The Japanese "can't go home again," although they may not yet be fully aware of it. Accordingly, he thinks that the Japanese have to begin creating a new culture of their own, and that the 1970s will see the beginning of this difficult task. Unfortunately, his highly relevant discussion ends without any suggestion as to the nature of this new Japanese culture.

In addition to the recent writers just quoted, one finds a plethora of books and articles on Japanese culture and people. Particularly during the last few years the Japanese seem to have been reading avidly about the nature of their culture and considering the question of their purpose as a nation. There seems, however, no clear answer as yet to these century old questions. Nevertheless, a strong collective feeling remains that the Japanese must cultivate and develop something uniquely theirs.

REFERENCES

1. Aida, Yuji. *Aaron Shuyojo* [War Prisoners' Camp in Ahlon]. Tokyo: Chuo Koron Sha, 1963.
2. Aida, Yuji. *Nippon Bunka no Joken* [Conditions of Japanese Culture]. Tokyo: Bancho Shobo, 1965.
3. Aida, Yuji. "Kosei Aru Kuni" [A Unique Country]. *PHP* (Special issue: *Nippon o Kangaeru* [Thinking about Japan]), no. 3, 10 October 1969, pp. 5-22.
4. Akutagawa, Ryunosuke. *Miteiko Shu* [A Collection of Unpublished Manuscripts]. Edited by Yoshitoshi Katsumaki. Tokyo: Iwanami Shoten, 1968.
5. Ashiwara, Yoshishige. "Nishi Doitsu de no Kenbun Kara" [From My Experiences in West Germany]. *PHP* (Special issue: *Nippon o Kangaeru*), no. 3, 10 October 1969, pp. 24-38.
6. Bellah, Robert. "Ienaga Saburo and the Search for Meaning in Modern Japan." In *Changing Japanese Attitudes toward Modernization,* edited by Marius Jansen, pp. 360-423. Princeton: Princeton University Press, 1965.
7. Bellah, Robert. "Japan's Cultural Identity: Some Reflections on the Work of Watsuji Tetsuo." *Journal of Asian Studies,* 24, 1965, pp. 573-594.
8. Chamberlain, Basil Hall. *Things Japanese.* London, 1891.
9. De Vos, George. *Socialization for Achievement: The Cultural Psychology of the Japanese.* Berkeley: University of California Press, 1973.
10. Fukasaku, Mitsusada. *Nippon Bunka oyobi Nipponjin Ron* [A Study in Japanese Culture and People]. Tokyo & Kyoto: San'itsu Shobo, 1972.
11. Fukuzawa, Yukichi. "Datsu-a Ron" [Getting out of Asia], first published in 1885. In *Fukuzawa Yukichi Zenshu* [Collected Works], vol. 10, pp. 238-240. Tokyo: Keio University Press. 1958-1964.
12. Inoue, Kaoru. "Ikensho" [Statement of Opinions]. 1887.
13. Ishida, Eiichiro. *Tozai Sho* [Essays on East and West]. Tokyo: Chikuma Shobo, 1965.
14. Ishida, Eiichiro. "Nipponjin no Ijin Ishiki" [Japanese Attitudes toward Foreigners]. *Ushio,* August 1967, pp. 78-86.

15. Iwakura, Tomomi. *Iwakura Tomomi Tokumei Zenken Taishi Bei-o Kairan Jikki* [Travel Report in America and Europe by Iwakura Tomomi, the Envoy Extraordinary and Minister Plenipotentiary], first published in 1878. Quoted in Shuichi,Kato, *Nippon no Uchi to Soto* [Inside and Outside Japan], pp. 69-113. Tokyo: Bungei Shunjusha, 1969.

16. Jansen, Marius. "Changing Japanese Attitudes toward Modernization." In *Changing Japanese Attitudes toward Modernization,* edited by Marius Jansen, pp. 43-89. Princeton: Princeton University Press, 1965.

17. Kase, Shun'ichi. "Tenshi no Gotoki Omoiyari" [Angelic sympathy]. *PHP* (Special issue: *Nippon o Kangaeru*), 10 October 1969, pp. 39-56.

18. Kato, Shuichi. "Nippon Bunka no Zasshu-sei" [The Hybrid Nature of the Japanese Culture]. *Shiso,* June 1955.

19. Kato, Shuichi. "Zasshu-teki Nippon Bunka no Kibo" [Hope for the Hybrid Japanese Culture]. *Chuo Koron,* July 1955.

20. Kato, Shuichi. "Kindai Nippon no Bunmei-shi Teki Ichi" [The Position of Modern Japan in the History of Civilizations]. *Chuo Koron,* March 1957.

21. Kato, Shuichi. "Japanese Writers and Modernization." In *Changing Japanese Attitudes toward Modernization,* edited by Marius Jansen, pp. 245-445. Princeton: Princeton University Press.

22. Kato, Shuichi. *Nippon no Uchi to Soto* [Inside and Outside Japan]. Tokyo: Bungei Shunjusha, 1969.

23. Kawashima, Takeyoshi. *Nihon Shakai no Kazoku-teki Kosei* [The Familial Structure of Japanese Society]. Tokyo: Yuhikaku, 1948.

24. Kosaka, Masaaki, et. al. "Meiji Bunka Shi" [Meiji Cultural History]. In *Shiso Genron Hen* [A Volume on Thoughts and Speech]. Tokyo: Yuzankaku, 1938.

25. Kosaka, Masataka. *Sekai Chizu no Naka de Kangaeru* [Thinking in the World Map]. Tokyo: Shincho Sha, 1968.

26. Kosaka, Masataka. "Amae to Amayakashi" [Need to be Loved and Lenience]. *PHP* (Special issue: *Nippon o Kangaeru*), 10 October 1969, pp. 73-90.

27. Kuga, Katsunan. "Tokyo Dempo." 9 June 1885 (quoted in Kenneth Pyle, *The New Generation in Meiji Japan.* Stanford: Stanford University Press, 1969).

28. Kuga, Katsunan. "Kokumin Teki no Kannen" [Nationalistic Notion], first published in 1889. In *Kuga Katsunan Bunshu* [Collected Papers], edited by Kaji Mori, pp. 9-13, Tokyo, 1910.

29. Kuwabara, Takeo. *Nippon Bunka no Kangae Kata* [The Way to Think About the Japanese Culture]. Tokyo: Hakusui Sha, 1963.

30. Maruyama, Masao. *Gendai Seiji no Shiso to Kodo* [Thoughts and Behavior in Contemporary Politics]. Tokyo: Shinzenbi Sha, 1957.

31. Masuda, Yoshio. *Junsui Bunka no Joken – Nippon Bunka wa Shogeki ni Do Taetaka* [The Conditions of A Pure Culture – How the Japanese Culture Has Survived Shocks]. Tokyo: Kodansha, 1967.

32. Matsushita, Konosuke. "Shuza o Tamochi Tsutsu" [Keeping our Autonomy]. *PHP* (Special issue: *Nippon o Kangaeru*), 10 October 1969, pp. 109-136.

33. Minami, Hiroshi. *Nipponjin no Shinri* [Psychology of the Japanese]. Tokyo: Iwanami Shoten, 1949.

34. Miyagi, Otoya. *Kindai teki Ningen* [Man of Modern Age]. Tokyo: Kaneko Shobo, 1950.

35. Miyagi, Otoya. *Atarashii Kankaku* [New Tastes]. Tokyo: Kawade Shobo, 1956.

36. Miyake, Setsurei. *Shin Zen Bi – Nipponjin* [Japanese – Truth, Good and Beauty], first published 1891. In *Miyake Setsurei Shu, Gendai Nippon Bungaku Zenshu* [Collection of Contemporary Japanese Literature]. Tokyo: Kaizo Sha, 1931.

37. Nagai, Michio. *Nihon no Daigaku – Sangyo Shakai ni Hatasu Yakuwari* [Japanese Universities – Their Roles in an Industrial Society]. Tokyo: Chuo Koron Sha, 1965.

38. Nagai, Michio. "Kenmei Na Sentaku O" [Let Us Make a Clever Choice]. *PHP* (Special issue: *Nippon o Kangaeru*), 10 October 1969, pp. 91-108.

39. Natsume, Soseki. "Sengo Bungaku no Keiko" [Trends in the Post-war Literature], first published 1905. In *Natsume Soseki Zenshu* [Collected Works]. Tokyo: Iwanami Shoten, 1928.

40. Natsume, Soseki. "Gendai Nippon no Kaika" [Civilization of Present-day Japan], first published 1911. In *Natsume Soseki Zenshu.* Tokyo: Iwanami Shoten, 1928.

41. Obe, Yutaka. Personal communication. 1970.

42. Passin, Herbert. "The Source of Protest in Japan." *The American Political Science Review* 54(2):391-403, 1962.

43. Pyle, Kenneth. *The New Generation in Meiji Japan – Problems of Cultural Identity 1885-1889.* Stanford: Stanford University Press, 1969.

44. Rosenthal, A. M. "New Japan – Future Beckons to Timorous Giant in Search of an Identity." *New York Times,* Western edition. June 1963.

45. Sabata, Toyoyuki. *Nippon o Minaosu – Sono Rekishi to Kokuminsei* [Japan Re-Examined – Its History and National Character]. Tokyo: Kodan Sha, 1964.

46. Sabata, Toyoyuki. *Nikushoku no Shiso – Yoroppa Seishin no Sai Hakken* [Meat Eaters' Thought – Rediscovery of the European Spirit]. Tokyo: Chuo Koron Sha, 1966.

47. Sabata, Toyoyuki. *Sekai no Naka no Nippon – Kokusaika Jidai no Kadai* [Japan in the World – Her Task in the Era of Internationalization]. Tokyo: Kenkyusha, 1971.

48. Sabata, Toyoyuki. *Bunmei no Joken – Nippon to Yoroppa* [Conditions for Civilizations – Japan and Europe]. Tokyo: Kodansha, 1972.

49. Seidensticker, Edward. *Kafu, the Scribbler.* Stanford: Stanford University Press, 1965.

50. Takagi, Masataka. *Nihonjin – Sono Seikatsu to Bunka no Shinri* [The Japanese – Psychology of Their Life and Culture]. Tokyo: Kawade Shobo, 1955.

51. Takahashi, Yoshio. *Nippon Jinshu Kaizyo Ron* [Proposal for Physical Improvement of the Japanese Race], first published 1883. Quoted in Ishii Ryoichi, *Population Pressure and Economic Life in Japan,* Chicago: University of Chicago Press, 1937.

52. Takayama, Chogyu. *Meiji Shiso no Hensen* [Vicissitudes of Meiji Thoughts]. In *Takayama Chogyu Zenshu* [Collected Works], vol. 4. Tokyo: Iwanami Shoten, 1905.

53. Takeuchi, Yoshiyuki. "Nippon to Ajiya" [Japan and Asia]. In *Kindai Nippon Shisoshi Koza* [Treatises on Contemporary Japanese Thoughts], vol. 8. Tokyo: Iwanami Shoten, 1961.

54. Tani, Tateki. "Ikensho" [Statement of opinion], first published 1887. Quoted in Shuichi Kato, *Nippon no Uchi to Soto* [Inside and Outside Japan], Tokyo: Bungei Shunjusha, 1969.

55. Tokutomi, Soho. *Shin Nihon no Seinen* [Youth of New Japan], first published 1885. *Gendai Nippon Bungaku Zenshu* [Contemporary Japanese Literature], vol. 5. Tokyo: Kaizosha, 1931.

56. Tokutomi, Soho. "Shorai no Nihon" [Japan in the Future], first published 1886. In *Gendai Nippon Bungaku Zenshu* [Contemporary Japanese Literature], vol. 5. Tokyo: Kaizosha, 1931.

57. Ueyama, Shunpei. *Nippon no Dochaku Shiso* [Indigenous Thoughts in Japan]. Tokyo: Kobundo, 1965.

58. Ueyama, Shunpei. *Nippon no Nashonarizumu* [Japanese Nationalism]. Tokyo: Shiseido, 1965.

59. Umezao, Tadao. "Bunmei no Seitai Shi Kan Josetsu" [An Introduction into the Ecological History of Civilizations]. *Chuo Koron,* February 1959.

60. Wagatsuma, Hiroshi. "Gesellschaftliche Bedeutung der Hartfarbe in Japan." In *Rassenkonflikte in der Welt,* edited by Rolf Italiander, pp. 186-195. Hamburg: Fischer Buecherei, 1966.

61. Wagatsuma, Hiroshi. "The Social Perception of Skin Color in Japan." *Daedalus,* Spring 1967, pp. 407-443.

62. Wagatsuma, Hiroshi. "Recent Trends in Social Psychology in Japan." *American Behavioral Scientists* 12(3):36-45, 1969.

63. Wagatsuma, Hiroshi. "Some Problems of Interracial Marriage for the Japanese." In *Interracial Marriage,* edited by L. E. Akt and I. R. Stuart. New York: Grossman, 1972 (forthcoming).

64. Wagatsuma, Hiroshi. "Mixed-Blood Children in Japan: an Exploratory Study." Paper prepared for the Conference on Ethnic Relations in Asian Countries, at the State University of New York, Buffalo, N.Y., on October 20-21, 1972.

65. Wagatsuma, Hiroshi and De Vos, George. "Alienation and the Authors: A Tryptich on Social Conformity and Deviancy in the Japanese Intellectuals." In *Socialization for Achievement,* edited by George De Vos. Berkeley: University of California Press, 1973.

66. Yazaki, Genkuro. *Nihon no Gairai Go* [Words of Foreign Origin in the Japanese Language]. Tokyo: Iwanami Shoten, 1964.

Ethnic Identity and Minority Status

PART FIVE

PART FIVE

ETHNIC IDENTITY AND MINORITY STATUS

We now turn to the area in which ethnic identity is most often considered an issue—the maintenance of ethnic identity of individuals living as members of minority groups within a pluralistic society.

Ethnic minorities buffeted between shifting political boundaries are principle features of Europe's unhappy history. We present only one example of the ethnic complexities found in both Eastern and Western Europe. Czeslaw Milosz presents, in the sensitive personal approach of a humanist whose specialty is Slavic literature, the case of individuals whose cultural identity is bound up with their residence in the Lithuanian city of Vilnius. The case illustrates without use of social science terminology a number of issues, raised in our introduction, to which we return in our conclusion.

Pluralistic societies with racially visible minorities pose special problems related to ethnic identity. The last chapter deals with issues of self reflection and self acceptance related to being racially different. This theme has already been anticipated by Wagatsuma in a previous chapter about ambivalence in Japanese identity vis-a-vis socially and politically aggressive Caucasians. Francois Raveau, an anthropologically oriented psychiatrist, exposes the processes involved in the internal adjustment of black migrants entering a white European society. He discusses the part that body image plays in the

psychopathological reactions that a black immigrant sometimes suffers as a response to social rejection.

The social and psychological problems resulting from reactions to minority status within a racially discriminating society are perhaps the most severe that minority individuals must face. However, one should not assume that these problems are qualitatively different from those met in other contexts where an individual, as part of his identification with a social group, must accept a complex of stigmatizing social attitudes directed toward him by members of a dominant social group. The processes are the same, whatever the peculiarities of historical context or the available excuses for social discrimination may be. Possible responses to a minority status position are limited and are defined by "universals" of psychological adaptation. There are, however, also differences in group traditions which either protect or expose the individual to the effects of negative social attitudes, as we have discussed in Chapter One. Again, these processes are limited in number. It is the task of a comparative social science to arrive at some generalizations. In our conclusions we explore the direction these papers have taken us.

Vilnius, Lithuania: An Ethnic Agglomerate

CZESLAW MILOSZ

13

This chapter represents the experience of a man who comes from a very unusual spot in Europe: the city of Lithuania known as Wilno or Vilnius, which in its mixture of languages, religions, and traditions is rivaled only, and not quite successfully, by Transylvania, Bukovina, or Trieste. My observations were made before World War II, but, as will be seen, the present appears again and again.

Today, if I call this city which is the capital of the Lithuanian Soviet Republic "Vilnius," I give a hint as to my Lithuanian identity. If I call it "Wilno," I present myself to the Lithuanians as probably a Pole or a Russian. Behind the double names lie the complex historical events of several centuries.

Before 1939 this city belonged to Poland, and the languages spoken by its inhabitants were first, Polish, and second, Yiddish. In the schools, instruction was in Polish, Yiddish, Hebrew, Lithuanian, Byelorussian, and Russian. The question of who was sent to each of these schools has much to do with the problem of ethnic divisions, for to assume that every ethnic group favored schools in which instruction was given in its own language would be far from the truth. Religious divisions cut across language divisions. Roman Catholicism, Judaism, Greek Catholicism, Orthodoxy, and Islam coexisted, and to these should be added the ethno-religious group of Karaites, a Judaic sect.

Lithuanians and Poles

The meaning of the statement "I am a Lithuanian" was undergoing a change at the end of the nineteenth and the beginning of the twentieth century. Previously it was used by the members of the upper class, the nobility or the petty gentry, whose ancestors had spoken Lithuanian or old Byelorussian, but who no longer used those languages at home. The "Polonization" of the upper classes, a result of the union between the Kingdom of Poland and the Grand Duchy of Lithuania in 1386, and of their gradual fusion, which was nearly complete by the seventeenth century. Thus, "I am a Lithuanian" was not opposed to "I am a Pole," but meant "I am from here" as opposed to "He is from there," namely, the Kingdom of Poland. The equivalent of such a feeling could perhaps be found in the British Commonwealth where there was opposition of Scottish and Irish to English, but not to British.

In Latin, which was in that area the language of liturgy, of many legal documents, and to a large extent, of literature, a "Lithuanian" was defined as a man who is *gente Lithuanus natione Polonus,* while the name of the state, embracing the Kingdom and the Duchy, was neither Poland nor Lithuania, but *Respublica.* As to the Lithuanian language, its fate was similar to that of the Gaelic. A non-Slavic language, and therefore already handicapped at the moment when, during the Middle Ages, the Grand Duchy of Lithuania absorbed large areas inhabited by Eastern Slavs, it was not used in writing. Paradoxically, before its union with Poland, the Grand Duchy adopted an Eastern Slavic dialect (which was to become Byelorussian in the north and Ukrainian in the south) for administrative purposes. Lithuanian, increasingly the language of the peasantry only, remained a low-status idiom. By the sixteenth century, it was used in writing only by those who wanted to descend to the people, in order to convert them to their religious domination. To that end, Protestants and Roman Catholics produced prayer-books and catechisms. A Polish-Latin-Lithuanian dictionary, published in 1629, was proof of a Jesuit's zeal. Literature in Lithuanian appeared late and was connected with a revival of national feeling, which challenged the "Lithuanianishness" of the upper classes and made the language spoken at home a distinctive mark.

The Lithuanian national movement, created by the new intelligentsia of peasant origin in the second half of the nineteenth century, regarded the formula *gente Lithuanus natione Polonus* as an unbearable reminder of defeat: the historical Lithuania had lost its upper classes through Polonization. The necessity of choosing between being a Lithuanian and being a Pole seems to be a result of the idea that nationality is defined by language. And indeed, in the twentieth century many families had to decide upon their nationality, with the not unusual consequence that one brother called himself Lithuanian, another a Pole, and the third Byelorussian. One has to go back in time in order to explain the strange myth about Lithuania that persists today in Polish cultural patterns.

Lithuania, the last country in Europe to become Christian, was converted in 1386. As a land of primeval forests, of abundant wildlife, and of pagan dieties, it fascinated Polish writers as early as the sixteenth century. This literature contributed to certain stereotypes. The Jesuit Academy of Wilno, founded in 1578, two centuries later became the best Polish university and a hotbed of romanticism. One of its pupils, Adam Mickiewicz (1798-1855) became the most important Polish poet of all time. The most cherished of Mickiewicz' work, a long tale in verse, *Pan Tadeusz,* opens with an invocation not to the Muse but to Lithuania: "Lithuania, my native land." Throughout all Mickiewicz' works, nature is Lithuanian. As a sort of emotional puzzle, consider the peasant child in Poland today who has to cope with a poet who called himself Lithuanian. Let us also add that the first history of Lithuania was written and published (nine volumes, 1835-1841) in Polish by another disciple of the University of Wilno, Teodor Narbutt.

A curious game of superiority-inferiority has been played by natives of Lithuania, speaking Polish with their half-compatriots from Poland. "Lithuanians" looked upon themselves as serious, obstinate, persistent, deep, conceding magnanimously some truth in their being in the eyes of the Poles bearish, uncouth, and miserly. It was assumed that great men of Polish letters could only come from Lithuania, and Mickiewicz' myth was a basic asset in such a contention. But there seems to have been something to the myth, since many eminent personalities come from ethnically Lithuanian families, as did, for instance, a precursor of modern Polish poetry, Cyprian Norwid (1821-1883), whose name in the Lithuanian form was once Norvidas. The question arises as to why a feeling of a separate identity did not express itself in Lithuania as it did in Ireland, where William Butler Yeats and others did not have to use Gaelic in order to be considered Irish patriots. One could go also to Finland, where the intelligentsia once had adopted Swedish, but where the use of Swedish did not exclude one from belonging to the Finnish nation.

That things evolved differently in Lithuania can be ascribed to many causes, but in all probability there is one primary cause underlying all the others. The Polish language was connected with a cultural pattern completely different from the pattern of the Lithuanian peasantry. It would be incorrect to maintain that only the nobility spoke Polish in Lithuania. It was also spoken by the petty gentry who tilled the land themselves and lived practically like peasants. The merchants and tradesmen, if they weren't Jewish, also used Polish at home, as did the non-Jewish artisans and workers in Vilno and in small towns, either because they were descended from the petty gentry or because they were former servants in the manors. All of those people were permeated, however, by the "culture of nobility" and considered their use of Polish a mark of the status that distinguished them from the Lithuanian-speaking boors. Thus, we observe a class hostility combined with a linguistic conflict. But to make the matter more difficult for investigators, the have-nots could be found on both sides, for rich Lithuanian peasants were often better off than the artisans or the laborers of a neighboring small town. Yet the very idea of an independent Lithuania was greeted by Polonized segments of its population with scorn and hostility: how could the boors pretend to become a nation and impose upon the rest of the people their boorish language? The new Lithuanian intelligentsia that appeared in the second half of the nineteenth century was, with very few exceptions, of purely peasant origin, and since, for a peasant family the only possible social advancement was to make one of their sons a Roman Catholic priest, clergymen were largely responsible for the emergence of the national movement. In the twentieth century educated members of the higher classes, who for a long time had proclaimed their loyalty to Lithuania for sentimental reasons, realized that they had to choose between Polish and Lithuanian loyalties, that one could no longer be at the same time a Lithuanian and a Pole. In 1918, when an independent Lithuania was being created, some of them opted for the country of their ancestors and started to learn the difficult, non-Slavic language. A very few looked for an intermediate solution, an equivalent of the relationship between English and Gaelic in Ireland. The majority, however, even if they became citizens of the new state, looked upon themselves as Poles. After World War I the region around Wilno leaned towards Independent Poland, and for a short time was a separate political entity, loosely bound to Poland, leaving in history a not very important but interesting trace in the form of postage stamps, a rarity today. That entity, "Middle Lithuania," was absorbed by Poland in 1922, but remained within the Polish borders only until 1939.

Relations between Polish-speaking Lithuanians and Poles displayed infinite ambiguities. On the one hand, Lithuanians indulged in a certain self-idealization, and on the other, owing to a myth transferred through literature, they were idealized by those outside it. Self-irony became an increasingly prominent ingredient of that peculiar Lithuanian ethnic identity. The difference was disguised as innocent snobbery. Yet it cannot be said that Lithuanian ethnic identity belongs completely to the past. Lithuanians, whether they lived in the region of Wilno or emigrated to ethnic Poland (which occurred *en masse* after World War II), have been bringing to Polish arts and letters a particular perspective. One may guess that a man who grows up surrounded by people who speak various languages and who belong to various cultures acquires a different personality than does a man brought up in a homogeneous ethnic milieu. Let us add also that Lithuanians were much more open to Russian thought and Russian literature than were Poles. This did not make them partisans of Russia, yet did endow them with some kind of openness to the seriousness of the "Russian phenomenon."

It would be interesting to examine modifications of the Lithuanian myth in Polish literature of the last few decades, including the avant-garde literature of the grotesque, the macabre, and the theatre of the absurd. In literature in which the aristocratic origin of a character is equated with degeneration and idiocy, a certain mocking respect is shown toward characters from Lithuania. After World War II, Poland became a melting pot of people with different languages and regional backgrounds, as a consequence of the shift of its borders from the east to the west. In this new melting pot, Lithuanians and Poles have been mixing. Even today, however, among some groups it is considered more dignified to marry within one's own group of emigrants from the East. A relatively small number of the Lithuanians who spoke Polish remained in Lithuania. Centered for the most part around Wilno, they represented the artisans and workers who had been inhabitants of that city for many generations.

Lithuanians

Among the peoples of Baltic stock only the Lithuanians succeeded in creating a state which, in the thirteenth and fourteenth centuries, expanded south and east, mostly thanks to the weakening of the Eastern Slavic principalities in the wake of Tartar invasions. The Lithuanian dukes had a strong army, since ethnic Lithuania seemed to be more densely populated than the regions of neighboring Slavs. Moreover, the Baltic Lithuanian ethnic area reached farther east and south than it does today. As a result of the conquest, the Grand Duchy of Lithuania, extending at one point as far south as the Black Sea, counted among its subjects people speaking an Eastern Slavic idiom (Ruthenian) and confessing the Orthodox faith, while the ruling Lithuanian ethnic group remained pagan. Penetration of the Duke's court by Eastern Orthodoxy, owing to marriages with Christian princesses, and the victory of the Eastern Slavic vernacular as the administrative language throughout the state, pre-figured, so to speak, what happened after the union with Poland in 1386. At that point ethnic Lithuania began to convert to Roman Catholicism, the Polish language slowly (though not before the sixteenth century) supplanted the Eastern Slavic idiom, and the Latin alphabet replaced the Cyrillic. Lithuanian survived as the language of folksongs of great beauty and antiquity. In some of these songs, called *dainos,* heroes are pagan planetary deities. Protestant and Catholic catechisms and hymns were the only documents of written Lithuanian until the second half of the eighteenth century, when an ethnically Lithuanian Protestant minister in a corner of East Prussia, Kristijonas Donelajtis (1714-1764), wrote his long poem *Four Seasons,* depicting the miseries and joys of peasant life. The national revival in the nineteenth century was indebted to partisans of Lithuania who wrote scholarly books in Polish, and to German collectors of Lithuanian folksongs, who were entranced to find in Europe a language still closely related to Sanskrit. But let us imagine the situation of a Lithuanian intellectual (usually a clergyman) in search of his ethnic identity: the glory of the country belonged to the past, for not only was his country a part of the Russian Tsarist empire, but Lithuania bore a strong Polish imprint; moreover, to be a Lithuanian carried the stigma of a boorish status.

It would not be an exaggeration to say that for such a man the language itself was both his fatherland and his passport. A desperate search went on for the names of illustrious men, which in their Polish spelling preserved Lithuanian vocables. There was also jealous competition with the Poles for the claim to some eminent writers. Thus, since Adam Mickiewicz invoked Lithuania as his muse, he was added to the Lithuanian pantheon. Typical of the Lithuanian language are family name endings in "as" or "ius." Thus Mickiewicz had to become Mickevicius. An eminent French poet, O. V. de L. Milosz, a relative of the author of this paper and a Lithuanian by option—in contrast to the other "Lithuanian" members of his family—had his tomb in Fontainebleau engraved with "Milasius." The extremely ambiguous state of ethnic identity among the Lithuanians often became hostility when confronted with the nationalism of the "boors." This is more understandable if we keep in mind that the word "Lithuania" designated both the Grand Duchy as a whole and the ethnic area alone. Many Polonized families, natives of the Grand Duchy, had nothing to do with the Lithuanian stock, since their ancestors were Eastern Slavs who spoke old Byelorussian. Animosity was also exacerbated, especially during World War I and immediately after, by the Wilno question. Once the capital of Lithuania, Wilno contained by the twentieth century only a small group of people who spoke Lithuanian, a fact which seemed to validate Poland's claim to it. The religious factor introduced an additional complication. Both those who spoke Lithuanian at home and those who spoke Polish were Roman Catholics, and the traditional attachment to the idea of the Commonwealth (*Respublica*) was strengthened in the minds of the Polonized by their sensitivity to the danger menacing their religious faith first from Russian Orthodoxy and then from Communism. The tiny Baltic states created in 1918 were too weak to provide protection. The question of Wilno, which was appropriated by Poland (with the support of its inhabitants) exacerbated the feud between the two groups in the period between the two World Wars.

The experience of Poles and Lithuanians as American immigrants forms a marked contrast to their life in Europe. In Lithuania everything Polish enjoyed prestige, but in America Poles enjoyed little social status, ranking well below such groups as the Scandinavians or even the Irish. As a consequence of the predominantly upper-class culture in the Polish-Lithuanian *Respublica,* illiterate Poles emigrating to America were particularly helpless in that industrialized nation, since they could rely neither on the status of the "Polish culture" nor on the relatively weak tradition of their own village. In all probability the Lithuanian ethnic group in America fared a little better. One may guess that the "boor," a Lithuanian peasant, left to himself and rooted in his folkloric tradition, proved to be less vulnerable and somehow in a position closer to that of a Scandinavian, German, or an Irish plebeian. Moreover, independent Lithuania between 1918 and 1939 produced a whole new educated class, an intelligentsia with peasant backgrounds. Thus every peasant family there wanted to give their children a high school and university education. This ambition affected the Lithuanian immigrants after 1945. Examples abound of rare tenacity and self-sacrifice on the part of Lithuanian parents when they found themselves in America. A typical example is the case of some friends of mine, both with university degrees, who became manual laborers in order to provide higher education for their children.

A kind of cold war between Lithuania, which claimed Wilno as its capital, and Poland, which held it, did not make life easy for the small Lithuanian ethnic group in the years between the two wars. One high school conducted in Lithuanian, some newspapers, and a fraternity of Lithuanian students at the university who steered clear of their Polish-speaking colleagues, serve to illustrate the situation of a city where Roman Catholic churches had no Lithuanian sermons and songs—except one, St. Nicholas, where the majority of the faithful was composed of servant women, transplanted from their native villages.

Jews

The great number of Jews in the Grand Duchy of Lithuania was for centuries completely separated from the rest of the population by their religion, language (Yiddish), profession (non-agricultural) and even dress. The frozen division between Jews and Christians was a phenomenon typical of several areas and therefore need not be discussed here. What should be mentioned, however, is the place of a non-rural group in a purely rural civilization. They monopolized many branches of handicraft and trade, acting as suppliers of goods to the manor and village, as innkeepers, and as buyers of agricultural products. Their religious communities were closely supervised by their elders, so that the contamination of Jews by the Christian milieu and vice versa was minimal. The one exception came toward the end of the sixteenth century, when a radical Protestant movement with an anti-trinitarian orientation (Arianism, Polish Brethren, the Minor Church) invoked the authority of the Old Testament against that of the New Testament. This led to friendly theological disputes between the sectarians and Jewish rabbis. In the eighteenth century a messianic sect founded by Jacob Frank found many followers among the Jews of the Grand Duchy. Frank, a Jew whose teachings bore a strong Manichean imprint, embraced Catholicism after he had been anathemized by the synagogue, an act which he conceived as a necessary preparation for the advent of a new world. This movement left some marks, since many upper-class families in Lithuania trace their ancestry to "Frankists," the Jewish followers of Frank, who had been baptized. In a way, Frank was a precursor of the Jewish rush beyond the confines of the ghetto. The Enlightenment touched the ghetto at the very end of the eighteenth century and the beginning of the nineteenth century, but here the political predicament of the area made the whole problem of Jewish assimilation a complex one. The entire area, as a consequence of the partitions of the *Respublica*, came under the domination of Russia. Of course, the choice of a language which would supplant Yiddish imposed itself upon the Jews. Polish had preserved throughout some three decades of the nineteenth century a half-official standing, and the *Haskalah* (Enlightenment) movement among the Wilno Jews turned at first to Polish as the instrument of written expression. The career of an interesting writer, Julian Klaczko (1825-1906) illustrates this. A native of Wilno, he started to write in Hebrew, then switched to Polish, only to change his language once again when he emigrated to Paris, where he remained a Polish patriot, though renowned as a contributor in French to the best Parisian reviews. Not many such instances, however, could be quoted in Lithuania. After the end of a liberal policy in St. Petersburg and when the official language was increasingly imposed upon reluctant subjects of the newly acquired territories, those Jews who were emancipating themselves from the traditional ghetto felt the attraction of a huge area with its unified culture. Things went a different way in other parts of the Polish-Lithuanian *Respublica* after its partition by foreign powers. In central Poland a considerable number of Jews entered the ranks of the intelligentsia, thus becoming Poles of Jewish origin. In the Hapsburg Empire, German and Polish competed for the allegiance of the Jews. The seductive power of Vienna was strong and the story of Sigmund Freud's family is rather typical. Yet many

Polish scholars and writers in Galicia had a Jewish background, especially at the time when the Polish intelligentsia was changing its character and absorbing groups which until now had been barred from access to higher education (peasants, Jews, and women); that process gathered momentum at the very end of the nineteenth century. The Russian orientation of the Lithuanian Jews produced a large group of the socalled Litvaks, namely those Jews who, instead of Yiddish or Polish, spoke Russian at home. Antagonism existed between Litvaks and the Jews from central Poland, not to mention the Jews from Galicia, for whom Russian was a completely alien tongue. Since the policy of St. Petersburg in Lithuania consisted of a forceful Russification, especially after the uprising of 1863, the non-Jews regarded Jews as allies of the Tsarist government by the very fact of their switching to the Russian language and spreading the gospel of great Russian literature. A continuation of that state of affairs was also noticeable in the revolutionary movement, beginning with the 1890s. The movement split into two socialist parties, the Polish Socialist Party and the Social-Democratic Party of the Kingdom of Poland and of Lithuania, with the two parties unequally dividing sympathies of emancipated Jews. Most favored the second party, since it rejected the national aspirations of ethnic groups that had been absorbed by the Russian Empire and relied upon the All-Russian Revolution which would solve all the problems automatically. The socialist Jewish organization, *Bund*, represented a specific program close to that of the Polish Socialist Party, yet its members were not Litvaks, but Jews clinging to Yiddish. In the period between the two wars, when Wilno belonged to Poland, the Jewish community was internally divided in a fantastic way. Russian schools in Wilno could count on Jewish pupils only because the number of Russian Christians was exceedingly small. However, Wilno was a strong center of studies in Yiddish and Hebrew. The Jewish Institute of Wilno was to be transferred during World War II to New York. Books and newspapers in Yiddish testified to the vigor of the language, but many young people were also trained in Hebrew and were subsequently instrumental in making Hebrew the official language of Israel. Polish schools did not attract many Jewish pupils, and in this respect the situation was different from that in Central Poland, where Poles whose fathers or grandfathers had used Yiddish were numerous. As to the Lithuanian and the Byelorussian languages, they attracted almost no Jews in the region of Wilno.

Politically, varieties of Zionism competed with socialism and communism; the latter was rather popular, since in this area it was a direct descendant of the Social Democratic Party of the Kingdom of Poland and Lithuania. The result was anti-Semitic slogans, since the Poles and the Lithuanians only rarely were sympathizers of Russia, in her tsarist or communist incarnation.

In the region of Wilno, anti-Semitism was not as strong as in Central Poland where there existed a class of non-Jewish small shopkeepers. The right-wing anti-Semitic Polish National Democratic Party (*Narodwa Demokracja*) scored successes primarily at the University, where Jews and non-Jews had separate student unions. The composition of the student body did not, however, correspond to the ethnic composition of the city, since it admitted students from all over Poland, thus representing rather a cross-section of the whole country. What was characteristic of Wilno was the prevalence of the type of Jew who was quite sure of his ethnic identity, whether he was Litvak or a speaker of Yiddish. If there were some Poles of Jewish extraction, they were mostly imports from Poland proper. In general, survivals of the traditional set-up were so strong until 1939 and the economic backwardness of the area so marked that it is difficult to guess what the probable course of Jewish assimilation would have been, had not the crime of genocide committed by the Nazis put an abrupt end to the centuries-old life of Jewish Wilno.

Byelorussians

To my knowledge there is practically no literature on this subject free from Polish or Lithuanian bias. It is also doubtful whether those few Byelorussians who wrote about their compatriots in the region of Wilno are any more reliable. The Byelorussian nationality was probably the last to appear in Europe. As to the identity of those who once used old Byelorussian in writing, the idea of calling themselves Byelorussians would not have occurred to them. If they belonged to the privileged class, they considered themselves for centuries nobles of Lithuania. Like their brethren of ethnic Lithuanian stock, they abandoned their tongue for Polish. For peasants the concept of nationality was alien up until the 1930s. Upon being asked during a census about nationality they answered either Catholic or Orthodox, or simply: "I am from here." That does not mean that the notion of an ethnic identity (of being "from here") was absent. Religious denomination served here as the dividing line. The Orthodox religion distinguished one village from a neighboring village inhabited by Roman Catholic Lithuanians. It also distinguished between the inhabitants of the village and those people in the neighborhood who represented a higher social status, i.e., those who spoke Polish, whether they belonged to the petty gentry, owned a manor, were foresters, or were craftsmen. Those people also confessed to Roman Catholicism. It should be mentioned here that peasants of Eastern Orthodox faith were former Greco-Catholics: the Greco-Catholic or Uniate Church, created as a consequence of the Union of Brest (1596) which had been engineered by the Polish Jesuits, was administratively destroyed by the Tsarist government; in other words, its independence from Rome was restored in the nineteenth century.

The Byelorussian peasant remained throughout all the turbulent history of the area the passive object of powers incomprehensible to him. He was gaining silent victories wherever his village neighbored on a Lithuanian village. For complex and little-elucidated reasons, the non-Slavic Baltic element had a tendency to recede territorially. Through intermarriage and gradual adaptation to Byelorussian, a Lithuanian village would melt into a Slavic and Orthodox mass. In such a fashion the area south and east of Wilno, once Lithuanian, became Byelorussian. Byelorussian villages, however, in the close neighborhood of Wilno, no longer in the twentieth century spoke Byelorussian, but rather a peculiar slang of "people from here," namely, Polish strongly influenced by Byelorussian and to some extent by Lithuanian. That idiom was somehow reminiscent of sixteenth century documents, many of which preserved a curious mixture of Polish and old Byelorussian, as well as a mixture of two alphabets, Latin and Cyrillic. The ethnic identity on the level of high school or university education was, during the period between the two wars, more or less closely related to Communism. A young Byelorussian who harbored strong class resentment looked with hostility at the manor and at the Polish administration and looked for his sense of history to the capital of the Soviet Byelorussian republic, Minsk, with its Byelorussian University, its press and books published in his native tongue. Stories of purges and persecutions related by escapees from the Soviet Republic contributed to the effort to create some sort of independent national movement. But the intolerance of the Polish authorities, for whom the Byelorussian nationality was a bizarre invention, strengthened the appeal of Communism. For other groups it was very difficult to understand what Byelorussianism was about. Traditionally, the language was considered a folk dialect closer to Polish than, let us say, Provencal is to French. To boost the national morale the young Byelorussian intelligentsia invoked the official language of the Grand Duchy of Lithuania, claiming it to be their own, although it differed considerably. These young enthusiasts also laid claim to literary monuments as the first printed translation of the Bible into the vernacular in the Polish-Lithuanian *Respublica,* since that vernacular was not Polish but old Byelorussian (Franciszek Skoryna's *Bible,* printed 1517-1525). Also the speeches of lords from Lithuania in the Polish Diet were frequently given in old Byelorussian. The past, however, was irretrievable, since the dialect had earlier been used by the nobility and some burghers in cities, classes which later switched to Polish. Thus, Byelorussian remained a language suddenly halted in its literary development and revived by nationalists only at the beginning of the twentieth century. Its rich folklore and particularly beautiful folk music have not been matched by literary works of genuine value, except by a small number of poems. Perhaps this judgment is unfair, since we should take into account the unenviable conditions of national life that still persist. Yet this perspective reflects the attitude toward the Byelorussians of all the other groups in the region of Wilno and explains why young Byelorussians identified education with training in nationalist-leftist militancy. As I said before, there were instances when in the same family one man heeded "the call of blood" to become a Byelorussian, his brother the same call to become a Lithuanian, the third to become a Pole. Yet even though we may debate the rank in the social hierarchy of any particular group, it was generally recognized that the lowest place on this scale was for the Byelorussians. This was certainly nothing new—Byelorussian folksongs are heart-rending in their melancholy tone and their images of centuries of oppression.

Tartars

Since no native inhabitants of Lithuania would have embraced the Moslem religion, the mosques in Wilno and in some neighboring villages testify to the presence of immigrants who arrived many years ago, mostly in the fourteenth and fifteenth centuries. Lithuanian Dukes had gladly used them as soldiers and recompensed them for their services with land. Because of their religion the Tartar villages preserved their separation from the surroundings. Their status was superior to that of peasant villages, because being settlers from outside, the Tartars were never just serfs of landlords. As to their native tongue, they abandoned it during the seventeenth century, preserving for quite a long time, however, the Arabic alphabet. Some extant religious books are written in a mixture of Polish and old Byelorussian, but in Arabic letters. Being quite energetic, many Tartars acquired estates and titles of nobility. In such a way the upper class in Lithuania numbered not only people of Lithuanian, Eastern Slavic, immigrant-Polish, and immigrant-German stock, but also Frankists and Tartars. The social peers of the Frankists and Tartars accepted them, but on different bases. The acceptance of the first was due to their being Christians, while for some strange reasons a noble of Tartar origin was accepted even if he remained a Moslem. Tartar villages, on the other hand, could be cited as a case of religious barriers that led to economic barriers. If certain professions were a distinctive mark for the Jews, something similar applies to the Tartar villages, which in certain districts monopolized the production of leather goods, such as sheepskin coats or gloves.

The ethnic identity of Moslems was well-preserved, taking the form of pride in their warrior ancestry. In the 1930s two periodicals (*The Tartar Yearbook* and *Tartar Life*) appeared in Wilno, both published in Polish. They are interesting by virtue of their catering to the ideal of the "Lithuanian

Tartar" (of Polish language) well-rooted in his adopted country. Those publications usually traced the history of the deeds of valor performed by the Tartars in the service of the Polish-Lithuanian commonwealth. The upper-class orientation on the part of the Moslems explains their being little attracted by the Lithuanian element and the Byelorussian element, though some Tartar villages spoke Byelorussian rather than Polish. In general, however, Moslems had a tendency to melt into the Polish-speaking intelligentsia of gentry origin.

Karaites (Karaim)

A tiny ethnic and religious group which in this century numbers barely a few thousand all over the world, the local Karaites were, like the Moslems, a relic of the Grand Duchy's expansion far to the south, to the shores of the Black Sea. At one time the Kievan Rus' dealt with the Khazars, an industrious tribe that had converted to Judaism. Karaites, a Judaic sect not recognizing the Talmud and the tradition, was a part of the Khazar scene. The history of the sect in the subsequent centuries is obscure, no less obscure than the circumstances in which some Karaites settled in Wilno and the surrounding neighborhood during the reign of the Grand Duke Vytautas at the end of the fourteenth century. Karaites created an exotic island, being neither Christians nor Jews. They were distinguished by their physical type and their language, which was incomprehensible to others. They were by tradition cucumber growers. They are mentioned here because their influence in Wilno was quite out of proportion to their small number. The most closed religious-ethnic group, they possessed a temple (*Kenessa*), a head of their religious hierarchy who was their spokesman, and published one periodical in Polish (*Karaite Thought*) and one in the Karaite language.

CONCLUSION

Wilno, as a city marked by the social transformations of the twentieth century, reflected to a large extent the ethnic differentiation in the countryside. A rural district possessed manors where Polish was spoken, a few gentry villages inhabited by Polish-speaking farmers with titles of nobility though they labored in their fields like ordinary peasants, a little town, Yiddish in its commercial center, Polish in its workers' and craftsmen's outskirts, and villages, either Lithuanian or Byelorussian. Since Wilno lacked villagers, Polish and Yiddish prevailed. The intelligentsia, white-collar workers, and merchants were either of noble origin or of Jewish origin. The local burgher class, although its traditions went back a couple of centuries, had become extremely weak. The core of the Wilno population lived either in the narrow, picturesque streets of the ghetto or were artisans and workers who lived in the village-like outskirts of the city. For the majority of the population in that area the modern idea of national identity that followed the lines of language and ethnic stock came as a surprise. Yet choices had to be made and for the most part they were made, thus creating a web of mutual resentments and mutual hostilities.

If one takes a detached view, the tragic fate of that corner of Europe acquires comic and macabre dimensions. Poland and Lithuania could not resolve peacefully the question of Wilno, which remained a bone of contention throughout the two decades between the two wars. The Soviet Union, in fulfilling the Molotov-Ribbentropp agreement, occupied Wilno in September 1939, only magnanimously to offer it two weeks later to Lithuania. However, already at that time the fate of all three Baltic states was sealed. The Nazi offensive in the summer of 1941 reached Lithuania in a couple of days and opened three long years of terror and genocide. The whole Jewish population of Wilno was first closed within the walls of the ghetto and then massacred. After the terror and mass deportations applied by the Soviet Union between 1939 and 1941, Lithuanians and Byelorussians, much like the Ukrainians in the South, for a while attached some hope to the arrival of the Germans. They were soon disillusioned, and the Nazi policy in that part of Europe was exemplary in its folly, though consistent in one respect—scorn for the sub-humans, i.e., any ethnic group other than German. It is difficult to know if the Germans were responsible for the hostilities that emerged between the ethnic groups, particularly between the Poles (or rather, "Lithuanians") and Lithuanians, before the Red Army entered Wilno again in 1944. Perhaps the massacre of Polish and Lithuanian guerilla units by each other in the name of patriotism were the result of old hatreds. The Poles maintained that Wilno should belong to Poland, the Lithuanians that Vilnius has always been and would be a part of Lithuania. Perhaps those sardines fighting each other in the mouth of a whale are not untypical of the relations between humans when they search for self-assertion through ethnic values magnified into absolutes.

Role of Color in Identification Processes

F. H. M. RAVEAU

14

The Social Psychiatry Center of the Ecole Pratique des Hautes Etudes has for several years been conducting research on the pathology of acculturation by studying minority populations in a situation of adaptation in France. In our research we have been concerned with the identification processes of a black African guest minority involved in assimilating the cultural models of the white majority in the industrial Western host society.

We have been struck by the importance of skin color for both failure and success in these processes. Observing African minorities in France is a unique situation, but we believe that we have assembled a set of experimental conditions relevant to the developing African countries which can perhaps lead to a complete structural study of the problems of identification with new cultural models. The dynamic of exchanges in psycho-social processes is often invisible in normal behavior, but is revealed through the disorder of disease, which magnifies certain of its aspects and may in this way provide valuable information towards an understanding of the behavior patterns of subjects or groups considered normal.

Over 1,000 Melano-Africans have been included in our studies. They come for the most part from French-speaking West African countries, since they were in the zone of influence of the former French colonial empire. We have also studied minorities from Madagascar, Vietnam, Haiti and the French West Indies by the same method, which involves making an inventory of incidents that could occur during their stay in the host society. We use the term "route of adaptation" because we have in mind a road strewn with obstacles of varying size. Resistance of the white milieu may show up, for example, in all kinds of discrimination: housing, sex, etc. Or the subject may resist this milieu, eventually overcoming his resistance or remaining bound by it.

The African coming from a tropical country to a temperate climate first encounters a different bioclimatic environment—the cold, the different amount of light affecting the opto-hypothalamic relays, the disturbances in diet—all at first convey in purely physically terms the difference of milieu. Simultaneously, he experiences modifications in the activity of his psycho-social rhythms due to modifications of the time schedule. The new immigrant is also faced with "color shock," an awareness of the color difference existing between the subject and the milieu in which he suddenly finds himself. This traumatic discovery can be interiorized without symptoms, or exteriorized in a phobic mode. For example, a person may experience an irrational fear of being shut in with many white people, a fear that will keep him away from public transport, cinemas, etc. Color shock may also take the form of an obsession in which the person practices various conjuration rites expressed in themes from his native culture. One of our cases was able to communicate, through drawings and paintings, the intense anxiety he felt when confronted with a crowd of whites. The dreams we collected at the outset during adaptation offer the first cultural syncretisms and valuable information on this "color experience." Scenes of daily activity in France show black characters in African surroundings, then black characters in white surroundings or whites in African surroundings, until colors and situations mingle in a chaotic kaleidoscope.

Thus biological and cultural experiences are associated in a sort of Pavlovian conditioning, and will be lived out simultaneously both in their affects and in their explicative rationalization:

"The weather is cold. I am cold. They are different. They are white. I am black."

"They eat different food. They are different. They are white. I have a stomach-ache. I am black."

"I am nervous (or tired). They are different. They are white. I am black."

After a little while, it could be read the other way round. The subject accounts for all his discomforts in terms of color difference: "It's because I'm black among white people that I'm anxious, asthenic, impotent."

A heightened evaluation of the body image is experienced, formulated in a psychosomatic language, learned through living out the experience of this change of milieu. The subject rationalizes discomforts in terms of evident difference, in other words, in terms of color.

The host milieu shares the same impression in reverse, and uses color, the most apparent difference, to account for the symptoms felt by the black man. There is a whole arsenal of preconceived ideas that are expressed by sentences beginning with "Blacks feel the cold. Blacks get tuberculosis. Blacks are no good in this climate, etc."

It is here that the idea of corporal schema is introduced. Franz Fanon had already wanted to use this idea as the basis for a physical perception of negritude, but on this level of color he confused intersubjective relations with purely intrasubjective relations. "Corporal schema" refers to the sum of exteroceptive, proprioceptive and interoceptive sensations, mixed with vestibulary and visual perceptions. The different paths meet at the level of the diencephalon, in the thalamic nuclei, and are projected into the parieto-temporal area, where the integration of these various elements takes place, from which each individual builds up the image of his own body. As is the case with all other sensorial areas, there exists a zone of projection (this "schema") and a zone of association (the image), here connected with the limbic system, of paramount importance in determining viscero-affective behavior. We do know that there exist no specific color receptors responsible for keeping this zone of the brain informed, so the information transported cannot therefore include the notion of color in the corporal schema. Circuits exist at the critical level which permit and control learning. It is thus possible to insert this realization of a difference of color—of the image—obtained by the retinohypothalamic relays, into a chain of behavior patterns.

The stresses of bioclimatic change lead to an entirely physiological alteration in perception of the corporal schema, thus creating a quite specific sensation of anxiety, conducive to learning processes and therefore to new associations. This anxiogenic modification due to the interpretation of the iterative stimulus of fresh needs leads to a new attitude, which is now anxiolytic since it is an anticipation either of the object of the need or of the relation to this object. The body image, thus restored at a new stage, is then completed by a new fantasy of objectal relation to color, which has been imprinted concomitantly with other stresses. In Pavlovian terms, this is a conditioning to the other color. In a way there is simultaneously an awareness both of his own color, anxiogenic in the new environment, in the acculturative situation in a context of stress, and an awareness of the different color of the reassuring models (anxiolytic, experienced as an achievement, a protection).

By favoring investment in a model, identification transforms the learning of new behavior patterns into a social relation which makes the change possible. However, for this to happen there must be a dialogue, and integration will depend on the success of different interactions, presupposing phenomena of reciprocity in the opposite members of the dominant milieu. This is the point at which the psychotherapist can apply effective action.

One of the important stages in this experience is the integration of the new body image, now including color, "somatized" in a way. It would seem that this gives us a possibility of formulating this language of the body (in a classic psychiatric nosography we could link it up with hysteria). Over 95 percent of our cases somatize their modes of entry into the adaptation neurosis, which becomes symbolic of the failure of the dialogue we mentioned above. The body becomes what it imagines itself to be, so as to anticipate what it might be able to do. The new image of the body thus appears as the center of reference for behavior. Psychologists applying the Rorschach test were struck by the high frequency of references to the body image. Neurotic symptomatology is almost entirely expressed at the level of the organs with a frequency which sets these black African groups apart from other hospital samples who have a similar cultural origin, in that they are able to draw on a stock of folk images to interpret their ills.

At this level we link up with the clinical observations of the first practitioners who had studied the mental pathology of Melano-Africans and who had been struck by the hysteroid character of the syndromes. In all the dreams of our cases we find, through a symbolism peculiar to the native culture, a meaning indicating the profound disturbance and confusion in applying colors to situations evoked: forms supposed to be white turn out to be black, or vice versa. Erotic investment with sex-objects ambiguous as to color sometimes occurs and lends itself to interpretation as homosexual fantasy. In a survey which Roger Bastide directed for UNESCO he often found among the black males questioned interdicts concerning women of their race, whom they looked upon as sisters, fenced off by all the taboos pertaining to sisterhood.

We think we have sufficiently emphasized the fact that even if the subject in the process of adaptation builds his body image and his anticipations on new cultural symbols offered by the host milieu, these symbols can become operative only if they imply a modified body image. The subject is thus led to change his needs and their expression, his interests, his reference system of values, his modes of knowledge of others and his system of relations, all by constructing in fantasy different plans of behavior and retaining the one which proves most gratifying. This process takes place through identification with reassuring social models presented by normative subjects, giving rise to the problem of criteria for model selection.

It is in the fantasies of identification that the new culture is seen to be linked with the new image of the body (plus color). The fantasies are induced by proposed socio-cultural models, and lead to the need to create a modified body image in order to achieve a satisfactory integration. It is here that color sets up a formidable barrier. For Africans, gratifying finality can be found in temporary models, and so all kinds of provisional patterns are created, which leads to scattered behavior. The subjects evolve more or less successfully from one to the other, according to Roger Bastide's "*principe de coupure*."

For a Sarakole worker, filling a humble job in Paris for two or three years in order to take some savings back to his country and buy his share of a herd, the new models will be found within his community, which is a sort of retribalization carried out in the midst of the city. Identification with a gratifying image of the same skin color, in the group provides a temporary answer to a temporary need. Mental pathology in these groups of workers is the lowest among all the Africans we studied in Paris. There is a situation of precarious adaptation, an autarchic life in the bosom of a vast protective community. On the other hand, the lone African becomes fragile: he requires other models and his problems begin.

For a student, a trainee, an isolated African, color becomes an obstacle, and if the new models and new images cannot be reconciled, the change becomes pathogenic. Removal of anxiety is then achieved through a narcissistic withdrawal which permits him to recuperate in a fantasy world that consists of the African cultural theme of bewitchment and the explicative exteriorization of his ills, that is, persecution.

The behavior patterns of the new milieu are very much desired, but are made incomprehensible or inaccessible by the impossibility of formulating an adequate fantasy, since the color of the body image blocks any successful identification. We often find this in the apparent absurdity of certain patterns of conduct characterized by behavior reminiscent of play-acting. These patterns rapidly wear thin with use, since they require the audience around them to contribute continual confirmation by an ever-exaggerated parodic attitude. We find these types of cultural mimicry among psychotics in our hospital, but also at large among our cases who at a further stage of their evolution show a type of apprenticeship either elementary (often linked with a low IQ) or badly lived (often linked to the secondary benefits of old, encysted neuroses).

This failure to achieve identification then produces feelings of inferiority and of guilt, which become obstacles in their turn and widen still further the distance between the subject and his goal. We then finally reach regression, resulting in incoherence through the apparent disorder of the symptomatic expressions, or notions of unworthiness caused by failure, which lead to depressive or suicidal behavior. The *bouffée délirante* in Africans can thus be clarified in its etiodynamics.

In our consultations we find that mental illness is almost invariably entered through somatization of conflicts; it is because we are witnessing a neuroticization of this pathology and we get further from the acute psychotic phase expressed in the *bouffée délirante.* This can be imputed to the fact that the African no longer seeks his models on the same level today as in the days of colonialism. The relations of authority reigning at that time led to radical failures in the acquisition of new models. Dr. Aubin's work on neuroses among black troops in the French army illustrates this point. He described a situation of frustration institutionalized by the authoritarian structure of the army or of the colonial hierarchy. Skin color therefore renders certain models inaccessible. A gulf separates the postulant subject from his model and creates frustration, anxiety, and hostility, which become obstacles to mastery of the proposed or desired model.

In *metis* societies where the high value put on one color—the whitening process, for example—facilitates the behavior of the palest and handicaps that of the darkest, all depends on the permanence of the normative patterns of conduct put forward by these societies. The socio-cultural problems of classes acquiring and settling into power, the weight of interpreted history, makes the situations less schematic. Politicization of color on the national level, as seen in the young African states, leads to preferential nationalisms, and color then assumes a positive role in adaptation within the African's own culture. It may lead to a rationalization, in which new nationalisms are explained in term of color, as Klineberg has shown in his last UNESCO survey.

Let us try to imagine how we might put color to a therapeutic use. Colored milieux in a situation of adaptation set up a resistance to a complete realization of their otherness, and express by an ambivalent attitude the feelings arising from a conflict in which the defense mechanisms of the ego often bring into play motivations incompatible with one another. "I accept myself as black so I may become white." That is to say, "I set a high value of my negritude so as to master forms of conduct which will ensure control of the milieu, and also techniques yielding high returns." What is agreeable for one system of values becomes inadequate in the other. To recognize oneself as black is to exclude oneself. Not to recognize oneself as black is an incomplete identification, source of neurogenic discomfort. Synthesis presupposes an ego with sturdy defenses and a socio-cultural framework in which these may operate.

Thus with the milieu acquiescent and guilty, a state of symbiosis may exist, in which color difference is utilized as an extra gain, a ploy similar to the secondary benefits of neurosis. Rather than outright libidinal satisfaction, it will often be a matter of narcissism linked with self-preservation: "Because I'm black they won't dare refuse me such and such a social gratification," or

"Because I'm black I can make use of the guilty conscience of the white milieu to arrange an existence, somewhat dependent but well protected." Indeed, we know that it is usual for a company to employ a certain quota of blacks, preferably in visible positions.

In cases where neurotic compensation indicates an inability to master such divergent lines of conduct, the psychotherapist's friendly neutrality can make things easier, helped by the phenomenon of transfer. Here arises the problem of the indications for using this vector of acculturation that the psychotherapist has become. These can be decisive for the social future of the subject. Also, if the sojourn in the white society is to be prolonged, the psychotherapist should be white; he should be black if the stay is short.

But we have to take into account the dominant milieu and the part it plays in the acquisition of new identities. This milieu seeks to repress, to retain in the unconscious, its reactions to the color of the minorities living in its midst. If it ventures to recognize this evidence, it exposes itself to unpleasant conflicts provoked by other exigencies, mainly ethical, which severely condemn such racist reactions. In turn, realization of this refusal leads the rejected colored minorities to edify mythic models—proteiform, and therefore easier to acquire. This may possibly explain the revendication of color as a culture model: the confusion arises from the need to confront a dominant culture with a dominated color.

REFERENCES

1. Bastide, R. "Problèmes de l'Entrecroisement des Civilisations et de leurs Sens." *Traite de Sociologie.* Paris: PUF, 1963.
2. Bastide, R. *Sociologie des Maladies Mentales.* Paris: Flammarion, 1965.
3. Berthaud-Gibello. "Schema Corporal et Image du Corps." *Perspectives Psychiatriques* 3(29), 1970.
4. Devereux, G. "La Rénonciation a l'Identite: Defense contre l'Aneantissement." *Rev Francaise de Psychanalyse* 31:101-142, 1967.
5. Dolto. "Personnologie et Image du Corps." *La Psychanalyse* 6(59), 1961.
6. Erikson, E. H. *Identity, Youth and Crisis.* New York: Norton, 1968.
7. Fisher, S. *Body Image and Personality.* Princeton, N.J.: Van Nostrand, 1958.
8. Raveau, F. "An Outline of the Color in Adaptation Phenomena." *Daedalus,* Spring 1967.
9. Richer, S. "La Notion d'Image du Corps et Certaines Recherches Recentes sur la Personnalite." *Entretiens Psychiatriques,* 10, 1964.
10. Schilder, P. *The Image and Appearance of the Human Body.* International University Press, 1951.

Conclusions

PART SIX

Ethnicity: Vessel of Meaning and Emblem of Contrast

GEORGE DE VOS and LOLA ROMANUCCI-ROSS

15

The preceding chapters were discussed together by their authors for several days. In this concluding chapter we attempt to integrate a number of themes which emerged during the course of these subsequent discussions. We begin with a consideration of the themes of origin, rules, and contrasts with respect to ethnic identity, followed by a brief discussion of ethnic leadership. Our third section discusses changes in ethnic identity through the life span of the individual—the intertwining problematics of ethnic and personal identity at various stages of the life cycle. Finally, we look at a large group of issues related to the instrumental and expressive uses of ethnicity.

ORIGINS, RULES, AND CONTRASTS IN ETHNIC IDENTITY

Where are we from?

As discussed in Chapter One, ethnic identity is in essence a past-oriented form of identity, embedded in the cultural heritage of the individual or group. This form of identity contrasts with a sense of belonging linked with citizenship within a political state, or present-oriented affiliations to specific groups demanding professional, occupational, or class loyalties. It also contrasts with those identities that reject both past and present in favor of a future-oriented ideological commitment to a cause or social goal. Ethnicity is symbolically represented in self-conscious variations in language and customs. It is symbolized in the ritual practices which are its affirmation, particularly by dramatic symbolic representation of a past. Ethnicity is explained by religious myth, since religious beliefs or myths are, in effect, very often attempts at explanation of group origin. To know one's origin is to have not only a sense of provenience, but perhaps more importantly, a sense of continuity in which one finds to some degree the personal and social meaning of human existence. It is to know *why* one behaves and acts in accordance with custom. To be without a sense of continuity is to be faced with one's own death. Extinction of a group occurs when, as a California Indian once remarked to anthropologist Alfred Kroeber, "the cup of custom is broken and we can no longer drink of life."

Two alternate forms of myth occur as explanations of origin among peoples of the world. There are the autochthonous myths of human origin from a given sacred place, and alternatively, the religious myths which dramatize "the journey"—an event buried in the distant past. The myths explaining origin buttress a conviction that one's group arrived "here" from elsewhere. Origin in this sense has a spatial dimension. One's sense of social meaning and social belonging also obtains from moving through time, both as an individual and as a member of a group and a culture. Traditions characteristically present a script for group continuity from the past into the future, taking great care to perpetuate factual fictions or fictional facts as links that bind the generations.

Concern with origins is a concern with parentage. To know who they are, individuals and groups look back "genealogically" to their progenitors. Some mythologies explain how men and women descended from a primordial mating event; others explain group diversity as totemically originating from different animals or plants. In Judeo-Christian mythology, the Tower of Babel marks the origin of linguistic diversification by punitively dividing groups from each other for their presumption to wish to know the Father. Explanations of origin help to explain present differences between groups as well as providing the rationale for such differences. The Judeo-Christian tradition, for example, purports to explain racial origins as a result of Noah's attitude toward his children. Human conflict emphasized contrast, and so out of unity springs diversity.

Curiously enough, a number of mythological traditions indirectly reveal the converse. They are attempts by a cultural group, for the sake of present cohesion, to deny previous diversity of origin by disguising evidence of past amalgams that occurred through conquest. Greek myths excel in disguising such past conflicts, including changes from matrilineal to patrilineal descent as a result of conquest. The book of Genesis in the Hebrew Bible, according to Freud, disguises the separate tribal origins of the Jews. It gives internal evidence suggesting that there occurred a blending of several deities into one Jehovah. Similarly, the ancient Japanese mythology preserved in the Kojiki and Nihongi gives internal evidence that prior political conflict was resolved religiously by producing a more unified pantheon of deities.

What must we do?

Origin myths establish who one is, and, because of one's progenitors, with which group one has rights and obligations. Such knowledge helps the individual resolve priorities of loyalty and allegiance. It helps to integrate and regulate his behavior. It defines the classes of persons toward whom he can express affection, or vent aggression.

The sense of history is celebrated in collective ritual. Ritual acts are also expressions of commitment, be it to a religion, to a nation of loyal citizens, or to an ethnic group. Such acts are a collective experience that teaches those who participate who they are. The redundancy of ritual goes beyond verbal expression by reinforcing emotional response. Participants identify with one another in the sharing of an implicit sense of purpose. Rituals of belonging are reaffirmations of origin, dramatizations of ancestral suffering and triumph, out of which future purpose is born and sustained. For example, for the Jews the sacred holidays commemorate historical occurrences that reaffirm reasons for continuity. The Communion ritual for the Christian (ingesting the body of Christ from a common vessel) represents both the historical fact of the beginning of Christianity and the sense of belonging to a group that moves forward with a purpose toward the last judgment.

In modern societies, as in folk cultures, the reasons for present rules are often explained mythologically. Taboos of foods and other constraints on behavior are explained in terms of past occurrences, usually a specific mythologized event. It seems that humans always have to know *why* something is or is not done, and so mythology provides the explanations that justify required behavior.

Many of the historical occurrences that are ritualized or become legend tend to be symbolic victories of survival, or attempts at revival. In American Indian history, the Ghost Dance was the revivalist ritual of a then defeated people.

Today the massacre at Wounded Knee and the long bloody marches of Indian families forced by the United States government from their eastern homes into western reservations serve as tales of ordeal stimulating a need for survival by the maintenance of group consciousness. Revivalist movements and legends of ordeal are an affirmation of the state of affairs that existed before a traumatic defeat which has marked a people. What is symbolized is an extension backwards in time to a time of group strength that existed prior to defeat. As we indicated in the introduction, the contemporary militant black movement among Negroes in the United States contains an explicit and an implicit affirmation of an African identity as a point of origin. Ancestry pre-dates the experience of slavery in the New World. In claiming group origin prior to defeat or degradation, the individual is asserting that defeat is temporary and one must create a new dignity by re-establishing the status that was disturbed by the vicissitudes of history.

In rituals of affirmation that re-enforce ethnic identity, there is often a reference to a mythical golden age before the fall. The Romanucci-Ross chapter mentions the recent example of Fascist Italy, which returned to Roman military insignias and titles in an attempt to re-establish a Roman Empire. Italy's invasion of Ethiopia might also be interpreted as an attempt to emulate the colonial strategy of England and France. Thus Italians symbolically wiped out millenia of foreign conquest and subjugation. For authentic Fascists (and there were some) this was an affirmation of pan-Italianism, as was their attempt to purge the Italian language of foreign idioms. Such uses of historical glory to assert cultural integrity are also discussed in the chapters by Hamamsy and Wagatsuma. In their zeal to eradicate borrowed impurities, some Japanese even became anti-Buddhist, since it was a foreign religion which had invaded Japan thirteen centuries earlier. Some French groups, alarmed by the threat of "franglais," are attempting to keep the French language "pure." The Academie Francaise must give its blessing to new words, to make them official, yet 5,000 to 8,000 forbidden words have subversively crept into the language without such approval. Such words include "weekend," "retired," "gangster," "hold-up," "self-service," words that are not considered acceptable because the casual world-view they suggest implies a degradation of the formal quality of a cultured elegant life.

Ethnic identity can be a positive affirmation containing a negative potential for becoming a hysterical or paranoid defense. As in all forms of belonging, it can be used to express one's humanness, or to deny the humanness of others; its use depends on collective and individual mental health. It also depends on the reality of external pressure and oppression.

In addition to creating a sense of common origin, ethnic identity also defines the rules of comportment. The essential correctness of one's own behavior and the behavior of one's group may or may not be contrasted with the behavior of outsiders. Groups differ greatly in the degree to which contrastive criteria are used. Social behavior in conformity to group expectation cannot be completely regulated through socialization. No culture can afford the absence of "reinforcers" of desired behavior. These are understood by all group members as having an inviolability even stronger than formal law. Social sanctioning reinforces group expectations; the individual is vulnerable to the reactions of his group should he break the rules. Membership is validated through attempts at correct behavior. Punishment is meted out to those who break the covenant of belonging through incorrect behavior, thereby destroying group cohesion and threatening group survival. Belonging to a group, then, means being aware of group expectations and group regulations—we know who we are through learning what we are expected to do. The embodiment of the group's identity may be found in periodic ritual religious acts as discussed by Durkheim in *The Elementary Forms of Religious Life* (*6*). It may also be embodied in a written tradition which is at the same time a body of laws, such as the Christian and Jewish Bible or the Koran.

The need to follow unique rules may permit a given people to maintain their identity despite their proximity to others. Indeed, as Schwartz pointed out in Chapter Four, such awareness of proximity and difference may cause the differences to be amplified and to become emblematic. Jews are a well-known case in point, for they have maintained their integrity by following their tribal regulations throughout their history. The Batak in Sumatra, by maintaining their *adat* ("law"), create an illusion of cultural continuity that enables them to move easily into culturally heterogeneous modern cities (*2*). Objectively (i.e., as seen by the outsider) their law changes, but those who identify themselves as Batak perceive no change in their law. Belief in the continuity of law keeps them identified as Batak.

In some ethnic groups recruitment is possible, often simply by bringing in members who will abide by the law. Candidates may be asked to experience a rebirth ritual signifying that they will henceforth recognize and obey the laws joyfully. In cultures where law is the major focus of identity can therefore recruit the outsider who has no birthright to the group. Such emphasis on law is characteristic of the boundary area between ethnic identity and citizenship. As more emphasis is placed on the political dimension of belongingness, a present orientation begins to supplant the past in the sense of social identity. But one finds considerable overlap in this area.

There is a variety of differences of emphasis between a commitment to a state and to an ethnic group. In a pluralistic society, a major sanctioning force of an ethnic group is ostracism. But in commitment to the state one accedes to submission to law and, by force if necessary, to the political authority which is rationalized by all as necessary to survival. One manages to suppress the outer expression of thought, if not repress thought itself, about the state of affairs.

It is possible to be simultaneously a loyal citizen of the state, a part of the superordinate political unit, and a member of an ethnic minority. Problems arise only if the rules are mutually antagonistic. When Jesus was asked about the coin of the Roman realm, he resolved what was supposed to be a conflict over Caesar's and God's possessions by giving to each his own. Many Christians were later persecuted because they insisted on mixing logical levels (to paraphrase Bertrand Russell and Gregory Bateson) and created a dialectic which the Romans took up in a gleeful collusion to send them on their journey to Paradise. For actually, the Romans expected and accepted ethnic and religious diversity, but would not brook the lack of respect implicit in repudiating the necessary symbolic acts of allegiance to the Roman hegemony.

Like other forms of loyalty, ethnic identity is experienced as a moral commitment, making rejection of conflicting moral and legal commitments mandatory. When a commitment becomes future oriented and therefore ideological or politicized, there is less necessity for maintaining ethnic concern with parentage and origin. The initiation ritual seems to suffice, a ritual in which the rebirth usually symbolizes rejection of actual ancestry and a pledge of allegiance to shared future goals of the new group.

How are we different?

A person's behavior tells him who he is, that is, what group he belongs to. Others who behave differently are not part of his group. Thus we know who we are by knowing who we are not. Contrastive roles and their attendant role expectations have a separating function within a society as well as between societies. Contrastive representations mark sex, age and class differences. How one learns about oneself by contrasting oneself to other individuals and groups is important, for only in this way does one develop a strong sense of self. The stances are various—pejorative, belligerent, peaceful, etc.—and their opposites. In his chapter on the English, Geoffrey Gorer raised the question "Who is the audience?" and added that the English, for example, do not pay too much attention to outsiders in trying to define who they are. Other groups create their image at the expense of outsiders. What are the mental health considerations to be extrapolated from considering such modes of group image manufacture and the antagonistic flouting of emblems of identity?

The use of contrast is not so much dictated by geographic proximity as by the nature of the contact with another group. In identity maintenance one has to assess the nature of the possible threat which close contact with an alien group implies. In a modern pluralistic society, where contact is intense and unavoidable, certain minor symbolic "emblematic" measures remain vitally necessary to maintain psychological distance from those outside one's group.

In constructing any theory of ethnic identity it is necessary to consider how external or social distance factors are related to internal or psychological distance factors in identity boundary maintenance. Any or all cultural features can be used emblematically for contrastive purposes: the prescribed and the tabooed, special foods, and social rituals, ideals of physical beauty, phonemic styles. According to Devereux, the Greeks called others "barbarians" because it seemed that everything uttered was "bar bar bar."

Many cultural effects become self-consciously contrastive only when contact with strangers suggests alternatives. Foods have seemed naturally edible or inedible; phonemic sequences natural and logical, standards of beauty divinely decreed. The manner and degree of reaction to newly discovered differences depends on the social or physiological threat posed by the contrastively perceived behavior. There are tolerable and intolerable differences within what is recognized as behavioral contrast. Others doing what is rigidly tabooed by one's own group will be most disturbing. Romanucci-Ross was told by Sori islanders of an event that took place between themselves and Harengan islanders (Admiralty Islands of the Bismarck Archipilago) a long time before culture contact with the West. The Sori were received with all due hospitality and given women, which the Sori thought was very nice indeed. But imagine how horrendously crude of the Harengan men to expect the Sori to lend Sori women when the Harengan paid them a reciprocal visit! The Sori were so offended they broke off all diplomatic and trade relations with the Harengan up to at least 1955 (7).

Projection of negative traits on an alien group is widespread. What is socially disavowed within one's own group is projected as prevalent among outsiders. In the Admiralties one group will often refer to the customs of other New Guinea groups by saying "as in the manner of pigs and dogs."

Contrasts may be viewed on a vertical or a horizontal dimension. Some contrasts neither elevate nor degrade outsiders. In other circumstances a particular pattern of behavior may be seen within a vertical framework of superiority/inferiority. For example, in noting racial difference, Europeans respond diversely depending on whether the subject is African or Chinese. Before the nineteenth century, Europeans were quite impressed by the achievements of the Chinese, and so found it easy to make invidious comparisons between the Chinese and Africans, whom they found primitive, since they understood nothing of the unperceivable (to them) complexities of some

African cultures. Only recently has the European been able to develop some appreciation of the aesthetics of African art as a highly developed alternative to the naturalist traditions which persisted until the end of the nineteenth century in Europe.

In the maintenance of ethnic boundaries, some groups are more insistent on contrastive exclusiveness while others are more open and inclusive. The latter are more apt to bring in individuals to become part of the group rather than continue to emphasize differences. Groups with members who develop a more secure sense of self are not as easily threatened by contrast. Some groups have developed no mechanisms by which new members may be included. One can only enter by birth. Polynesians, for example, exhibit an easy sense of inclusiveness, while the Melanesians are acutely sensitive to differences. Melanesian cultures amplify all possible differences in continually creating new ethnic distinctions. Throughout Polynesia, language is characterized by homogeneity, whereas Melanesians, over similar periods of time, have evolved great linguistic differentiation. Hawaiians consider anyone Polynesian who has had any Polynesian ancestor, no matter how far distant, if he chooses to become a member of the group. Similarly, white American attitudes have dictated that anyone with a black ancestor, no matter how remote, could not be considered white. Margaret Mead's chapter discusses the attempt to maintain contrastive racial distinctions that has been an obvious part of the dilemma of American identity.

One factor determining criteria for exclusion or inclusion is reckoning of descent, whether lineage is traced bilaterally or unilineally. Among Jews, for example, group belonging hinges on whether the mother is a group member, since, according to some scholars, the mother is considered the major disciplinary socializing influence on the children. She is the assurance that the child recognizes and adheres to the law through his formative years. A non-Jewish woman could not properly inculcate "being Jewish" in the child. This reasoning is in accordance with the emphasis in Jewish culture on the regulatory nature of belonging rather than simply on awareness of blood lineage through the mother.

At times a contrastive sense of ethnic identity actually came about through conflict. For example, the Hutterites, who emphasize a contrastive exclusiveness, had their origin in religious protest against the larger society. They owe their continuity not only to their maintenance of separatist behavioral practices, but also to their persecution by a hostile state. When they were no longer meeting with sufficient opposition in Russia to help them sustain the proper group moral tone, they migrated to Canada. Here they again met considerable opposition and developed a stronger sense of cohesiveness. In Melanesia the cargo cult phenomenon, according to

Schwartz, depended on the believers *and* on the non-believers, who provided the dynamic contrastive tensions necessary for the movement to sustain itself. Some cultures seem to thrive on continual internal perturbation. The sense of one's existence in such a culture depends upon a continual rivalry and confrontation within the system. The subjective experience of self in cultures based on contrastive moieties or lineages is dependent upon the continual opposition of subgroups which set the tone of social life.

The internal or external sense of contrast in a culture may, as noted above, be emphasized in either a vertical or horizontal direction. Contrastive ethnic feelings can be directed toward individuals considered equal antagonists, or the sense of ethnic separateness may be based on viewing another group as inferior. In the course of time such a disparaged group may indeed come to view themselves as inferior. They exhibit, in Kardiner's terms (*8*) some internalized "mark of oppression" in their self-concepts.

It is psychologically difficult for groups whose self-esteem has been based on physical prowess to avoid interpreting military and political defeat as proof of personal worthlessness. An unhappy history of ethnic identity is exemplified by the American Indian. As a defeated warrior people forced to live with their conquerors, they have not as yet devised a satisfactory means of escaping the collective psychological effects of the destruction of their own cultural identity in the course of the past century. Jews, on the other hand, defeated and dispersed, nevertheless sustained a pride in the relative invulnerability of their intellectual-religious attainments which buffered the effects of political annihilation. Scots, ambivalent as they have remained over their forced political union with the English, have found compensatory ethnic pride in commercial enterprise, with the added advantage of allowed regional self-sustenance.

Finally, the study of contrast in ethnic identity leads us back to the discussions in Chapter One of stratification in systems of ethnic pluralism. It also relates to the entire question of ethnic ascendancy which we briefly introduced in Part Four. Viewing European history in ethnic terms, one notes the gradual cultural ascendancy of the French, culminating with the reign of Louis XIV. The ascendant French in Europe developed non-reciprocal relations with others, and the French language became internationally dominant. Throughout Europe it became the language of the nobility, and nobility transcended specific ethnic loyalties.

ETHNIC LEADERSHIP

A topic merely broached in this book but needing further exploration is that of the psycho-cultural characteristics of legendary heroes and actual leaders of ethnic movements. How does their behavior, real or mythical, actual or imputed, correspond to the central social issues of highly desirable group traits? "Stagalie," a folk legend of black Americans, is a heroic figure capable of exaggerated violence with bravado and dominance. Such prowess is deemed necessary to survival in the harsh underworld of black counter-culture, a culture developed partially as a result of the denial to blacks of access to the majority society. Clever, cunning and cruel, rogue and outlaw, he is the symmetrical inversion of the traditional, acceptable "Black Sambo," who symbolized to whites the subordinate status of Blacks.

American Indians have a store of heroes ranging from the scheming Apache Geronimo to the religious leader Handsome Lake, all serving as symbols of violent resistance or some form of religious revival that might allow one to avoid acknowledging final defeat. In modern times, Charles de Gaulle represented an attempt at ethnic ascendancy by France, the final resistance to becoming a co-equal rather than a dominant partner in forming a European multi-ethnic community. For Turks, Kamal Ataturk has been a symbol of modern rebirth, a figure of transition through which to be "Turkish" could also mean to be modern. Mussolini was a symbol of an Italian attempt to recapture ethnic pride, an attempt to reassert a past cultural ascendancy which had suffered severely from the seventeenth century on. The Mussolini phenomenon, now repudiated by most Italians as an embarrassing historical incident, symbolized unification and a source of self-esteem. But later his failures also symbolized all the negative traits Italians saw in themselves. In looking for "living space" and a "place in the sun" under Hitler, Germans dreamed of re-creating the Roman Empire, which through the centuries had been a German dream comparable to French dreams from the time of Charlemagne to the Emperor Napoleon.

It is curious that in numerous instances the leader who personifies an ethnic group is an outsider. Such a leader often vehemently affirms his allegiance as the means of overcoming his questionable legitimacy of belonging. Ataturk was of Anatolian ancestry, a minority group within the old Turkish empire. Hitler was an Austrian, possibly of Jewish descent, Napoleon was a Corsican of Italian origin and De Gaulle's ancestors were Flemings who had taken on a new, more French-sounding name to emphasize their loyalty to France. Malcolm X, a leader of the black movement in the United States, was all the more motivated toward a black identity by the previous excruciating ambivalence he experienced when he once attempted to identify strongly with the majority whites (*8*). The reaffirmation of his black identity was a positive resolution of a deep psychological stress—internal tensions were transmuted into a strong need to affirm the black man's right to dignity. The autobiography of Valiers (*11*), a French-Canadian ethnic leader, is a highly poignant parallel to that of Malcolm X, demonstrating the functional similarity between racially or culturally mixed inheritances in producing a divided self, a problem which for some people can be resolved only by an exemplary affirmation which may result in the appearance of a group hero.

A potential sense of alienation in many members of a minority group can be overcome by witnessing in the behavior of the hero the way to become a "true" person. Such a person can bend events to a realization of common purpose. Ethnic identity movements therefore are usually led by individuals who, at given points in their careers, manifest in their own personalities some resolution of previously disturbing internal states, which are also experienced by many other members of the group at large. Such movements also represent collective alternatives to isolated individual attempts at "passing" or guarding one's ethnic feelings in silence. Uchendu in his chapter makes the point that it is not the individual who succeeds, but that success is ultimately a group process that allows for resolution of the dilemmas of minority status. It remains difficult indeed to overcome the history of past conflict. The sense of defeat far outlasts the memory of victory.

SUBJECTIVE CHANGES IN THE INDIVIDUAL EXPERIENCE OF ETHNIC IDENTITY

Just as ethnicity in pluralistic societies cannot be seen apart from the history of a group, so the origins of a person's sense of identity must be traced through the life cycle of an individual. In the introductory chapter we said that vicissitudes in identity occur in different stages of the life cycle in given subcultures within pluralistic societies. Sometimes the essential problem is how to maintain one's identity in spite of change in role definition. Conversely, in some situations, as we shall shortly discuss, the attempt to take on other social attributes for instrumental and expressive reasons brings about a change in behavior.

In modern complex societies, it has become possible to take on behavioral alternatives, varying behavior with changes in reference group, so much so that as Robert Lifton has described it, one sees many examples of "Protean" man, that is, individuals who seem as capable as the mythological Greek, Proteus, of changing social behavior with context. While this capacity has certain adaptive advantages, especially for disguise, it is actualized at some cost to the individual's sense of personal integrity. It is related to the extreme form of "other directedness" discussed by David Riesman.

Society in general expects the individual to maintain some behavioral consistency. He must remain recognizable or social interaction is impossible. In moral terms, an individual is supposed to maintain his "integrity." Ethnic identity, like any form of identity, is not only a question of knowing who one is subjectively, but also of how one is seen from the outside. Ethnic identity requires the maintenance of sufficiently consistent behavior to enable others to place an individual or a group in some given social category, thus permitting appropriate interactive behavior.

Extremes of mobility—social, geographic, or ethnic—are socially disruptive. Society needs consistency in attribution for interpersonal functioning. In other words, identity involves some internally socialized consistency with respect to behavioral norms, so that the individual and the others with whom he is in contact know what to expect in interpersonal relationships. One finds it uncomfortable to be part of a social scene or watch a dramatic presentation in which the players change their designated parts in some inconsistent fashion. To some degree, people have to be able to relate in terms of approximations or stereotypic expectations. Complete unpredictability in another's behavior makes social communication impossible. Internally, an individual also has to maintain his sense of self by certain patterns of consistency. The work of George Herbert Mead describes how a "generalized other" is internalized in the composition of a consistent sense of self.

Self consistency within given cultures is related to the use of altered states of consciousness, which allow a person to overcome the limitations imposed by conscious control of a consistent self. Individuals in trance, for example, are able to act out roles which are too inconsistent with the usual self to be tolerated in an ordinary state of consciousness. A striking example of this process is found in the documentary film by Jean Rouch, "Les Maîtres Fous." On their weekends natives of Ghana who are working in modern industrialized factories participate in a new religion which consists of a communal feast. A live dog is dismembered. The individuals in trance eat and share this "communion." In their trance state they become white officials, exemplifying social power and prestige. Such role behavior was impossible for these people to assume in their ordinary state of consciousness. In trance, however, they could emulate the members of the dominant white culture, strutting and assuming other postures of self-importance. The internal structuring of these assumed roles, of course, remained a foreign mystery to the participants of the feast.

Edward Sapir (*9*) talked about cultures as "genuine" or "spurious," stating, in effect, that a person is only "natural" in one language. A second acquired language never takes on the internal natural emotional richness afforded by one's language of nativity or childhood. Changes of ethnic identity therefore may appear to be somewhat artificial and external if the changes are assumed after personality structure has rigidified into the consistent pattern of an adult. To be subjectively genuine, changes in identity must start sufficiently early to make the assumption of the particular behavior feel natural to the individual.

For the individual, ethnicity is part of the gradual and continual definition of self that occurs as part of psycho-sexual development. It is not our purpose here to discuss the psychological mechanisms through which the process occurs. Suffice it to say that what we term "identity" is to be distinguished from what is discussed psychoanalytically as the mechanism of identification. A sense of identity is, by definition and by implication, a conscious part of the self rather than the operation of unperceived automatic mechanisms. It is a conscious awareness of what and who one is in relation to a social group. An ethnic identity is developed through time and takes on various meanings in the course of one's life experience, as one contrasts one's social group in some measure against the dominant culture and against other groups within it.

Romanucci-Ross discusses briefly in her chapter the continuing internal and external feedback in identity affirmation that is received and acted upon. Primary family and face-to-face identity is influenced in modern society by the multitudinous recordings of experience received through print and other message media. There is a continual onslaught of socially perceived information and continual "editorializing" about it, keeping a person in touch with the past history of his group and its present circumstances. The reverberations of such experiences may not be immediate but rather become particularly significant at crisis periods in the trajectory of a lifetime. The social feedback mechanisms that establish, develop and maintain an ethnic identity have immediate effects and delayed effects which may only become manifest much later in the life cycle.

For some people, crises occur at points of challenge or choice; for others, choice or commitment is gradual or cumulative. Considered figuratively, these points of choice may be imperceptible or highly dramatic. The individual can identify himself by gradually taking on a certain way of behaving, but by so doing he eliminates the possibility of alternate ways of behaving. The process need not be painful, though it can be agonistic over inconsistent and conflictful modes of behavior. Identity theory, therefore, must be related to some concepts of a continuing need for closure, for self-consistency, which embodies both the cognitive and the affective. Some individuals, however, learn to live with ambiguity and dissonance (and as a matter of fact, it is not unknown for this to eventually become a survival tactic, or a means of manipulating others). These internal inconsistencies may find expression in collective social movements as well as in complex forms of individual adjustment or maladjustment.

Choice points are not only related to alternatives between two modes of behavior, they are also related to the levels of inclusiveness to which the individual refers his behavior. The individual may learn to identify with expanding circles of inclusiveness. His first level of inclusiveness is with himself alone, the next perhaps with his family, and other face-to-face relationships in the community. He may transcend his community by identifying with a professional world. The psychological investment in each of these widening or segmenting circles will vary in strength. Ultimately, individual identity may expand to encompass all forms of life, (as in Buddhism).

Our focus in this volume is on the level of belonging related to ethnicity as we have defined it—levels and modes of cultural separateness in one's sense of self. We cannot therefore consider the other realms of identity except insofar as they reflect our particular concern. As discussed by Uchendu in the case of black Africans, there are several alternative levels of belonging in modern societies. One goes from the community or socalled tribal group into a broader identity with a nation-state or a group of similar nations (identification with black Africa, for example) or even with an entire continent (identification with the African continent as a whole in contrast with Europe, Asia or the Americas). Usually an individual can move from one such realm of identity to another without conflict, for one of these identities can be contained within the other. In the case of mutually exclusive ethnic identities, however, there can be crises in which the behavior demanded on one level is inconsistent with the behavior expected on another. It may be that the individual can find no stable position from which to resolve the resulting tensions.

It may be possible to predict the priorities of loyalty in an individual and to determine whether his ethnic identity is given priority over another more inclusive form of identity. To do so, one must understand the functional uses of identity by the individual on both a psychological and a social level. In the following section of our conclusions we discuss what we term the instrumental and expressive uses of identity.

Tensions in ethnic identity are particularly likely when a person attempts to resolve the ambiguity of mixed parentage. In some cultures, the culture itself has a well established pattern on how to handle mixed ancestry. The priority may be given either to the father or to the mother. The son or daughter is supposed to decide to whom he or she belongs in terms of the prior claims of lineage. In a mixed cultural situation, it may not be as easy to find one's identity in terms of lineage. We know this psychological resolution does not always happen, however. We find in some societies tragic representations of conflict related to priority of parental loyalty. The Greek culture, described in Devereux's chapter, produced tragic myths concerning dilemmas of loyalty. For example, the tragedy of Orestes as presented in the Greek plays grows out of the conflict produced by the competing claims of his mother and father for his loyalty. This tragedy embodies a residual problem of Greek cultural history in which patrilineal invaders overran groups with matrilineal descent. In killing his mother to avenge his father, Orestes is affirming his ultimate membership in a more newly established patrilineal system. Symbolically, in the modern age we find tragic dilemmas of belonging related to social racial or ethnic marginality, such as the dilemma of the Eurasian in the novel *Love is a Many Splendored Thing.* There are many tragic instances described in Eastern Europe of members of the same family deciding to be loyal to one or another of the political divisions into which subordinate ethnic groups were arbitrarily divided. Milosz's chapter is one brief glimpse into this highly complex history of ethnic conflict.

The mestizo in Mexico is often seen as an individual who is caught between an Indian and Spanish sense of belonging. In Mexico the condition of being a mestizo in culture and in personality is a complex one. Physical appearance is important but not conclusive. Mexicans rank themselves according to skin color and physical types: at the pinnacle are the most Caucasian, the most "Spanish" looking; at the bottom are the most "Indian" looking. In between there are various degrees of "Indianness" in skin color and in comportment. These racial and behavioral-cultural traits are almost always correlated with socio-economic status. In Mexico as elsewhere one finds a positive correlation between being darker and being poorer.

In this context in Mexico, a sufficient amount of money or power can compensate for skin color. Questions arise as to how external social ascriptions fit or do not fit the inner identity of the person who is accorded or denied status by the ascribing group, for the social power of ascription in Mexico is quite evident. It is the contention of Romanucci-Ross that the social reality, that is to say the prevailing attitudes, allow very few individuals in this culture to develop an inner sense of self which is radically out of line with social expectations (*11*).

The present situation in the United States is more confused. There are so many standards and so much flux in regard to ethnic pluralism that individuals can transmit and receive many false signals. Passing is widespread. Names are changed. Modern plastic surgery even allows one to pick out a new physiognomy, in an attempt to change one's social acceptability.

In studying the subjective sense of ethnic identity cross-culturally, the contrasting examples of Mexico and the United States raise an interesting issue. Where there are two or more rigidly defined life styles, as in the Indian and the Spanish Mexican, the force of group ascription may make almost irrelevant the subjective experience of the individual who is being defined. In situations where external standards are themselves in transition or lack universality, a sense of inner conflict arises out of the greater measure of choice placed upon the individual himself. He is constrained to define as best he can where he fits in, or who he is. Thus there are probably differences from one culture to another in the degree to which subjective conflict is a relevant variable, because the nature of the resolution of the subjective conflict will have as much force in determining behavior or attempted behavior as will the external force of ascription exercised by the society.

In some circumstances, a dual or combined identity is not denied but encouraged. In Hawaii, for example, individuals of mixed Hawaiian and Chinese ancestry make a point of affirming themselves as a group, differing from either the pure Chinese or Hawaiian. Similarly the mestizos in Mexico are a recognized ethnic group whose members are graded according to degree of racial mixture and the degree of Spanish or Indian cultural behavior. It is interesting to note that in the context of a strong resurgence of ethnic specificity among the students at the University of California, a group of Eurasian students who had never united with others on the basis of their mixed ancestry found it expedient to come together as a small group to self-consciously discuss whether they identified more strongly with the heritage of their Caucasian parent or with that of their Asian parent. It may be a sign of the times that the majority of decisions as to essential identity were made in the direction of the minority Asian parent. This type of identity decision refers to the issues raised about a contemporary democratic sense of integrity reflected in a felt necessity to affirm rather than deny the less prestigious segment of one's ancestry. This sense of integrity runs counter to previous patterns which emphasized identification with one's more socially elevated ancestors—a common mode of tracing geneologies practiced in aristocratically oriented societies.

INSTRUMENTAL AND EXPRESSIVE USES OF ETHNICITY

As a final attempt to unify and systematize a number of issues, this section relates ethnic identity to basic concerns in interpersonal relationships. This scheme of social interactional concerns has been used by George De Vos in his previous work in understanding social role behavior in Japan (*4*). It is a conceptual framework which has evolved out of analyses of the Thematic Apperception Test in different cultural settings. Of the ten elemental concerns identified in the analysis, five are "instrumental," five "expressive" (see Chart 1).

Instrumental interpersonal behavior is principally goal oriented—what one does, or what one is concerned with is seen as a means to an end. Expressive behavior, by contrast, is an end in itself. Such behavior is a result of a prior need or emotional state. The five basic instrumental concerns are "achievement," "competence," "responsibility," "control," and "mutuality" (cooperation or competition in problem solving). Expressive concerns include "harmony" (or its opposite, "discord-aggression"), "affiliation" (or "isolation"), appreciation (or degradation) and "pleasure" (versus "suffering"). Each of these vectors has what are socially perceived as positively or negatively sanctioned features. There are both active and passive social roles played in respect to each of these behavioral dimensions. Although one could discuss ethnic identity at great length in regard to each of these concerns, we shall merely sketch some of the issues raised related to each of these concerns.

Instrumental Behavior and Ethnic Identity

Social definitions of success or achievement are found in every society. In a pluralistic society success may require one to emphasize ethnic belonging or to disguise it. In Chapter One we discussed "passing," in which a person changes his behavior or appearance in order to attain what is defined as success. We have also mentioned how minority status can, in some instances, stimulate compensatory striving. In other instances, however, a minority identity can prevent an individual from trying to succeed.

Crises in identity maintenance occur when one must choose between conflicting group loyalties, such as between the demands of ethnic group membership and of professional integrity. Individually successful American black teachers, for example, are under severe pressure to put ethnic allegiance ahead of professional integrity when grading black students. In the United States as elsewhere there are continuing dilemmas over "taking care of" members of one's own ethnic group versus a priority of responsibility to inculcated professional standards. In Nigeria the Ibos did so well professionally and economically that the other major ethnic groups finally responded by driving them out of non-Ibo regions of Nigeria. Many other examples of the forceful suppression of too successful ethnic minorities are easily brought to mind. The ethnic composition of various professions and trades in the United States has changed over the years. Some, however, continue to manifest ethnic differences due to earlier patterns of exclusion. The exclusion-inclusion process in trades and professions begins with admittance or non-admittance to training programs. Patterns of ethnic prejudice, however, readily may shift to more subtle forms of "recognition" or non-recognition through appointments. Advancement related to "quality in

CHART I Basic Thematic Concerns in Human Relations

Thematic Concerns	Positive (Socially Sanctioned)	Indeterminate	Negative (Socially Unsanctioned)	
	Active, initiated and/or resolved	Inactive or unresolved	Active, initiated and/or resolved	Passive, withdrawal and/or resolution
		INSTRUMENTAL BEHAVIOR		
Achievement (will do) internalized goals (S)	Goal-oriented activity	Internal conflict, over-commitment, role diffusion, daydreaming	Goal-oriented criminal activity	Anomic withdrawal, alienation
Competence (can do) internalized standards of excellence (S)	Avowal of capacity	Doubt about capacity, worry, diffuse anxiety, chagrin	Failure due to personal inadequacy	Sense of incapacity and inadequacy
Responsibility (ought to do) internalized moral standards and controls (S)	Sense of duty, assumption of obligation	Remorse, guilt, regrets over acts of commission or omission	Profligacy, irresponsibility	Avoidance, escape
Control-Power (must do) external power				
superordinate:	Legitimate authority, power-mastery, persuasion	Defensive insecurity	Authoritarian dominance, security, control through destruction of feared object	Failure to assert proper authority, spineless
subordinate:	Liberation, autonomy	Ambivalence about authority or power	Rebellion, trickery	Submission, compliance
(V)				
Mutuality (with or against) interpersonal ethics				
competitive:	Regulated competition, games, contests	Envy	Unethical competitive behavior	Capitulation, withdrawal from competitive situation
cooperative:	Concerted behavior (mutual trust)	Distrust, disagreement	Plotting, deception of a cohort	Sense of betrayal

CHART I Basic Thematic Concerns in Human Relations (continued)

Thematic Concerns	Positive (Socially Sanctioned)	Indeterminate	Negative (Socially Unsanctioned)	
	Active, initiated and/or resolved	Inactive or unresolved	Active, initiated and/or resolved	Passive, withdrawal and/or resolution
		EXPRESSIVE BEHAVIOR		
Harmony (with, emotionally) (H–V)	Harmony, peaceful relationships	Jealousy, fear of threat, emotional discord	Violence, injury, revenge	Withdrawal into hostility and resentment
Affiliation (toward someone) (H)	Affiliation intimacy, union, responsiveness, contact	Isolation, loneliness, alienation	Rejection of another	Sense of loss due to rejection or separation
Nurturance (for someone) (V)	Nurturance, care, help, comfort, succor	Dependency	Withholding	Sense of personal, social or economic deprivation
Appreciation (from someone)				
other:	Recognition of achieved or ascribed status	Feeling ignored, neglected, unappreciated	Disdain, disparagement	Sense of degradation
self:	Self-respect	Doubt about worth, sense of shame	Self-abasement, self-depreciation	Sense of worthlessness
(S, H–V)				
Pleasure (within oneself) self-expression	Satisfaction, sense of curiosity or creativity, enjoyment	Indifference, boredom	Masochistic behavior, asceticism	Suffering
		FATE		
Fortune Health, social economic conditions	Good luck, fortunate circumstances	Anxiety over environmental or health conditions	Bad fortune, accident, injury, bad economic circumstances	Handicap, illness, death

Note: In each category the relationship between actor and others changes relative to the observer's perspective in the thematic concerns. Some categories are actor-initiated and some are actor-responsive. There are internalized concerns (self-oriented) coded (S) and other-oriented themes concerned either with horizontal interactions (H) or vertical interactions coded (H–V).

From: George De Vos, "Social Role Relationships in Changing Japan" in (*4*).

professional performance" can be and often is ethnically controlled. The pure notion of professional integrity, therefore, is somehow lost in a labyrinth of multiple causal loops, and the achievement process over time will display many of the characteristics of a self-fulfilling prophecy. "Opportunity" will be better used by those whose personality has been cultivated to understand and exploit ethnically biased opportunities to maximal advantage.

Competence Ethnic identity may determine a person's confidence in his capacities to take on socially acceptable goal oriented activities. Expectations of self are shaped by the capacities or incapacities attributed by others to one's ethnic group. As part of one's ethnic identity one may be faced with a prevalence of situations that demonstrate personal inadequacy rather than increasing confidence. In other instances, an inherited high social status is at the same time an avowal of one's potential capacity.

It is therefore psychologically easier for members of certain ethnic groups to move up to expectations of group competence if there is a collective confidence shared by the group. The social self in such a group is developed around supportive attitudes. It is more difficult for an individual to assert (his) competence when he is a member of a group that has no such supportive tradition. The minority group individual who has unusual competence has to depend more upon his independent capacities for status than do members inheriting such psychological support simply by being born into a group.

Responsibility As we have indicated, being a member of a group is partially defined by feeling compelled to obey its moral codes. Individuals who identify ethnically with a group also identify ethically with it. They feel constrained to assume certain obligations. They may become subject to guilt or remorse for acts of omission or commission which are related to the well-being of their group. Not only the responsibilities, but what is irresponsible and reprehensible is defined in group terms. As in the case of the Italians already cited, some groups have as part of their traditions both positive definitions of expectations and fears of how individuals, characteristically for the group, fail in meeting responsibilities. The dilemma of identity within many groups is this awareness of traditional avoidance of duty, as well as the heroic representations of what one should do to be truly moral.

As defined in ethnic terms, therefore, responsibility in all groups has an internalized moral dimension. Some who seek to escape ethnicity do so because they judge that the negative social and personal features of their inheritance far outweigh the positive. In times of crisis however they find themselves vulnerable to falling into a negative destiny—they may come to define their own moral failings as culturally inherited traits.

In other instances, the positive expectations of what it is to be a member of a group are considered a burden to be avoided. One seeks to identify with a less demanding subgroup as a way out of the constraints of one's own tradition. But George Santayana, in his brilliant novel, *The Last Puritan* (*12*), suggests that a conscious disavowal of a tradition does not erase deeper layers of socialization. De Vos (*2*) in describing "psychological lag" in Japanese arranged marriages points out how conscious avowals of a right to "free marriage" do not result in any great decrease in arranged marriages in Japan. Many Japanese do not *feel* morally right about a free marriage for themselves although they consider it acceptable intellectually for other Japanese.

In an ethnically pluralistic society an individual may wish to take on a minority identity to take advantage of the seemingly freer pattern enjoyed by members of another group. Such individuals may attempt to take part in minority group activities, but they are usually not accepted and remain outsiders. They are not considered to have the necessary "soul" to be included.

In short, one's sense of ethnic identity invariably implies some assumption or avoidance of responsibility and guilt. A minority group member, by introjecting a negative ethnic self-image, may take on an internal conflict about ethical standards. Some therefore seek to avoid an ethnic identity as morally distasteful, or burdensome, as well as use it as an external explanation for personal failings.

Control We have already indicated in several instances throughout this volume how ethnicity is related to concepts of power. One tends to assess oneself, as well as one's group, as being placed by society in a superordinate or in a subordinate position with respect to other groups. If placed in a superordinate status, the individual can view as legitimate the authority he wields in assuming dominance over members of other groups. Such individuals may come to experience some social insecurities related to an inculcated need to maintain control over others. A sense of an emphasis on group ascendancy can be used to hide individual impotence.

When the dominant group feels its authority threatened, the subordinate but the feared group may be subjected to pressure to extract symbolic signals of its continuing subordination. The more insecure, the more the need to manifest symbolically one's dominance, and the more need to receive symbolic gestures of submission from members of subordinate groups. The emphasis on German superiority in Nazism, for example, followed upon past defeats, including the social and economic impotence of the lower middle class Germans during the economic chaos of the last Weimar Republic. These groups found some psychological and social assuagement in the ideology advocated by Hitler: German ethnicity imparted a right to feel powerful and dominant—it relieved the individual of his own sense of weakness. Belonging to a "superior" group helps resolve questions of individual assertion.

For a person of subordinate status to espouse an ethnic identity may be to assume a moral imperative to seek liberation and autonomy, to re-assert a necessary independence of oneself and one's group from the oppressor. In a negative sense, there may be ambivalence over "rebellion." An individual may feel impelled to rebel while at the same time he senses the rebellion to be an illegitimate act of infantile origin. The psychodynamics of submission, rebellion, or autonomy are complex. The same social acts may spring from different levels of maturity—submission, for example, may be an instrumental, mature decision to survive, or it may be an infantile form of dependency uncalled for by social circumstance. In most instances, however, motives are complex and not easily reducible to a simple psychological explanation.

An individual, as part of his tradition, may inherit modes of social trickery employed by subordinates in somehow maintaining themselves vis-a-vis individuals of superior status (e.g., the "laughing barrel" of American blacks). There may also be ambivalences about social submission and compliance which an individual may project outward as a problem of group identity. The relation of ethnic identity to power and exploitation is a large topic that needs no further illustration to indicate its relevance.

Mutuality Ethnic or subcultural traditions define modes of competition as well as modes of cooperation expected of the individual by his group. Competitive activity may be de-emphasized within the group at the same time that competition with individuals outside the group is encouraged. For example, among the *burakumin,* minority outcastes of Japan, competitive activities or expressions of aggression among children were discouraged within the group but were implicitly and explicitly encouraged toward the majority children.

Standards of ethical competition within a group are quite different from those permitted when the individual is dealing with people outside his group. Behavior considered unethical when expressed toward members of one's group might be condoned if expressed toward an outsider. Very often within-group activities of an instrumental nature emphasize the need for concerted behavior and mutual trust in acting together toward the realization of goals. At the same time, some groups realize that they may be betrayed from within the group. This makes it difficult for the group to unite itself to attain political or social goals. American Mexicans for example have shown continual distrust of their leadership.

With respect to each of these dimensions of instrumental activity, the individual may be faced with a dilemma of identity, since maintaining oneself within one's own group may be a disadvantage to the individual when he seeks to realize his own goals. He must then decide whether it is worthwhile to him to give up his group identity or to maintain it and seek to realize his goals despite the inconveniences of his ethnic status. In some cases, on the other hand, allegiance to a group is reinforced because group membership affords support in the cooperative or competitive realization of goals.

Expressive Behavior and Ethnic Identity

Maintenance of one's ethnic loyalty is very often an expressive, emotional need. As such the psychological rewards of remaining a minority outweigh the instrumental advantages of leaving or changing behavior to gain occupational or social advantage. Such decisions are very complex. In each instance one has to assess the relative strength of a variety of expressive vectors in understanding behavior related to group affiliation. The following are some fragments of topics that deserve more than the cursory comments we include. A fuller exposition of a psycho-cultural theory of ethnic identity would explore these motivational features in much greater depth.

Harmony A universal need of group living is some kind of peacefulness or harmony within one's group relationships. Feelings of conflict and contention are muted within the group; whenever possible, hostilities are displaced onto individuals not belonging to a group. It is the unfortunate destiny of many groups, however, also to embody in their traditions of membership, forms of discord, hostility and resentment that are more internally rather than externally directed.

Social movements arising from within minority groups very often are attempts to unite the group to achieve a new sense of harmony within. The most expedient mechanism for effecting internal harmony is to find some means of deflecting socially disruptive behavior onto outside individuals. Thus, considerable emotional benefits can be gained by certain church memberships, such as the Black Muslims. Membership permits a new conceptualization of one's ethnic self in such a way that internal brotherhood is reinforced while at the same time the individual is given a means of deflecting his aggressive needs onto legitimately hated outsiders.

Most groups use mechanisms of this type in one way or another to maintain their continuance. By so doing one reaches for a greater sense of peacefulness and ease within the group. But as a consequence there is an increase in uneasiness, wariness, and suspicions in relation to given outsiders who are cast in the role of enemy. Scapegoating is a well established mechanism central to any social psychological study of prejudice and ethnocentrism. It is a characteristic both of majority *and* minority groups in plural societies.

Affiliation The sense of affiliative belonging involved in ethnicity has been discussed throughout this volume. Social isolation is an intolerable state for most humans. The threat of separation from the group is one of the most stringent of human sanctions. An ethnic group can provide for a mutual sense of contact possible only in some areas of communication to those sharing common past experiences. In this regard a generalized ethnic identity may in some instances supplant more direct personally intimate one-to-one relationships.

There can arise a generation gap in ethnic identity. An individual may find satisfying if not intimate companionship more readily with peers of similar ethnic origin than in contacts with primary family members of a different generation. For many Mexican American youths, for example, an ethnic peer group quickly replaces the primary family as the primary reference group.

Problems of ethnic identity can arise if self-affirmation signals that one is leaving one's group. This in turn can lead to rejection by, and enforced isolation from, others of one's group. A choice to go it alone involves severe psychological strain. In *Japan's Invisible Race* (*6*) De Vos and Wagatsuma cite examples of Japanese former outcastes who tried to pass for some time, but finally returned to their own group, giving up promising professional careers bought at the cost of social estrangement.

The whole topic of individualism and alienation related to problems over a sense of group belonging deserves more exposition here than can be given here. De Vos has covered some of these features with Hiroshi Wagatsuma in exploring alienation and suicide among Japanese (*3*).

Nurturance Interdependency of ethnic group members is a large topic. Here are some suggested psychological fragments, each needing more exposition.

Ethnic relationships very often are expected to supply care, help, and comfort in times of need. A member of an ethnic group does not only expect sociability or "brotherhood," he expects to be able to express his dependency needs to other members.

Ethnic membership for some people also provide a field for the expression of benevolence. Many find within themselves a need to care for others—to care for the more helpless of one's own kind.

Whereas individuals expect nurturance and care from their group and often feel responsible for caring for others within their own group, they may within the larger society find themselves relatively deprived personally, socially, or economically, because of their minority or ethnic group status.

Nurturance is the transmission of care from the older to the younger generations. This sense of nurturance may not extend beyond ethnic boundaries. The parental attitude, if genuine, assumes the younger individual needs *temporary* assistance, not that he is permanently incapable of taking care of himself. This attitude between groups may slip over into one of a permanent paternalism that is psychologically damaging to the recipients.

Many ethnic groups in plural societies set up special benevolent societies to take care of distressed members. The American Jews have been pioneers in professional welfare agencies in the United States.

A major problem in public welfare programs has been an incapacity of professionally trained workers to reach people across ethnic barriers. Similar problems arise in public health programs. The recent interest in "medical anthropology" is a recognition that ethnic identity and differences in cultural traditions are important social issues in reaching and aiding the disadvantaged. Members of one's own ethnic group, when professionally trained, have the advantage in reaching people who need help. All psychiatry or medicine in this sense requires some feeling of mutual trust and mutual belief. It is psychologically very difficult to become dependent on an outsider.

The dependent role of wards of the government forced upon American Indians has helped perpetuate in one way or another chronic identity problems that have been socially debilitating for the groups which they were supposedly designed to aid.

Finally, in some groups one might find that there is the unhappy perception that members are mutually depriving of one another. This may not be overtly stated to outsiders but a felt experience which adds to an ambivalence about maintaining group membership.

Appreciation Ethnic identity is related basically to pride in an affirmative direction, or to shame and degradation in a negative one. Each group seeks to create for itself a sense of humanity, dignity, self respect, and proper status. Any human being resents the possibility of being neglected, ignored, unappreciated—or worse, actively degraded, disparaged, debased, and depreciated.

Ethnic identity often involves vulnerable feelings about self respect or a potential sense of worthlessness. Some groups are particularly sensitive to the opinions of others, to their public image. Other groups are more self sufficient. Perhaps the English as described by Gorer and the Japanese as seen by Wagatsuma are extremes of this continuum. English self-sufficience is related to a need for appreciation limited to those within their class system. In both the English and Japanese, a deep sense of shame may be aroused by improper behavior on the part of a member of one's own group. A readiness to take on external values often critically curtails the self sufficiency of Japanese. As a nation they are particularly vulnerable to external criticism or inadvertent disparagement.

Expressive feelings concerned with appreciation are central to understanding many difficulties that arise in intragroup and intergroup relationships. Culture traits cannot help but be evaluated. What is seen in highly positive terms within a group may, with alien contact, lose its value as soon as it is perceived by others in a devalued way. Theodore Schwartz has with great cogency discussed the origin and development of cargo cults, not as some individuals would have it, as a reaction to an external dominance of Western culture but much more directly related to the devaluation of what was of value in Melanesia in their economic interaction. That is, the Melanesians could no longer believe in their symbols of economic worth when they were faced with the knowledge of a much superior technology producing goods of greater worth than they could possibly imagine within their traditional culture. Resultant crises in the sense of self felt acutely by Melanesians led into the development of the cargo cult preoccupation, in which they hoped for the arrival of superior cargo from some supernatural source. They could not countenance without extreme self devaluation the idea that these superior material artifacts were simply the products of men like themselves.

One of the great problems of culture contact is such crises of self assessment. These occur when a group is forced to recognize the relative merits and sometimes the superior technology of an alien group. Within pluralistic societies there is constant mutual evaluation. Such collective evaluative comparisons can add to or detract from the individual's appraisal of personal worth as a member of a group. Hamamsy's and Wagatsuma's chapters were related to this issue.

Pleasure and Suffering Finally, ethnic identity is ultimately related to questions concerning the satisfaction afforded by social life, and to the problem of arriving at a mature capacity to tolerate the suffering and death which is the destiny of all men in all societies, no matter how they identify themselves. As in the metaphor of the California Indian, sadly commenting on the death of his culture, ethnic identity is found in the "cup of custom" passed on by one's parents, from which one drinks the meaning of existence. Once the cup is broken one can no longer taste of life. It is a light-scattering prism through which one envisions life with a sense of curiosity and creativity. It is both a means and an end, insofar as one develops a capacity to enjoy.

An ethnic identity gives savor, the taste of one's past. The tastelessness of instant artifice is what the younger generation today describes as "plastic;" it is the opposite of the sense of past accumulations, of meanings husbanded and passed on to a new generation. Stripped of these, the individual faces indifference, boredom, and a sense of normlessness or "anomie," which is the result not only of a lack of regulation governing life but of the lack of savor and seasoning which occurs with the heedless casting out of past custom.

Ultimately, ethnic identity is the unexpressed meaning of anthropology. Anthropologists intellectualize about human culture, yet they try to preserve in their own modes of pursuing knowledge the value of man's past, and so to assert, that without a consciousness of the past, the present becomes devoid of meaning.

In ethnic identity there is a commitment to endure suffering. In Christian context, to change the Indian metaphor, one's culture is also the common chalice in which suffering blood becomes redemptive wine. To some few, identity can be a commitment to masochism, but to most it is simply a necessary stigmatic emblem one must learn to carry without disguise. Each group perhaps thinks that in maintaining itself it has to undergo certain forms of unique suffering not experienced by others. It may be reassuring to some and perhaps deflating to others to recognize that consciousness of suffering is not unique to any one group, but is the destiny of our common humanity, whatever our separate cultural origins.

REFERENCES

1. Bruner, Edward. "Some Observations on Cultural Change and Psychological Stress in Indonesia." In *Responses to Change: Adjustment and Adaptation in Personality and Culture,* edited by George A. De Vos, n.d.
2. De Vos, George. "Some Observations of Guilt in Relation to Achievement and Arranged Marriage in the Japanese." In *Socialization for Achievement: The Cultural Psychology of the Japanese,* edited by George De Vos. Berkeley: University of California Press, 1973.
3. De Vos, George. "Role Narcissism and the Etiology of Japanese Suicide." In *Socialization for Achievement: The Cultural Psychology of the Japanese,* edited by George De Vos. Berkeley: University of California Press, 1973.
4. De Vos, George, ed. *Socialization for Achievement: The Cultural Psychology of the Japanese.* Berkeley: University of California Press, 1973.
5. De Vos, George and Wagatsuma, Hiroshi. *Japan's Invisible Race.* Berkeley: University of California Press, 1966.
6. Durkheim, Emile. *The Elementary Forms of Religious Life,* translated by J. W. Swain. Glencoe, Ill.: Free Press, 1947.
7. Haley, Alex. *The Autobiography of Malcolm X.* New York: Grove Press, 1966.

8. Kardiner, Abram and Ovesey, Lionel. *The Mark of Oppression.* Cleveland and New York: World, 1962.

9. Romanucci-Ross, Lola. "Conflits Fonciers a Mokerang village Matankor des iles de l'Amiraute." In *L'Homme,* 6, no. 2 (1966) 32-52.

10. Romanucci-Ross, Lola. *Conflict, Violence, and Morality in a Mexican Village.* Palo Alto: National Press Books, 1973.

11. Santayana, George. *The Last Puritan.*

12. Sapir, Edward. "Contributions to Cultural Anthropology." *International Encyclopedia of the Social Sciences.* MacMillan, 1968.

13. Valiers, Pierre. *Negres Blancs d'Amerique: Autobiographie Precoce d'un "Terroriste" Quebecois.* Montreal: Parti Tris, 1968.

Index